INVESTED NARRATIVES

SPEKTRUM: Publications of the German Studies Association
Series editor: David M. Luebke, University of Oregon

Published under the auspices of the German Studies Association, *Spektrum* offers current perspectives on culture, society, and political life in the German-speaking lands of central Europe—Austria, Switzerland, and the Federal Republic—from the late Middle Ages to the present day. Its titles and themes reflect the composition of the GSA and the work of its members within and across the disciplines to which they belong—literary criticism, history, cultural studies, political science, and anthropology.

Recent volumes:

Volume 26
Invested Narratives
German Responses to Economic Crisis
Edited by Jill E. Twark

Volume 25
Football Nation
The Playing Fields of German Culture, History, and Society
Edited by Rebeccah Dawson, Baston Heinsohn, Oliver Knabe, and Alan McDougall

Volume 24
What Remains
Responses to the Legacy of Christa Wolf
Edited by Gerald A. Fetz and Patricia Herminghouse

Volume 23
Minority Discourses in Germany since 1990
Edited by Ela Gezen, Priscilla Layne, and Jonathan Skolnik

Volume 22
Beyond Posthumanism
The German Humanist Tradition and the Future of the Humanities
Alexander Mathäs

Volume 21
Feelings Materialized
Emotions, Bodies, and Things in Germany, 1500–1950
Edited by Derek Hillard, Heikki Lempa, and Russell Spinney

Volume 20
Names and Naming in Early Modern Germany
Edited by Marjorie Elizabeth Plummer and Joel F. Harrington

Volume 19
Views of Violence
Representing the Second World War in German and European Museums and Memorials
Edited by Jörg Echternkamp and Stephan Jaeger

Volume 18
Dreams of Germany
Musical Imaginaries from the Concert Hall to the Dance Floor
Edited by Neil Gregor and Thomas Irvine

Volume 17
Money in the German-Speaking Lands
Edited by Mary Lindemann and Jared Poley

For a full volume listing, please see the series page on our website:
http://berghahnbooks.com/series/spektrum

Invested Narratives

German Responses to Economic Crisis

Edited by Jill E. Twark

berghahn
NEW YORK • OXFORD
www.berghahnbooks.com

First published in 2023 by
Berghahn Books
www.berghahnbooks.com

Library of Congress Cataloging-in-Publication Data
Names: Twark, Jill E., 1968- editor.
Title: Invested narratives : German responses to economic crisis / edited by Jill E. Twark.
Description: [New York] : Berghahn Books, 2023. | Series: Spektrum: publications of the German Studies Association ; volume 26 | Includes bibliographical references and index.
Identifiers: LCCN 2022028512 (print) | LCCN 2022028513 (ebook) | ISBN 9781800736931 (hardback) | ISBN 9781800736948 (ebook)
Subjects: LCSH: Financial crises--Germany--History. | Germany--Economic conditions--History.
Classification: LCC HB3722 .I589 2023 (print) | LCC HB3722 (ebook) | DDC 38.5/420943--dc23/eng/20220630
LC record available at https://lccn.loc.gov/2022028512
LC ebook record available at https://lccn.loc.gov/2022028513

British Library Cataloguing in Publication Data
A catalogue record for this book is available from the British Library

ISBN 978-1-80073-693-1 hardback
ISBN 978-1-80073-694-8 ebook

https://doi.org/10.3167/9781800736931

~: CONTENTS :~

~: FIGURES :~

ACKNOWLEDGMENTS

This volume is dedicated posthumously to Crister S. Garrett, a former Professor of American Culture and History at the University of Leipzig. Crister, Monika Albrecht, and I conceived of this project together in fall 2015 and brought it to life with our German Studies Association seminar, "Contemporary German Narratives of Economic Crisis and *Ordnung*," in 2016. The seminar participants and contributors to this volume who knew Crister are grateful for his inspirational spark and lively personality, taken away much too soon with his passing in 2019.

Thanks also to the Berghahn Books Spektrum Series editor David Luebke, former Berghahn Books editor Chris Chappell, and its current editors, Sulaiman Ahmad and Caroline Kuhtz, as well as our two helpful, blind peer reviewers, for carrying this book forward with diligence and grace throughout the coronavirus pandemic. The contributors to this volume also deserve praise for having to wait patiently for this book to appear. Some authors had to rush to finish chapters—one added to replace Crister's—and others to substitute chapters promised by those who dropped out for various reasons.

Among the numerous outside readers of various drafts of my Introduction and the individual chapters—who contributed to their readability and interpretive depth—I would like to mention Robert Blankenship, Susan Pearce, James Skidmore, Caleb Joseph, and Lily Johnson, who told me that learning about "cruel optimism" helped her understand and live her own life better.

My partner, Charles Jenkins, who was quite supportive throughout the final push to the finish line, also deserves to be acknowledged for his loving care, lots of long walks, various necessary home repairs, and cooking skills!

Introduction

Narrating Economics as Crisis

JILL E. TWARK

> I was head over heels in debt back then. I was constantly receiving letters from my bank, sometimes two or three a week. I crossed out my name and wrote "address unknown" on the envelopes, then I threw them in the next mailbox. The bank people called me, but I told them I was not myself. I wasn't there. . . . A few months earlier the bank had gone bankrupt by speculating on businesses in the US, and the government jumped in with a couple million to help out. The bosses responsible for it were let go with a huge severance package and a stately pension. *60,000 Euros a month for the Chief Indian. . . . Till he drops dead.* (Italics in original)
>
> —André Pilz, *Man Down*

As the German-Austrian author André Pilz demonstrates, in this brief synopsis of the 2007/8 financial crisis as it affected his unemployed, working-class protagonist in the 2010 novel *Man Down*, storytelling brings economics to life. By means of this fictional character, Pilz denounces the German economic and governmental "system" (p. 113) for protecting banks, as well as business owners such as this man's employer, while allowing them to dismiss their employees and leave them destitute. Whereas Pilz's narrator calls this system into question, the German historian of capitalism, Jürgen Kocka (2016), underscores how societies also construct narratives to legitimate such systems. Narratives can help us make sense of a large amount of information by depicting it as a series of events with identified actors and a plot, rather than just as collected "data." Narratives provide links between causes and their effects (Prince 1982; Onega and García Landa 1996; Bal 1997). No longer presumed to be confined to the domain of fiction, what constitutes a narrative can be understood broadly as a sociocultural practice that involves both "sense making" and "worldmaking" (Herman 2009: viii).[1] In recent decades, this viewpoint has led to a growing interest in the "forms, role and function of narrative and storytelling in a wide array of disciplines across the humanities, social sciences and even disciplines in other faculties" (Nünning 2012: 149).[2] In the wake of this "narrative turn" (Kreiswirth 2005), the narrativity of economic and political specialist discourse likewise has come under scrutiny (Horvath 2011: 333), generating the need to look also at non-fiction narratives in greater depth.

Exploring economic narratives from various sources can in fact serve as a paradigm of cross-disciplinary work, as no single area of study can cope fully with the complexity of narrative worldbuilding (Herman 2009: ix). Narrative analysis performs the useful function of questioning the motivations for depicting historically significant events in certain ways. It helps us take a step back and explain *how* and *for which purposes* these stories are created, and which effects they produce. Such analysis can determine how these representations affect perceptions, actions, and outcomes in the immediate aftermath of an event that threatens the existing order of any given society, and how these effects linger later on.[3] As Robert J. Shiller (2020: 3) argues in his groundbreaking book, *Narrative Economics: How Stories Go Viral and Drive Major Economic Events*, "the study of the viral spread of popular narratives that affect economic behavior . . . can improve our ability to anticipate and prepare for economic events. It can also help us structure economic institutions and policy." Contemplating economic narratives, of course, also requires us to scrutinize the types of narrative we construct with our own analyses.

Economic crisis narratives run the gamut from expressing panic and tragedy to illustrating a crisis as a brief disruption followed by a restoration of the status quo. One type of narrative construes the financial system as too complex and abstract to be fully comprehensible or formally regulated. Such narratives "suspend knowledge and description of that world by claiming its mechanisms are beyond our collective cognitive, linguistic, and epistemological reach" (La Berge 2014: 93), and can lead to a feeling of helplessness in the face of financial market dynamics. Referring to financial investment activities as fundamentally incomprehensible also makes it difficult to lay blame on the actual perpetrators. Economic systems and their boom-and-bust cycles can, however, also be presented rationally and transparently. Reinhart and Rogoff (2009), for example, provide the big picture in their straightforward analysis of worldwide historical and more recent financial disasters, whereas Illing (2013) homes in on Germany with his chronological account of its political responses to the dot-com and subprime mortgage crises. One predominant account pinpoints economic crises as a moral problem involving human greed, reckless risk-taking, corruption, the obsession with seeking loopholes, and so forth. Like the novelist André Pilz cited above, many German authors, filmmakers, and journalists, writing in the wake of the Great Recession, directed their wrath similarly at the seemingly unconscionable behavior of bankers and investors, "spotlighting facets of the banking crisis by reporting on personal failures, greed, and examples of abysmal human character" (Sinn 2010: xiii; see also Funke et al. 2016; Krasni 2017).[4]

One recent, prevalent economic crisis narrative is informed primarily by neoliberal ideas, which engendered an ongoing, international process of economic liberalization beginning in the Global North in the 1970s and 1980s. This liberalization is exhibited in national and international development policies "involving the promotion of free markets, individual responsibility, and global homogeneity" (Birch 2015: 571; see also Bourdieu and Wacquant 2001). The state's primary role in fostering this systemic transformation is to "protect and/or create markets and competition" (Birch 2015: 572). Neoliberal economic crisis narratives can be divided into two camps. On the one hand, a crisis such as the Great Recession is described as the result of excessive government regulation and interventionist polices that prevented the free market from working efficiently. On the other hand, the crisis is seen as emerging from the failure of neoliberal policies to regulate the market stringently enough (see, e.g., Kahler and Lake 2013). In its most extreme form, this narrative depicts the government as part of an elite system in which politicians and the banking industry are colluding to manipulate the economy. Along with disparaging financial actors and the current capitalist system—which John Maynard Keynes referred to in the 1930s as "casino capitalism" (see Strange 1986; Sinn 2010; Schäfer 2013)—attention is directed here toward government interventions and regulatory plans, often without providing much orientation as to which of these measures will be most effective in overcoming and preventing future economic crises (Quiring et al. 2012; see also Mast 2012). Where do the Germans fit in, among the multifaceted, international, and often contradictory discursive approaches to explaining economic crises, both in recent times and in the past?

The objective of this volume is to assess historical and neoteric narratives from Germany, both non-fictional and literary-fictional, that depict the origins, effects, and responses to economic crises. Such narratives may or may not also promote stability in the wake of a crisis (see, e.g., Hertner and Miskimmon 2015). In interpreting these diverse economic narratives, contributors approach the crisis topic and disciplinary genre from various angles, spanning the nineteenth, twentieth, and early twenty-first centuries. Three contributions examine narratives that negotiate German government policy responses to major world economic crises (Köster, Kurzer/Cooper, Konoe); three look at literary narratives that depict the main actors in the financial sector—bankers and financial advisers—and their culpability (Albrecht, Tönsing, Kaipainen); and four analyze literary or sociological narratives that highlight the precarious plight of the working class and unemployed (Brambora, Delianidou, Matthies, Twark). These analyses of economic crisis narratives are prefaced by Reinhard H. Schmidt's chronological account of the 150-year, up- and downward trajectory of Germany's most important financial institution, Deutsche Bank. This narrative history serves as a useful overview of the evolution of the German financial system, and it contextualizes many of the chapters that follow. Our broad spectrum of perspectives thus offers an aggregate assessment of a variety of economic crises and their resulting narratives from multiple vantage points.

What binds these temporally and generically different German economic crisis narratives together is that they were spawned as reactions to a widespread perception that the existing sociopolitical order was under threat by a system-wide economic transformation or upheaval, and that there was a need to adapt to such insecurity. Whether affecting an individual, an entire geographic region or nation, or the entire world, this "threatened order" was then captured in narrative form. In adopting this definition of "crisis" as a "threat to order"—as opposed to its various other, often subjective definitions as, for example, a turning point or a time when a decision must be made (see Siemens 2012)—we recognize that a crisis emerges "when agents become convinced that their options for action are uncertain, when behavior and routines are called into question, when agents feel they cannot rely on each other, and when agents manage to establish a threat discourse" (Collaborative Research Center 2022). Defined in this way, diverse disciplinary approaches and economic crisis narratives can be united, as we have done in this volume. To connect their contributions further, the contributors kept in mind that engaging with such narratives requires addressing themes fundamental to German identity, interests, institutions, and international initiatives. The following questions thus guided us while writing our respective contributions:

- How do the framers of German-language economic narratives from various political, economic, social, and cultural realms depict an "economic crisis"?
- Why did the framers of an economic crisis narrative produce this particular narrative?
- How did these speakers draw from, and respond to, the prevailing narrative discourse of their time?
- Which narrative strategies did these speakers use to depict economic crises and their solutions?
- How do they connect their proposed solutions to the quest for freedom of economic activity and the struggle for greater socioeconomic equality and justice?

Some contributors also compare economic crisis narratives from earlier times with those produced more recently, and others point out how German crisis narratives resemble or differ from those generated in other European countries in both their messages and real-world outcomes.

Whether responding to the eurozone crisis, the rules and norms for the European Union more broadly, or national debates about *Wohlstand* and *Solidarität*, the contesting of economic crisis and the maintenance or restoration of order inform German debates and the construction of multidisciplinary narratives for both domestic and international consumption. The national media debate that emerged from literary scholar Joseph Vogl's *Das Gespenst des Kapitals* (2010; *The Specter of Capital* 2014), which received animated attention in the economic sections of mass media outlets such as the *Süddeutsche Zeitung* and the *Frankfurter Allgemeine Zeitung*, is just one example of the intersection between culture, capitalist critiques, and the construction of economic narratives in Germany. At first, Vogl was praised highly for his critiques of the notion that financial markets can function rationally to produce "self-balancing market forces," for which he coined the neologism "oikodicy" (Vogl 2014: 36). He soon drew criticism, however, for, among other reasons, having derived his conclusions primarily from historical economic-theoretical texts (e.g., by Adam Smith, G.W.F. Hegel, and Marx/Engels). In doing so, Vogl neglected more recent economic research, including economic modeling (see Pahl and Sparsam 2013; Halsmayer and Huber 2013). Despite the shortcomings in Vogl's approach, several contributors here pick up on his ideas as a successful synthesis of interdisciplinary research bridging the humanities, philosophy, and economics, and use these ideas as a springboard for their interpretations of literary narratives.

Our focus here is not on exposing "fake news" or "viral narratives," and the ways they produce recurring, archetypal "epidemics," as Robert J. Shiller does. We have chosen instead to limit our analyses to economic crisis narratives produced by the public policymakers of the German government and the financial giants of Germany's major institutions such as Deutsche Bank, as well as those narratives disseminated by social scientists and literary writers. The effects of economic crises on "ordinary" people are nevertheless addressed by the creators of many of these narratives, for financial ups and downs leave their mark on most, if not all, people in any given country, even the wealthiest such as Germany.

Part I of our volume, titled "Shaping Economic Knowledge from Historical Perspectives," contains four contributions that set the stage for the later chapters that focus on more recent financial crises. Reinhard H. Schmidt's narrative history of the most powerful and influential German bank, Deutsche Bank, introduces this section, as it provides an overview of German financial history from the bank's founding in 1870 to the end of the euro-crisis decade. Although his chapter differs from the other contributions in taking the form of a narrative chronicle of significant Deutsche Bank events, leaders, and what influenced these leaders' financial decisions—rather than a meta-analysis of their discourse—it prefaces the other contributions as a useful, overarching survey of German financial crisis history.

As Schmidt dissects Deutsche Bank's role in the German financial system during the first 150 years of its history, he explains how this institution was shaped by various wars and economic crises, and by the efforts to overcome them. The evolution of Deutsche Bank has always been tied closely to that of the German financial system, and Schmidt demonstrates how this bank has had a stronger influence on its character than any other German institution. Three specific aspects of the bank's history considered in this chapter are: its varying degrees of internationalization; the extent to which it has focused on investment banking as opposed to commercial banking; and the consistency of the bank's business model across different times. Decisions made in the late twentieth and early twenty-first century by Deutsche Bank's CEOs, Supervisory Board, and Management Board have destabilized the German financial system for the foreseeable future (see also Schmidt 2019). Schmidt explains in a systematic narrative history how this destabilization occurred.

Following Schmidt's vast tour of German economic history from the founding of Deutsche Bank to the present time, Johannes Brambora steps back chronologically to show us the forms that the economic crises of the working classes took in the mid-to-late nineteenth century, when German workers suffered under the birth pangs of its relatively rapid industrialization. Brambora brings the economic crises of the factories and workers to light by discussing how three mostly forgotten nineteenth-century novelists represent these crises in their fictional narratives. In "Narrative Confrontations with Socioeconomic Crisis: Ideas for Building Community in the Mid-Nineteenth-Century German Social Novel," Brambora analyzes how the authors Ernst Willkomm, Luise Otto-Peters, and Robert Prutz depict the devastating effects of industrialization, and conceive solutions to these problems. Their solutions are based on what they recognize as a need to develop a strong sense of social cohesiveness and community both among the factory workers and between them and the factory owners who otherwise exploit them. Brambora looks specifically at how these authors depict socioeconomic contradictions, which ideas of community they set up to counter these contradictions, and what chances of success they give to these ideas.

Brambora's novelists were writing in a divided Germany prior to Bismarck's creation of the Second German Empire. The last two chapters in Part I of this volume evaluate real and fictionalized reactions, respectively, to the series of economic crises that struck Germany during the interwar period. Especially after the 1929 stock market crash, while the Great Depression ran its course, economic decisions were often blamed by historians of economics on "old ideologies" and a fundamentally antidemocratic stance of politicians. In "Economic Knowledge and the Failure to Alleviate the Great Depression in Weimar Germany," Roman Köster argues that such interpretations are misleading, because they neglect the importance of the insights gained during the eventful times after World War I began in 1914. The Weimar Republic's economic austerity policies and *Inflationsangst* (fear of inflation) were not primarily the result of dogmatism or a right-wing ideology, but instead conclusions drawn from the economic and political turmoil that German society experienced after this war began.

Along with these economic and political narratives, the worldwide economic crisis of the late 1920s and early 1930s has also been dealt with in many German fictional texts. Written in the style of *Neue Sachlichkeit* (New Objectivity), these literary works chronicle the daily lives of factory workers and low-level bureaucrats in a matter-of-fact writing style resembling that of newspaper journalists. One such novel, *Fabian: The Story of a Moralist* (1931) by Erich Kästner, critiques the economic policies of the Weimar Republic as well as the theory that capital markets are self-regulating and fair. In highlighting the moral emptiness connected to money that he perceived in Germany's interwar period, Kästner describes how the value order of high capitalism began to reduce human interactions to a set of commercial exchanges. In her chapter, "The Moral Equation Works Out Differently: The Great Depression, the Crisis of Knowledge, and Value Order in Erich Kästner's *Fabian: The Story of a Moralist*," Simela Delianidou examines how Kästner exposes the economic system as socially constructed, highlighting the ambiguous multiplicity of moral values and crisis of knowledge that emerged in Germany between the two world wars. These topics have recently been dealt with again in a series of German and American novels that ensued from the 2007/8 financial crisis, such as Rainald Goetz's *Johann Holtrop* (2012), Don DeLillo's *Cosmopolis* (2012), and Jonas Lüscher's *Frühling der Barbaren* (2013; *Barbarian Spring*, 2015), the third of which is discussed by Joel Kaipainen later in this volume.

Vitally connected to these economic crisis narratives is the question of what happens to the labor force and how labor is perceived in times of crisis.In Part II of this volume, "German Narratives of Work and Unemployment," such narratives are discussed from sociological and literary perspectives, moving from the big picture of German theories of labor's societal functions down to the scale of the individual, micromanaged human body. In her chapter, "Unemployment as Crisis: Past and Present German-Language Sociological Narratives on the Loss of Work," Annemarie Matthies traces the views of German sociologists toward labor and unemployment from the 1930s to the age of neoliberalism, which began to be adopted in Germany in the 1980s. On the one hand, sociologists refer to unemployment as a *social crisis*, and on the other, they, along with psychologists, write about unemployment as a *crisis of the subject*. In the early 1990s, a narrative on the psychosocial consequences of unemployment evolved out of the disciplinary merge of psychology and sociology. This narrative has as its theoretical premise that work not only integrates the subject into society, but it also lends the subject his or her identity as a social being. After recounting these differing perspectives, Matthies points out the major paradox of how work functions in capitalist societies. Whereas work is seen to benefit society because it is necessary for social cohesion and the formation of identities, empirical studies as well as historical data show paradoxically that much political and economic effort is put into the reduction of work. Matthies reflects on these paradoxes, assessing the arguments of sociological narratives of unemployment as crisis.

Along with sociologists and other scholars who study these phenomena from a scientific perspective, fiction writers reacted to the 2007/8 financial crisis with plots fueled by financial disaster, unemployment, and economic desperation. These authors recognized that it is important to tell stories about the financial "losers" that enable their suffering to be seen (Greaney 2007: 7). In her contribution, "Cruel Optimism as Plot Driver in German and Austrian Economic Crisis Novels with Adult and Child Protagonists Thrust into Poverty," Jill E. Twark delves into the literary aesthetics of narrating poverty in a series of German and Austrian social novels published from 2010 to 2014 by André Pilz, Inger-Maria Mahlke, Christoph Dolgan, Mathias Nawrat, and Thomas Melle. Her analyses focus on how the authors tell stories of poverty from both adult and child perspectives, with the adult characters falling into the trap of what Lauren Berlant (2011) calls "cruel optimism," a psychological state of hope that they can improve their condition, but that ironically contributes to their inability to escape from it. The narrative techniques these authors employ allow them to give a voice to the powerless while condemning socioeconomic and legal institutions as well as familial and interpersonal dynamics for contributing actively to their misery. Their narratives compel readers to take a step back from crisis discourses, which often focus on those at the top of the economic ladder, and see the devastating consequences of economic crises for those struggling to survive at the bottom.

As capitalism extends beyond the economic sphere into non-economic spheres (see Marx 1959; Schumpeter 1994; Boltanski and Chiapello 2005; Foucault 2008; Kocka 2016), capitalist discourse, as one cultural manifestation of capitalist systems, impacts the way individuals construct their narrative identities. On the opposite end of the poverty narratives that Twark discusses are those such as that of the fictional corporate consultant depicted by John von Düffel in his 2001 novel *Ego*. Working with Paul Ricœur's concept of the "narrative self," Johanna Tönsing explores what has changed in the ways individuals narrate their selves in the contemporary neoliberal era. In "John von Düffel's *Ego* (2001) as a Seismographic Recorder of the Neoliberal Crisis of the Self," Tönsing observes a shift from identities focused on mental growth and development to those obsessed with personal characteristics that are quantifiable. Fictional narratives not only represent this transformation, but also reflect on it, criticize it, and modify it. Instead of focusing on inner progress and development—like the traditional *Bildungsroman*—the emergence of a narration of the self, based on numbers, can be observed in some early twenty-first-century novels. John von Düffel's novel is an early German example of this type of narrative. Decisive in constructing his protagonist's identity is the man's physical attractiveness, which he observes through seemingly objective numbers, and then turns into a narration of his self that is wrapped around the quantification and optimization of his body. Looking at the way von Düffel's protagonist narrates his self is not only a narratological investigation, but also an analysis of contemporary neoliberal discourse.

Part III contains two chapters that focus on "German 'Exceptionalism' in Contemporary European Crisis Situations." The first contribution calls into question the coherence that many observers of EU politics and social affairs point out in German government fiscal responses to the eurozone crisis, and the second finds coherence in Germany's stable housing policies. Looking back to 1992, the year of the signing of the Maastricht Treaty and the launching of the long-disputed framing of the EU common currency, one finds a plurality of German voices and judgments regarding financial policies in the eurozone. Even after the full-fledged start of the global financial crisis in 2008, a sharp difference can be detected between the Keynesian public policy stimulus orientation taken in the December 2008 meeting of the European Council, already clearly under German leadership, and the somber call for fiscal discipline and debt control a year later. In her chapter, titled "Germany's Compromises: The Impact of Crisis Narratives on the European Central Bank and Euro Governance," Sara Konoe shows how European Central Bank (ECB) leaders, facing dire financial circumstances, convinced Germany to bend its otherwise rigid policies toward this bank. Exploring how the euro crisis induced changes in the roles played by the ECB, Konoe focuses on the extent to which Germany's policy community tolerated the ECB's wider discretion in financial stabilization policies.

When the European Monetary Union and the ECB were negotiated and instituted during the 1990s, upon Germany's insistence, price stability became an absolute priority for the ECB, which could not be compromised for other policy purposes. In these pre-crisis years, the ECB adhered to conservative monetary policies, and these policies were considered of paramount necessity for stable management of the eurozone. However, because of the ECB's own initiatives in defending the euro as well as other eurozone members' demands for the ECB to expand its role, Germany had to accept the ECB's widened discretions during the period of crisis management after the 2008 stock market crash. Konoe examines how this crisis impacted policymakers' discussions about the ECB in Germany, and analyzes the extent to which the ECB's changing roles were tolerated there. How and why did the German government and German members of the ECB react differently to the need for the ECB to expand its role? What traditional and new narratives emerged from the discussions? Konoe explores how creditors' responsibilities in fueling such crises were perceived in Germany, and how the policy discourse on creditors' and debtors' responsibilities impacted Germany's stance toward the ECB's changing roles.

The second chapter in Part III turns to another major topic that received much attention in the United States and Europe after the 2007/8 financial crisis: the high number of housing foreclosures that both initiated the crisis and continued to impact people's lives for several years thereafter. Germany is a nation renowned for low levels of property ownership, which stands at around 43 percent of housing stock. By comparison, American homeownership is over 60 percent. In contrast to Anglo-liberal societies or even other coordinated market economies, German leaders do not promote homeownership, and German governments have pursued tenure-neutral housing policies over the last decades. The wide acceptance of renting by German households and leaders raises interesting questions about the global financial crisis and the euro crisis. In both cases, the bust of the property market preceded the insolvency of lenders, and revealed enormous amounts of debt undertaken by households and financial institutions. In their contribution, "Housing Crises and the Crisis of Housing: German Experiences with Neoliberal Reforms," Paulette Kurzer and Alice H. Cooper first look at how the German political elite and media interpreted the collapse of the housing market in the US and various EU member states, given the absence of widespread homeownership and, more recently, since 2016, the rising rental costs in large urban areas. They then assess how the events in the US and Europe affirmed the expediency of Germany's preference for long-term rental housing, which allowed it to avoid highly leveraged households whose wealth is tied up in "concrete."

Part IV starts by grappling with "The Tricky Question of Cause and Effect" in financial crisis narratives. Who is to blame for financial crises? How can we determine their guilt? What should be their punishment, if any? Monika Albrecht begins by looking at a novel written during the rise of financial capitalism in Germany in the late 1980s and published in 1991: Uwe Timm's *Kopfjäger* (published in English as *Headhunter*, 1994). In his novel, Timm not only predicts what may happen as a result of unrestrained financial activities, but he also reveals strategies that justify and muddle the real causes of economic crises. In order to do this, he creates a reality in which the status quo of financial affairs appears to be natural and without alternatives. In "Literature against the 'Profit-Friendly Ideological Defense System': Entertainment and Sociopolitical Enlightenment in Uwe Timm's *Headhunter*," Albrecht interprets *Kopfjäger* as revealing the learning process the narrator undergoes in acknowledging that his crimes were not inevitable, and thus that alternatives to exploitative economic activities do exist. According to Timm, the simple law of cause and effect can still be used to explain international financial activities and their consequences for culture and society.

In the final chapter, "An Imaginary of Blame: The Representation of Crisis, the Crisis of Representation, and Jonas Lüscher's *Barbarian Spring*," Joel Kaipainen looks at a novel whose author, like Timm, mobilizes the "imaginary of blame" that was directed against major actors involved in the production of the 2007/8 financial crisis. Instead of resorting to blaming these financial actors unequivocally for the crisis, however, Swiss author Lüscher's tale undermines the very stereotypes of financial actors it puts on display, thereby advancing a more fundamental critique of the narrative representation of major financial events. Kaipainen explains how, as the novel's plot unfolds at a wedding party of London financial professionals that devolves into scenes of violent chaos, Lüscher suggests that financial accumulation is plagued with problems of governance, agency, and accountability. The novelist thus shuns an unequivocal crisis narrative with wholly culpable protagonists, as well as clearly defined causes and effects. *Barbarian Spring* contrasts with predominant accounts of the crisis promulgating the greed or incompetence of financial professionals as its cause.

In subverting a simplistic moral legibility of the crisis and its pre-crisis economic order, Lüscher's novel aligns its critical thrust with claims that certain economic phenomena cannot be represented or narrated (Lipshaw 2009; Vogl 2010). After discussing what he calls an "imaginary of blame" as the (re-)emergence of a familiar strategy of complexity reduction and appeasement in representing financial crises, Kaipainen demonstrates how Lüscher's representation of the crisis serves as a nuanced examination of culpability in a world permeated by finance. Rather than providing a one-sided critique of "barbaric" bankers, Lüscher's carefully constructed text draws attention to a larger crisis of representation in depictions of the financial system.

Questions of blame and cause and effect that Albrecht and Kaipainen ponder have likewise been foregrounded in J.C. Chandor's fictional film *Margin Call* (United States, 2011) and Marc Bauder's documentary *Der Banker – Master of the Universe* (Germany, 2013), among many others. These films not only home in on *what*, but also *who* caused the financial crisis of 2007/8. Although just a handful of bankers and financial traders have thus far been punished as criminals in either the United States or Germany for their irresponsible actions, they do receive their comeuppance in cinematic portrayals of the crisis. Willingly or not, they take on the moral responsibility, thereby distracting from the need to pose systemic questions of neoliberal capitalism. Quinn Slobodian's (2020) research into the origins of what he calls "neoliberal globalism" represents a significant step forward in posing—and answering—questions of culpability for neoliberalism's failings. In *Globalists: The End of Empire and the Birth of Neoliberalism,* Slobodian reveals that twentieth-century European neoliberal theorists from the now mostly forgotten Geneva School viewed democracy as a threat to producing their vision of a world economic order. These theorists produced a narrative that advocates for political and legal institutions to maintain economic stability by integrating the world's economies into a global world order. They attempted to superimpose a seemingly stable "constitutional" order over an economic system that is hopelessly out of balance with respect to global wealth and power disparities. Economic crises make this lack of balance painfully visible.

In this volume, using Germany as a case study, we see how economic crisis narratives constantly shift their focus as new crises emerge across the globe, and how all are inevitably tied to an immense humanitarian and monetary cost. After the immediate efforts to overcome the stock-market crash of 2007/8 kicked in, debates on the sovereign debt crisis and bailouts in the European Union arose. In the third decade of the twenty-first century, the worldwide "climate crisis" and the "coronavirus crisis" are also affecting the global economy, dominating the media and political discourse such that we seem to have entered into a perpetual, worldwide state of crisis. Georgio Agamben's (1998: 9, 12) assertion that the "state of emergency has become the rule" in government maintenance of state security since World War I begs the analogy that a perpetual state of financial emergency runs in tandem with it.

This foreboding discourse has captured the popular imagination. Authors such as Marc Friedrich and Matthias Weik (2019), for example, continue to fuel the flames of fear of the next financial crash. Their bestselling book *Der größte Crash aller Zeiten: Wirtschaft, Politik, Gesellschaft – Wie Sie Ihr Geld noch schützen können* (The biggest crash of all time: Economy, politics, society – how you can still protect your money) points to the insanity (*Irrsinn*) of government manipulation of bank note value, and warns that the world's financial system is teetering on the brink of collapse. Friedrich and Weik buttress their arguments by alluding to the popular HBO television fantasy series *Game of Thrones* and its rulers' need to band together and prepare for the coming winter and the pending White Walker zombie invasion. Not only do Friedrich and Weik draw on existing "real" financial crisis narratives such as those blaming the causes of crisis on high national debt, but they also produce their own account by comparing the current economic climate to an established, fictional doomsday narrative with an archetypal plot of struggle, sacrifice, and final triumph. The purpose of their story is to enthrall their readers and jolt them out of their ostrich-in-the-sand mentality of underpreparing for disasters (see Meyer and Kunreuther 2017). In the twenty-first century, as Friedrich and Weik suggest, it is important to take stock of the causes, reactions to, and ongoing results of recurring crises.

Can the inability to soften the egregious impact of economic booms and busts be linked to how crises have been explained in predominant crisis narratives? Do narratives that buttress neoliberalism drown out alternatives to this ideological conviction, preserving the flaws of the capitalist system and the fact that it is perpetually prone to instability (see, e.g., Piketty 2021)? Narratives can be invested in propagating a status-quo agenda that leads to greater economic precarity and cyclical crises. But we can also choose to invest in narratives that have the power to effect change on behalf of greater economic equality and stability.

Jill E. Twark is Associate Professor of German at East Carolina University in North Carolina. Her research interests include twentieth- and twenty-first-century German literature and culture, including the representation of history in German film. She has published widely on humor and satire, including the book *Humor, Satire, and Identity: Eastern German Literature in the 1990s* and the edited volume *Strategies of Humor in Post-Unification German Literature, Film, and Other Media*. She focused on social justice dilemmas in the volume *Envisioning Social Justice in Contemporary German Culture*. She serves as a German Studies editor for *The Literary Encyclopedia*.

Notes

1. "Sensemaking" produces reality by means of cognitive and verbal patterns as "an ongoing accomplishment that emerges from efforts to create order and make retrospective sense of what occurs" (Weick 1993: 635; Weick 1995: 1–16). It allows people to construct and preserve "images of a wider reality, in part to rationalize what they are doing" (Morgan, Frost, and Pondy 1983: 24) and to serve as "a springboard into action" (Weick, Sutcliffe, and Obstfeld 2005: 409). "Worldmaking" is the process of creating multiple versions of the world using language or symbolism (as in the visual arts), all of which may be true, and they are projected onto the world as we conceptualize it (Goodman 1978; see also Cohnitz and Rossberg 2019).
2. German authors who have taken an interdisciplinary approach to assessing economics that takes storytelling into account include Joseph Vogl (2010; English translation 2014), Gereon Rausch (2012), Jochen Hörisch (2013), and Tomáš Sedláček and Oliver Tanzer (2015).
3. The University of Tübingen's Collaborative Research Center 923, created in 2011, is dedicated to researching "threatened orders" (i.e., societies around the world, past and present, that have experienced various catastrophes), as well as to analyzing the concurrent discourses and their effects. Their mission and publications can be found

at: https://uni-tuebingen.de/en/research/core-research/collaborative-research-centers/crc-923/scientific-profile/.

4. The German pulp-fiction crime thriller *Bad Banker* by Markus A. Will (2010); the 2013 documentary film *Master of the Universe* and 2016 feature film *Dead Man Working*, both directed by Marc Bauder; and the 2018–20 ZDF/ARTE TV series *Bad Banks* reproduce this narrative. Note that all of these titles are in English, alluding to the English-speaking world as the source of criminal banking activities. See Sorkin (2009), Sinn (2010), Lewis (2010), Bauert (2014), and Tooze (2018) for thorough analyses of the 2007/8 crisis causes and results.

References

Agamben, Giorgio. 1998. *Homo Sacer: Sovereign Power and Bare Life*. translated by D. Heller-Roazen. Stanford, CA: Stanford University Press.

Bal, Mieke. 1997. *Narratology: An Introduction to the Theory of Narrative*. Toronto: University of Toronto Press.

Bauert, Ann-Katrin. 2014. *Die Finanzkrise seit 2008 im Kontext ausgewählter Marktteilnehmer: Konsequenzen und Auswirkungen auf Banken und Privatanleger*. Hamburg: Diplomica.

Berlant, Lauren. 2011. *Cruel Optimism*. Durham, NC: Duke University Press.

Birch, Kean. 2015. "Neoliberalism: The Whys and Wherefores . . . and Future Directions." *Sociology Compass* 9(7): 571–84. doi.org/10.1111/soc4.12277.

Boltanski, Luc, and Eve Chiapello. 2005. *The New Spirit of Capitalism*, translated by Gregory Elliott. London: Verso (orig. *Le nouvel esprit du capitalism*. Paris: Gallimard, 1999).

Bourdieu, Pierre, and Loïc Wacquant. 2001. "New Liberal Speak: Notes on the New Planetary Vulgate." *Radical Philosophy* 105: 2–5.

Cohnitz, Daniel, and Marcus Rossberg. 2019. "Nelson Goodman." *Stanford Encyclopedia of Philosophy*. Retrieved 20 May 2022 from https://plato.stanford.edu/entries/goodman/.

Collaborative Research Center 923. 2022. "Scientific Profile." Eberhard Karls Universität Tübingen. Retrieved 16 January 2022 from https://uni-tuebingen.de/en/research/core-research/collaborative-research-centers/crc-923/scientific-profile.

Foucault, Michel. 2008. *The Birth of Biopolitics: Lectures at the Collège de France 1978–1979*, translated by Graham Burchell. London: Palgrave Macmillan.

Friedrich, Marc, and Matthias Weik. 2019. *Der größte Crash aller Zeiten: Wirtschaft, Politik, Gesellschaft – Wie Sie Ihr Geld noch schützen können*. Cologne: Eichborn Verlag, 2019.

Funke, Manuel, Moritz Schularick, and Christoph Trebesch. 2016. "Going to Extremes: Politics after Financial Crises, 1870–2014." *European Economic Review* (88): 227–60.

Game of Thrones. Written by George R.R. Martin. Produced by David Benioff et al. HBO, 2011–2019.

Goodman, Nelson. 1978. *Ways of Worldmaking*. Indianapolis, IN: Hackett.

Greaney, Patrick. 2007. *Untimely Beggar: Poverty and Power from Baudelaire to Benjamin*. Minneapolis: University of Minnesota Press.

Halsmayer, Verena, and Florian Huber. 2013. "Ökonomische Modelle und brüchige Welten – Joseph Vogls *Das Gespenst des Kapitals*." In *Wirtschaftswissenschaft als Oikodizee?: Diskussionen im Anschluss an Joseph Vogls Gespenst des Kapitals*, edited by Hanno Pahl and Jan Sparsam, 27–52. Wiesbaden: Springer Fachmedien.

Herman, David. 2009. "Editor's Column: The Scope and Aims of *Storyworlds*." *Storyworlds: A Journal of Narrative Studies* 1: vii–x.

Hertner, Isabelle, and Alister Miskimmon. 2015. "Germany's Strategic Narrative of the Eurozone Crisis." *German Politics and Society* 33(1–2) (Spring and Summer): 42–57.

Hörisch, Jochen. 2013. *Man muss dran glauben: Die Theologie der Märkte*. Munich: Wilhelm Fink.

Horvath, Michael. 2011. "Die Herausforderung der Interdisziplinarität: Erwägungen zum Verhältnis von Literatur- und Wirtschaftswissenschaft anhand von Joseph Vogls *Das Gespenst des Kapitals*." *Scientia Poetica. Jahrbuch für Geschichte der Literatur und Wissenschaften* 15: 331–48.

Illing, Falk. 2013. *Deutschland in der Finanzkrise: Chronologie der deutschen Wirtschaftspolitik 2007–2012*. Wiesbaden: Springer Fachmedien.

Kahler, Miles, and David A. Lake, eds. 2013. *Politics in the New Hard Times: The Great Recession in Comparative Perspective*. Ithaca, NY: Cornell University Press.

Kocka, Jürgen. 2016. *Capitalism: A Short History*. Princeton, NJ: Princeton University Press (orig. *Geschichte des Kapitalismus*. Munich: C.H. Beck, 2013).

Krasni, Jan. 2017. *Schuld und Krise: Bonuszahlungen und Verantwortung in Mediendarstellungen der Finanzkrise*. Wiesbaden: Springer Fachmedien.

Kreiswirth, Martin. 2005. "Narrative Turn in the Humanities." In *Routledge Encyclopedia of Narrative Theory*, ed. David Herman, Manfred Jahn, and Marie-Laure Ryan, 377–82. London: Routledge.

La Berge, Leigh Claire. 2014. "The Rules of Abstraction: Methods and Discourses of Finance." *Radical History Review* 118: 93–112.

Lewis, Michael. 2010. *The Big Short: Inside the Doomsday Machine*. New York: W.W. Norton.

Lipshaw, Jeffrey M. 2009. "The Epistemology of the Financial Crisis: Complexity, Causation, Law, and Judgment." *Southern California Interdisciplinary Law Journal* 19(2) (August): 299–351. Retrieved 20 May 2022 from https://dx.doi.org/10.2139/ssrn.1421837.

Margin Call. 2011. Dir. J.C. Chandor. Lionsgate.

Marx, Karl. 1959. *Economic and Philosophic Manuscripts of 1844*, translated by Martin Milligan, rev. Dirk J. Struik. Moscow: Progress Publishers.

Mast, Claudia, ed. 2012. *Neuorientierung im Wirtschaftsjournalismus: Redaktionelle Strategien und Publikumserwartungen*. Wiesbaden: Springer Verlag für Sozialwissenschaften.

Master of the Universe. Dir. Marc Bauder. Arsenal Filmverleih, 2014.

Meyer, Robert, and Howard Kunreuther. 2017. *The Ostrich Paradox: Why We Underprepare for Disasters*. Philadelphia, PA: Wharton School Press.

Morgan, Gareth, Peter J. Frost, and Louis R. Pondy. 1983. "Organizational Symbolism." In *Organizational Symbolism*, ed. Louis R. Pondy, Peter J. Frost, Gareth Morgan, and T.C. Dandridge, 3–35. Greenwich, CT: JAI Press.

Noonan, Laura, et al. 2018. "Who Went to Jail for Their Role in the Financial Crisis?" *The Financial Times*, 20 September. Retrieved 5 December 2019 from https://ig.ft.com/jailed-bankers/.

Nünning, Ansgar. 2012. "Narrativist Approaches and Narratological Concepts for the Study of Culture." In *Travelling Concepts for the Study of Culture*, ed. Birgit Neumann and Ansgar Nünning, 145–83. Boston, MA: Walter de Gruyter.

Onega, Susana, and Jose Angel García Landa. 1996. "Introduction." In *Narratology: An Introduction*, ed. Susana Onega and Jose Angel García Landa, 1–41. London: Longman.

Pahl, Hanno, and Jan Sparsam, eds. 2013. "Einleitung: Diskussionen im Anschluss an Joseph Vogls *Das Gespenst des Kapitals*." In *Wirtschaftswissenschaft als Oikodizee?: Diskussionen im Anschluss an Joseph Vogls Gespenst des Kapitals*, ed. Hanno Pahl and Jan Sparsam, 7–23. Wiesbaden: Springer Fachmedien.

Piketty, Thomas. 2021. *Time for Socialism: Dispatches from a World on Fire, 2016–2021*, trans. Kristin Couper. New Haven, CT: Yale University Press.

Pilz, André. 2010. *Man Down*. Innsbruck: Haymon Verlag.

Prince, Gerald. 1982. *Narratology: The Form and Functioning of Narrative*. Berlin: Mouton.

Quiring, Oliver, Hans Mathias Kepplinger, Mathias Weber, and Stefan Geiss. 2012. *Lehmann Brothers und die Folgen: Berichterstattung zu wirtschaftlichen Interventionen des Staates*. Wiesbaden: Springer Verlag.

Rausch, Gereon. 2012. *2010 – Nach der Krise ist vor der Krise*. Berlin: Epubli GmbH.

Reinhart, Carmen M., and Kenneth S. Rogoff. 2009. *This Time Is Different: Eight Centuries of Financial Folly*. Princeton, NJ: Princeton University Press.

Rudrum, David. 2005. "From Narrative Representation to Narrative Use: Towards the Limits of Definition." *Narrative* 13(2) (May): 195–204.

Ryan, Marie-Laure. 2007. "Toward a Definition of Narrative." In *The Cambridge Companion to Narrative*, ed. David Herman, 22–35. Cambridge: Cambridge University Press.

Schäfer, Ulrich. 2013. "Schwierige Aufräumarbeiten bei der Deutschen Bank." *Süddeutsche Zeitung*, 30 October. Retrieved 20 June 2022 from https://www.sueddeutsche.de/wirtschaft/spuren-der-finanzkrise-schwierige-aufraeumarbeiten-bei-der-deutschen-bank-1.1807051.

Schmidt, Reinhard H. 2019. "Zur Veränderung des deutschen Finanzsystems." In *Zentralbanken, Währungsunion und stabiles Finanzsystem*, ed. Theodor Baums et al., 355–72. Berlin: Duncker & Humblot (English version: "On the Change of the German Financial System," SAFE White Paper 61 [July 2019]: 1–20).

Schumpeter, Joseph A. 1994. *Capitalism, Socialism and Democracy*. Intro. Richard Swedberg. New York: Routledge (orig. New York and London: Harper, 1942).

Sedláček, Tomáš, and Oliver Tanzer. 2015. *Lilith und die Dämonen des Kapitals: Die Ökonomie auf Freuds Couch*. Munich: Carl Hanser Verlag.

Shiller, Robert J. (2019) 2020. *Narrative Economics: How Stories Go Viral and Drive Major Economic Events*. Princeton, NJ: Princeton University Press.

Siemens, Daniel. 2012. "Das Narrativ der Krise in der deutschen Geschichte des 20. Jahrhunderts." In *Sicherheit und Krise: Interdisziplinäre Beiträge der Forschungstage 2009 und 2010 des Jungen Kollegs der Nordrhein-Westfälischen Akademie der Wissenschaften und der Künste*, ed. Cornel Zwierlein, 63–82. Paderborn: Schöningh.

Sinn, Hans-Werner. 2010. *Casino Capitalism: How the Financial Crisis Came About and What Needs to be Done Now*. Oxford: Oxford University Press (orig. *Kasino-Kapitalismus: Wie es zur Finanzkrise kam, und was jetzt zu tun ist*. Berlin: Econ, 2009).

Slobodian, Quinn. (2018) 2020. *Globalists: The End of Empire and the Birth of Neoliberalism*. Cambridge, MA: Harvard University Press.

Sorkin, Andrew Ross. 2009. *Too Big To Fail: The Inside Story of How Wall Street and Washington Fought to Save the Financial System—and Themselves*. New York: Viking.

Strange, Susan. 1986. *Casino Capitalism*. Oxford, UK: Basil Blackwell.

Timm, Uwe. 1991. *Kopfjäger*. Cologne: Kiepenheuer & Witsch. (English edition: *Headhunter*, translated by Peter Tegel. New York: New Directions Publishing, 1994).

Tooze, Adam. 2018. *Crashed: How a Decade of Financial Crises Changed the World*. New York: Viking.

Vogl, Joseph. 2014. *The Specter of Capital*. Stanford, CA: Stanford University Press (orig. *Das Gespenst des Kapitals*. Zurich: Diaphanes Verlag, 2010).

Weick, Karl E. 1993. "The Collapse of Sensemaking in Organizations: The Mann Gulch Disaster." *Administrative Science Quarterly* 38: 628–52.

———. 1995. *Sensemaking in Organizations*. Thousand Oaks, CA: Sage Publishing.

Weick, Karl E., Kathleen M. Sutcliffe, and David Obstfeld. 2005. "Organizing and the Process of Sensemaking." *Organization Science* 16(4) (July/August): 409–21.

PART I

Shaping Economic Knowledge from Historical Perspectives

CHAPTER 1

German *Finanzkapitalismus*

A Narrative of Deutsche Bank and Its Role in the German Financial System

REINHARD H. SCHMIDT

The idea underlying this volume of "narratives" about Germany and crises is appealing, and the case of Deutsche Bank is particularly well suited for this methodological approach.[1] For many years, Deutsche Bank has been the flagship of German banking; but its roles in the German financial system, the German economy, and German politics have often been the objects of heated controversies. It offers a rich menu of dramatic events about which one can tell stories of ups and downs, of crises, and of attempts to overcome them. The evolution of Deutsche Bank is closely related to the development of the entire German financial system and, in fact, it strongly shaped the development of this system. This is why telling its history in narrative form may interest many readers, not only experts in banking and finance.

Narratives rely not merely on facts and figures[2] but also on the author's personal assessments and on what relevant people, actors as well as outside observers, have told him or others about the subject. A narrative on economics is neither an outright historical account nor a strict economic analysis, even though a clear line of separation between writing about hard facts and "storytelling" does not exist. Consequently, the following account of the history of Deutsche Bank is strongly shaped by my interpretation of what seems to be the raw facts and by interviews and other confidential conversations with relevant actors from Deutsche Bank, including four of its former CEOs.

One might be inclined to think that narratives are not what an economist is supposed to offer his or her readers. However, this orthodoxy is not appropriate, for it would exclude nearly all economic writing. McCloskey (1985, 1990) has argued convincingly that even rather formal economic research is more akin to narratives or rhetoric than most economists believe. The following narrative of Deutsche Bank makes its history accessible to readers, and its leaders' choices visible and logical, rather than diabolical as German journalist Dirk Laabs depicts them in *Bad Bank: Aufstieg und Fall der Deutschen Bank*

(2018) or David Enrich in *Dark Towers: Deutsche Bank, Donald Trump, and an Epic Trail of Destruction* (2020).

These introductory remarks aim to distinguish this chapter from others in this volume, as it is a narrative in the sense described above and not an analysis of narratives concerning Deutsche Bank, even though it refers to what others, in particular the bank's leaders, have said or written about the bank. I focus here on four features of the bank's history, tracing each forward chronologically in a series of subsections: (1) its degree of internationalization, which has varied greatly over time; (2) the extent to which it has engaged in investment banking (as opposed to commercial banking), which has also varied greatly over time; (3) the important role that ups and downs—or crises and efforts to overcome them—have played in the bank's development; and (4) the consistency of the bank's business model at different stages in its history. From the end of the nineteenth century until the 2008–2010 financial crisis struck, Deutsche Bank had contributed more than any other financial institution to the expansion and stabilization of the entire German financial system. Mistakes made by its leaders at the turn of the twenty-first century, however, led to a reduction in its power following this crisis. Understanding what motivated Deutsche Bank's leaders over the past 150 years, and how their decisions have impacted its losses and recoveries, helps us understand the German financial system as a whole.

The Early History and "Original Roots" of Deutsche Bank

After the Prussian/German victory over France in the war of 1870/71, Prussia's chancellor Otto von Bismarck proclaimed the Prussian king Wilhelm as the German emperor Wilhelm I in the French Palace of Versailles, and by so doing completed the protracted process of establishing a new German Empire. The creation of this "Second German Reich" coincided with Germany's ascent to the ranks of a leading export-oriented industrial nation, which had been preceded by a fundamental reform of the law of corporations in 1865 and the modernization of the German stock exchange system in the 1860s.[3] The new political, economic, and legal opportunities inspired the development of new technologies and the emergence of large industrial firms that wanted to use these technologies worldwide and benefit from the German stock exchange as a source of funding.

These developments fostered the creation of big banks as joint-stock corporations that did not require government authorization, a legal form that had not existed in German banking up to that time. Deutsche Bank was founded in Berlin in 1870 by a group of bankers and industrialists. Two competitors established at the same time were Commerzbank (founded in Hamburg in 1870) and Dresdner Bank (founded in Dresden in 1871). Together with Deutsche Bank, they shaped private commercial banking for more than 150 years—however, Deutsche Bank soon became the uncontested leader.

Deutsche Bank was not created as just another bank like those that had already existed in the mid-nineteenth century. It was supposed to add a truly novel institution to the German banking system and to supplement the range of services provided by the existing private banks. Its original mandate was to support the large new industrial corporations in their efforts to internationalize and to access the stock market, two banking services that the existing banks were neither large enough nor sophisticated enough to provide. This origin explains why internationalization and capital-market orientation are "the roots" or "in the DNA" of Deutsche Bank, as it has often been described metaphorically, and why, together with industrialists, private bankers stood behind the creation of Deutsche Bank.[4]

On the eve of World War I, Deutsche Bank had established numerous branches and subsidiaries in various countries and assumed a dominant role in the German stock exchange system. Its most important clients were the newly created industrial corporations. Thus, in its early years Deutsche Bank was essentially what came to be called a century later an international investment bank. Like the other big German banks of that time, Deutsche Bank also soon started to lend money to its corporate clients on a grand scale and thereby created close working relationships with them. Out of these transactions grew the system of "house banks." At that time, combining the provision of capital market-related services with lending to large corporate clients, and therefore being their house bank, was compatible, and it constituted a sound business model. Investment banking "à la 1900" was for the most part advisory-based, and therefore client-centered, rather than based on trading, as investment banking was to become a century later.

The German House Bank System as Facilitator of Deutsche Bank's Rise to the Top

What exactly is a house bank? Above all, a house bank is the preferred bank with which a corporation interacts by having its payments executed by it, using it to issue securities, borrowing heavily from it, and, last but not least, employing its bankers as financial advisors. This multiplicity of services provided to its corporate clients gives the house bank access to much more information than other banks could ever acquire, let alone the general investing public. This close relationship allows a house bank to lend more freely than other banks and also to continue lending in situations in which less-informed banks would hesitate to do so. The resulting close relationship leads to a mutual dependence, with all its pros and cons. This form of relationship banking has been practiced for many years by banks all over the world. However, being a house bank is more than simply relationship banking. In the past, three additional features of the bank–client relationship supported and stabilized house bank relationships. The first feature is that Deutsche Bank—along with its German peers—often held large equity stakes in many of the corporations for which it served as the house bank.[5] The second is that these banks possessed extensive voting rights at the corporations' annual shareholder meetings. These voting rights derived either from the banks' own shareholdings or they were so-called depository voting rights, transferred to the banks by shareholders whose shares it held in custody. The banks were essentially free to use these depository voting rights however they wanted—that is, in their own best interest.

The third, and arguably most important, feature of the house bank–client relationship was that top bankers used to be members of the supervisory boards of their partner corporations. In the German legal system, the supervisory board is distinct from the management board. It endorses the general strategy of a corporation, monitors the management board's actions, and appoints and dismisses its members. The role of supervisory board chair is particularly powerful. For many years, there were no exchange-listed German corporations without at least one top banker on the supervisory board, and at times close to half of these boards had a banker as chair. Deutsche Bank sent more members to corporate supervisory boards than any other German bank.

Even though the German house bank system only reached its peak in the years after World War II in the form described above,[6] it is actually much older. As Rudolf Hilferding (2000; orig. 1910) reported in detail, it was already in place around the turn of the twentieth century, and Deutsche Bank was the paragon of that system. However, as will be described below, in the late twentieth century Deutsche Bank moved away from house banking when it shifted its focus from commercial banking to investment banking.

The Interwar, Nazi, and Post-World War II Years

The era from its genesis in the 1870s until 1914 was a nearly uninterrupted Up phase for Deutsche Bank. When World War I ended with the total defeat of Germany, however, the nation entered a precipitous Down period, which affected Deutsche Bank along with its corporate clients. The 1919 Treaty of Versailles dictated that Germany lose almost all it had come to own—in one form or another—outside of its pre-1871 borders, plus a portion of East Prussia. Deutsche Bank's foreign branches and subsidiaries were seized by the victorious powers, its credit claims on foreign borrowers were declared void or simply became unenforceable, and it lost most of its international business connections.

Still, Deutsche Bank managed to recover quickly, initiating a decade that was, from the perspective of the bank, another Up period. Deutsche Bank also survived the great inflation of 1923 better than other German banks, and it soon built up a new network of foreign offices and connections. It expanded enormously by taking over many formerly independent local banks. When the great financial and banking crisis of 1929 to 1932 struck, Deutsche Bank once again suffered significantly fewer losses than other institutions. In Germany, the banking crisis started with the collapse of Nordwolle, a large textile company, and of DaNat-Bank, Nordwolle's house bank. Other large German banks soon experienced serious difficulties as well. Deutsche Bank, however, seized the opportunity in 1929 to merge with Disconto Gesellschaft, for many years its biggest competitor, in order to assert its position as Germany's leading bank. From the perspective of Deutsche Bank, the interwar years until 1933 were another Up phase.

During the Nazi period from 1933 to 1945, Deutsche Bank—like the others mentioned above—cooperated willingly and shamelessly with the Nazi regime, financing war preparations and war activities, and continuing its policy of snapping up other banks (mainly those with Jewish owners) in Germany and in countries occupied by the German army. In business terms this was also a period with an Up trend, but morally it was a very deep Down.

After World War II ended, the moral Down continued, at least at first, along with the general economic Down experienced in Germany after losing the war. When the Western Allied Powers investigated the war-related crimes of Germany's three remaining large commercial banks, to which Deutsche Bank belonged, all were found guilty. The Allies therefore split each bank into ten regional banks, with an additional one located in Berlin. The foreign operations of Deutsche Bank were once again discontinued, and foreign holdings, claims, and other belongings were seized, including the parts of Deutsche Bank located in East Germany, which was separated definitively from West Germany in 1949.

Despite the need to restructure and find new leadership for Deutsche Bank in the postwar years, it did not take long until a new Up phase got underway. When tensions between the Western Allies and the Soviet Union intensified after 1948 in the lead-up to the Cold War, the US government started to regard Deutsche Bank and its peers as indispensable for the reconstruction of West Germany, which had become an ally of the Western powers in this new conflict. The reintegration of the big private banks started in 1953 and was completed by 1957.

The Postwar "Economic Miracle" Years

In the next twenty or so years, Germany underwent the so-called *Wirtschaftswunder*, the economic miracle. During these two decades, Deutsche Bank and its peers managed once again to strengthen their ties to the large German industrial and commercial companies. They moreover systematically forged close connections in the financial sector in the form of cross shareholding and personal alliances. These efforts resulted in what came to be known as "Deutschland AG"—or, in English, "Germany Inc." Because the German capital market had not yet recovered from its decline during the interwar and Nazi periods, bank lending was needed more urgently than ever before for corporate reconstruction. This explains why banks were so important for German industry growth and why, for thirty years, Deutsche Bank remained at the peak of its "power and glory."

Two important differences stand out, however, in comparison to the bank's early years. First, capital-market orientation was at a very low level, as the capital market was essentially dormant. Second, the degree of internationalization was once again very low, and much lower than that of big banks from other West European countries.[7] Based on the experience of two world wars and their respective aftermaths, the longtime leader of Deutsche Bank during the 1960s and 1970s, Herrmann Josef Abs, was convinced that internationalization would simply be too risky. Thus, in the postwar period, the phrase "the roots of the bank" or "its DNA" took on an entirely different meaning from what had been appropriate a hundred years earlier: the roots of Deutsche Bank were now seen as being geared strongly toward providing reliable credit to Germany's large and mid-sized corporations.

Deutsche Bank as the Center of the German Financial System

To understand fully how Deutsche Bank reached its peak success and influence during the postwar reconstruction years, one needs to see how it fit into the entire German financial system. The term "financial system" refers to more than just the banking system or the financial sector. A country's "banking system" consists of all banks in that country. The "financial sector," by contrast, is made up of the banks plus all other financial institutions, such as investment companies, private equity firms, other financial intermediaries, and organized capital markets. It represents all economic institutions that provide financial services to the non-financial sectors of an economy, such as private households and firms. The financial sector nevertheless does not encompass the entire financial system—or the entire market for financial services—because it only covers the supply of financial services. The financial system also includes the demand side, which is shaped by the savings and investment decisions of households, and by the financing decisions and the resulting financing patterns of firms.

Three core elements make up a financial system: the financial sector (as just defined), the financing patterns of large firms, and the corporate governance of corporations. Including the corporate governance regime of a given country in the description of its financial system is necessary for the following reason: the ability of non-financial firms to attract external financing depends on how the use of external funds obtained from the financial sector or from shareholders, bondholders, and private creditors is monitored and controlled.

Until the late twentieth century, the German financial system had an important characteristic: it was "consistent," both internally and with respect to its economic environment. A system is consistent if its main components fit together well. These individual components must take on values such that their respective strengths reinforce each other, and their respective weaknesses mitigate each other. A consistent financial system is more stable and beneficial for an entire economy than an inconsistent one. As can be shown, shortly before the year 2000:

- the major German commercial banks dominated the entire German financial sector. Other parts, including the organized capital market, were largely bank-dependent and thus under the control of the big banks;
- as a source of funding for firms and an outlet for household savings, the capital market was underdeveloped and in fact almost irrelevant. This underdevelopment was apparently a consequence of the big banks' policy of holding back competition from the organized capital markets to ensure sufficient funding for corporations;
- large German corporations mainly used long-term bank loans, provided by the big private commercial banks, to finance their investments;
- corporations could rely on the support of their house banks even in difficult situations, which enabled them to pursue long-term strategies. These strategies were important for the banks, as they helped keep the banks' exposure to credit within reasonable limits, in turn permitting them to lend on a grand scale;
- by law and in practice, the governance of most German corporations—both in the financial and the non-financial sector[8]—and corporate policies were not shareholder-oriented but stakeholder-oriented, which again is in line with what banks as an important group of stakeholders wanted and requested; and
- the big banks played the central coordinating role in the stakeholder-oriented corporate governance regime of Germany's large non-financial

> corporations, and thereby could obtain the information and exert the influence they needed in order to protect their loans. (Schmidt and Tyrell 2004)

To understand this latter point, one must know that since the mid-1950s German corporate law has prescribed a co-determination regime, according to which half the seats and voting rights in the supervisory boards of large joint-stock corporations are held by employee representatives. The people who occupy the other half of the seats in the supervisory boards—and who have the right to appoint the chair of the supervisory board—are elected by the shareholders. However, this does not mean that these shareholder-elected board members are supposed to use their influence strictly in the interest of the shareholders. Instead, according to German corporate law, all members of both boards, the supervisory board and the management board, are supposed to act "in the interest of the corporation," which was understood for many years by almost all academic lawyers and most top managers to be different from the mere interest of most shareholders in maximizing profits (Rieckers and Spindler 2004).

Between 1955 and the late 1990s, there were two highly influential groups among the supervisory board members elected by the shareholders: people representing the holders of blocks of shares (the strategic investors), and representatives of large banks and insurance companies. Other shareholders did not play a significant role in corporate governance. Thus, the three main influential groups on the supervisory boards of German corporations used to consist of representatives of labor (i.e., the aforementioned appointed employee representatives), plus the elected blockholders (large shareholders) and bank representatives. All three groups had a largely common interest in maintaining a steady, healthy development of the corporations for which they were responsible.

Among these three influential governing groups, banks have traditionally played the central role in making business decisions. The main reason for this is their position as mediator between company employees and shareholders. That labor is more interested in steady growth than high profits is obvious: it usually secures stable jobs and opportunities for internal advancement for the core employees. Although most blockholders also have a strategic interest in securing their lasting influence for various reasons, they are, of course, also interested in high profits. Being important lenders to corporations, banks are mainly interested in profitability and stable growth, because this ensures their loans will not be put at risk. Thus, German banks' dominant, fact-based interest more closely resembled that of the employees than that of the shareholders. At the same time, bankers were professionally and ideologically closer to the big shareholders than to labor. This intermediate position made them ideally suited to holding a central position on the supervisory boards and bridging the gaps that might exist between the other two groups. It also explains why bankers were members and often chairs of most German supervisory boards.

Toward the end of the twentieth century, the German financial system was indeed a consistent system of complementary segments, and at least in this specific sense it was a good financial system. But what exactly was the role of Deutsche Bank in this context? Deutsche Bank was more than just one part of this system and more than merely one among several big banks: it was the central player. It was the uncontested market leader among German banks and the trendsetter whose peers at that time, Dresdner Bank and Commerzbank, essentially imitated what it was doing (see Janssen 2009). Thus, the fact that Deutsche Bank had for a long time shaped and represented the system of house bank relationships, embedded in a bank-based financial system with a stakeholder-oriented corporate governance regime for large corporations, was crucial in upholding the consistency of the German financial system.

The Fundamental Strategy Switch of the Late 1980s: Identifying Weaknesses

Apparent success often harbors the seeds of decline. In the mid-1980s, Deutsche Bank was still quite successful. However, its success was based on a business model that continued to be shaped by the bank's postwar history: like its two peers, Dresdner Bank and Commerzbank, it was one-sidedly credit-oriented and almost fully Germany-centered—and, according to a widely held perception at that time, it had become overly complacent. Being essentially Germany-centered meant that none of the three big private German banks succeeded in supporting—nor did they even try to support—German non-financial corporations in their efforts to become more export-oriented and globalized.[9] Moreover, in the 1980s Deutsche Bank was still heavily decentralized, as the allied forces had required it to be after World War II. This structure had far-reaching consequences for the bank's internal power distribution and management strategy.[10]

The most important decisions made at Deutsche Bank in the late twentieth century were lending decisions. They were made by the people at the helm of the regional centers—internally called the "regional barons"—and not by the bank's management board at its headquarters. Individual management board members merely had to sanction the general policy of those regional centers, for which they bore responsibility under the auspices of the entire management board. At least to a certain extent, the reputation of management board members also depended on the profits earned by the regional centers whose "godfathers" they were. In accordance with the allocation of decision-making authority, earnings from lending operations were booked as revenue at the respective regional center. Of course, Deutsche Bank also provided capital market-related services to its corporate clients, even though the scale of these services was quite limited. Providing such services was important for maintaining close, stable relationships with corporate clients, and indirectly served the purpose of making these clients borrow more from the bank. Thus, this service provision supported both the bank headquarters and its regional centers.

But which part of the bank provided these services and how were they recorded in the bank's internal accounting system? Headquarter units provided capital-market services, and even though this may appear strange, the bank offered and provided these services almost for free and, as compensation, expected its corporate clients to accept slightly higher interest rates on their loans. In the internal accounting system, the regional centers were treated as profit centers, whereas the headquarters was merely a cost center. Thus, the cost of providing capital-market services was charged at the headquarters, and the indirect benefits increased the accounting profits of the regional centers, thereby providing a clear case of internal profit-shifting. As a consequence, the headquarter account was notoriously in the red, and its deficit was in turn compensated by allocating the headquarter costs as an overhead charge to all regional centers, regardless of how much these regional offices benefited from the activities of the headquarters.

Understandably, the "regional barons" resented these overhead charges, and they often succeeded in enlisting their respective "godfathers" among the management board members to support their opposition to all headquarter activities, including those referred to today as investment banking. Much the same applied to all business conducted outside Germany, which was also coordinated at the headquarters. This structural state of affairs explains why, in the early postwar years, Deutsche Bank shied away from the capital market-related banking services and international activities of its early years.

This policy bias became a serious burden for the bank during the 1980s, when capital markets were gaining in importance in Germany and many other nations, and several large European banks, became much more active in international markets. Observing these developments, Deutsche Bank leaders feared they would miss out on new opportunities to expand the bank's profits, as their internal strategy group leader told us[11] later in an interview.

Getting the Bank Back on Track: Alfred Herrhausen's Vision

In 1985, Alfred Herrhausen was appointed as the new CEO of Deutsche Bank.[12] He had strong views of what had gone wrong, and therefore wanted to overhaul the bank in a fundamental way, seizing the opportunities that had been neglected in prior years. According to his vision, Deutsche Bank should get much more involved in investment banking, become active on the international stage again, and stop being old-fashioned and complacent. In particular, he and his core team of forward-looking advisors were acutely aware of the profoundly conservative consequences of the existing power distribution in Deutsche Bank. He therefore wanted to take away the power of the "regional barons" to block decisions made at the bank's headquarters. This was not an easy task, however, because an old rule of the management board mandated that its decisions be made unanimously. Herrhausen's efforts to transform the bank met with strong resistance within the board. Tragically, Herrhausen was assassinated in November 1989 by members of the militant left-wing German terrorist group, the Red Army Faction.

Shortly before his death, Herrhausen initiated negotiations to take over Morgan Grenfell, a leading British merchant bank, in order to strengthen Deutsche Bank's investment banking competence, and he had planned to buy commercial banks in Italy and Spain in order to expand the bank's international scope. His vision of strengthening its investment banking activities and its international orientation, and his initial steps in both directions, were later often lauded as "bold" (see Sattler 2019, passim). This positive assessment is justified, as what he aspired to do represented a fundamental break with the bank's post-World War II business model. His untimely tragic death meant that his successors inherited the task of implementing his vision and demonstrating its feasibility and strengths from a business perspective. Accepting this challenge, they adopted various strategies to carry out his plans. This corporate policy shift turned out to be an enormous challenge, for it was by no means clear how, or even if, it could be met.

The Organizational Challenges behind Herrhausen's Vision

Herrhausen's push for a greater internationalization of Deutsche Bank was bold, but also timely, and thus does not appear controversial in retrospect. But as far as the aspiration of getting involved in investment banking on a grand scale—including all modern forms of investment banking[13]—is concerned, the assessment is less clear-cut. Would it be compatible with what, up to that time, had been the bank's mainstay, relationship-based corporate banking, which Herrhausen certainly did not want to give up? And how should the two parts of a restructured Deutsche Bank, with commercial and corporate banking on the one hand, and investment banking on the other, be organized in the future? Could both function as closely interacting parts of a single integrated institution, in which resources such as equity capital, liquidity, and reputation are needed and employed by both parts and shifted freely from one to the other? Or would a substantial expansion of the bank's investment banking activities require a holding structure with two largely independent divisions whose relationships would be governed by market-like transfer prices?

An integrated structure can create synergies that result from close cooperation and shared resources. At the same time, such a structure can also lead to conflicts and rivalry. Conflicts are especially likely to arise if one bank division provides substantial resources to the other without possessing a well-defined, transparent transfer-pricing system. Transfer prices are a crucial determinant of the accounting profits of the various divisions of any bank, and indirectly also of the bank's power distribution and allocation of the bonus pool.

As far as we know,[14] in the years after Herrhausen's death, when investment banking had indeed been boosted at Deutsche Bank, substantial resources were transferred from the commercial to the investment banking divisions, and these transfers were not accounted for by transfer prices that would have reflected market prices for the transferred resources. Moreover, as the bank expanded its investment activities, it began to be plagued by internal power struggles between the traditional corporate bankers and the new breed of investment bankers, and over the years it established huge bonus pools. Thus, the preconditions for serious conflicts were met. Still, despite often using the term "divisions" for its different parts, Deutsche Bank has always maintained an integrated structure. As Jan Krahnen recently argued in an address delivered to the Historical Society of Deutsche Bank, to think this arrangement would function well was not only "bold" (*kühn*) but "overly bold" (*tollkühn*).[15]

Deutsche Bank under Hilmar Kopper: Increasing Size and Declining Profitability

Herrhausen's successor as CEO was Hilmar Kopper. He had cooperated closely with Herrhausen and was therefore familiar with his vision and plans. Kopper implemented many of these plans surprisingly quickly, without meeting the earlier resistance of other board members. Under Kopper, who held office until 1997, when he retired because of his age as planned, Deutsche Bank purchased the British investment bank Morgan Grenfell, acquired commercial banks in Italy and Spain, and, most importantly, consolidated power in its Frankfurt headquarters over the regional centers. These steps were necessary for a bank with international ambitions and an increasing orientation toward investment banking.

Under Kopper, the bank grew with breathtaking speed, becoming Europe's largest commercial bank and much more international (Slager 2006). At the same time, it strengthened its ties with Germany's largest non-financial corporations and with other important players in the financial sector. In retrospect, one can say that Kopper was successful: he strove for growth in all areas, making inroads into investment banking and expanding the bank's commercial banking activities. In this respect, the Kopper years seemed to be another Up period.

This growth came at a cost, however. The bank's expenses rose faster than its scope, scale, and revenue. Profitability declined, along with the bank's stock market value compared to relevant peer groups. In our unfinished study mentioned above, we compared the stock price performance of Deutsche Bank under the three CEOs who succeeded Herrhausen with that of two peer groups. One peer group comprised the leading international investment banks of the time, and the other was a group of large commercial (or universal) banks. We compared their performance both with and without risk adjustment. All four measurements yielded the same result: under Kopper, Deutsche Bank's *relative* stock price performance was poor, and it trailed that of the banks in the two peer groups by a wide margin.

It seems that Kopper was aware of this problem. Together with a few other management board members, in June 1994 he devised a detailed plan to develop what at that time seemed to be the most attractive line of business for a large bank: investment banking. A stronger focus on investment banking also meant more internationalization, because investment banking is almost by definition international business. Accepted by the full board, this plan indicated that a looming crisis—in this case a profitability crisis—prompted a fundamental policy reorientation. What did this imply for the "roots" or "DNA" of Deutsche Bank? The decision to focus more on international (and) investment banking, and less on corporate (and domestic) lending, was a step back to the late nineteenth-century roots of the bank and away from what might have become the new roots in the early postwar years—and this is how Kopper apparently viewed it.

One fundamental question was not given the consideration it deserved, however: are the features that would make Deutsche Bank successful as an investment bank—features Kopper wanted to strengthen—compatible with its universal bank features, which he also wanted to retain, within an integrated institution? If this question had been asked—which I as an outside observer cannot know—the bank leaders who devised this plan would most likely have given a positive answer. Stock market investors, by contrast, were evidently not convinced that this was a good business model.

Turbulent Times for Deutsche Bank under Rolf-E. Breuer

When Kopper resigned as CEO in 1997, he took over as chair of the supervisory board. Much of the envisioned bank restructuring was thus left to his successor, Dr. Rolf-E. Breuer. Breuer indeed continued to internationalize the bank and to shift its focus more toward investment banking. The early Breuer years did not bode well for many corporate bankers at Deutsche Bank, who had formerly been its most highly respected employees, because corporate banking activities were downsized. Investment banking was strengthened most notably by acquiring the American investment bank Bankers Trust and thus establishing Deutsche Bank as a "bulge bracket bank" on the international investment banking market. In the jargon of investment bankers, the term "bulge bracket bank" refers to the half-dozen market leaders in this line of business. The stock market performance of Deutsche Bank's shares, relative to the two peer groups mentioned above, was better during Breuer's tenure than under Kopper, but the slight gain in relative performance did not make up for the earlier losses.

The Breuer years were difficult, both for the bank and for Dr. Breuer personally. What led to the end of his tenure as CEO in 2002 was his plan to change Deutsche Bank's business model yet again. Breuer had negotiated a merger with Mr. Walter, the CEO of Dresdner Bank, Germany's second largest private bank, without involving other high-ranking decision makers at Deutsche Bank. Because, at that time, an important block of Dresdner Bank shares was held by Allianz, Germany's largest insurance company, the CEO of Allianz had to be involved in the negotiations. Breuer and Walter's plan was to merge the corporate and investment banking activities of the two banks, then spin off the entire retail business and give it to Allianz in exchange for its block of Dresdner Bank shares. When this plan was presented to the full management board of Deutsche Bank, it was rejected mainly because of opposition from the board's investment bankers. Dresdner Bank's leadership responded by revoking its earlier approval of the planned merger, and CEO Walter resigned. Although Breuer was not forced to resign, his position was weakened considerably when the board nominated Dr. Josef Ackermann as his soon-to-be successor.

How would Breuer's plan have fit the pattern of the roots/DNA of Deutsche Bank if it had been accepted and implemented successfully? Giving up retail banking and concentrating on corporate and investment banking would have been a drastic strategic shift, making Deutsche Bank an extreme version of what it had been in its first eighty years: a "corporate bank" and no longer the universal bank into which it had transformed itself since the 1960s. It would have been a return to the bank's late nineteenth-century roots and a divergence from those of the postwar years.[16] Investment banking, as it was developing around the turn of the millennium, however, was quite different from the capital market-oriented type of banking from a hundred years earlier. Investment banking "à la 1900" was not trading-oriented, but geared toward supporting the bank's core clients, and therefore compatible with corporate banking. Investment banking "à la 2000" was trading-oriented, as is illustrated well by the primary activity of Bankers Trust, the American investment bank that Breuer had just purchased. There are good reasons to question whether this type of "modern" investment banking is compatible with Deutsche Bank's traditional corporate banking strategy.

Deutsche Bank under Josef Ackermann: A Smooth Start and a Hard Landing

Herrhausen provided the vision to transform a complacent, Germany-centered universal bank into an international bank that was also competent in investment banking. Kopper contributed greatly to making this vision a reality, though he did not assign priority either to corporate and universal banking or to investment banking. Breuer pushed investment banking at the expense of corporate banking. Dr. Josef Ackermann, CEO from 2002 to 2012, went even further during his early years at the bank's helm, providing support for investment banking—and the investment bankers in Deutsche Bank—and shifting resources from traditional banking activities to capital-market fields. By the early twenty-first century, investment banking had come to shape the bank's image and self-image. Investment bankers gained influence, and most of the bank's sizable bonus pool landed in their pockets. Edson Mitchell and later Anshu Jain, the top investment bankers at Deutsche Bank, and their staff were the "rainmakers." In terms of (divisional) accounting profits, investment banking was the main contributor to corporate profits.

In contrast to the two CEOs before him, Ackermann, a Swiss national, had not spent his entire career at Deutsche Bank. Instead, he had formerly held a high position at Credit Swisse. Upon joining Deutsche Bank in 1996, he was immediately appointed to the management board and soon given responsibility for investment banking. In this role, he earned respect by integrating Bankers Trust into Deutsche Bank quickly and efficiently. After Breuer's failure to merge Deutsche Bank and Dresdner Bank, the management board decided to appoint Ackermann as its "speaker" in 2002, and in 2006 his position was strengthened by changing his status from speaker to chair, a position no other CEO of Deutsche Bank had held before.

Numerous events and developments show how Ackermann transformed Deutsche Bank into a leading international investment bank. Most of these events occurred from 2002 to 2004, the time of the Mannesmann trial discussed below. All demonstrate the strong determination of Deutsche Bank to abandon the old house-bank regime. Being merely the house bank of some large German industrial firms was rightly considered incompatible with the business model of a modern investment bank. Because the close bank–client relationship in house banking allows the house bank to obtain considerable internal information, it would be difficult, if not impossible, to sell investment banking services to other corporations in the same industry for which it is not the house bank. One management board decision from the early twenty-first century illustrates how Deutsche Bank distanced itself from its former role as a house bank: its leadership agreed to prevent any members from assuming a new position as chair of a client's supervisory board, and discouraged all from joining a client's supervisory board.

More important, however, was Deutsche Bank's decision to sell most of its industrial holdings. Over decades, Deutsche Bank had acquired substantial blocks of shares in many important German corporations. Typically, these shares had been acquired at prices way below those at the turn to the twenty-first century. Experts estimated that the value of the bank's industrial holdings constituted at least half of its stock market value at the time when its leadership decided to convert it into an international investment bank. During this transformation, Deutsche Bank wanted to sell its industrial holdings, because being a major shareholder in individual corporations was also deemed incompatible with the "deal-based" business model of a twenty-first-century investment bank. Moreover, substantial capital reserves were tied up in these holdings, and this capital was considered necessary to fund the investments required to build up the bank's investment capacity.[17] For many years, however, there was a major hurdle to selling the bank's shares for cash in the German tax and accounting system. According to German accounting rules of the time, blocks of shares had to be carried on the balance sheet at their acquisition values. Thus, selling the industrial holdings would have implied huge accounting profits with the corresponding negative tax consequences.

In this situation, Deutsche Bank received a generous "gift" from the German government under Chancellor Gerhard Schroeder. As a true surprise to everyone, including the top management of Deutsche Bank, the tax code was changed in 2003, allowing Deutsche Bank—and others in a comparable situation—to sell their industrial holdings without having to pay tax on the accounting profits. This tax revision was motivated by the German government's desire to unravel the net of cross holdings, which had been a cornerstone of the so-called Deutschland-AG described above, and it coincided perfectly with Deutsche Bank's plans at that time. Jumping on this unexpected windfall, it reduced its portfolio of industrial holdings swiftly and substantially. Within two years, this portfolio shrank to about one-third of its former size. The proceeds from the sale of shares were close to 25 billion euros, of which 17 billion were used for a share buy-back program intended to raise Deutsche Bank's share prices. Thus, only a relatively small part of the proceeds was in fact used to fund the expansion of investment banking activities.

During the early Ackermann years, as Deutsche Bank's investment banking activities expanded, investment bankers gained the upper hand in the internal power struggle that had been taking place in the early 2000s. They succeeded in making Deutsche Bank an important player on the international investment banking market, and investment banking contributed the major portion of its corporate profits. In the Thomson Financial "league tables," showing which bank holds which position in the various subfields of investment banking, Deutsche Bank was consistently moving upward. Its stock price also improved substantially in absolute and in relative terms. Investors who bought Deutsche Bank shares in 2002, when Ackermann took over as the bank's CEO (or at a later date), and held them for any period up to 2011, his last full year as the CEO, fared substantially better than any investors who had bought a portfolio of shares of other investment banks or of large commercial banks. Note that this time span includes the Great Recession of 2007/8 and the start of the euro crisis.

The Mannesmann Trial and Its Implications for Deutsche Bank

The Mannesmann trial was the major event of the year 2004 for Deutsche Bank, and also a turning point in its development and strategy. Together with three other people, Ackermann was accused of having misappropriated Mannesmann AG funds and tried in court in Düsseldorf, where Mannesmann was based. As is well known, the British telecom giant Vodafone had attempted to take over Mannesmann, a former steel-making company that had turned into a mobile phone service provider. Vodafone finally succeeded in the year 2000, and the price agreed was the highest paid to date by a bidder in a takeover contest. It was truly remarkable that Mr. Josef Esser, Mannesmann's CEO, had negotiated extremely successfully from the perspective of Mannesmann shareholders: the final price of 180 billion euros was more than double Vodafone's initial offer.

Ackermann was a member of Mannesmann's supervisory board and also of that board's remuneration committee. After the transaction was completed, the remuneration committee granted CEO Esser a special bonus of 30 million euros. Compared to what he had achieved for his shareholders, a gain of more than 100 billion euros, this bonus was a mere 0.3 percent. Nevertheless, the public prosecutor argued that giving this bonus to Esser was an abuse of corporate funds and thus a criminal offence. After many months on trial, all four defendants were acquitted. During the trial, however, Ackermann had been attacked vigorously by the media and the general public. In my view and that of most of my colleagues, these attacks were unfair. What matters, though, is that the trial and the related public attacks taught Ackermann a lesson: a bank as important as Deutsche Bank has some features of a public institution, and as such it depends on political support in its home country.[18] I also assume that Ackermann understood that the extremely one-sided investment banking orientation adopted by the bank under his leadership implied a turn away from its former supporting role for German clients, in particular for Germany's mid-sized and large corporations. By the turn of the twenty-first century, the international investment bank Deutsche Bank thus no longer appeared to be the German bank it had once been, and this invited a loss of political support at home and of respect from the local German business community.

Ackermann's conclusion may have been that the turn to international investment banking and away from the bank's traditional focus on credit for German firms had gone too far. His actions support this assumption. In the years after the Mannesmann trial, Ackermann changed course and initiated a limited revival of Germany-oriented banking. Organizational structures were adjusted; Deutsche Bank acquired a stockholder majority in Postbank AG, a purely Germany-focused retail bank with a large branch network; and again the bank promoted high-ranking, Germany-focused and credit-oriented employees. This reversal was important, even though investment banking was not simultaneously downgraded. After all, the top management and many employees maintained the view that Deutsche Bank should become a leading international investment bank. The new strategic concept was to create more synergies between (Anglo-Saxon) investment banking and traditional (German) commercial banking. Deutsche Bank's later CEO, Anshu Jain, emphasized how achieving such synergies between the bank's investment and commercial banking divisions would be possible, and how these synergies would give Deutsche Bank a competitive advantage over other bulge-bracket investment banks organized as holding companies.[19]

Other interpretations and explanations as to why this reversal of the bank's focus was merely half-hearted are, of course, also possible. Perhaps the investment bankers had become so powerful that they were able to resist a more drastic return to a balanced business model. There are also reasons for assuming that the 'post-Mannesmann' reorientation of the bank's strategy, moderate though it was, produced tension between Ackermann and the leaders of the investment bankers at Deutsche Bank. The events in the run-up to the Great Recession and during this severe crisis might serve as indicators that Ackermann lost full control of what was happening in the investment banking division before and during the crisis years.

Two Conclusions Concerning the Ackermann Years

The Mannesmann trial, the half-baked strategic reorientation, and possibly also his loss of control over the investment bankers weakened Ackermann's position in the bank. This became visible when he first considered stepping down as chair of the management board and instead becoming chair of the supervisory board, as most of his predecessors had done, and tried to install Axel Weber as his successor. These plans failed, however, and Ackermann left the bank abruptly, on bad terms (see Knight 2011).

Any assessment of the Ackermann years must distinguish between what his leadership meant for the bank and what it implied for the entire German financial system. During his time as CEO, Ackermann did succeed in putting the bank back on track, restoring its profitability, and transforming it into a leading international investment bank. The first years of his leadership in particular were once more a long-awaited Up period. Moreover, Ackermann's policies helped Deutsche Bank survive the financial crisis better than most other comparable big banks.

A big question mark must be added to this overall positive assessment, however, because during the post-crisis years and after Ackermann left, Deutsche Bank entered turbulent waters. US authorities became critical of the bank's conduct and of its investment banking division before, during, and after the crisis, and several US and European institutions filed claims against it that were extremely costly to settle. If these "misconduct costs" had been reflected properly in the bank's accounting system and stock market value, the Ackermann years would no longer appear financially successful. Equally, Deutsche Bank's short-lived rise to becoming a leading investment bank must be reassessed. Not much of its "interim glory" remains today. Thus, the second half of Ackermann's tenure must be assessed as a Down period, though this only became visible after he had left the bank.

Turning to the German banking and financial systems, under Ackermann, Deutsche Bank definitively discontinued its support of, and participation in, "Germany Inc." It relinquished its former role as a significant provider of credit to large corporate clients; it stopped playing a central role in the corporate governance of large German corporations, thereby undermining the former stakeholder orientation of German corporate governance; and it voluntarily relinquished control over most other parts of the financial sector. In this respect, Deutsche Bank was not alone.

What happened to the other former big German banks? Dresdner Bank no longer exists. Soon after the failed merger with Deutsche Bank, it was acquired by Germany's largest insurance company, Allianz. Allianz failed to generate the aspired synergies between its old insurance and new banking business, and therefore sold its new subsidiary Dresdner Bank to Commerzbank on the eve of the financial crisis in August 2008. Dresdner's banking activities were then integrated into Commerzbank, which was hit hard by the crisis and rescued by the German government. After the crisis was over, Commerzbank changed its strategy and now focuses on retail banking and credit for small and medium firms. Thus, the "triumvirate" of the former big banks, which had mainly served large corporations, cooperated closely in matters of corporate governance, and together dominated the entire German financial sector, no longer exists.

Even earlier, the two other big private commercial banks had developed a habit of largely trying, with varying success, to imitate what the market leader Deutsche Bank was doing. They also purchased British investment banks, cut back lending to large corporate clients, and pulled out of their respective roles of co-owning and monitoring large corporations and of shaping the entire financial sector. Thus, Deutsche Bank as the "prime mover," followed by its peers, indeed brought down the old German financial system. By now, this system is much less bank-dominated and it has lost its former vital feature of being a consistent system.

The "Post-Ackermann Years" under Jain/Fitschen and Cryan

Ackermann stepped down after he lost an open conflict with Clemens Börsig, then chair of the supervisory board, and probably also a not-so-open conflict with Anshu Jain and the bank's other leading investment bankers. One issue in this conflict was Ackermann's future role at the bank and on its supervisory board; another was who should be his successor. There was likely also a third conflict concerning the role and standing of the investment bankers. Ackermann wanted this role to be scaled back to a level similar to that of the late Breuer years.

Ackermann had two successors sharing the role of the bank's CEO: Anshu Jain and Jürgen Fitschen. Jain had been the leader of the investment bankers after Edson Mitchell died in a plane crash in 2000. Fitschen was an experienced corporate banker who had close contacts with top German managers. Installing both men as co-CEOs may have been meant to serve as a signal to the outside world and to the staff that, from now on, investment, corporate, and retail banking would have near-equal importance within the bank. This structure did not materialize, however. Investment banking remained the dominant focus, and Jain was clearly the dominant leader, whereas Fitschen's role was to act as a German counterweight to the dominance of Jain and his London-based investment bankers.

My internal sources at the bank have stated quite frankly that Ackermann had wanted neither Jain nor Fitschen as his successor. His clear preference was Axel Weber, a former economics professor and later president of the Deutsche Bundesbank. The same sources said that the idea of making Weber the sole CEO of Deutsche Bank had met with considerable resistance, presumably mainly from the investment bankers.

The joint leadership did not last long, and it is difficult in retrospect to recognize any substantial changes brought about by the co-CEOs Jain and Fitschen. Investment banking remained at the same level as before, and Fitschen did not re-establish the bank's former relationships with corporate clients. One thing did change, however: after the financial crisis, the heyday of investment banking was over and Deutsche Bank's investment bankers could no longer generate huge profits. At the same time, the bank had to pay substantial sums to settle the various lawsuits connected to the financial crisis years. The bank's operating costs were moreover quite high in comparison to those of the other big banks. As a consequence, profits fell dramatically, and the stock price more or less stagnated at around 20 euros. All of this, plus Jain's unwillingness or inability to establish a positive relationship with the German government, as well as with most people in the bank and on its two boards, led to the supervisory board decision to terminate both him and Fitschen after three years.

After the dismissal of Jain and Fitschen, the supervisory board under its new chair Paul Achleitner,[20] appointed John Cryan as the new, and sole, CEO. As I learned from various internal sources in Deutsche Bank, Cryan was welcomed there; he had some success in restoring order and internal peace, and was regarded as a competent cost-cutter. However, he neither achieved a full turnaround nor restored profitability. Profits fell even further and the stock price reached its lowest level in decades, leading once more to a CEO's dismissal after only three years.

Neither Jain/Fitschen nor Cryan gave the bank what it needed most: a new orientation. None of these leaders could inspire enthusiasm like Herrhausen, Kopper, Breuer, and Ackermann had done at times. Given the resulting staff demotivation, a tarnished reputation, no profits then or in the foreseeable future, and the unbelievably low stock price of around 6 euros in 2018, anyone becoming the next CEO would have a troubled starting point.

Christian Sewing and the Return to "the Roots" of Deutsche Bank

Christian Sewing has faced this trouble head on since he was appointed as the new CEO in June 2018. Sewing has spent his whole working life at Deutsche Bank.[21] After one year in office, he proclaimed a fundamental shift in the bank's strategy after finally obtaining supervisory board approval. Its crux was to cut much of the bank's investment banking activities. At the same time, those parts of the bank's activity portfolio that had been the mainstay of Deutsche Bank's business twenty-five to thirty years ago, in particular lending to large and mid-sized German and European corporate clients, should be expanded, despite a planned staff reduction of eighteen thousand full-time employees. This is indeed a profound transformation, because it will take power away from the investment bankers and return it to the commercial and corporate bankers. This change might well be exactly what the bank needed for a long time to get back on track.

Sewing called this shift in strategy a "return to the roots of Deutsche Bank" at the press conference at which it was announced, without, however, making it clear to which roots he was referring. Did he mean those of the 1950s to 1970s, when Deutsche Bank was essentially a Germany-focused commercial bank, or those from the late nineteenth century, when the bank was founded with the mission to become an international bank with a strong capital market-orientation? In my view, what Sewing proclaimed as his vision is a return to Deutsche Bank's late twentieth-century business model as a universal bank with a moderate dose of investment banking. This is why his plan indeed portends a fundamental reorientation. In any event, the press and all other observers were impressed by the reference to the "roots of Deutsche Bank," and keep quoting it despite its ambiguity.[22] This newly announced strategy shift raises three questions: Can it be successful? What does it mean for the bank and its shareholders, staff, and clients? And what does it imply for the entire German financial system?

Whether this proclaimed major strategy change can put an end to the many years of decline of a bank that had for a long time been regarded as a model of success, and even lead to a recovery, is an open issue. Its success is in no way assured. Deutsche Bank is perhaps still strong enough to succeed in making this turnaround. But it is also possible that the financial losses of recent years, the loss of the bank's former reputation and of its clients' trust, the tremendous cost of this restructuring, and staff frustration and demotivation at all levels weigh so heavily that its failure is inevitable. Despite all such doubts, and if one disregards the options of being bought by a foreign competitor or merging with another large European bank, there is no sensible alternative to what Mr. Sewing and his team are now trying to do. The crucial issues at this time are how the turnaround will be implemented in detail: which parts of investment banking will be scrapped altogether; and if and how the remaining parts can be made to generate synergies, or at least be compatible, with the bank's primary business of serving German corporations and private clients.

Several years ago, after Ackermann first considered leaving office, a similar strategy shift was already needed. At the latest, the financial crisis of 2007/8 made it clear that the heyday of investment banking was over. One example of an equally radical strategic reorientation, that of the large Swiss banking group UBS, which shed most of its risk-prone investment banking activities in 2012, suggests that a similar strategy switch at that time would also have been possible and successful for Deutsche Bank. Interestingly, the turnaround at UBS was initiated and implemented after Axel Weber, Ackerman's preferred choice as his successor at Deutsche Bank, had become the president of UBS. Because Anshu Jain, Deutsche Bank's highest-ranking investment banker, became one of the two new CEOs instead of Axel Weber, Deutsche Bank was not likely to cut back investment banking, even though this would have made sense at that time.

What will Sewing's planned fundamental strategy shift mean for the German financial system if implemented successfully? The last fundamental change in Deutsche Bank's strategy, three decades ago, had a profoundly negative effect on the entire German financial system. The transformation of Deutsche Bank under Breuer and Ackermann deprived this financial system of its prior consistency. Several factors led to this loss of consistency, some external and some internal to the financial system. Among the external factors were the usual suspects: globalization, European integration, and advances in information and communication technology. By far the most important internal driver of change was the strategy switch that Deutsche Bank undertook under its CEOs Rolf-E. Breuer and Josef Ackermann. They rightly regarded the bank's former roles as the main lender and "house bank" of large corporations and as the pivotal player in the old corporate governance regime as incompatible with its new ambition to become an important trading-based investment bank. Thus, the role that Deutsche Bank played in transforming the German financial system around the turn of the twenty-first century was in one sense equal to the bank's former role in the old German financial system: Deutsche Bank shaped this system more than any other institution. At the same time and in a different sense, the way it shaped the German financial system was fundamentally opposed to this system. Whereas it had formerly kept the system going, it later made the first and most decisive move leading to its destabilization.

Would—and could—a successful turnaround of Deutsche Bank, reversing those developments that led to the loss of consistency in the German financial system, help restore this consistency? The answer is straightforward: even if Deutsche Bank succeeds in abandoning many segments of the investment banking market, its former "house bank" relationships with large corporations cannot simply be brought back to life.[23] Deutsche Bank can no longer buy back its blocks of shares that were essential for the functioning of the old system, and other banks are highly unlikely to accept a revived Deutsche Bank again as a market leader and trendsetter. Large and mid-sized non-financial corporations can also not be expected to react with enthusiasm to more generous offers of long-term loans that Deutsche Bank might now be inclined to make. It is equally difficult to imagine that clients and other business partners would all of a sudden trust Deutsche Bank again if it were to pull out of some areas of investment banking. There is, moreover, no reason to expect that its envisioned strategy switch—even if it were implemented successfully—would again make Deutsche Bank the leading force in the German financial sector and allow it to recover its formerly strong role in the governance of large non-financial corporations. Other players are unlikely to give up the positional gains they have made in the course of the past two decades.

All of this can be summed up by saying that what has changed in the German financial system since the turn of this century—with Deutsche Bank as the most influential change agent—is not reversible. For the bank itself as an entity, its shareholders, its clients, and its employees, top management efforts to "get back to the roots" would be beneficial. However, for the quality of the German financial system—and, more precisely, for its consistency as a determinant of quality—these efforts are by now irrelevant.

Reinhard H. Schmidt is Professor Emeritus of International Banking and Finance at the Goethe University of Frankfurt. He has written or edited twenty-five books and numerous articles on the topics of institutional economics; the strategy and structure of international firms; finance theory; international economic relationships and regulation; financial systems in industrial and developing countries, especially European financial systems in comparison; and development financing. He has held guest professorships at Stanford University and the Université Paris Nanterre, among other universities in the United States and Europe.

Notes

1. This chapter draws from an unpublished study on the transformation of Deutsche Bank. I thank my co-authors of this study, Jan Krahnen and Marti Subrahmanyam, for many discussions about Deutsche Bank, helpful comments on this chapter, and their permission to use material originally written for our joint project.
2. For 'facts and figures,' see the homepage of the Historische Gesellschaft der Deutschen Bank.
3. Organized, regulated markets for securities and other financial assets, called "Exchanges," had existed long before that time. However, most transactions on these exchanges involved currencies, government bonds, or similar securities, and not stocks or equity shares. As in most other European countries, stock trading on the various German exchanges was limited to the trading of shares in those companies that had a government authorization or concession. It only gained in importance with the rise of private railroad corporations (which had a government concession)

in the mid-nineteenth century. As stock trading grew in importance, it became regulated more strictly, until a more liberal regulatory regime for stock exchanges was implemented in the 1860s. For more information on the history of stock exchanges in Germany, see Gömmel 1992.

4. Among the many historical accounts of Deutsche Bank, the most authoritative are those by Lothar Gall et al. (1995), written for the 125th anniversary of Deutsche Bank, and by Alexander Nützenadel, Werner Plumpe, and Catherine R. Schenk (2020), prepared for the 150th anniversary. Both volumes are available in German and English. See the homepage of the Historische Gesellschaft, mentioned above, for further sources.
5. In many cases, these equity stakes were created when a corporate client borrower had come under pressure and bank debt had to be converted into equity, or when a house bank had not been able to sell all shares in an Initial or Secondary Public Offering (IPO/SPO) and had to honor its obligation as an underwriter. In other words, rarely have house banks acquired their blocks of shares on the open market.
6. At the end of the 1980s, the number of supervisory board seats held by Deutsche Bank board members was reported to be around four hundred (see Schwarz 2003: 58).
7. The Dutch economist Alfred Slager was the first researcher to apply the so-called Transnationalization Index (TNI)—a measure of internationalization originally developed for non-financial corporations—to big European banks. As Slager reports, in the late 1960s, the TNI-value of Deutsche Bank was lower than that of all other comparable European banks, while thirty years later this value exceeded that of its peers (see Slager 2006).
8. Kotz and Schmidt (2016) discuss the corporate governance regimes of the various German banking groups.
9. Wolfram Engels, an academic teacher of the present author, often said in his lectures that, whereas German non-financial corporations were on their way to becoming "economic and technological giants" in the world market, German banks were, at least in relative terms and by international standards, merely "financial dwarfs."
10. In his excellent book on Deutsche Bank, financial journalist Friedhelm Schwarz (2003: 26) makes a similar point, arguing that Deutsche Bank was, until the end of the twentieth century, a federation of largely independent regional banks, rather than one single, integrated bank.
11. "Us" refers to the authors of the unpublished study mentioned in Note 1; the same authors report below about Herrhausen's views and aspirations.
12. From 1985 to 1988, Herrhausen shared the role of management board speaker with Wilfried Guth, in line with the bank's recent tradition of having two speakers. When Guth retired in 1988, Herrhausen became the sole speaker.
13. The attribute "modern" refers to the focus of today's investment banking on market trading and financial engineering (i.e., on market-oriented activities), in contrast to its former focus on advisory and security issues (i.e., on activities geared more toward solving the capital market-related problems of individual bank customers). The development of Goldman Sachs, the world's best-known investment bank, in the past thirty years, illustrates this transition from traditional to modern investment banking. Morgan Grenfell, the British merchant (or investment) bank acquired by Deutsche Bank in 1990, represents the traditional approach to investment bank-

ing, whereas the US-based investment bank Bankers Trust, acquired by Deutsche Bank about ten years later, was a premier market- and trading-oriented investment bank.

14. "We" again refers to the authors mentioned in Note 1.
15. Krahnen's unpublished speech was delivered at the book launch of Friederike Sattler's impressive biography of Alfred Herrhausen (2019), which coincided with the thirtieth anniversary of Herrhausen's assassination. Raising the issue of how corporate and investment banking could be coordinated in a substantially reshaped Deutsche Bank was not meant by Krahnen as a criticism of Herrhausen, whose merits in having developed his vision and in leaving behind a powerful legacy are well established. It is striking that neither the originator of this grand vision nor any of the bank's top managers were aware of the importance of this vital structural problem for many years.
16. Interestingly, the reason Deutsche Bank's management board rejected Breuer's merger plan was not that it entailed shedding almost the entire retail division, but rather a controversy about how the investment bankers of Dresdner Bank would be integrated into the new entity. Deutsche Bank's by then powerful investment bankers purportedly rejected the idea of taking over Dresdner's investment bankers because they did not want to share their bonus pool with them.
17. A possible third reason may have been that 'unlocking' the hidden reserves might have helped boost the share price, which was much too low according to how the top management of Deutsche Bank, and especially CEO Ackermann, saw it. However, the economic logic of this motive is questionable. The argument would have presupposed that 'the capital market' (i.e., the investing public), was not aware of the value of these industrial holdings—an incorrect assumption, because the size and value of the bank's industrial holdings were public knowledge.
18. This assessment is based on several extended conversations we had with Dr. Ackermann while preparing our unpublished study (see Note 1).
19. Anshu Jain expressed this view in an interview with us, while we were preparing our study mentioned in Note 1. Jain called this "the platform strategy" of Deutsche Bank, which he evidently found promising.
20. In his former capacity as the chief financial officer of Allianz, Achleitner had pushed for its unfortunate acquisition of Dresdner Bank.
21. This section draws on Schmidt 2019.
22. Almost all German media stated in the headlines that Sewing used the expression "Zurück zu den Wurzeln" (back to the roots) when he announced this strategy shift at the 25 April 2019 press conference. See, among others, *Frankfurter Allgemeine Zeitung*, *Süddeutsche Zeitung* and *Deutsche Welle* on 26 April 2019.
23. Today, house bank relationships still exist—not between large banks and major corporate clients, but between savings banks or cooperative banks/credit unions and the relatively large *Mittelstandsunternehmen*.

References

"Chronik Deutsche Bank 1870–2010." 2022. Historische Gesellschaft der Deutschen Bank. Retrieved 10 May 2022 from http://www.bankgeschichte.de/.

Enrich, David. 2020. *Dark Towers: Deutsche Bank, Donald Trump, and an Epic Trail of Destruction*. New York: Harper Collins.
Gall, Lothar, et al. 1995. *The Deutsche Bank, 1870–1995*. London: Weidenfeld & Nicholson.
Gömmel, Rainer. 1992. "Entstehung und Entwicklung der Effektenbörse im 19. Jahrhundert bis 1914." In *Deutsche Börsengeschichte*, ed. Hans Pohl, 135–201. Frankfurt am Main: Fritz Knapp-Verlag.
Hilferding, Rudolf. 2000 reprint. *Das Finanzkapital*. Düsseldorf: Verlag Wirtschaft und Finanzen (orig. in *Marx-Studien. Blätter zur Theorie und Politik des wissenschaftlichen Sozialismus*. Band 3, Vienna 1910).
Janssen, Sven. 2009. *British and German Banking Strategies*. London: Palgrave Macmillan.
Knight, John. 2011. "Axel Weber Snubs Deutsche Bank for Swiss Financial Giant." Deutsche Welle, 1 July. Retrieved 8 December 2021 from https://www.dw.com/en/axel-weber-snubs-deutsche-bank-for-swiss-financial-giant/a-15204477.
Kotz, Hans-Helmut, and Reinhard H. Schmidt. 2016. "Corporate Governance: A German Alternative to the Standard Model." *Zeitschrift für Bankrecht und Bankwirtschaft* 28: 427–44.
Laabs, Dirk. 2018. *Bad Bank: Aufstieg und Fall der Deutschen Bank*. Munich: Deutsche Verlags-Anstalt.
McCloskey, Deirdre. 1985. *The Rhetoric of Economics*. Madison: University of Wisconsin Press.
———. 1990. *If You're So Smart: The Narrative of Economic Expertise*. Chicago: University of Chicago Press.
Nützenadel, Alexander, Werner Plumpe, and Catherine R. Schenk. 2020. *Deutsche Bank: The Global Hausbank*. London: Bloomsbury.
Riekers, Oliver, and Gerald Spindler. 2004. "Corporate Governance: Legal Aspects." In *The German Financial System*, ed. Jan Pieter Krahnen and Reinhard H. Schmidt, 350–87. Oxford: Oxford University Press.
Sattler, Friederike. 2019. *Herrhausen: Banker, Querdenker, Global Player*. Berlin: Siedler.
Schmidt, Reinhard H. 2019. "Die Deutsche Bank im deutschen Finanzsystem." Frankfurter Allgemeine Zeitung, 20 July, p. 26.
Schmidt, Reinhard H., and Marcel Tyrell. 2004. "What Constitutes a Financial System in General and the German Financial System in Particular?" In *The German Financial System*, ed. Jan Pieter Krahnen and Reinhard H. Schmidt, 19–67. Oxford: Oxford University Press.
Schwarz, Friedhelm. 2003. *Die Deutsche Bank – Riese auf tönernen Füßen*. Frankfurt: Campus-Verlag.
Slager, Alfred. 2006. *Internationalization of Banks: Patterns, Strategies and Performance*. Berlin: Springer.

CHAPTER 2

Narrative Confrontations with Socioeconomic Crisis

Ideas for Building Community in the Mid-Nineteenth-Century German Social Novel

JOHANNES BRAMBORA

German social novels of the nineteenth century tell sensational stories of forged testaments and children exchanged at birth, of honorable workers and wicked factory owners, of dark secrets and dastardly intrigues in the industrial milieu (see Brambora 2020). "From a historical viewpoint, the industrial novel played an exceptional role in the reader's mind from Goethe to the grinderies" (Edler 1977: 15). From the mid-1840s to the end of the century, such novels became bestsellers, demonstrating the widespread interest of readers in this genre (Kocka and Schmidt 2015: 343). Today, only literature scholars are aware of these novels' existence; they do not belong to the literary canon. They are considered aesthetically inferior and thus unworthy of scholarly interest.[1] Even recent studies following the seminal work carried out by Joseph Vogl (2011a, 2011b) and Jochen Hörisch (1996, 2013), examining the economic knowledge conveyed by nineteenth-century literary texts, for the most part ignore the social novel (Rakow 2013; M. Bauer 2015; Agethen 2017).

But these novels deserve our attention, for despite their sensationalized plots, their authors tackle one of history's most radical transformations—the Industrial Revolution with all its contradictions (Wehler 1989: 589). The social sciences emerged concurrently in the late nineteenth century; but long before the first global financial crisis in 1857, German social novels diagnosed a *social* crisis tied to localized *economic* crises. Their authors put narrative coping forward as an answer to the theoretical and practical questions of how to maintain a sense of community while facing the pressures of industrialism's economic antagonisms, which are at the root of factory workers' individual financial difficulties. It is important to note that every social novel discussed here depicts a unique vision of community. Therefore, a specific definition of community cannot be given here,[2] but instead its various *possible* definitions will be investigated. Although these novels do not share a common concept, they do pose the same questions: How might the emerging industrial antagonisms such as those between factory owners and workers be reconciled? What might an integration of the workers into bourgeois society look like? In asking such questions, the novels insert themselves into a widespread, vehement nineteenth-century socioeconomic discourse surrounding these topics.

When the Industrial Revolution first took hold in Germany,[3] two opinions came to dominate the national debate regarding the societal benefits of manufacturing machines. First, from an overarchingly positive perspective, it was believed that the new machines would lead to great societal improvements by fostering economic growth and individual welfare. This view was shared by critics such as the lawyer Johannes Alois Perthaler (1965: 347), who, although he also developed ideas promoting the shutting down of the machines, understood simultaneously that this step backward could not be taken, "because [factories] initiated a great era for the entire history of the world." But there was, secondly, the public belief that the strong record of industrial success also "casts a huge shadow" on society, as the political scientist Robert Mohl (1965b: 295) described it, which consists in "the wide deplorable impacts the big factory system exerted on the economic, moral, civilian, and political conditions of the numerous everyday factory workers" (ibid.: 296). This situation, according to political scientist Karl Biedermann (1847: 15–16), "is almost ruining the enjoyment of the fundamental success of our civilization, and it often seems as if those successes and achievements were reached at the sacrifice of well-being, freedom, even the existence of our millions of brothers." It was moreover feared that the workers themselves would gradually identify less and less with this community, and begin to combat society instead. "I will not have to prove for long that poverty has turned dangerous," Swiss writer Jeremias Gotthelf (1965: 377) states in 1841, and he continues, "the relations of so-called proletarians to the owners, or the have-nots to those who have, are so tense that they portend a rupture that would cover all of Europe with blood and flames, [and] poverty is the hostile entity that threatens old Europe the most."

It was the avowed aim of several middle-class groups, mainly government civil servants and intellectuals, to surmount this social crisis by counteracting the workers' self-proclaimed exclusion and reintegrating them into civil society. The so-called "problem of the 'naturalisation' of proletarians" (Baader 1965: 292),[4] seen by many as "absolutely unsolvable" (ibid.), kept the whole century in suspense regarding what was then called the *social question* or *worker's question*.[5] Answers and ideas for remedies were put forth in large numbers. Some of them concerned the enlightenment and education of workers, who should be kept informed about economic rules and the equal standing of their interests and those of the manufacturers, to give them a sense of being members of civil society. But it was well known that such an undertaking would be impossible without simultaneously improving the workers' material situation. To a large extent, the suggestions made at the time not only focused on explaining and interpreting industrial realities, but also on changing them. Socially conscious intellectuals thus proposed to strengthen the legal position of factory workers and to create organizational structures that could ensure a fair wage for them. These intellectuals considered various forms of profit-sharing, making changes in the structure of wage payments, and reforming the internal organization of factories, among other strategies. The overall aim was that "capitalists, entrepreneurs, and workers are united as a whole" (Mohl 1965a: 331), "creat[ing] an organization . . . by means of which the opposing interests of hostile, separate classes of factory owners and factory workers can be mediated, structured and brought together" (Perthaler 1965: 347). It is this concept of community—a unified group of factory owners and workers that mediates antagonisms and diminishes hostilities, overcoming opposing interests, or at least mitigating them—that nineteenth-century social novels have in common with the then-emerging social sciences.

The fact that literature provides its own kind of knowledge has been discussed abundantly in recent literary studies (Hörisch 2007; Klausnitzer 2008; Köppe 2011; Kley 2018). Unlike scientific texts, however, novels do not recount their ideas in a logical, argumentative fashion. Instead, they employ the medium of narrative in order to enact their ideas in a fictional framework, bringing them to life and putting them to the test at the same time. In this way they act as a kind of corrective in relation to the "established and recognized (e.g., common-sense or scientific) discourses" offering "alternative versions of reality" (Hörisch 2007: 10). In other words, "[t]he worlds that imaginary texts project thus entertain possibilities and alternative perspectives to be reckoned with in the academic articulation and public discussion of pertinent social issues" (Kley 2018: 10). This function of envisioning different realities also applies to nineteenth-century German social novels. Despite their trivial plots, these novels put forth ideas of community that are not entirely unrealistic. In fact, they scrutinize ideas of community painstakingly in the framework of industrial production, and describe the profit calculations and devastating mental and physical effects on the working population with surprising accuracy. How the authors of these novels grasp the social contradictions causing this social crisis; which ideas of community they confront their protagonists with; and what chances of success they give to these ideas—these are the questions that will be addressed in the following analyses of three German social novels.

White Slaves or the Sorrows of the People by Ernst Willkomm (1845)

Ernst Willkomm is the founder of the factory novel genre in Germany.[6] His five-volume novel called *Weisse Sclaven oder die Leiden des Volkes* (White Slaves or the Sorrows of the People)[7] is said to be "the earliest and perhaps most felicitous experiment of a German factory novel trying to describe capitalist exploitation and the resistance against it" (Halter 1983: 263). Willkomm's work is seen as a paragon: "All the later-known authors mostly kept moving in the lines drawn by Willkomm" (Edler 1977: 224).

"A great stir" (Hinnah 1915: 127) was caused by *White Slaves* at the time of its release in Leipzig in 1845. This uproar is apparent in the legal proceedings that were imposed on Willkomm shortly after he had published the first parts of his novel. The lawsuit caused a delay in the release of the latter volumes, and government authorities in Austria imposed censorship on the sale of his first two books by requiring purchasers to acquire an official permit to buy them (Bachleitner 1993: 412).[8] The fact that Willkomm had his finger directly on the pulse of his time can be seen in the preserved literary reviews of his work. Critics not only praised his "detailed knowledge about the everyday life of the proletarian people" (A.B. 1845: 312) and inclusion of rigorous descriptions of "the main sorrows of the people" (Marggraff 1990: 196). They also stressed that Willkomm's novel develops a "peaceful" (Dingelstedt 1990: 196), "natural and organic solution to the described circumstances" (A.B. 1845: 311), and presents a "comfortable and indeed Christian reconciliation in the end, which cures all fractures, cracks and wounds that have been disclosed by the author on the body of suffering mankind" (Marggraff 1990: 195).

White Slaves is based on a definition of conflict in the factory that would have been familiar to many contemporaries (Eiden-Offe 2014). It compares a modern-day type of poverty, which is marked by the abject dependence of workers on factory owners, to preindustrial serfdom, even though this was thought to have been overcome by the nominal freedom granted to the workers. One of the protagonists remarks sarcastically: "The people are as free as the masters: they are perfectly free to drown, hang, shoot or starve themselves. They say that the freedom to starve is the most common, which is why there are hundreds who offer it up for a pittance and become the willing slaves of humans and machines alike" (I, 100f.). Although serfdom had gradually been abolished in German territories from the late eighteenth to the mid-nineteenth century (Kitchen 1978: 9–15; Schäfer 2019), and no one was supposed to exert so much power over others, there were other chains of bondage. Freed laborers still feared hunger (Kitchen 1978: 9), and former bondsmen, without possessing any means of production or owning much, if any, land, could not work independently for a living and were thus turned again into slave laborers.

Willkomm's novel underscores this predicament with its description of working people's living conditions, which are characterized by absolute deprivation. The workers' wages do not support their basic needs: their clothes are "lousy, scratched and patched" (I, 139); they live in dark and tumbledown huts, which they cannot heat properly (III, 234);[9] they are supposed to eat "dry potatoes and their peel with salt, and which has been cooked in chicory coffee in the morning, at noon, and in the evening, every day" (III, 237); throughout the novel, several children die of starvation (IV, 146). But the work in the factory not only barely allows the workers to survive; it also endangers their lives. The novel marks factory work as a permanent attack on the workers' health, as they are not even able to breathe properly in the sticky factory halls. There is, furthermore, the ever-present danger of injury: the novel tells of a ten-year-old boy whose "left foot was half destroyed by a machine" (III, 239) and who eventually died from his injury.[10]

The novel does not end with this diagnosis, however. This is not its final judgment on factory life. Instead, it asks what interests lie behind this enslavement of the workers. Can the workers not be treated with a modicum of consideration? Ironically, it is a bookkeeping clerk who tests his employer's patience by asking this basic question. It is this functionary of capitalist calculation himself who insists on fair payment for the workers, to which he claims they are entitled for various reasons. He lists these reasons as the cost of living, the strenuousness of the work, or the increased profits due to the use of machines: "Give all those poor people, most of them your factory invalids anyway, a few pennies more, because you are receiving a way bigger benefit through your use of machines" (I, 115). His employer, however, cites business inevitabilities as a justification for wage cuts, such as his standing with the competition, the wages paid by other factory owners, or his own expenses: "The machines cost money, a lot of money, and till the workers know how to use them, they may ruin me a bunch of yarn balls" (I, 115). The clerk does not question these necessities. He treats the conditions governing his master's business success as unchangeable laws. But then, does he not also have to accept wage cuts for the workers as a natural consequence of such laws? This is one of the novel's core paradoxes: on the one hand, wage policy appears unacceptable and inhumane; on the other, it represents nothing but the natural logic of business.

The novel nevertheless manages to reconcile this paradox—capitalist business logic and fair payment—by giving the factory owner an added ulterior motive: it gradually reveals that he is not primarily interested in riches, but in the power that comes with them. As a member of the aristocracy, he wants to use the factory as a means of restoring power and recognition to his social class. Hence, he abuses the factory system in order to declassify and debase the workers. The novel suggests that it is this additional motive alone that leads the factory owner to disregard the workers' interests. It is one of the novel's inherent contradictions that, in fact, all he eventually does is follow modern capitalist business logic.

The aristocratic factory owner's plans do not pan out in Willkomm's tale, but this does not mean that the novel turns the ideal of fair wages into reality. It counters the industrialist's personal hubris by gradually revealing that he has familial ties among some of the workers. His proletarian siblings indeed go on to claim ownership of the factory and eventually become its new heirs. However, there is nothing in the novel to suggest that a universal enforcement of adequate payment might become a reality outside this particular factory. The new heirs merely express the earnest intention of paying decent wages in the future.

One of Ernst Willkomm's primary purposes in writing *White Slaves* was to set up the possibility of fair payment against the utterly unbearable living conditions of the factory workers of his day. Although the workers' wage demands may conflict with the factory owners' calculations, the author demonstrates that a fair wage would not, in the end, be bad for business. In the novel, at any rate, it is not capitalism that is the problem, but the aristocrat's aspirations to power. As soon as these immoral aspirations are eliminated, the workers are able to make their peace with the factory system. This, at least, is what the narrator claims at the end, when the doubling of wages has made sure that no worker is ever again "unhappy with his lot" (V, 361). The novel categorically precludes the possibility that this reconciliation might become universal in the existing order of business, however. It is only some higher authority such as a "state law" (V, 317) that would guarantee fair wages by forcing modern factory owners to take an interest in their workers' survival.

Castle and Factory by Louise Otto-Peters (1848)

Louise Otto-Peters has been "occupied by all sections of the middle-class and proletarian women's movement, as initiator, foundress and leading figure of this movement" (Gerhard, Pommerenke, and Wischermann 2008: 63). She notably published *Frauen-Zeitung* (Women's paper) in 1848, and founded the Allgemeiner Deutscher Frauenverein (General German women's club) in 1865, as well as the club's organ of speech, *Neue Bahnen* (New paths), and was a popular fiction writer (B. Bauer 1995: 47). Being the daughter of upper-middle-class parents, who allowed her to achieve financial independence by suddenly leaving her a substantial inheritance, she began writing prolifically. Besides her dedication to the Women's Rights Movement, she also published "not less than 27, often multivolume novels, 11 volumes containing tales, novellas, two opera libretti, works about art and music as well as numerous contributions, articles and reviews in journals and papers" (Gerhard, Pommerenke, and Wischermann 2008: 63). Today, her literary works are "virtually unknown" (B. Bauer 1995: 47)—except for one "socialist novel,"[11] as Louise Otto-Peters calls it in her diary, the three-volume *Castle and Factory*.[12]

As reported by the *Demokratisches Wochenblatt* (Democratic weekly), which published two reviews recommending warmly that readers purchase the novel, reprinted in 1868, she received a lot of support from the workers for it. The *Demokratisches Wochenblatt* called it a "tremendous sensation in its time, factory owners and capitalists became alarmed, and even the liberals regretfully viewed Louise Otto-Peters as 'going socialistically astray,' but workers from all cities in the German territories sent her delegations and salutations" ("Zur Geschichte" 1869: 116). The author of this particular review also unveiled the fact that even the national censorship authority made claims against some parts of the book, and forced Louise Otto-Peters to make substantial changes to the text (ibid.).[13]

Whereas Ernst Willkomm discusses capitalist business logic in some detail, and debates possible objections to it, Otto-Peters ignores overarching economic issues from the outset of her novel (Adler 1980: 134; C. Otto 1995: 249). The devastating effects of business practices on workers' lives are well known, but in Otto-Peters' novel they do not engender a critical interest in the workings of capitalism. The novel relegates wider socioeconomic policies to the sidelines of factory life: a system of organized philanthropy is supposed to compensate for the damage done and to reconcile the workers. That this private solution does not come across as cynical from the outset—after all, the potential philanthropists are also in charge of the factory regime—is because the protagonist, Pauline, who embodies this idea, is the seventeen-year-old daughter of a factory owner and she does not form part of the factory's workings.

Castle and Factory chronicles the failure of Pauline's philanthropic plan, intended to improve the workers' lives. She does not receive any support from her father, who rather harshly defeats the first of her suggestions for a charity project: "This is a dumb idea, I do not have any money for such foolish jokes, it goes against my fundamental principles" (74). But more than this, the workers themselves do not appreciate Pauline's efforts. In fact, their reaction is downright hostile, as the following case of a female worker illustrates. When the worker's child is mutilated by a machine, the factory owner's daughter tries to help by bringing bandages. The mother rails: "[I]f only your clean white canvas could repair what your damned machines destroy, . . . but I'm telling you, we will not wait until doomsday until we get our judgment . . . our fists are strong enough to put an end to your machines one day" (119). The novel does not take the mother's accusation seriously, however. It also does not point out the absurdity of the industrialist family's desire to be helpful, although they are responsible for their workers' destitution. Instead, it asks why the workers do not accept help. Why do they refuse to be moved by the kind gestures of their oppressor's daughter? The novel concludes that it must be the workers' fault; it is they who need to be changed in some way. The novel bolsters this conclusion by presenting the workers—who are, by now, the only obstacle preventing a reconciliation with the factory owners—as emotionally damaged. Their indignation against any kind of reconciliation is presented as a form of mental illness, to which they are nearly driven by their desperate situation. "She went crazy, didn't she?" asks the manufacturer's daughter about the working woman referred to above, and got corrected directly: "No, not in particular, but this is her way of acting; she is in pure despair over her children" (158).

The solution Otto-Peters devises from the workers' situation is to reclaim them by means of education, for which purpose a workers' association is founded. Here they are taught that it is possible to live on any wage, however pitiful, if only one is virtuous enough to cut down on costly leisure pursuits such as drinking spirits and betting on card games. The workers' association also advocates sending the workers' children to school, arguing that this does not mean depriving the factory of cheap labor, but instead ensuring its future. Educating the workers' children is good for society as a whole, one member of the association argues, because "everybody benefits if good plants are sprouted and grown everywhere. Nobody, after all, cultivates weeds in his own garden—if people would only consider this, all would be well" (158). Nothing would stand in the way of reconciliation, if only the factory owner understood schooling as the gardener understands weeding.

This assessment of the poor as incorrigible, as the novel suggests, and its practical consequences, which its characters draw from their situation, found vast support at the time it emerged. One visible reaction to the Silesian Weavers' Uprising of June 1844 against the mechanization of textile manufacturing, for example, was the founding of the Centralverein für das Wohl der arbeitenden Classen (Association for the Welfare of Workers) in Berlin in October of that same year (Reulecke 1985). Otto-Peters does not grant this concept of workers' welfare associations any chance of success, however. The factory owners see no reason why they should spare the workers' children, because they are a cheap source of labor. Neither do the children's parents wish to forgo their children's contribution to the family income. The novel therefore imagines a third force that should apply the necessary coercion to create the basis of community: the state. But the state, mentioned as "wise legislators and lawful governments" (129), which the novel implies will carry out this task, cannot be won over. Its representative is an ambitious and overzealous government informer, who suspects a communist conspiracy behind everything the workers do. His spying and slander escalate the existing factory conflicts to the point that the embittered workers eventually resort to rioting. Among the casualties is the factory owner's daughter, who meets a tragic fate—a result that clearly evokes the reader's empathy.

Otto-Peters' novel *Castle and Factory* does not propose an ideal of reconciling opposing parties in the factory, because the idea of organized philanthropy, on which her concept of community is based, does not acknowledge these parties' antagonistic economic relations. The factory managers in the novel are aware that their business, as it is run using machines, prevents them from taking the workers' well-being into consideration. However, they also believe it is impossible to object to this situation. Instead, they try to compensate the workers for the damage caused in the factory after the fact, and, at the same time, to reconcile the opposing parties. If the workers oppose such an idea of community, then—so Otto-Peters reasons—they are damaged, antisocial individuals, which makes them doubly in need of help. The novel imposes an educational program on them directed solely at creating a will to reconcile with those who exploit them, and would in fact subject them to state force to achieve this aim by requiring them to attend school. However, it fails to imagine substantial support for this idea among its protagonists. Because all options the novel presents to reconcile workers and factory owners, such as political repression or a communist revolution, would lead to catastrophe, the idea of reconciliation via philanthropy remains the only conceivable solution.

The Angel by Robert Prutz (1851)

Born in 1816 in Stettin, Prussia (now Szczecin, Poland) as the son of a merchandiser, Robert Prutz was a well-known German intellectual who commented in a liberal-oppositional manner on nearly every question of public interest in the mid-nineteenth century. "From 1840 (accession to the throne of Friedrich Wilhelm IV) to 1866, we do not find any decisive moment of the German people at which P. had not raised his voice as a journalist, author, or speaker" (Mähly 1888: 679). Prutz (1981) proclaimed the genre of light fiction useful for spreading his ideas and criticized its general negligence among German authors in an essay published in 1845.[14] As a major desideratum for German national literature, he mentions the social novel as particularly relevant. It is, therefore, not surprising that his essay was later recognized as programmatic scripture and his novel *The Angel*,[15] which he started writing in the year of the essay's release, was viewed as an attempt to start this campaign (Edler 1970; Prümm 1980).[16]

In *The Angel*, Prutz rejects any ideas of fair payment that are voluntarily agreed upon, as well as any reconciliation brought about by philanthropy or workers' associations. His rejection is expressed in his depiction of the factory laborers, whose moral degeneracy is so advanced that the novel judges it to be incorrigible. From quarreling on payment day to drinking mindlessly in the local pub and prostituting themselves on the side, the workers are portrayed as remarkably unappealing, causing some literary scholars to call *The Angel* a "pre-naturalistic" (Liptzin 1990: 219) text. The omniscient narrator in *The Angel* states explicitly that these kinds of behavior constitute ways of coping with factory life, and that the factory system necessarily produces them. The excesses in bars are, for example, not "justified" in the narrator's view, "but," he asks rhetorically:

> [I]sn't the only thing that still makes them human that they keep on living to the bitter end of their lives, as wildly, as amusing to enjoy, as they can? That they are chasing after every cheer, every joy, no matter how transient, with insane speed, how void, how disgraceful it may be, just to be able to at least numb their consciousness of their despair? (I, 130f.)

The novel depicts the brutalization of the workers as a necessary consequence of factory work—indeed, an inherent hostility toward community appears as the central principle of the factory. In order to prove this thesis, Prutz puts forth a convoluted plot that reveals countless secrets and stretches the reader's credulity with the most bizarre coincidences and discoveries. At the center of the narrative is an old weaver who boldly resists the competition brought to his village by the factory. That he is motivated by love for his time-honored craft, rather than money alone, is illustrated by the fact that he hardly earns any. He barely makes enough to secure his family's survival. His moral integrity thus forms the counterpart to the debauchery of the factory workers, who have, in his view, "[sold themselves] to the devil of the machines" (I, 138). The weaver's competition with the factory's mass production personalizes the antagonism between factory and community. The factory owner, who is in immediate competition with the weaver, does not simply pursue the same commercial interests as he, albeit with superior equipment. Rather, he seeks directly to destroy him. He "placed a high stake . . . on demolishing the master's pride," who, from his point of view, "must be carried away from his weaver chair, . . . to the same machine that he, as a stooge, had incited the crowds to lean up against, in sacrilegious foolishness, with impetuous, stupid speeches" (I, 331f.). He will do anything to sabotage the weaver's business. But he has no commercial motive for this: it is solely the craftsman's opposition to the factory's moral degeneracy that earns him the industrialist's hatred.

From one coincidence to another, the factory owner's base intrigues are gradually revealed by the narrative. He has not only crossed the line of legality in his competition with the weaver, but is also guilty of contraband, forging testaments, and theft—the "most horrible villain the planet has ever seen" (III, 454), as another character in the novel calls him. His crimes are legion, and his punishment becomes inevitable. Caught up in a hopeless situation, he commits suicide. His end also marks the end of the factory. The weaver's craft is restored, and with it, public morals, as the narrator points out at the end: "[T]o the sturdy young settlers, the master is an example in word and deed. The splendid inn has disappeared from the village . . ., but so has drunkenness, gambling, and crime; a new race, industrious, chaste, and moral, is coming forth, full of reverence for every domestic and public virtue" (III, 460f.).

Prutz considers the antagonisms of modern industrialism to be irreconcilable with any positive concept of community. His novel argues for a return to preindustrial times, which he imagines as a sanitized idyll, populated by poor but decent folks. However, the sheer literary effort he needs to construct this fictional return to a feudal society is enough to make one wonder if he actually thought it could be successful. Literature scholars differ in their evaluations of the novel, ranging from accusing it of "naiveté" (Edler 1970: 30*) to considering it a "conscious unlikelihood" (Kirchner-Klemperer 1962: 263). But its conclusion is not arbitrary; in fact, it can be seen as the logical result of Prutz's narrative analysis of the industrial reality of his day. To the celebration of prior traditional morals belongs, at the same time, their enactment in reality, which means the recovery of a former "decent poverty."

Conclusion

Why do these novels, long-forgotten by literary studies nowadays, deserve our attention? What do they contribute to understanding the concept of economic and social crisis in the mid-nineteenth century? There are several answers to these questions. First, the three popular novels analyzed here represent the emerging lives and occupations in the factory in various German territories during the initial transition to industrial modes of production in an unembellished way. The novels thereby reveal the nature of the individual economic crisis experienced by the factory workers. With their focus on the stunning antagonisms between owners and laborers, these texts demonstrate that the workers cannot live on the wages they earn, and that they suffer from exploitation: factory life damages their health and, in some cases, their ability to act as morally upright individuals. In this respect, the knowledge the novels convey corresponds to that of the emerging social sciences.

Second, the authors' aim in writing these novels was to illustrate and promote ideas that might bring about a reconciliation of these antagonisms in the factory context. They do not aim primarily to eliminate individual destitution but are concerned with the cohesion of society as a whole—it is the social crisis they want to resolve. Keeping the economic antagonisms and their consequences for workers' lives in mind, the authors describe and argue emphatically for ideals of community that would bind workers and industrialists together in healthy socioeconomic relations. Although their novels differ in the concrete ideas of reconciliation they present, the authors share the view that a harmonious community *must* be possible in the newly established economic circumstances. In this respect, too, their ideas resemble those put forth by the social sciences, emerging simultaneously in the mid-nineteenth century.

Third, however, the authors can imagine no hopeful realization of such ideals. This is where the novels' conclusions differ from the conclusions of the social sciences. Authors of fictional texts can "play out" new social ideas, and can thus also let them fail. None of the authors discussed here is bold enough to turn the factory into a site of reconciliation. In Ernst Willkomm's novel from 1845, reconciliation only exists in the forms of a bookkeeper's claims and a vague promise for the future. Louise Otto-Peters' novel from 1846 does not attempt to assuage antagonisms on an economic level, concentrating instead exclusively on fixing personal relationships—and even these relationships fail. Robert Prutz contends, moreover, in 1851, that reconciliation is an impossible goal. He argues for a return to preindustrial times, while strongly suggesting that this ideal is in fact based on wishful thinking. At the very moment that these novels dare to give shape to any idea of social harmony, they immediately enact its failure. This is the "alternative knowledge" (Hörisch 2007: 10) provided by social novels.

Last but not least, regardless of this failure of social ideals in the mid-nineteenth-century factory context, these authors express in their novels a belief that a mutually beneficial arrangement should be possible under the existing circumstances. It is noteworthy that the only solution then considered seriously, however, would be for the state to coerce groups living in economic antagonism to coexist peacefully. This is a sobering conclusion. As far as the economic workings of the factory system were concerned, these authors could envision no basis on which a harmonious and just community might be built. In reality, social welfare policies intended to improve work and living conditions were not implemented in Germany until the end of the nineteenth century under Bismarck's leadership. At that time, however, "neither humanism nor solidarity" were the driving forces behind these initiatives, but instead the "fear that Social Democracy would succeed" (Dobner 2007: 93). Such success would not only have unseated the conservative and center parties, which represented the wealthier classes and the landed nobility, but it would also have overthrown the existing society.

Johannes Brambora earned a PhD in German Literature from the Martin Luther University of Halle-Wittenberg, Germany. His book, *Von Hungerlöhnern, Fabriktyrannen und dem Ideal ihrer Versöhnung: Der Beitrag des populären Romans zur Entstehung eines sozialen Erklärungsmusters ökonomischer Gegensätze der Industrialisierung, 1845–1862*, was published in 2020. He currently teaches German, Ethics, and Social Studies at a vocational school in Leipzig.

Notes

1. The few published studies share a concern for the need to raise the reputation and recognition of this genre. "The historians of literature do not have a reasonable cause to exclude this important type of literary analysis of society," states Adler (1990a: 14). International scholars such as Bullivant (2005: 44–45) underscore this argument in the case of English social novels: "Although they may be not the best literary achievement of those times, their place in literary history is ensured: they are still available, partly in inexpensive paperback editions, the novels of Elizabeth Gaskell and Charles Dickens have been made into movies, and all of them are on the reading lists of English literature seminars." This is why Rink (2014: 24) pursues the goal to "examine the lesser and not very recently edited novels, sometimes referred to as trivial, to (re)evaluate them for contemporary and future studies."
2. Opielka (2006: 11) testifies to the fact that this question has not yet been answered: "[Y]ou cannot find consensus in the sociological 'scientific community' about this concept [of community]—which also denominates the group of scientists themselves."
3. Scholars disagree as to the periodization of the Industrial Revolution in Germany. I adhere to Hans-Werner Hahn's (2011: 24–25) view that it began in 1845.
4. This 1835 quote from Franz Baader is considered the first evidence of the use of the word "proletarian" in Germany. Baader apparently extracted it from the discussion in France.
5. At the turn of the twentieth century, "people in the social reformer circle were of the opinion that the reintegration and renaturalization of the proletariat, created by capitalism and industrialization, 'within the *Kulturgemeinschaft* [cultural community] of the modern states as an independent element was an undeniable problem of overall politics at that time'" (Ritter 2010: 19; orig. qtd. in Jaffé, Sombart, and Weber 1904: iv).
6. The factory was depicted before *White Slaves* in novels such as Goethe's *Wilhelm Meisters Wanderjahre* [*Wilhelm Meister's Years of Travel or the Renunciants*] in 1829; *Die Epigonen* [*The Epigones*] by Immermann in 1836; and in Willkomm's novel *Eisen, Gold und Geist* [*Iron, Gold and Spirit*] in 1843. But in none of these texts is it at the center of the action.
7. Henceforth, this novel is referenced parenthetically by volume and page number. All volumes are available for free in the online library Zeno.org.
8. A reference to the fact that "legal press proceedings" prevented the release of volumes four and five can be found in Franz Dingelstedt's (1990: 181) review. However, Dingelstedt makes no reference to the reason for the dispute. Hermann Marggraff's

(1990: 195) review speaks of a public declaration by Willkomm that led the authorities to suspect him of being unchristian. Hans Adler (1990b: 295), who studied the censored documents in the state archive in Dresden, stresses that religious descriptions made up the main parts of the text that were criticized.

9. In his novel, Willkomm also describes the living conditions of the urban proletariat. In one scene, the narrator describes the Hamburg Gängeviertel as housing the "poorest quarters of the great trading city" (III, 39) in apartments resembling "smoky cellar caves" (III, 41). Kurzer and Cooper's contribution to this volume discusses socioeconomic policies in Germany and other north-east European countries intended to improve housing conditions from the post-World War II era to the early twenty-first century.
10. Willkomm's description matches contemporary impressions of the textile factories: "Being rather poorly paid, extremely controlled by others, degraded to appendixes of ruthless machines, mostly influenced by bad conditions, the work in the textile factories was already for contemporaries an 'embodiment of relentless employment'" (Emsbach 1982: 295; qtd. in Kocka 1990: 448).
11. Qtd. by Ludwig (Otto-Peters 1996: 347–64) in the epilogue to the 1996 edition of *Castle and Factory.*
12. After complaints from the censorship authority, the novel was published in 1846 in a redacted version as Louise Otto, *Castle and Factory: Novel,* 3 vols (Leipzig: Adolph Wienbrack, 1846). It was reprinted in 1996, edited by Johanna Ludwig, as *Castle and Factory: Novel,* 1st complete edition of the 1846 censored novel, Louiseum (Leipzig: LKG, 1996). All citations below are from the 1996 edition.
13. For more details, see Ludwig 2004.
14. Prutz published this article in 1845 in the *Literarhistorisches Taschenbuch* [Literary historical paperback], and included it in 1847 in *Kleine Schriften* [Short papers]. In his article, Prutz anticipates some of the thoughts later formulated by researchers on the genre of "trivial literature" (see Langenbucher 1968).
15. Prutz, *Das Engelchen: Roman* [The Angel: Novel] (1851), is referred to hereafter by referencing volume number and page directly after each quote.
16. Although literature scholars in later years have viewed the success of Prutz's undertaking critically, contemporary judgments of his novel were rather euphoric, as in the following statement: "*The Angel* is a social novel, if one gets the idea of social right, and is one of the best German novels of all times" (Balde 1854: 76).

References

A.B. 1845. "Neueste Erzählungsliteratur." *Die Grenzboten* 46(4): 307–14.

Adler, Hans. 1980. *Soziale Romane im Vormärz: Literatursemiotische Studie.* Munich: W. Fink.

———. 1990a. "Einleitung." In *Der deutsche soziale Roman im 18. und 19. Jahrhundert,* ed. Hans Adler, 1–14. Darmstadt: Wissenschaftliche Buchgesellschaft.

———. 1990b. "Literatur und Sozialkritik: Versuch einer historischen Spezifikation des sozialen Romans." In *Der deutsche soziale Roman im 18. und 19. Jahrhundert,* ed. Hans Adler, 280–309. Darmstadt: Wissenschaftliche Buchgesellschaft.

Agethen, Matthias. 2017. *Vergemeinschaftung, Modernisierung, Verausgabung: Nationalökonomie und Erzählliteratur in der zweiten Hälfte des 19. Jahrhunderts.* Göttingen: Vandenhoeck & Ruprecht.

Baader, Franz. (1835) 1965. "Über das dermalige Mißverhältnis der Vermögenslosen oder Proletairs zu den Vermögen besitzenden Klassen der Sozietät in betreff ihres Auskommens, sowohl in materieller als intellektueller Hinsicht, aus dem Standpunkt des Rechts betrachtet." In *Die Eigentumslosen: Der deutsche Pauperismus und die Emanzipationskrise in Darstellungen und Deutungen der zeitgenössischen Literatur,* ed. Carl Jantke and Dietrich Hilger, 286–93. Munich: Karl Alber.

Bachleitner, Norbert. 1993. *Der englische und französische Sozialroman des 19. Jahrhunderts und seine Rezeption in Deutschland.* Amsterdam and Atlanta, GA: Rodopi.

Balde, Ernst. 1854. *Robert Eduard Prutz.* Cassel: Verlag der modernen Klassiker.

Bauer, Barbara. 1995. "Louise Ottos Romane." In *Louise Otto-Peters. Ihr literarisches und publizistisches Werk: Katalog zur Ausstellung,* ed. Johanna Ludwig and Rita Jorek, 45–53. Leipzig: Leipziger Universitätsverlag.

Bauer, Manuel. 2015. *Ökonomische Menschen: Literarische Wirtschaftsanthropologie des 19. Jahrhunderts.* Göttingen: Vandenhoeck & Ruprecht unipress.

Biedermann, Karl. 1847. *Vorlesungen über Sozialismus und soziale Fragen.* Leipzig: Biedermannsche Verlagsbuchhandlung.

Brambora, Johannes. 2020. *Von Hungerlöhnern, Fabriktyrannen und dem Ideal ihrer Versöhnung: Der Beitrag des populären Romans zur Entstehung eines sozialen Erklärungsmusters ökonomischer Gegensätze der Industrialisierung, 1845–1862.* Vormärz-Studien XLIII. Bielefeld: Aisthesis Verlag.

Bullivant, Keith. 2005. "Der deutsche Gesellschaftsroman des neunzehnten Jahrhunderts." In *Das verschlafene 19. Jahrhundert? Zur deutschen Literatur zwischen Klassik und Moderne,* ed. Hans-Jörg Knobloch and Helmut Koopmann, 43–51. Würzburg: Königshausen & Neumann.

Dingelstedt, Franz. 1990. "Kritische Gastrollen II." In *Der deutsche soziale Roman im 18. und 19. Jahrhundert,* ed. Hans Adler, 173–85. Darmstadt: Wissenschaftliche Buchgesellschaft.

Dobner, Petra. 2007. *Neue soziale Frage und Sozialpolitik.* Wiesbaden: VS, Verlag für Sozialwissenschaften.

Edler, Erich. 1970. "Nachwort." In *Robert Prutz: Das Engelchen. Dritter Theil. Faksimiledruck nach der 1. Auflage von 1851,* 1*–30*. Göttingen: Vandenhoeck & Ruprecht.

———. 1977. *Die Anfänge des sozialen Romans und der sozialen Novelle in Deutschland.* Frankfurt am Main: Klostermann.

Eiden-Offe, Patrick. 2014. "Weisse Sclaven, oder: Wie frei ist die Lohnarbeit? Freie und unfreie Arbeit in den ökonomisch-literarischen Debatten des Vormärz." In *Geld und Ökonomie im Vormärz,* ed. Jutta Nickel, 183–214. Bielefeld: Aisthesis Verlag.

Emsbach, Karl. 1982. *Die soziale Betriebsverfassung der rheinischen Baumwollindustrie im 19. Jahrhundert.* Bonn: Röhrscheid.

Gerhard, Ute, Petra Pommerenke, and Ulla Wischermann. 2008. "Louise Otto. Wegbereiterin der deutschen Frauenbewegung und Schriftstellerin." In *Klassikerinnen feministischer Theorie: Grundlagentexte*, ed. Ute Gerhard, Petra Pommerenke, and Ulla Wischermann, 63–67. Königstein im Taunus: Ulrike Helmer Verlag.

Gotthelf, Jeremias. 1965. "Die Armennot." In *Die Eigentumslosen: Der deutsche Pauperismus und die Emanzipationskrise in Darstellungen und Deutungen der zeitgenössischen Literatur*, ed. Carl Jantke and Dietrich Hilger, 377–89. Munich: Karl Alber.

Hahn, Hans-Werner. 2011. *Die Industrielle Revolution in Deutschland*. 3rd edn. Munich: Oldenbourg.

Halter, Martin. 1983. *Sklaven der Arbeit—Ritter vom Geiste: Arbeit und Arbeiter im deutschen Sozialroman zwischen 1840 und 1880*. Frankfurt am Main: Peter Lang.

Hinnah, Fritz. 1915. *Ernst Willkomm: Ein Beitrag zur Geschichte des "Jungen Deutschland."* Bocholt: Temming.

Hörisch, Jochen. 1996. *Kopf oder Zahl: Die Poesie des Geldes*. Frankfurt am Main: Suhrkamp.

———. 2007. *Das Wissen der Literatur*. Munich: Fink.

———. 2013. *Man muss dran glauben: Die Theologie der Märkte*. Munich: Fink.

Jaffé, Edgar, Werner Sombart, and Max Weber. 1904. "Geleitwort." *Archiv für Sozialwissenschaften und Sozialpolitik* 19(1): i–vii.

Kirchner-Klemperer, Hadwig. 1962. "Der deutsche soziale Roman der vierziger Jahre des vorigen Jahrhunderts, repräsentiert durch Ernst Willkomm und Robert Prutz einerseits und Alexander Sternberg andererseits, unter besonderer Berücksichtigung seiner Beziehung zum französischen Roman." *Wissenschaftliche Zeitschrift der Humboldt-Universität zu Berlin. Gesellschafts- und sprachwissenschaftliche Reihe* 11(2): 241–80.

Kitchen, Martin. 1978. *The Political Economy of Germany 1815–1914*. London: Croom Helm.

Klausnitzer, Ralf. 2008. *Literatur und Wissen. Zugänge – Modelle – Analysen*. Berlin: De Gruyter.

Kley, Antje. 2018. "What Literature Knows: An Introduction." In *What Literature Knows: Forays into Literary Knowledge Production*, ed. Antje Kley and Kai Mertens, 9–25. Berlin: Peter Lang.

Kocka, Jürgen. 1990. *Arbeitsverhältnisse und Arbeiterexistenzen: Grundlagen der Klassenbildung im 19. Jahrhundert*. Bonn: Dietz.

Kocka, Jürgen, and Jürgen Schmidt. 2015. *Arbeiterleben und Arbeiterkultur: Die Entstehung einer sozialen Klasse*. Bonn: Verlag J.H.W. Dietz Nachf.

Köppe, Tilman. 2011. *Literatur und Wissen: Theoretisch-methodische Zugänge*. Berlin: De Gruyter.

Langenbucher, Wolfgang R. 1968. "Robert Prutz als Theoretiker und Historiker der Unterhaltungsliteratur: Eine wissenschaftsgeschichtliche Erinnerung." In

Studien zur Trivialliteratur, ed. Heinz O. Burger, 117–36. Frankfurt am Main: Vittorio Klostermann.

Liptzin, Solomon. 1990. "Die Weber im deutschen Roman." Trans. Hans Adler. In *Der deutsche soziale Roman im 18. und 19. Jahrhundert*, ed. Hans Adler, 204–27. Darmstadt: Wissenschaftliche Buchgesellschaft.

Ludwig, Johanna. 2004. "'Ich martere mich selbst mit diesen Problemen . . .': Die Zensurgeschichte und zeitgenössische Bewertung des Romans 'Schloß und Fabrik' von Louise Otto." In *Bürgerliche Gesellschaft – Idee und Wirklichkeit: Festschrift für Manfred Hahn*, ed. Eva Schöck-Quinteros, 179–200. Berlin: Trafo-Verlag.

Mähly, Jacob Achilles. 1888. "Prutz, Robert." In *Allgemeine Deutsche Biographie*, vol. 26, ed. Historische Kommission bei der Bayerischen Akademie der Wissenschaften, 678–82. Leipzig: Duncker & Humblot. Retrieved 26 October 2017 from https://de.wikisource.org/w/index.php?title=ADB:Prutz,_Robert&oldid=2493269.

Marggraff, Hermann. 1990. "Proletarierpoesie in Deutschland." In *Der deutsche soziale Roman im 18. und 19. Jahrhundert*, ed. Hans Adler, 186–203. Darmstadt: Wissenschaftliche Buchgesellschaft.

Mohl, Robert. 1965a. "Die Vergangenheit, Gegenwart und Zukunft der politischen Ökonomie." In *Die Eigentumslosen: Der deutsche Pauperismus und die Emanzipationskrise in Darstellungen und Deutungen der zeitgenössischen Literatur*, ed. Carl Jantke and Dietrich Hilger, 319–37. Munich: Karl Alber.

———. 1965b. "Über die Nachteile, welche sowohl den Arbeitern selbst als dem Wohlstande und der Sicherheit der gesamten bürgerlichen Gesellschaft von dem fabrikmäßigen Betriebe der Industrie zugehen und über die Notwendigkeit gründlicher Vorbeugungsmittel." In *Die Eigentumslosen: Der deutsche Pauperismus und die Emanzipationskrise in Darstellungen und Deutungen der zeitgenössischen Literatur*, ed. Carl Jantke and Dietrich Hilger, 294–318. Munich: Karl Alber.

Opielka, Michael. 2006. *Gemeinschaft in Gesellschaft. Soziologie nach Hegel und Parsons*. 2nd rev. edn. Wiesbaden: VS Verlag für Sozialwissenschaften.

Otto, Christine. 1995. *Variationen des "poetischen Tendenzromans": Das Erzählwerk von Louise Otto-Peters*. Pfaffenweiler: Centaurus.

Otto, Louise. 1846. *Schloß und Fabrik: Roman*. 3 vols. Leipzig: Adolph Wienbrack.

Otto-Peters, Louise. 1996. *Schloß und Fabrik: Roman*. Leipzig: LKG.

Perthaler, Johannes Alois. 1965. "Ein Standpunkt zur Vermittlung sozialer Mißstände im Fabriksbetriebe." In *Die Eigentumslosen: Der deutsche Pauperismus und die Emanzipationskrise in Darstellungen und Deutungen der zeitgenössischen Literatur*, ed. Carl Jantke and Dietrich Hilger, 338–60. Munich: Karl Alber.

Prümm, Karl. 1980. "Robert Prutz: Das Engelchen (1851): Experiment eines 'mittleren Romans': Unterhaltung zu den höchsten Zwecken." In *Romane und Erzählungen des bürgerlichen Realismus: Neue Interpretationen*, ed. Horst Denkler, 40–64. Stuttgart: Reclam.

Prutz, Robert. 1851. *Das Engelchen: Roman*. 3 vols. Leipzig: F.A. Brockhaus.

———. 1981. "Über die Unterhaltungsliteratur, insbesondere der Deutschen." In *Robert Prutz: Zu Theorie und Geschichte der Literatur*, ed. Ingrid Pepperle, 108–28. Berlin: Akademie-Verlag.

Rakow, Christian. 2013. *Die Ökonomien des Realismus: Kulturpoetische Untersuchungen zur Literatur und Volkswirtschaftslehre 1850–1900*. Berlin: De Gruyter.

Reulecke, Jürgen. 1985. "Die Anfänge der organisierten Sozialreform in Deutschland." In *Weder Kommunismus noch Kapitalismus: Bürgerliche Sozialreform in Deutschland vom Vormärz bis zur Ära Adenauer*, ed. Rüdiger vom Bruch, 21–59. Munich: C.H. Beck.

Rink, Elisabeth. 2014. *"Arbeit" und "Proletariat" im deutschen und französischen Roman vor 1848*. Essen: Klartext.

Ritter, Gerhard Albert. 2010. *Der Sozialstaat: Entstehung und Entwicklung im internationalen Vergleich*. 3rd exp. edn. Munich: Oldenbourg.

Schäfer, Frank. 2019. "Transition from Feudal to Modern Society: The Impact of Abolition of Serfdom on German Private Law." In *Legal Science: Functions, Significance and Future in Legal Systems. Collected conference papers of the 7th International Scientific Conference of the Faculty of Law of the University of Latvia*, ed. Agita Kazakeviča and Andra Damberga, 25–34. Riga: University of Latvia Press.

Vogl, Joseph. 2011a. *Das Gespenst des Kapitals*. 4th edn. Zurich: Diaphanes.

———. 2011b. *Kalkül und Leidenschaft: Poetik des ökonomischen Menschen*. 4th edn. Zurich: Diaphanes.

Wehler, Hans-Ulrich. 1989. *Von der Reformära bis zur industriellen und politischen "Deutschen Doppelrevolution" 1815–1845/49*. 2nd edn. Munich: Beck.

Willkomm, Ernst. 1845. *Weisse Sclaven oder die Leiden des Volkes: Ein Roman*. 5 vols. Leipzig: Chr. E. Kollmann.

"Zur Geschichte eines Romans und unserer Zeit." *Demokratisches Wochenblatt* 10 (1869): 115–16.

CHAPTER 3

Economic Knowledge and the Failure to Alleviate the Great Depression in Weimar Germany

ROMAN KÖSTER

A majority of historians agree that the Weimar Republic's massive economic problems were among the main reasons why the first German democracy failed. The sheer number of severe economic crises (inflation until 1923, the intermediate crisis of 1925/26, and finally the Great Depression beginning in autumn 1929) would probably have overburdened more stable societies without the massive political and social tensions that Weimar Germany faced. Economic crises, however, are not simply fateful events; they can be intensified or mitigated by government policies. It is thus important to answer the question: what role did government economic policies play in Germany's massive economic turmoil of the 1920s decade? The inflation as well as many other deleterious effects of the Great Depression are usually ascribed to policy mistakes. Chancellor Heinrich Brüning's austerity policies during the Great Depression are perceived by many observers as a particularly significant reason why the Weimar Republic failed (e.g., Büttner 2008: 428ff.).

But why did Weimar politicians such as Brüning act the way they did? Historians have a strong tendency to ascribe specific decisions to political stances. Recent debates about Brüning's motives to pursue austerity policies during the Great Depression make this clear: Paul Köppen (2014) and Tim B. Müller (2014 and 2015) perceive his economic measures as an attempt to supersede the democratic system and to use the crisis to steer Germany in a more authoritarian direction (see also Tooze 2014: 493ff.). This point of view ascribes a dominance of political over economic reasons for the decisions that were made. The fact that, until the banking crisis of July 1931, Brüning was backed by leading circles of industrialists, who had no love for the Weimar democracy and were concerned about the bargaining power of trade unions, merely underlines how widespread antidemocratic attitudes were among the German elite (Kim 1997). Another explanation some scholars provide for the move toward fiscal austerity is that Weimar politicians were trapped in their adherence to outdated economic doctrines. From this perspective, a lack of imagination and flexibility rather than a weak moral character were culpable for their disastrous political decisions. This latter argument is more problematic than the former, however, because several visionary economists, such as Wilhelm Lautenbach and Wladimir Woytinsky, did develop practical solutions to overcome the Great Depression—the leaders in power just did not listen to them (Krohn 1981).

Both of the above explanations for the failed economic policies of the Weimar Republic are not particularly convincing. To this day, it remains highly disputed whether an alternative economic policy was feasible at all during the Great Depression (see the "Borchardt Debate" that commenced in the late 1970s [Ritschl 2003]). Of the two proposed explanations for the policy failures, the first faces the problem of ascribing economic decisions to specific political attitudes without considering the actual, underlying economic motives behind them. The second explanation operates by means of a rather simplistic notion of economic knowledge that is more or less reduced to a kind of "textbook wisdom." Scholars relying on these assumptions to buttress their arguments almost never ask what people at that time actually knew about the economy and how it functions; or how they acquired this knowledge; or whether something like a "common opinion" existed on certain topics. Perhaps most politicians in the 1920s did not gain an understanding of how the economy works by studying academic treatises, but instead from practical life experience.

I will address these problems related to economic knowledge by illustrating what can be learned by analyzing three debates that historians have been engaged in for decades in seeking explanations for the political decisions that crippled the Weimar Republic. First, I delve into what the term "economic knowledge" means in this context: how it can be used for historiographical purposes; and what the relationship was between "economic knowledge" and "economic narratives" in the early twentieth century. Next, I describe three issues that have emerged from these debates, and that are vital for understanding these political decisions. These issues are related to what is called "inflation trauma"; to the dispute over balancing the budget and various work-creation schemes; and to the presumption that the market tends to regulate itself and thus that the 1920s economic crises created the preconditions for an upswing that should have followed in their wake. My arguments demonstrate how taking a closer look at economic ideas, the narratives that propagate them, and assumptions about them, in their temporal context, enables us to understand why politicians take certain actions as leaders.

Economic Knowledge and Fundamental Learning in the Weimar Republic

"Economic knowledge" consists of a set of assumptions about how the economy works, what factors drive it, and to what degree economic policies may influence it (Arnsperger 2010: 21–27). These assumptions do not necessarily translate into precise theoretical doctrines. Even today, most politicians engaged with economic policy are not economists in any strict sense, but practitioners with a certain "working knowledge." This basic understanding of the economy normally suffices for them to perform their job, and it is occasionally observed that an academic background can be a disadvantage in a political context (Krueger 1999: 37–42). Keeping this point of view in mind, it makes sense to abstract from the state of academic knowledge in the Weimar Republic (which was in itself highly contested), and to take a look at which conclusions were likely to have been drawn from economic events since the end of the Kaiserreich.

Before coming to logical conclusions about the state of economic knowledge in the Weimar Republic, we must first figure out how this knowledge was acquired. Of course, there is no simple answer, but practical experience played an important role. In this case, Weimar politicians drew conclusions from the economic turmoil that Germany had experienced since the outbreak of World War I in 1914, especially by observing the failures and inefficiencies of wartime economic planning. These failures not only demonstrated the alleged absence of patriotic solidarity among large companies, but also a severe lack of economic expertise in the administration, which further undermined the reputation of the old, monarchic order (Feldman 1993: 76–81). War financing and subsequent international political conflicts contributed to a dynamic inflation, which remained more or less latent until 1918, gained acceleration until 1922, and then ended in a disastrous hyperinflation that lasted until the fall of 1923 (Holtfrerich 1986; Feldman 1993). Many contemporary observers concluded that these phenomena were caused by extraordinary circumstances that would probably straighten themselves out in the coming years. But nevertheless, those who experienced these financial vagaries believed these events had to be kept in mind so that similar perils could be avoided in the future.

In the newly created democratic society of the Weimar Republic, economic questions soon became an urgent public issue. Regarding the question of inflation, politicians had to be aware that the vast majority of citizens were hostile to any measures that could produce it (Mergel 2002: 83–120). For this reason, "economic knowledge" in the political realm had to include an idea of what the public "thought" about certain economic questions, and which policy measures appeared legitimate in the public discourse. This sudden attention paid to public opinion marked an important shift from the Kaiserreich, in which politicians had enacted economic legislation more autonomously, with less public input. Even though legitimation in the realm of public opinion had already been important before 1914, after World War I the requirement to ensure the democratic legitimacy of the government became considerably stronger. As Adam Tooze (2001) demonstrates in *Statistics and the German State*, economic questions and ideas rose to much greater prominence in Germany in the 1920s, conveyed by means of economic journals and public debates.

Practical experience alone, however, does not deliver explanations for events, as the Austrian economist Joseph Schumpeter announced in 1926 with regard to historical facts; they need a salient idea to bind them together (Schumpeter 1926: 363f.). Whereas it is unlikely that many politicians, journalists, or the public acquire economic ideas directly from academic textbooks, economic doctrines do nevertheless eventually permeate the public discourse. John Maynard Keynes famously concluded his most important book, *The General Theory of Employment, Interest and Money*, with the statement: "Practical men, who believe themselves to be quite exempt from any intellectual influence, are usually the slaves of some defunct economist" (Keynes 1936: 383). Keynes believed that politicians hold commonly shared ideas about how the economy works, and that these ideas derive from economic doctrines that have been transformed over the course of time into broadly held societal assumptions.

Such basic ideas can, for instance, be identified in common models such as the liberal notion of a self-regulating economy, in which the self-interested actions of individuals have the best possible outcome, led by an invisible hand, or socialist ideas of the advantages of economic planning. Quite typical for the 1920s was the idea that self-organizing tendencies in the economy were beneficial. Until the Great Depression struck, for instance, cartelization (as a typical form of "self-organizing") in Germany was frequently perceived as a healthy reaction to the unreliability of markets (Beckerath 1927: 1119f.). Various ideas about whether the state had the means to influence economic developments or not played a role in the 1920s as well. These ideas were usually connected to specific narratives that, in many cases, drew from the reservoir of "classical" economics (for instance, the "invisible hand"). In many cases, however, new narratives emerged during public debates that made a strong impression on their audience and were repeated by other speakers and authors. A good example of this is the explanations for the recent hyperinflation, which provoked vivid descriptions and metaphors, but left observers without historical models as reference points.

Another question to consider is whether these basic notions were static or if they could adapt easily to new developments. A helpful way to come to terms with this problem is to apply the concept of "fundamental learning," developed by Swiss historian Hans-Jörg Siegenthaler. In his view, people continue to develop fundamental ideas about the functioning of the world throughout their lives. The result is a so-called "*Regelvertrauen*" (rule confidence), which has a strong emotional component and can be reconciled with facts and experiences that deviate from it. Such facts and experiences can, for example, be treated as exceptions or used to justify the occasional need to discharge extraordinary political interventions. According to Siegenthaler, however, these fundamental ideas can undergo major transformations under certain circumstances. Particularly shocking, groundbreaking experiences, which he interprets as *Aktivierungsereignisse* (activation events), can set in motion processes of "fundamental learning" that bring people to change their attitudes and the categories with which they perceive and arrange a complex reality (Siegenthaler 1993).

With regard to the development of economic knowledge, hyperinflation as well as the Great Depression likely served as "activation events" for the Germans in the sense that Siegenthaler describes them. These were not merely grave economic crises, but also—at least in Germany—the first of their kind. The country had, in modern times, never before experienced such an extreme inflation or such a severe economic crisis as the Great Depression. This claim should not, however, automatically determine what conclusions are drawn from these events, or what kind of "fundamental learning" was taking place. To answer these questions, it is necessary to take a closer look at the first major German experience with inflation. Only then can we understand why the depreciation and eventual currency collapse could impact German society so profoundly.

Inflation Trauma: Was It Real or Just a Pretext for Anti-Democratic Policies?

One highly controversial issue, discussed in debates on why the Weimar Republic failed, is whether German inflation trauma existed or not. Was it perhaps just an argument used by politicians during the Great Depression to justify certain political actions? Viewed in hindsight, one can say with confidence that there was actually no real danger of inflation occurring during the Great Depression, for the main problem was, on the contrary, deflation. This debate has nevertheless been waged fiercely among historians, for some of them have seized upon the fear of inflation to justify Brüning's austerity policies during the Great Depression (Borchardt 1982). German inflation trauma is moreover used as a popular argument to explain the rather conservative economic policies implemented under Chancellor Angela Merkel's leadership during the financial crisis that began in 2007/8 (Eichengreen 2015: 9 f.).

Until the year 1923, inflation was experienced generally as a shock that had severe negative economic effects on German society. One should not, however, neglect to mention the fact that inflation, at least for some time, stabilized the German economy by improving its "terms of trade" and creating artificial purchasing power, which protected the economy from the global economic crisis of 1920–21. Some historians claim, with solid arguments, that without the inflation the Weimar democracy probably would not have survived the first years of its existence (Holtfrerich 2016: 224f.). The final consequences of the inflation, however, turned out to be disastrous: it impoverished the *Mittelstand* (middle class); eradicated personal savings; and forced many pensioners, who were important for the cultural life of the Kaiserreich, back into the labor market. Inflation undermined all the certainties and expectations usually connected with stable prices and the proper functioning of economic life.

It is, for obvious reasons, complicated to measure how traumatized German citizens actually became as a result of the inflation they experienced. A possible way to approach this problem, however, is to observe what can be learned from the inflation experience, and how it was narrated in various media during the 1920s. In taking this approach, it is first of all important to consider that the inflation did not last just a few months, but extended over several years, and only in the summer of 1922 did it accelerate to what we call hyperinflation. Inflation was already a matter of public debate during and immediately after World War I, when observers noted the massive drop in value of the German mark in foreign markets, especially in the significant Dutch stock exchange in Amsterdam. In successive years, the German currency depreciated with considerable fluctuations until the summer of 1922, when inflation became rampant and the value loss started to accelerate. The "Ruhr strike," initiated in January 1923, was the last aggravating provocation in an economic crisis that, at this point, could no longer be avoided (Feldman 1993: 631–97).

Germany was certainly not the only European country to experience severe inflation in the 1920s. At least four others—Russia, Poland, Austria, and Bulgaria—had to deal with hyperinflation and a complete currency ruin. Except for Great Britain, Switzerland, and the Scandinavian states (excluding Finland), all European countries endured inflation in one way or another (Köster 2020: 269–73). Even France, a war victor, faced this problem until it stabilized its currency in 1926 by introducing the Franc Poincaré. Thus the French developed their own "inflation trauma," even though their currency depreciation was much less drastic than in Germany (Straumann 2010: 129f.). It was severe enough, though, to have devastating effects on personal savings, and to reduce the prominence of Paris as a financial market.

The main German economic debate of the early 1920s revolved around the question of why the currency was depreciating—this was, once again, a characteristic of European economies (Ufermann 1924: 53f.). Some observers, aligned with the Social Democratic Party or the communists, suspected that the government was manipulating the currency in order to benefit "big business." Others, however, highlighted the advantages of inflation, whereas the early currency stabilization in Great Britain and Czechoslovakia demonstrated the high social costs that such a reverse situation could bring about. In both cases, it appeared that inflation processes had gained a dynamic momentum that eventually made them impossible to manage. These processes brought with them the new insight that, in most cases, inflation would progress along typical paths, but that it was an illusion to think that governments could keep them in check. Economist Eleonor Dulles summarized this conclusion in her dissertation on the French franc: "The transition from mild to severe depreciation is usually sudden. It is possible for the money of a nation to be relatively stable through months of slight depreciation, and then suddenly break away from its former limits and decline with lightning rapidity" (Dulles 1929: 113).

This economic debate comprised merely one aspect of inflationary dynamics, however. While the inflation was still raging, a related broad debate and a literary treatment of its social consequences were also taking place. In novels, dramatic plays, and non-fiction books it was portrayed as a kind of absurd, "hellish carnival" (Ostwald 1931: 7) that produced its own illustrious cast. It allegedly spawned a new type of entrepreneur who profited from the extraordinary circumstances via fraud, corruption, and blackmail, or simply because the "rules" of inflation were better suited to certain kinds of shady business dealings that sidelined the "honest merchants." Thus neologisms such as "*Inflationskönige*" (inflation kings) were spawned, with the diversified industrialist and parliament member Hugo Stinnes being the most prominent example (Feldman 1998: 739–41).

The numerous corruption scandals of the Weimar Republic, described by Martin Geyer (2018: 85–142), furthermore contributed to an overarching perception that inflation led to conditions in which the traditional rules of business conduct would be trampled on. This impression was connected closely to the unbridled nightlife in Berlin: the same figures purportedly drinking absinthe and otherwise enjoying themselves in shady dives were suspected of being inflation profiteers. A good example of the type of narrative that captured this milieu is Hans Ostwald's *Sittengeschichte der Inflation* (A Moral History of the Inflation, 1931), which processed this theme in a paradigmatic manner, uniting economic profiteering with dancing, drinking, and sexual licentiousness. These inflation stories often had strong antisemitic undertones or overtly racist references: although the industrialist Hugo Stinnes was not Jewish, he was often portrayed with facial features that mirrored racist clichés of Jewish men. The morally ambiguous protagonists of Hans Fallada's novel

Wolf unter Wölfen (Wolf among Wolves), published in 1937, flee Berlin in haste to the countryside, like refugees running from the bubonic plague epidemics of the fourteenth century (Fallada 1937).

Inflation was thus not only an individual experience, but also a cultural phenomenon that was present in the Weimar Republic from its inception. The fear of inflation was not fueled solely by the concrete experience of inflation, but also by how it was narrated in literary fiction-writing and the daily press. At the same time, inflation represented both economic turmoil and the disastrous endangerment of an already fragile social order. Typical metaphors like the "dance of the zeros" (Krell 1961: 109) underlined this perception. A decisive feature of this juxtaposition of economic debate and cultural interpretation was that inflation was connected not so much to governmental or Reichsbank policy decisions, but instead to the behavior of individuals. Inflation created favorable circumstances for a certain kind of business behavior that actually fueled its dynamic progression: people were not saving their money but instead spending it without thinking, because they (correctly) expected it would not be worth much in the near future (Feldman 1993: 504f.). Despite this precarious situation, German economists in the mid-1930s objected to the idea of Keynesian deficit spending, arguing that it would provoke the inflation-related behavior of citizens spending their money heedlessly (Salz 1944).

These roughly sketched-out developments provided the background for certain features of German politics in the 1920s and early 1930s: the solid management of state finances and private enterprise became part of an "anti-inflation" rhetoric that should legitimate political decisions. Politicians not only had to deal with their own inflation anxiety, however. For Hans Schäffer, state secretary of the Ministry of Finance, it was obvious that the Weimar government also had to avoid economic policies that might provoke public apprehension (Borchardt 1982: 221–24). Schäffer knew very well how powerfully inflation can affect mass psychology, and how inflation fear can influence public behavior—as a kind of self-fulfilling prophecy—and bring about inflation where it would not otherwise occur (Heyde 1992: 294f.). Many economists asserted in later decades that Weimar politicians did not grasp the "mechanics" of inflation (Winkel 1977: 118). However, they did grasp that inflation was a sensitive topic with psychological repercussions, and that how it manifested itself had much to do with the economic behavior and confidence of ordinary citizens. As Brüning stated in spring 1932: "Woe to those who would start a currency experiment in a country that has experienced an inflation like ours" (qtd. in Heyde 1992: 294f., 384f.).

The result of such fears was that even left-wing economic theorists, who advocated for more assertive governmental economic support policies during the Great Depression, had to assure the public constantly that the measures they recommended would not cause inflation, or that they at least knew the proper strategies to keep inflation in check, despite increases in state spending (von Bischoff 1931; Sturm 1931). Nazi activists, by contrast, produced publications attempting to fuel the public's fear of inflation (Franke 1932). But a group of leftist economists—among them Adolph Lowe—also submitted a petition to the Ministry of Finance in the summer of 1931 advocating against reducing the discount rate (the rate at which the central bank could lend money to banks). Reducing the lending rate is considered a classic countercyclical measure, but observers feared that it would carry with it a risk of provoking inflation (Köster 2011: 267). Anton Erkelenz, founder and party chairman of the German Democratic Party (DDP), aligned with the Social Democratic Party, moreover advocated for avoiding the severe dangers of deflation. He outlined why the measures he suggested would not bring about any inflationary dynamics (Erkelenz 1932: 34f.). The plethora of references like these to inflation, running the gamut from Nazi fearmongering to Social Democratic reassurances that their policies would avert it, demonstrate a preoccupation with inflation anxiety in the Weimar Republic, and can be considered to belong to the economic knowledge held by both politicians and the general public.

The fear of inflation can thus not be considered just an illusion or an argument used to justify an antidemocratic agenda in the Weimar Republic. It had a strong influence on German politics, and it played a particularly decisive role during the Great Depression. Inflation was perceived as nearly impossible to manage because public fears of inflation could and did bring about behaviors that caused inflations. Even if, viewed in hindsight today, there was no actual danger of inflation during the Great Depression, German experiences throughout the 1920s can explain why there was a concrete fear of it—one that influenced political decisions and provoked crucial political and economic debates (Borchardt 1982).

The Function of the State and the "Reichsreform"

Since it was formally founded in 1919, the Weimar democracy understood itself to be a "welfare state." This does not mean that the government created a social safety net for lazy people, as some staunch liberals suspected at that time, but it does mean that the state assumed responsibility for mitigating social tensions and helping people in financial need (Abelshauser 1987). After World War I, in fact, no European government that had participated was able to elude such demands: millions of war invalids had to be provided for, and international economic relations lay in tatters. At the same time, paradoxically, it was the war itself that gave governments the means to play a more active role in boosting socioeconomic equality. In Germany, for instance, the public spending ratio—which measures the share of public expenditures in the Gross Domestic Product (GDP)—had been about 15 percent before 1914. During the war this ratio rose to more than 60 percent, and remained above 30 percent throughout the 1920s. To finance these higher expenditures, the state implemented a tax reform in 1919 initiated by Minister of Finance Matthias Erzberger, who was assassinated by right-wing activists shortly afterward for his involvement in the Paris Peace Conference (Dowe 1994: 33f.). Without the war it would have been nearly impossible to implement such a substantial tax increase.

The growing public spending ratio made it possible to enlarge the welfare state. This meant upgrading the social measures that Bismarck had first put into place in the 1880s, but also introducing federal unemployment insurance in 1927. For many contemporary observers, this was the apex of a welfare state that actually deserved its name (Führer 1990: 524f.). It remained a complicated question, however, how to finance this expanded safety net. During the inflation years this did not pose a real problem, but the inflation did destroy the projected government financing scheme. This scheme had included a two-year buffer so that, for instance, old age insurance and benefits for war invalids in 1922 would be paid from revenues collected in 1920. Starting in 1924, however, such benefits had to be paid out directly from incoming tax revenues. This policy proved to be a primary reason for the rapid breakdown of the social security net during the Great Depression. By autumn 1931, for example, unemployment benefits could only be paid for four months, or sometimes for an even shorter time period (James 1986: 67).

The so-called *Zwischenkrise* (intermediate crisis) of 1925/26 provoked a further government policy response in the form of a new job-creation scheme launched by the minister of finance, Peter Reinhold (of the German Democratic Party). This countercyclical work-creation scheme massively strained state finances. Historian Dieter Hertz-Eichenrode (1982: 209ff.) has noted that this scheme came at an inopportune time: the annual Dawes Plan payments, agreed upon in 1924, were comparatively low during the years 1925 and 1926, but they rose from 1927 onward. Beginning in 1926, the Weimar government started to have massive problems balancing the state budget, and this turned into a yearly spectacle with uncertain results.

The policy of deficit spending during the *Zwischenkrise* led to a debate among economists and in the daily news press about the efficacy of work-creation schemes. Some voices advocated strongly for such measures, but the majority remained skeptical (Lampe 1927). At least the "bourgeois camp" was—as in other European countries—decidedly distrustful of high state expenditures that they believed would result in a lack of state autonomy and a dependence on the vested interests of employers' associations or trade unions

(Eucken 1932; Marx 2013: 308–15). At the same time, this camp feared that democracy would generate incentives for politicians to ensure their re-election by making spending promises. One event that exacerbated these debates turned out to be the *Ruhreisenstreit* (Ruhr iron strike), provoked in autumn 1928 when employers from the Ruhr region's industrial plants rejected a new state-guaranteed wage tariff, and locked out more than a hundred thousand workers (Bähr 1989: 250–74). Although some observers saw this behavior as proof of the antidemocratic stance of industrialists from the Ruhr region, for the "bourgeois camp" the *Ruhreisenstreit* and what they viewed as a scandalously high wage tariff demonstrated that the state had been taken hostage by the trade unions (Kim 1997: 15–20).

These developments served as the backdrop of intense debates on a proposed *Reichsreform*, which would mean a reorganization of the state, a new allocation of duties among the various ministries, and a restructuring of the relationship between the federal government and the municipalities, the latter of which had accrued high debts in the second half of the 1920s (James 1986: 85–109). The goal of the *Reichsreform* was to create a more stable basis for state and municipal finances, and to install a more precisely defined state structure. Behind the impetus for these reforms lay common ideas of a "lean state" that would also be autonomous and possess enough authority to steer clear of the influence of vested interests. From this point of view, a lean state was the precondition for a smoothly working free-market economy (Kim 1997: 11–20; Plumpe 2007: 129–35).

Such ideas were hotly contested, of course, but the need for an overarching *Reichsreform* was broadly accepted by representatives from the various democratic parties. What this restructuring should entail, however, and whether such a reform package could be implemented without creating winners and losers, remained unclear and was highly disputed.[1] Significantly, the government of Chancellor Hermann Müller (SPD, 1928–30) did not succeed in passing such a reform. These debates nevertheless demonstrate that Brüning's agenda, after he became chancellor in late March 1930, existed along the spectrum of the democratic discourse. He could latch onto these democratic debates during his chancellorship and, when he later declared in his memoirs that he had wanted to "seize" the crisis as a weapon to reorganize the government and the state, this did not necessarily mean that he wanted to produce an authoritarian state. His words might also be interpreted as expressing the intention to reorganize the state's finances and create a government that could protect its autonomy from vested interests and enjoy a greater financial "solidity" (Brüning 1972: 177–92).

It is important to be aware of the fact that the meaning of the general term *Reichsreform* changed as the economic crises of the 1920s played out. In the late 1920s, as demonstrated above, the term described a plan to reorganize the state so as to create a more solid financial framework and to avoid the annual tussle to balance the national budget. This stance was contested by left-wing political parties, but it remained a legitimate position in the democratic discourse. During the most severe economic crisis period, however, this meaning of *Reichsreform* shifted: starting in 1931, when the Great Depression intensified, it increasingly began to signify the end of the democratic experiment, and to stipulate the conversion of Germany to an authoritarian state (cf. Braatz 1973). The abandonment of democracy was not, however, what Brüning had in mind when he came to power in 1930, nor why he was backed by leading industrial circles. The main goal of this contingent was to reorganize the state so that it would possess solid financing and produce a favorable environment for economic growth (Kim 1997: 11–20). This was a classic liberal economic agenda. The political radicalization and polarization during the Great Depression, however, permitted a significantly different narrative to be produced and circulated.

The Concept of a Self-Regulating Business Cycle and "Fundamental Learning" during the Great Depression

Cyclical fluctuations in the economy have been observed since the mid-nineteenth century. In the 1860s, the French economist Clement Juglar identified business cycles with a duration of seven to eleven years, which later came to be called "Juglar cycles" (Juglar [1889] 1969). Starting in the year 1900, economic debates related to business cycles increasingly attracted attention, eventually becoming the dominant topic during the 1920s. Adam Tooze (2001: 98f.) demonstrates how the language of business cycle research and economic forecasting "trickled down" into the public discourse, and shaped debates about everyday life and government economic policies during the 1920s. Economists such as Adolph Lowe have wondered why business cycle research attracted so much attention during the 1920s, considering that no "normal" business cycle took place in Germany after 1918 (Lowe 1989: 80). Contemporary political and economic observers, however, were aware that they did not live in "normal times," which to them meant the years prior to 1914. The economic fluctuations they were experiencing were, at least in part, caused by extraordinary political and economic circumstances (Köster 2011: 229f.).

This concept of the steadily revolving business cycle had a variety of implications for Weimar politics and society. The most important implication was how this concept contributed to the widespread belief that economic development is self-adjusting. Upswings were assumed to create conditions (price hikes or high interest rates) that would bring about a depression, which would then sort out inefficient and unprofitable firms and—by lowering prices and interest rates—create the preconditions for a new upswing. Many observers thus considered crises to have a "purifying" influence on the economy. Connected to this notion of the cyclical nature of economic developments was the idea that crises would not be protracted, and that the economy would recuperate after a while, even without political interventions (Löwe/Lowe 1925).

The experience of economic crises up to the Great Depression seemed to confirm this opinion. The global economic crisis of 1920/21 did not last long. Even if its impact in Great Britain, with a GDP plunge of 20 percent, had been more severe than that of the Great Depression, the British economy had rebounded by the following year. The German crisis of 1925/26 did not even last a year, and the recovery was not ascribed to the countercyclical policies implemented by the government, but instead to the economy's self-healing powers. Many observers interpreted this crisis as an adjustment exercise to remove structural distortions brought about by the inflation years. What buttressed this interpretation was the powerful upswing that followed, making 1927 by far the best year economically in the history of the Weimar Republic (Knortz 2010: 115–25).

During the 1920s, the idea of a self-regulating business cycle was a de facto "*opinio communis*" among economists and politicians. As business cycle theories gained evermore traction, several *Konjunkturforschungsinstitute* (economic research institutes) were founded to provide the public with economic reports and forecasts (Kulla 1996: 9–21; Tooze 2001: 103–5). As the Austrian school liberal economist Ludwig von Mises remarked in 1928, this dissemination of economic data led to a situation in which "these issues, which are among the most complicated in economics, have become almost folkloric" (Mises 1928: 1). Economists and politicians from the left side of the political spectrum also argued along these lines, and even socialist thinkers such as Henryk Grossmann affirmed the cyclical structure of the capitalist process (Köster 2011: 233–41; Lenhard 2019: 100f.). What distinguished the Marxists from those with other political views was their prediction that a series of economic crises would inevitably lead to the breakdown of the capitalist order, and that this breakdown would be propelled further by the growing "organic" composition of the industrial process, which was dominated increasingly by machines and Fordist modes of production (Zinn 2002: 84).

While intellectuals debated the theoretical bases for economic fluctuations from various perspectives, the international political negotiations that took place throughout the 1920s aimed at creating a new international economic order that should in turn produce the conditions for the "normal" capitalist process to operate efficiently once again. This can be said in regard to the conferences in Genoa, Italy in 1922 and Geneva, Switzerland in 1927, as well as the numerous bilateral conferences held throughout the 1920s. Such gatherings of international leaders demonstrated an acute awareness of the urgent need for stable institutional arrangements to improve the economic situation. Political leaders were also attuned to the fact that the pre-1914 economic situation could not be restored quickly. Nevertheless, numerous trade agreements were made during the second half of the 1920s; the gold standard was restored; and several organizations such as the international "Rohstahlgemeinschaft" (a cooperation of French and German steel producers founded in 1926) were established to alleviate the scarcity of natural resources and raw materials needed for industrial production (Henrich-Franke 2014: 97–101).

It should thus not seem surprising that the general opinion shared by the German public in 1927 and 1928 was that the economic and political situation was about to stabilize. Some conservative observers ascribed this to a tendency of the business world to consolidate itself (i.e., to cartelize), while others saw the normalization of the political situation as the reason why the German economy had apparently overcome the crisis-ridden decade that followed World War I. The economist Adolf Weber even stated publicly that economic cycles had turned into "soft ripples," and that German capitalism had reached a state of "powerful manhood," leaving its former "adolescent" vulnerability behind (Weber 1929: 54). His metaphors of tranquility, masculine strength, and maturity reflect the optimism of the time, and demonstrate that, since the political and economic stabilization of 1923/24, the outlook of most economists had become much more optimistic.

This background on German attitudes toward the economy can help us understand what a novel, shocking state of affairs the Great Depression represented when it was triggered by the collapse of the US stock exchange in the fall of 1929. It was not only the most severe economic crisis of the industrial age, but also a crisis with an utterly atypical development. Although the Wall Street financial decline in October 1929 was sizable, the crisis took off slowly, only becoming a global depression in the year 1931. Up to this point, countries such as Britain and France had only been affected mildly by the slump, but as 1931 unfolded, they had to face growing economic problems, unemployment, and social unrest.

Starting around November 1930, German politicians, economists, and citizens became increasingly aware that this was no "normal" crisis, but instead a type of disaster the world had never seen before. Hans Schäffer, state secretary in the Ministry of Finance, expressed the pressure and helplessness he felt as a government official in a letter from autumn 1931: "You have to believe me: for someone in a responsible position it is difficult to bear mentally, to let the crisis 'consume itself,' when he learns on a daily basis what is also consumed with it."[2] Public debates roiled around the question of whether the economy would recuperate or if the world would linger in a perpetual crisis because the capitalist system had reached its limits of success. Notions of "secular stagnation" became fashionable, while the formerly predominant narrative of self-regulating business cycles lost credibility (Lederer 1931). Economists and business journalists began to revise their concepts of the business cycle, struggling to come to terms with the conundrum that an economic downswing does not automatically create the conditions for a subsequent upswing. The federal government was simultaneously bombarded with dozens of citizen suggestions for work-creation schemes—simply too many to check the efficacy of each. Overwhelmed by the public response to the crisis, the Ministry of Finance began answering these proposals merely with a form letter instead of producing individual responses.[3] This deluge of proposals demonstrated a fading faith in the economy's self-healing powers.

Eventually, the notion of a self-regulating economy fell completely out of fashion, and this reaction is likely the most profound example of "fundamental learning" to have taken place in the Weimar Republic. When citizens recognized that the crisis was neither going away nor curing itself, the general perspective on the economy started to change. Beginning in the autumn of 1930, the debate intensified as to whether the state should intervene more actively to dig Germany out of its slump. Reflecting later on what he had experienced in the early 1930s, economist Walter Eucken said that starting in 1931 the government was basically coerced into implementing countercyclical measures, because public pressure had become too strong to resist (Eucken 1951: 67). Other economists argued, however, that the crisis had stripped the government of all instruments it would have needed to combat the crisis with any efficacy. This desperate situation provided a breeding ground for the Nazis to use power politics in 1933 as a means to overcome the economic crisis and to present the state as the vanquisher of the failing functionality of the market (Schivelbusch 2006).

Here is not the place to rehash the debate on how much room the Weimar Republic had to maneuver its economic policy after 1929 (for a summary of this debate, see Ritschl 2003). The most important point to be made here is that a process of fundamental learning about how the economy works took place during the Great Depression, and was a major result of these hard economic times. Throughout the 1930s, German citizens understood only roughly how the state might intervene in the economy to regulate it, and this was probably the reason why John Maynard Keynes's book, *The General Theory of Employment, Interest and Money*, was received in 1936 as a message of salvation, because it appeared to provide instructions on how to carry out rational economic interventions (Kesting 1997: 166).

Conclusion

To sum up the attitude of many historians toward economic policy during the Weimar Republic, it is helpful to draw on an article from 1964 published by banker and economist L. Albert Hahn (b. 1889) in the German weekly newspaper *Die Zeit*, titled "Brüning war an allem Schuld" (It was all Brüning's fault). Hahn asserted that the German government had ignored all available theoretical options to fight the crisis actively during the Great Depression. From Hahn's perspective, Weimar politicians were held prisoner by their preconceived economic doctrines and anticipation of public fears of inflation. In the end, they were unable to liberate themselves from their intellectual prison, because they lacked courage and open-mindedness (Hahn 1963).

Hahn was anything but an impartial observer of the crisis, however. He belonged to a small group of people who advocated strongly for a completely different economic policy from that which Weimar politicians carried out. The Keynesian *Zeitgeist* of the 1960s and 1970s brought many of these concepts of countercyclical economic policy to light, which prove the openness of the intellectual debates during the Great Depression (Bombach 1976). But aside from the intense debates, still raging today, about whether an alternative economic policy was actually feasible, Hahn's arguments represent, in a rather archetypical manner, the assertion that there is no need to take a closer look at certain intellectual positions adhered to in the Weimar Republic, because Weimar politicians were just ignorant, stubborn, and at worst antidemocratic.

In this chapter I have brought forward two arguments: first, it is necessary to take a closer look at economic ideas, which gain traction in the narratives and assumptions about them, in their temporal context in order to gain a deeper understanding of why politicians take certain actions. To date, it appears that we are still at a point in the historical debate where many people simply claim that Brüning is to blame for the failure of the Weimar Republic, which unduly diminishes the complexity of the historical situation in its final years. My second argument, however, is that this economic knowledge cannot be explained adequately if we do not consider in detail the concrete experiences that contemporaries had with the Weimar economy. I argue that, for instance, with regard to the problem of the *Reichsreform*, a "bourgeois" stance existed, and that Brüning represented this stance. This is the reason why he was backed for several years by leading German industrialists and by various bourgeois political parties.

Taking this *Erfahrungsraum* (range of experience; Koselleck 1989) into consideration also leads to clearer, more differentiated explanations as to why Germany's first republic failed. I argue that such a re-evaluation of historical events can only be successful if scholars reintroduce the economy back into their narratives, and refrain from rehashing the debates of the 1970s and 1980s, as well as the clash of Keynesian vs. supply-side economics. It is essential to be aware of the fact that economic knowledge played an important role in political decision making in the Weimar Republic. In most cases, moreover, these conceptions were not the result of "ideologies" but instead of learning processes that resulted from concrete experiences gained after the outbreak of World War I. Such an interpretation complicates historical debates on the end of the Weimar Republic, and also enables us to draw a more complex, ambivalent image of key political players such as Heinrich Brüning, who was probably not the antidemocratic "villain" he is often made out to be.

Roman Köster is Senior Researcher at the Bavarian Academy of Science in Munich. Recent previous positions include Senior Researcher at the Universität der Bundeswehr in Munich and Visiting Professor at the University of Freiburg. His dissertation covered the "crisis" of German economics during the 1920s, and his habilitation dealt with the history of waste management in West Germany after 1945. His research areas include the economic history of the interwar period, the history of economic thought in the twentieth century, and the environmental history of waste management. His book, *The Global History of Waste*, will appear in 2022.

Notes

1. Letter from Staatssekretär Pünder to the Reichsminister des Innern (10 October 1928). Federal Archive Berlin, R 43 I/1878.
2. Letter from H. Schäffer to M.J. Bonn (26 October 1931). Federal Archive Koblenz, Bonn Papers, 82/52.
3. Moritz Julius Bonn: Notations concerning the memorandum from the 2nd September 1931. Federal Archive Koblenz, Bonn Papers, 82/51.

References

Abelshauser, Werner, ed. 1987. *Die Weimarer Republik als Wohlfahrtsstaat. Zum Verhältnis von Wirtschafts- und Sozialpolitik in der Industriegesellschaft*. Stuttgart: Steiner.

Arnsperger, Christian. 2010. *Full-Spectrum Economics: Toward an Inclusive and Emancipatory Social Science*. London: Routledge.

Bähr, Johannes. 1989. *Staatliche Schlichtung in der Weimarer Republik. Tarifpolitik, Korporatismus und industrieller Konflikt zwischen Inflation und Deflation, 1919–1932*. Berlin: Akademie.

Beckerath, Herbert von. 1927. "Der Inhaltswandel des Kartellbegriffs und seine wirtschaftspolitischen Folgen." *Wirtschaftsdienst* 12(30): 1119–22.

Bischoff, Friedrich von. 1931. *Krise oder Inflation?* Munich: Voglrieder.

Bombach, Gottfried, ed. 1976. *Der Keynesianismus. Vol. 2: Die beschäftigungspolitische Diskussion vor Keynes in Deutschland – Dokumente und Kommentare.* Berlin: Springer.

Borchardt, Knut. 1982. "Zur Frage der währungspolitischen Optionen Deutschlands in der Weltwirtschaftskrise." In *Wachstum, Krisen, Handlungsspielräume der Wirtschaftspolitik. Studien zur Wirtschaftsgeschichte des 19. und 20. Jahrhunderts,* ed. Knut Borchardt, 206–24. Göttingen: Vandenhoeck & Ruprecht.

Braatz, Werner E. 1973. "Franz von Papen and the Preussenschlag, 20 July 1932: A Move by the 'New State' toward Reichsreform." *European Studies Review* 2: 157–80.

Brüning, Heinrich. 1972. *Memoiren.* Munich: DTV.

Büttner, Ursula. 2008. *Weimar. Die überforderte Republik 1918–1933. Leistung und Versagen in Staat, Gesellschaft, Wirtschaft und Kultur.* Stuttgart: Klett-Cotta.

Dowe, Christopher. 1994. "Ein föderaler Unitarist? Matthias Erzberger und seine Vorstellungen von Reichsreform und Einheitsstaat." *Historisch Politische Mitteilungen* 24(1): 15–35.

Dulles, Eleonor. 1929. *The French Franc: 1914–1928: The Facts and their Interpretation.* New York: Macmillan.

Eichengreen, Barry. 2015. *Hall of Mirrors: The Great Depression, the Great Recession, and the Uses and Misuses of History.* New York: Oxford University Press.

Erkelenz, Anton. 1932. *Der Abbauwahn. Gegen Deflation. Gegen Inflation. Für Stabilität.* Berlin: Bott.

Eucken, Walter. 1932. "Staatliche Strukturwandlungen und die Krisis des Kapitalismus." *Weltwirtschaftliches Archiv* 36: 297–321.

———. 1951. "Unser Zeitalter der Misserfolge. Fünf Vorträge zur Wirtschaftspolitik." Tübingen: Mohr.

Fallada, Hans. 1937. *Wolf unter Wölfen.* 2 vols. Berlin: Rowohlt (English: *Wolf among Wolves,* translated by Philip Owens, Thorsten Carstensen, and Nicholas Jacobs. Brooklyn, NY and London: Melville House, 2010.).

Feldman, Gerald D. 1993. *The Great Disorder: Politics, Economics and Society in the German Inflation, 1914–1924.* New York: Oxford University Press.

———. 1998. *Hugo Stinnes. Biographie eines Industriellen, 1870–1924.* Munich: C.H. Beck.

Franke, Heinz. 1932. *Die Journaille lügt!: Katastrophenpolitiker! Inflation! Kriegshetzer –Reaktionäre.* Munich: Franz Eher.

Führer, Karl Christian. 1990. *Arbeitslosigkeit und die Entstehung der Arbeitslosenversicherung in Deutschland, 1902–1927.* Berlin: Akademie.

Geyer, Martin H. 2018. *Kapitalismus und politische Moral in der Zwischenkriegszeit oder: Wer war Julius Barmat?* Hamburg: Hamburger Edition.

Hahn, L. Albert. 1963. "'Brüning war an allem Schuld.' Eine falsche Wirtschaftspolitik ebnete den Weg für die Massenverführer." *Die Zeit* 14 (5 April). Retrieved 22 December 2021 from https://www.zeit.de/1963/14/bruening-war-an-allem-schuld.

Henrich-Franke, Christian, ed. 2014. *Die "Schaffung" Europas in der Zwischenkriegszeit. Politische, wirtschaftliche und gesellschaftliche Konstruktionen eines vereinten Europas*. Münster: Lit.
Hertz-Eichenrode, Dieter. 1982. *Wirtschaftskrise und Arbeitsbeschaffung. Konjunkturpolitik 1925/26 und die Grundlagen der Krisenpolitik Brünings*. Frankfurt am Main: Campus.
Heyde, Philipp. 1992. *Das Ende der Reparationen. Deutschland, Frankreich und der Youngplan, 1929–1932*. Paderborn: Schöningh.
Holtfrerich, Carl-Ludwig. 1986. *The German Inflation 1914–1923: Causes and Effects in International Perspectives*. Berlin: De Gruyter.
———. 2016. "Aus dem Alltag des Reichswirtschaftsministeriums während der Großen Inflation, 1919–1923/24." In *Das Reichswirtschaftsministerium der Weimarer Republik und seine Vorläufer. Strukturen, Akteure, Handlungsfelder*, ed. Carl-Ludwig Holtfrerich, 224–360. Berlin: De Gruyter.
James, Harold. 1986. *The German Slump: Politics and Economics, 1924–1936*. Oxford: Clarendon.
Juglar, Clément. (1889) 1967. *Des crises commerciales et de leur retour périodique en France, en Angleterre et aux États-Unis*. Reprint of 2nd edn. New York: Kelley.
Kesting, Peter. 1997. *Zwischen Neoklassik und Historismus: das ökonomische Werk Joseph A. Schumpeters aus methodologischer und theoriegeschichtlicher Perspektive*. Marburg: Metropolis.
Keynes, John Maynard. 1936. *General Theory of Employment, Interest and Money*. London: Macmillan.
Kim, Hak-Ie. 1997. *Industrie, Staat und Wirtschaftspolitik. Die konjunkturpolitische Diskussion in der Endphase der Weimarer Republik, 1930–1932/33*. Berlin: Duncker & Humblot.
Knortz, Heike. 2010. *Wirtschaftsgeschichte der Weimarer Republik. Eine Einführung in Ökonomie und Gesellschaft der ersten Deutschen Republik*. Göttingen: Vandenhoeck & Ruprecht.
Köppen, Paul. 2014. "'Aus der Krankheit konnten wir unsere Waffe machen.' Heinrich Brünings Spardiktat und die Ablehnung der französischen Kreditangebote 1930/31." *Vierteljahrshefte für Zeitgeschichte* 62(3): 349–75.
Koselleck, Reinhart. 1989. "Erfahrungsraum und Erwartungshorizont. Zwei historische Kategorien." In *Vergangene Zukunft. Zur Semantik geschichtlicher Zeiten*, ed. R. Koselleck, 349–75. Frankfurt am Main: Suhrkamp.
Köster, Roman. 2011. *Die Wissenschaft der Außenseiter. Die Krise der Nationalökonomie in der Weimarer Republik*. Göttingen: Vandenhoeck & Ruprecht.
———. 2020. "Krise als Erfahrungsraum. Die Weimarer Republik und die europäische Wirtschaftsordnung während der Großen Depression." In *Weimar und die Neurordnung der Welt. Politik, Wirtschaft, Völkerrecht nach 1918*, ed. Andreas Braune and Michael Dreyer, 267–89. Stuttgart: Steiner.
Krell, Max. 1961. *Das alles gab es einmal*. Leipzig: Deutscher Bücherbund.

Krohn, Claus Dieter. 1981. *Wirtschaftstheorien als politische Interessen. Die akademische Nationalökonomie in Deutschland, 1918–1933.* Frankfurt am Main: Campus.
Krueger, Anne. 1999. "The Use and Misuse of Theory in the Transfer Process." In *The Transfer of Economic Knowledge*, ed. Ernst Mohr, 32–44. Cheltenham: Edward Elgar.
Kulla, Bernd. 1996. *Die Anfänge der empirischen Konjunkturforschung in Deutschland 1925–1933.* Berlin: Duncker & Humblot.
Lampe, Adolf. 1927. *Notstandsarbeiten oder Lohnabbau? Kritik der Wirtschaftstheorie an der Arbeitslosenpolitik.* Jena: G. Fischer.
Lederer, Emil. 1931. *Technischer Fortschritt und Arbeitslosigkeit.* Tübingen: Mohr.
Lenhard, Philipp. 2019. *Friedrich Pollock. Die graue Eminenz der Frankfurter Schule.* Berlin: Suhrkamp.
Löwe, Adolf (Adolph Lowe). 1925. "Der gegenwärtige Stand der Konjunkturforschung in Deutschland." In *Die Wirtschaftswissenschaft nach dem Kriege*, Vol. 2, ed. Moritz Julius Bonn and Melchior Palyi, 329–77. Berlin: Duncker & Humblot.
Lowe, Adolph. 1989. "Konjunkturtheorie in Deutschland in den Zwanziger Jahren." In *Studien zur Entwicklung der ökonomischen Theorie VIII*, ed. Bertram Schedold, 75–86. Berlin: Duncker & Humblot.
Marx, Christian. 2013. *Paul Reusch und die Gutehoffnungshütte. Leitung eines deutschen Großunternehmens.* Göttingen: Wallstein.
Mergel, Thomas. 2002. *Parlamentarische Kultur in der Weimarer Republik: politische Kommunikation, symbolische Politik und Öffentlichkeit im Reichstag.* Düsseldorf: Droste.
Mises, Ludwig. 1928. *Geldwertstabilisierung und Konjunkturpolitik.* Jena: G. Fischer.
Müller, Tim B. 2014. *Nach dem Ersten Weltkrieg. Lebensversuche moderner Demokratien.* Hamburg: Hamburger Edition.
———. 2015. "Demokratie und Wirtschaftspolitik in der Weimarer Republik." *Vierteljahrshefte für Zeitgeschichte* 62(4): 569–601.
Ostwald, Hans. 1931. *Sittengeschichte der Inflation. Ein Kulturdokument aus den Jahren des Marktsturzes.* Berlin: Neufeld und Henius Verlag. (English excerpt: "A Moral History of the Inflation," in *The Weimar Republic Sourcebook*, ed. Anton Kaes, Martin Jay, and Edward Dimendberg, 77–78. Berkeley: University of California Press, 1994.)
Plumpe, Werner. 2007. "Der Reichsverband der Deutschen Industrie und die Krise der Weimarer Wirtschaft." In *Herausforderungen der parlamentarischen Demokratie. Die Weimarer Republik im internationalen Vergleich*, ed. Andreas Wirsching, 129–57. Munich: Oldenbourg.
Ritschl, Albrecht. 2003. "Knut Borchardts Interpretation der Weimarer Wirtschaft. Zur Geschichte und Wirkung einer wirtschaftsgeschichtlichen Kontroverse." In *Historische Debatten und Kontroversen im 19. und 20. Jahrhundert*, ed. Jürgen Elvert and Susanne Krauß, 234–44. Stuttgart: Steiner.
Salz, Arthur. 1944. "The Present Position of Economics." *American Economic Review* 34(1): 15–24.

Schivelbusch, Wolfgang. 2006. *Three New Deals: Reflections on Roosevelt's America, Mussolini's Italy, and Hitler's Germany, 1933–1939*. New York: Metropolitan Books.

Schumpeter, Joseph. 1926. "Gustav von Schmoller und die Probleme von heute." *Schmollers Jahrbuch* 50: 337–88.

Siegenthaler, Hans-Jörg. 1993. *Regelvertrauen, Prosperität und Krisen. Die Ungleichmäßigkeit wirtschaftlicher und sozialer Entwicklung als Ergebnis individuellen Handelns und sozialen Lernens*. Tübingen: Mohr Siebeck.

Straumann, Tobias. 2010. *Fixed Ideas of Money: Small States and Exchange Rate Regimes in Twentieth-Century Europe*. Cambridge: Cambridge University Press.

Sturm, Hans. 1931. *Los von Wallstreet. Die Behebung der Arbeitslosigkeit und die Wirtschaftskrise durch eine Hilfswährung ohne Inflation*. Flarchheim: Die Kommenden.

Tooze, Adam. 2001. *Statistics and the German State: 1900–1945: The Making of Modern Economic Knowledge*. Cambridge: Cambridge University Press.

———. 2014. *The Deluge: The Great War and the Remaking of Global Order, 1916–1931*. New York: Penguin.

Ufermann, Paul. 1924. *Könige der Inflation*. Berlin: Verlag für Sozialwissenschaft.

Weber, Adolf. 1929. *Das Ende des Kapitalismus? Die Notwendigkeit freier Erwerbswirtschaft*. Munich: Hueber.

Winkel, Harald. 1977. *Die deutsche Nationalökonomie im 19. Jahrhundert*. Darmstadt: Wissenschaftliche Buchgesellschaft.

Zinn, Karl Georg. 2002. *Konjunktur und Wachstum*. 5th rev. edn. Aachen: Riese-Springer.

CHAPTER 4

The Moral Equation Works Out Differently

The Great Depression, the Crisis of Knowledge, and Value Order in Erich Kästner's Fabian: The Story of a Moralist

SIMELA DELIANIDOU

Today the internationally acclaimed author Erich Kästner (1899–1974) is best known for his children's and young adult literature, rather than as the widely popular, prolific journalist and satirist who critiqued German society in the 1920s and early 1930s, while it experienced multiple economic crises.[1] This chapter takes a fresh look at Kästner's most important socially critical text from the latter years of the Weimar Republic, *Fabian: The Story of a Moralist* (1931),[2] which has thus far received little attention from literature scholars. The novel is a political and economic satire that will be analyzed here from economic and mass media perspectives. Incorporating an objective, documentary-like authenticity and journalistic texts such as news reports, satires, and essays,[3] Kästner makes daily life and its economic reality in the Weimar Republic tangible. The author moreover demonstrates successfully in *Fabian* that the economic system is socially constructed. The novel shines light on the confusing mix of moral values and the crisis of knowledge in the interwar years, as well as on the factual and fictional nature of the value system of the time, and its discursive connection to the "medium of money."[4] It is thus helpful to investigate Kästner's novel by drawing on the theory and methodology of New Economic Criticism,[5] which contributes to the production of knowledge related to the economy:

> Economics is (also) fiction, literature, reflection and not (only) a mathematically precise likeness of the social world, but (also) the construction of reality. The world, science and formulas need to be explained and interpreted just like

> literary texts. And interpretation always means diversity: there is not just one truth or one applicable argument; different interpretations can and must be tolerated, particularly in tension with each other. (Horvath 2011: 59)

We can thus assume that economics—like all systems of knowledge—is governed by its specific historical context. Even if economics "was established ahistorically at its core, based on the methods of the natural sciences" (ibid.: 52), which appears necessary for the production of knowledge, the knowledge it produces is limited by discourse. It is furthermore influenced by any given economy's historical context and is thus also socially constructed. Economics as a social science tends to downplay this fact (see Horvath 2011; Künzel 2014: 143–57), but this perspective is problematic. Kästner's literary text, discussed here, focuses explicitly on the problems with viewing economics strictly as a science.

In *Fabian*, Kästner furthermore reflects on the transactional medium of money, its symbolic power, and the politics surrounding it in the Weimar Republic. He thereby demonstrates that the economic knowledge attached to it developed historically, was in a constant state of flux, and was not always dependent on an ethical value system. In order to prove his point, he introduces various gift-giving practices into the novel's plot. According to one of Kästner's contemporaries, the sociologist Marcel Mauss (2002, orig. 1923–24), the earliest form of exchange consisted of gift-giving. Mauss's explanations of gift-giving practices as a social form of exchange are applied here to Kästner's novel to interpret the alternatives Kästner provides to the market exchange economy based on capitalism.

The Global Economic Crisis in the Interwar Years as the End of the "Oikodicy" and Catalyst of a Crisis of Knowledge

In the years between the two world wars, after having experienced the economic boom of the late nineteenth-century *Gründerzeit* and the short-lived Golden Years of the Twenties, people in Germany were once again confronted with the phenomenon of economic crisis. It is thus no coincidence that representatives of the New Objectivity movement cast a sharp eye on economic issues. Economic crises had certainly occurred since preindustrial times, but new crises such as that which triggered the Great Depression differed from this familiar pattern. Since the 1830s, stock market crashes have tended to develop into global economic crises (Plumpe 2013: 45). The global economic crisis that struck between 1928 and 1930, and lasted in its core phase until 1932, is thus logically the focus of many New Objectivity texts. With its epicenter in the United States, this crisis took a heavier toll on Germany than on other European countries (ibid.: 81–91), and the novel *Fabian* reacts to its effects there.

Kästner's economic satire is directed at specific, contemporary micro- and macroeconomic crisis zones, and anticipates the end of what Joseph Vogl (2015: 33–34, 16) calls the "oikodicy," referring to the belief that the self-regulating market is the "best of all possible [economic] worlds." The protagonist Jakob Fabian observes the economic system's failures to produce wealth for everyone, and how these failures come about, on his walks around Berlin and in his own life.[6] The newspaper headlines Fabian reads convey the global dimensions of the disaster: "Election of Premier—Another Fiasco, . . . Ruhr Coal-Sales Falling, . . . Coffee Markets Uncertain, . . . Expected Strike of 140,000 Metal Workers, . . . Timber Dumping—Negotiations in Moscow, . . . The usual thing. Nothing special" (Kästner 5; 11). Fabian summarizes the news sarcastically because he has a doctorate in German literature, anticipates losing his advertising job, and thus expects to become one of the newspaper's unemployment statistics. His detached, sober descriptions of the shabby Berlin cityscape document its poverty and crime (16; 26, 91f.; 125f.), as well as the daily street battles between Communists and National Socialists that resemble a kind of civil war (45; 63). Fabian is no longer an avant-garde bohemian flâneur akin to Arthur Rimbaud or Charles Baudelaire; he does not enjoy the metropolis as a constant source of titillation and intensely subjective aesthetic experiences.[7] He works in advertising, designing profane placards for cigarettes and prize competitions, and thus is an integrated actor in the capitalist system who increases its profits while it rationalizes him out of his job in order to cut expenses (79; 107, 94; 128). Thus, he becomes one of the many unemployed academics of his time (91; 124).

The microeconomy of the Weimar Republic is characterized by precarious working conditions (Kästner 28f.; 42, 31; 45, 94; 128) and high unemployment, as Kästner demonstrates. In a slapstick scene featuring the homeless inventor Professor Kollrepp (82; 111f.), technological progress and Fordism are blamed for having caused the unemployment of over five million people (38; 54f.). Even in the realm of academia, competition for jobs leads to antisocial behavior, as is exemplified in the fate of the character Labude, Fabian's friend who becomes the unwitting victim of intrigue, and commits suicide as a result (152; 207). *Fabian* exposes the value system of a purportedly liberal economic system, and its economic subjects, as fundamentally unethical and inhumane. Only a few people profit from this system, one of whom is the careerist character Zacharias, a stereotypical manager who works for a newspaper publisher and wishes to instrumentalize Fabian by turning him into his private work-slave (116f.; 158f.). The description of Fabian's visit to the employment office shows starkly the reasons why unemployment policies in the Weimar Republic were doomed to fail. The Weimar government could not combat social problems, because there were neither enough jobs nor money, and it was stifled by its Kafkaesque bureaucracy. It was inevitably condemned to inefficiency, as Kästner confirms with the experiences of his fictional character Fabian (90–93; 122–27).

The failure of contemporary German economic policies in the 1920s and early 1930s resulted from a fundamental societal deficit in ethical values and social justice. The "fields," according to Pierre Bourdieu's (2013) definition,[8] of politics, economics, education, and the mass media should usually guarantee democratic structures and public welfare in a republic. These fields broke down, however, in their function of representing an ethical value system. Because the political system also found itself suffering from a crisis of knowledge (see Delianidou 2018), the Weimar government could not halt the economic crisis, instead driving it forward catalytically. Many politically erroneous decisions were made, as the fictional editors of the politics and economics sections of a local newspaper, Münzer and Malmy, affirm to Fabian (18–27; 28–40). Even Fabian's friend Labude laments in his suicide letter that the "political experts . . . let the continent die under their hands, while they potter about with their petty remedies" (137; 186). The medical metaphor stands out blatantly here in Labude's desperate situation. Instead of curing the European patient with proper medicine,

> [t]he state bolsters up the bankrupt landowners. The state supports the heavy industries. The industrialists sell their goods to foreign countries at a loss and to the home market at a figure above the world price-level. Raw materials are too dear; the manufacturers reduce wages; the state accelerates the decline in the purchasing power of the masses by imposing taxes which it dare not impose on the rich; capital still flees by the milliard across the frontiers. Isn't that consistency? Can you say that madness has no method? (23f.; 35f.)

This insanity, which Malmy unmasks as the "softening of the public brain" (24; 37) of technocrats,[9] has already reached global dimensions. According to him, concealed behind this insanity are not only "villainous" but also "weak-minded" contemporaries, and the "spiritual slothfulness" of those "who manage the affairs of this globe" (24; 37):

> Technical improvements increase production. Technical improvements decimate the ranks of labor. The purchasing power of the masses is attacked by galloping consumption. Grain and coffee are being burnt in America to keep up the prices. In France the winegrowers are grumbling because the harvest is too good. Just think of it! Mankind is desperate because the earth is too fruitful! Too much grain – and elsewhere people are starving! (24; 36)

Malmy's argument reveals how intently political and economic decision makers are focused on maximizing profits at the expense of social concerns such as feeding the hungry.

Fraudulent politics contribute to the radicalization of society and promote populism and totalitarianism on both the right and left of the political spectrum, which the masses follow blindly (Kästner 25; 38). The popular press, whose mission should be to contribute to the formation of critical opinion, does not do justice to this role, and nor do the schools or universities (19–21; 29–32).[10] The mass media have become degraded to the level of the tabloid press because of censorship and other limits on press freedom, along with their self-imposed silence and the falsehoods propagated by newspeople (20; 31). Dieter Wrobel (2005: 279) describes *Fabian* as a mass media satire that functions "as a document opposing the threats to and usurpation of journalism and the mass media, as well as against the self-imposed disenfranchisement of journalists." Britta Jürgs (1995) points out that Kästner's narrative style resembles journalistic writing. The headline-like chapter titles, quick narrative rhythm, and recognizable intersections between the author's journalistic texts and the novel's fictional story characterize this hybrid style, which Jürgs analyzes in detail (198f.). Jürgs and Erhard Schütz (Jürgs 1995: 199; Schütz 1986: 152) both assert that this journalistic writing style becomes an end in itself, "whereas the warning loses credibility" (Jürgs 1995: 199). In their view, Fabian's concept of a better society appears to be a ridiculous caricature. Kästner was purportedly not interested in developing alternative social models, but only in describing society's decline. Jürgs (ibid.: 207) writes that unemployment does not appear to be a social problem in the novel—despite the fact that Kästner focuses on it specifically. I argue the opposite, here and in my 2018 article: although Jürgs's detailed literary analyses of the text are correct, in the end she comes to the wrong conclusions. Analyzing *Fabian* from an economic perspective shows how critical Kästner is of the society in which he lived.

The representatives of educational institutions in *Fabian* are equally responsible for the intellectual crisis. They either become criminals themselves—like the professor of sinology who becomes a thief (35; 50)—and thus can no longer serve as role models, or they work to militarize the youth of Germany, indoctrinating them so that they take on a subordinate mentality, national chauvinism, and a penchant for violence. Instead of promoting critical thinking, the teachers educate "whole generations of children into obedient officials and narrow-minded bourgeois" (161; 219), who allow themselves to be drawn into one war after another.

Renegotiating the Role of Money or the Search for New (Old) Value Orders

Fabian's nightmare (107–13; 146–54), which can be interpreted as a kind of surreal Faustian Walpurgisnacht, exposes in particular the grotesque, upside-down world of advanced capitalism.[11] The nightmare depicts a decadent, consumer-oriented, greedy, and violent society[12] that uses machines to clone people and forces them to engage in sadistic sexual acts. This dystopia functions as a surreal distorting mirror of Weimar society, showing the sordid underbelly of the Golden Twenties, and anticipating its calamitous end allegorically in the form of an apocalyptic poison gas war. In depicting this nightmarish scenario, Kästner employed not only innovative, avant-garde stylistic devices but also traditional, fantastical motifs of Romanticism to expose his contemporary societal situation as highly pathological.

The novel's introductory scene, depicting an advertising campaign stunt, suggests a direct connection between the desire for money and the erosion of moral values, both of which become more pronounced during financial crises. Here, Kästner alludes to the German Romantic fairytale tradition in an intertextual reference to the Grimm Brothers' fairytale "The Star Money." Many Romantic texts written in the early 1800s feature early capitalism and the concomitant loss of a moral compass as their main topic. Two such fairytales are "The Poor Maiden" (1812) and "The Star Money" (1819), the latter being one of the most famous "children's and household" tales, as the Grimm Brothers referred to them, and partly based on Achim von Arnim's novella *The Three Loving Sisters and the Lucky Dyer* (1812). Kästner describes the advertising campaign thus:

> The town was like a fairground. The house-fronts were bathed in garish light to shame the stars in the sky. An aeroplane droned above the roofs. Suddenly there was a shower of aluminium thalers. The passers-by looked up, laughed and bent to pick them up. Fabian fleetingly recalled the story of the little girl who lifted her frock to catch the small change that fell from heaven. Then he took one of the thalers from the stiff brim of a stranger's hat. It bore the words: "Come to the Exotic Bar, 3 Nollendorfplatz, Beautiful girls, Nude tableaux, Pension Condor in same house." (6; 12–13)

The values propagated in the "Star Money" fairytale have become perverted in advanced capitalism: instead of brotherly love and altruism, in *Fabian* a love that can be bought and sold is advertised. The religion of the market and advertising dominate society. Even the stars, which traditionally represent transcendence and piety, end up in the background, feeling ashamed of having to exist alongside the artificial lights of the surrounding businesses. The splitting of the subject that the protagonist experiences when confronting the world of consumption (Kästner 6; 13) alludes to the Romantic theme of the doppelgänger.[13] It refers to the loss of the self in modern mass society, in which the individual only has value as a consumer. Consumer behavior is tied to a "radical hedonism," as Erich Fromm (1976) describes it in his sociological study *To Have or To Be?* In trying "to find a meaning to life in unlimited pleasure" (3), the hedonist embodies a behavior that was encouraged starting in the eighteenth century, but could not be fully implemented until after World War I. During this phase of human history, "economic behavior became separate from ethics and human values" (ibid.: 7):

> In medieval society, as in many other highly developed as well as "primitive" societies, economic behavior was determined by ethical principles. Thus, for the scholastic theologians, such economic categories as price and private property were part of moral theology. Granted that the theologians found formulations to adapt their moral code to the new economic demands . . .; nevertheless, economic behavior remained *human* behavior and, hence, was subject to the values of humanistic ethics. (Ibid.: 7; italics in original)

According to Michel Foucault (2002: 191f.), a discursive shift occurred in the seventeenth century with the advent of mercantilism, because since then the value of money has no longer been based on the material (a precious metal) of which it was made. Its value now lies only in its function as a symbolic, representational object:

> Money (and even the metal of which it is made) receives its value from its pure function as a sign. This entails two consequences. First, the value of things will no longer proceed from the metal itself; it establishes itself by itself, without reference to the coinage, according to the criteria of utility, pleasure, or rarity. Things take on value, then, in relation to one another; the metal merely enables this value to be represented, as a name represents an image or an idea, yet does not constitute it: "Gold is merely the sign and the instrument commonly used to convey the value of things in practice; but the true estimation of that value has its source in human judgment and in that faculty termed the estimative."[14] (Ibid.: 191)

As this transition took place, the connection between the medium of money and traditional concepts of morality also gradually got lost. This shift in the system of values toward purely representational symbols in economics, language, and natural history is tied to the advent of modern thought and the end of metaphysics (ibid.: 344f.).

The early twentieth-century French sociologist Marcel Mauss, a contemporary of Erich Kästner, traces the history of various types of human exchange systems, as they relate to social structures, from an ethnological perspective. In his influential book *The Gift*, first published in 1925, Mauss (2002) describes the magical-religious dimension attributed to money in tribal cultures, in which not only precious metals but also stones and seashells were used as currency for payments and trade. In both later phases of historical development, however, one can observe how money lost its ethical-religious value:

> At the same time as its value became detached from its expression in gold and silver, the facts and ideas tied to this value shifted and became secularized: in this sense, they separated it [money] from the ethical-religious values to which it had been tied or subordinated—just like the economic part of social life with its ethical-religious part, which had a greater standing and regulated all of life, was tied or subordinated to it. (Simiand 2015: 75)

Mauss and his colleague François Simiand (ibid.: 108, 110) emphasize that money is a social representation, a social belief based on trust in its value, during all three phases of anthropological development (see also Seitz 2015: 64–67).

Felix Martin also views money as a social technology that is based on the belief in its value. This perspective diverges from conventional concepts of it, such as that put forth by the seventeenth-century English philosopher and physician John Locke, which remains influential to this day. The group of scholars to which Locke belongs presumes falsely that money is merely a thing, an object, and that "economic value is just a property of the natural world, like length, or weight, or volume" (Martin 2013: 144). If, however, "money was a thing and value a physical property, to discuss either in ethical terms no longer even made sense" (ibid.: 145; also 150).

Joseph Vogl makes similar arguments when examining economic history in the context of the anthropological revolution that has taken place since the seventeenth century. Vogl concludes that economic knowledge is oriented toward a set of general guiding principles. It corresponds to "the idea that there is a specific rationality to be found in political and social life once it has detached itself from the exemplary model of divine world government to seek its principles in itself" (Vogl 2015: 17). The secularization of money as a social technology, which has made ethical questions about it obsolete, is not ignored in the novel *Fabian*. To date, no literature scholar has recognized Kästner's thematization of this perspectival shift.

The consequences of this "new" value system, which had been asserting itself evermore forcefully since the seventeenth century and became manifest in the medium of money, is problematized by Kästner in *Fabian*. The galloping inflation that was reined in in Germany in 1924 with the introduction of the Reichsmark, and then followed by a deflation in 1927–28 (see Plumpe 2013: 76f., 80f.), allowed the question of the exchange value of money to be posed again in a new iteration in the novel. *Fabian* connects this question with that of the fundamental loss of moral values that were observable at all levels of society. Even the most intimate, private relationships were affected by this loss, and its varied effects are made visible in such relationships. Kästner's characters Irene Moll and her husband, for example, expose the bourgeois institution of marriage in advanced capitalism as a pecuniary, consumer-oriented exchange. Between them, even sexuality is regulated by contract and degraded to the level of a consumer good that assumes the formula "C(ommodity)-M(oney)-C(ommodity)."[15] Mrs. Moll, a nymphomaniac, reduces the male body to its most basic function in the circulation of wares. To her, Fabian is like a piece of cake to be bought and consumed, or a bobsled to be ridden (Kästner 12; 21). Irene and her husband, a lawyer, think they have him at their disposal financially and contractually to satisfy her sexual desires.[16] At the end of their first year of marriage, her husband stipulated in a contract the conditions under which his wife would be allowed to cheat on him, cutting her allowance in half if she should break the rules (13; 22). Both the immoral offer that Irene makes to Fabian to prostitute himself as her sex slave, and the fact that she later becomes the successful owner of a brothel, demonstrate how sexuality serves as a medium of monetary exchange in advanced capitalism. In the C-M-C constellation of the brothel, however, the body as commodity loses its status as the main focus of interest: money becomes capital, the end in itself and the means to an end—solely the acquisition of wealth (see Kästner 102; 139f.).

The other main female character in Kästner's novel, Fräulein Battenberg,[17] gets straight to the point when talking about what gets lost in "exchange relationships" that are shaped purely by economics. She describes the love relationships of her time as deficient. People no longer know what to do with the gift of love, because it is tied to social duties that paying consumer-individuals are no longer capable of fulfilling:

> Formerly a woman gave herself and was valued as a gift. Now we are paid, and the day comes when we are thrown aside, like all goods that are bought and made use of. It's cheaper to pay cash, thinks the man.
>
> Formerly a gift and a commodity were two quite different things. Now a gift is merely a commodity that can be bought for nothing. Its cheapness makes the purchaser suspicious. It must be a bad bargain, he thinks. And generally he is right. For later the woman presents him with the bill. Suddenly he is called on to refund the moral price of the gift. In moral currency. As a pension for life. (Kästner 68; 91)

In Fräulein Battenberg's explanation of the ways her contemporaries treat the gift of love, the historical development of the gift's significance becomes apparent. In the past, the granting of love had been a social practice based on a shared social responsibility, drawing its high value from this feature. In modern consumer societies, by contrast, love has become degraded to a short-lived consumer product that can only be experienced as such. If love is suddenly given selflessly, as a gift without pecuniary value, this act of giving provokes suspicion because this social practice is no longer customary. This suspicion then proves to be justified, according to Fräulein Battenberg, because individuals are only familiar with one-dimensional economic exchanges and can no longer make sense of complex social relationships.

An exchange of gifts, as Mauss (2002) calls it, is a social phenomenon no longer befitting the modern, rational economic system. In his ethnological studies, with which he initiated an "ethnological turn in sociology" (Ritter 1990: 198), Mauss concludes that the gift-giving practices in archaic societies are "total social phenomena" (Mauss 2002: 3). "All these phenomena are at the same time juridical, economic, religious, and even aesthetic and morphological" (ibid.: 101):

> First, it is not individuals but collectivities that impose obligations of exchange and contract upon each other. The contracting parties are legal entities: clans, tribes, and families who confront and oppose one another in groups. . . . Moreover, what they exchange is not solely property and wealth, movable and immovable goods, and things economically useful. In particular, such exchanges are acts of politeness: banquets, rituals, military services, women, children, dances, festivals, and fairs, in which economic transaction is only one element, and in which the passing on of wealth is only one feature of a much more general and enduring contract. Finally, these total services and counter-services are committed to in a somewhat voluntary form by presents and gifts, although in the final analysis they are strictly compulsory, on pain of private or public warfare. We propose to call all this the *system of total services*. (Ibid.: 6–7; italics in original)

The gift requires a return gift, as it forges a connection of the "soul" and thus is tied to an obligation (ibid.: 16–18). The purpose of the gifts "is above all a moral one, the object being to foster friendly feelings between the two persons in question, and if the exercise failed to do so, everything had failed" (Radcliffe-Brown 1922: 83; qtd. in Mauss 2002: 25). The exchanged object also possessed a religious character that has since become lost (Mauss 2002: 16). If a gift is not given, delayed, or inappropriate, then honor and prestige are lost (ibid.: 47). But the refusal to accept a gift also leads to a loss of honor, because the objects given as gifts "are always, and in every tribe, spiritual in origin and of a spiritual nature" (ibid.: 56); and as things with a "soul" that follows them around (ibid.: 84), they not only possess magical-religious power, but they can also bring good fortune or, used inappropriately, misfortune (ibid.: 58, 84).[18]

But by the interwar period, Mauss considers humanity no longer capable of fulfilling these "total services" to society. This period is dictated by the third phase of monetary value theory (Mauss 2002: 128, fn 29), whereas, by contrast, "the system of 'total services' . . . constitutes the most ancient system of economy and law that we can find or of which we can conceive" (ibid.: 90).[19] The incompatibility of these two value systems becomes apparent when Fräulein Battenberg chooses to pursue a film career as an actress rather than giving her love for Fabian a chance. In Fabian's view, she thus loses her dignity and lowers herself to the status of an object of exchange. Thus, he accuses her of selling herself to the movie industry:

> You have found a powerful man to finance you. He is not only financing you, but giving you a chance to make good in your profession. . . . [H]e will get back the money he has, so to speak, invested in you; you will also earn money yourself. . . . You will become more and more successful, more and more ambitious, but the higher you climb the greater danger of falling. Probably you will have to give yourself to other men. (Kästner 130–31; 178)[20]

In an earlier conversation with her, Fabian uses a mathematical metaphor to make his point, claiming: "The moral and the arithmetical equations work out differently" (105; 144). He suspects the arithmetical equation that Fräulein Battenberg sets up by betting that her film career will neither bring her luck nor make them happy in their shared relationship (see Kästner 106; 145). A comparable relationship, based primarily on money, led to the complete alienation of Labude from his parents (57f., 143; 77f., 195).

Mauss comes to similar conclusions in *The Gift* as the author and "moralist" Kästner does in Chapter X of his novel *Fabian,* and in his Preface to the 1950 German edition. Mauss argued for a return to archaic, elementary principles. A few key phrases he uses to reference these principles include "group morality" (87), "more care for the individual" (88), "generosity" (88), "disinterestedness" (89), and "corporate solidarity" (89). He implores his fellow citizens to "humanize . . . occupational groupings" (89). Kästner's novel, published just a few years after Mauss's study, also highlights the gift as an ideal of human communitarianism: gifted love, as well as monetary gifts exchanged by the partners Fabian and Fräulein Battenberg, the friends Labude and Fabian, or Fabian and his mother, are governed by a different, more humane value system than that based purely on monetary exchange. Labude regularly gives his needy friend Fabian money, without Fabian having to ask for it, because Labude has more than he needs (see Kästner 55–56, 58, 137; 76, 78, 187). Labude's suicide note ends with his giving Fabian a monetary gift so that he can afford to take a short vacation; facing his imminent death, Labude is full of benevolence toward his friend. Fabian accepts this gift (138; 188) but is not attached to its material value, instead giving some of it away. He sends half of it to his former girlfriend Fräulein Battenberg so she can use it to get away from the film producer Markart, in case she decides to do so. Giving and reciprocating gifts are characterized here by generosity and not calculated to be doled out equally. Such monetary gifts, as "things with a soul," are signs of mutual love and possess a moral, even magical, power intended to protect the loved one from misfortune. The moral power of such gifts is made visible in a scene where Fabian and his mother give each other some cash, even though both are barely surviving financially:

> He put the twenty-mark note in his pocket. There was his mother in the train; very soon she would find the twenty-mark note he had slipped into her handbag. Mathematically considered, the result equalled [sic.] nothing. For both were now as poor as they had been before. But good deeds are beyond bookkeeping. The moral and the arithmetical equations work out differently. (Kästner 105; 144)

From a mathematical perspective, such a gift does not result in a profit. There is a moral gain, however, as both protagonists receive an enormous amount of mutual love and concern.[21] Fabian lives expressly according to a new value system based on an older tradition: money's purpose is not just to function as a simple medium of exchange in the sense of reciprocation for an object or a service. It is not just an object whose value can get lost as it did during the Great Depression. In *Fabian,* money is recognized as a social technology based on trust and mutual affection. It represents a form of social behavior and a belief in society, and can thus be elevated to the status of a "gift" as Mauss defined it. It thereby retains its original meaning, regaining its magical character, which does not dissipate so rapidly. One purpose of the novel is to reverse the circumstance of money having lost its referent—money being a representation, a sign that lost its referent. The ethical-moral vacuum of the interwar period should thereby also recover its values. Should this project fail, the "waiting room" of Europe (Kästner 44; 62) would plunge toward its downfall (e.g., 32; 46) in the form of another war (44, 46; 61, 64), a prediction that unfortunately became reality.

Erich Kästner considers it an author's mission to serve as a "moralist" who warns against adverse societal developments. His concept of a "moralist" writer encompasses writing on economics and politics to free the reader of a "lethargy of the heart" and thus perform a kind of ethical-political activism (see Delianidou 2018: 194–96). The economists, politicians, journalists, and educators of his time, with all their education and knowledge, proved inadequate to fulfill this mission. In his 1994 book *The Age of Extremes,* historian Eric J. Hobsbawm speaks at the end of the twentieth century of a collapse of values and institutions in all of Europe during the first half of that century. The contemporaries Marcel Mauss and Erich Kästner made a case for drawing on wisdom and solidarity in the so-called civilized world in the 1920s and early 1930s. In this context, Mauss calls to mind the (not only Christian and

European) tradition and symbolic image of a collective round table that seems to have been forgotten by organizations such as the International Monetary Fund, the European Central Bank, and the Organization for Economic Co-operation and Development, although their members continue to meet at a table:

> Peoples, social classes, families, and individuals will be able to grow rich, and will only be happy when they have learnt to sit down, like the knights, around the common store of wealth. It is useless to seek goodness and happiness in distant places. It is there already, in peace that has been imposed, in well-organized work, alternately in common and separately, in wealth amassed and then redistributed, in the mutual respect and reciprocating generosity that is taught by education. (Mauss 2002: 106)

In his novel *Fabian*, Kästner critiques modern civilization, demanding a return to the tried and true ethical and moral values that got lost when capitalism and massification came to dominate society.

Simela Delianidou is Assistant Professor of German Literature and Culture in the Department of German Language and Literature at Aristotle University of Thessaloniki, Greece. Her research interests include German literature of the twentieth and twenty-first century, gender studies, intercultural studies, literature written in exile, employee culture in the literature of the Weimar Republic, the working world in literature, and literature and the economy. Her most recent publication is titled "Das räumliche Wissen der Literatur über Armut: Hans Fallada *Kleiner Mann – was nun?* (1932)," published in *Literatur für Leser* in 2022.

Notes

1. The numerous translations and film adaptations of Kästner's young adult novels *Emil und die Detektive* (Emil and the detective, [1930] 2018a), *Das doppelte Lottchen* (The double lottery, [1949] 2018b), *Pünktchen und Anton* (Annaluise & Anton, [1931] 2018c), and *Das fliegende Klassenzimmer* (The flying classroom, [1933] 2018d) contributed to his fame. For a complete bibliography of the first editions and filmography, see Hanuschek 2017: 468–76.
2. The original German title is *Fabian. Die Geschichte eines Moralisten*. It was first published in English in a slightly cropped version as *Fabian: The Story of a Moralist* (1932) and republished in 1990 without omissions as *Going to the Dogs: The Story of a Moralist*. English in-text citations in this chapter are taken from the 1990 version, and are followed by page numbers from the 2007 dtv German edition.
3. Since the turn of the twenty-first century, essays have also now been considered a "literary" genre, adding to the previous epic, lyric, and dramatic genres (see Jeßing and Köhnen 2003: 137–43).

4. Many German and American novels from the past three decades treat similar themes related to value systems, the crisis of knowledge, and the resulting emptiness connected to money as a medium of exchange. Such novels include Uwe Timm's *Kopfjäger* (1991; *Headhunter*, 1994), Martin Walser's *Angstblüte* (2008), Rainald Goetz's *Johann Holtrop* (2012), Don DeLillo's *Cosmopolis* (2012), and Jonas Lüscher's *Frühling der Barbaren* (2013; *Barbarian Spring*, 2015). These authors' creative, aesthetic approaches are more sophisticated than Kästner's, but my goal here is to demonstrate that this topic did not first become virulent in the 1990s, but was also prevalent during past financial crises such as that triggered by the 1929 stock market crash.
5. For a definition of "New Economic Criticism," see Urbatsch 2011: 236, fn 1.
6. Gabriele Tergit comes to similar conclusions in her novel *Käsebier erobert den Kurfürstendamm* (Käsebier conquers the Kurfürstendamm, 1931) (see also Delianidou 2022).
7. Reckwitz writes about the transgressive subject in avant-garde movements from 1890 to 1930 in *Das hybride Subjekt* (2006: 289–317).
8. See esp. the chapters "Das politische Feld" (97ff.) and "Politik, Sozialwissenschaften und Journalismus" (265ff.). According to Bourdieu, politics, the social sciences, and journalism are fields that constitute "jeweils ein autonomer Mikrokosmos innerhalb des sozialen Makrokosmos" (each an autonomous microcosm within the social macrocosm) (97). These fields function according to their own rules, though all are interdependent. Their agents have specific types of capital at their disposal—e.g., economic and cultural—as well as particular habits, skills, and dispositions. They do, however, have a tendency to exclude and thus disenfranchise the individual from politics. As a philosopher and politically engaged sociologist, Bourdieu resists this disenfranchisement by presenting a "coalition of critical intellectuals, union members and . . . left-wing parties on a European-wide level as a constructive alternative" (Spitz 2015). Bourdieu's suggestions resemble those Kästner puts forth in his novel.
9. The hopes of the Weimar Republic, to overcome its political crisis with the help of technocrats of the economic crisis, failed miserably. This failure was repeated nearly eighty years later during the financial/euro crisis, because this crisis, too, resulted from an analogous, ineffectual politics of austerity that was imposed on the countries of Southern Europe. The disastrous results of such political measures can be seen in the case of Greece, which continues to struggle with the dire social consequences. Once again, the presumed fiscal experts (*Kapitalversteher*), the "hermeneuticists of capital" in our knowledge society, have proven themselves to be power elites pursuing their own self-interests (see Streeck 2012: 776–87).
10. Kästner's text blames the popular press not only for contributing to the crisis of knowledge but also for experiencing its own, similar crisis, because it lacks certainty in the rules of orthography, a proficiency one should expect of academically educated journalists (see Kästner 22; 34).
11. Economic historians divide capitalism into several phases of development. Here, I refer to the phases described by Gerhard Willke as "early capitalism," which originated around 1780; "advanced capitalism" (*Hochkapitalismus*), which commenced in 1870 and expanded when an initially cartelized "financial capitalism" gained traction shortly before World War I; and "globalized capitalism," which began after World War II as the economy expanded rapidly and eventually led to mass prosperity (Willke 2006: 25–64).

12. Siegfried Kracauer first wrote about such consumer behavior, which emerged in the early twentieth century, in the *Frankfurter Zeitung*, in a 1929 article in which he introduced his study on white-collar workers in the Weimar Republic. In the chapter "Asylum for the Homeless," he describes the "mental homelessness" of the salaried class and their increasing demand for consumer goods and mass entertainment, which was threatening to spread to the other social classes and accompanied by an evolving value system (Kracauer 1980: see esp. 91–101).
13. The name of the street on which this scene takes place, "Jo-achims-thaler Straße," is another intertextual reference to Achim von Arnim's "Star Money" fairytale. Kästner uses this reference, as well as the doppelgänger and android/machine human in the nightmare scene, to demonstrate what had become of these Romantic motifs a century later. Romantic writers conceived such motifs in various forms to show the external controls over humans that came about during the technical revolution, with its accompanying pitfalls for the individual and his/her identity. The self-alienation that both motifs represent reached its height in the 1920s, when they became a mass phenomenon. Now they possess only a profane dimension, detached from any artistic referents.
14. Foucault cites de Grammont (1620: 46–47).
15. I refer here to Karl Marx's distinction between money as money and money as capital with its various forms of circulation in *Capital*, Volume I, Part II, Chapter 4: "The Transformation of Money into Capital" (1998: 211–15).
16. Fabian asks Mr. Moll with irony: "Perhaps you'd like to guarantee me a regular income?" The answer he receives heightens the scene's cynicism: "We might talk that over. I am not without means" (Kästner 14; 23).
17. For an in-depth analysis of these two main female characters, Irene Moll and Cornelia Battenberg, see Britta Jürgs (1995: 204–6) and esp. Anna Burgdorf (2013: 171–84). The findings of both scholars complement my own, although Burgdorf focuses specifically on the economization of love in *Fabian*, and recognizes the "tendency of an evermore capitalized society to favor the exclusive advancement of stupidly economic-minded individuals" (182).
18. The notion of a gifted object possessing an innate power can also be seen, for example, in early Roman law pertaining to theft, and in contracts (Mauss 2002: 65). It consists of a strong, irrevocable, and dangerous bond between donor and recipient (ibid.: 76).
19. Mauss distinguishes three phases of monetary value. In the first, human beings "found that certain things, almost all magic and precious, were not destroyed by use, and to these was given purchasing power. . . . [I]n a second phase, after having succeeded in putting these objects into circulation, within the tribe and in a wide area outside it, humanity found that these instruments of purchase could serve as a means of setting a figure on riches, and for putting these riches into circulation. This is the stage that we are describing. It is beyond this stage, in a fairly early era in Semitic societies, but doubtless not a very ancient one elsewhere, that—in a third phase—there was discovered the means of separating these precious objects from groups and people, in order to turn them into permanent instruments for the measure of value, and even a universal measure, although not a rational one—whilst waiting for something better to come along. Thus there has been, in our opinion, a form of money that has preceded our own" (Mauss 2002: 128–29, fn 29).
20. The moral finger that Fabian points at Irene Moll and Fräulein Battenberg is problematic from the perspective of gender, especially because he is not innocent in his

own sexual affairs. The text does, however, allow for multiple interpretations in its depictions of various gender relations.

21. In a parallel scene, Fabian gives a prostitute two marks and she surreptitiously returns them to him (170; 229), indicating that money should not only be seen as a medium of exchange, but also as a sign of affection and respect.

References

Bourdieu, Pierre. 2013. *Politik: Schriften zur Politischen Ökonomie 2*, ed. Franz Schultheis and Stephan Egger. *Pierre Bourdieu. Schriften*. Vol. 7. Berlin: Suhrkamp Verlag.

Burgdorf, Anna. 2013. "Sexuelle Progression und ökonomischer Progress: Zur Darstellung unmoralischer Frauen in Erich Kästners *Fabian: Die Geschichte eines Moralisten*." *Erzählte Wirtschaftssachen (JUNI. Magazin für Literatur und Kultur)*, ed. Gregor Ackermann, Michael Grisko, and Walter Delabar. Volume 47/48, 171–84. Bielefeld: Aisthesis.

Delianidou, Simela. 2018. "Erich Kästners neusachlicher Roman *Fabian: Die Geschichte eines Moralisten* (1931) als '(wirtschafts-)politische Literatur.'" In *Politische Literatur. Begriffe, Debatten, Aktualität*, ed. Christine Lubkoll, Manuel Illi, and Anna Hampel, 183–97. Stuttgart: J.B. Metzler.

———. 2022. "Krise – nicht nur – des Managements in Gabriele Tergits *Käsebier erobert den Kurfürstendamm* (1931)." In *Narrative der Krise: Literatur und Kino in Italien, Griechenland, Deutschland (2000–2015)*, ed. Sergio Corrado, Anastasia Antonopoulou, Uta Felten, Tanja Schwan, and Franziska Andraschik. Frankfurt a.M.: Peter Lang.

Foucault, Michel. 2002. *The Order of Things: An Archaeology of the Human Sciences*. London: Routledge Classics (orig. Paris: Editions Gallimard, 1966).

Fromm, Erich. 1976. *To Have or To Be?* New York: Continuum.

Grammont, Scipion de. 1620. *Le Denier royal, traité curioux de l'or et de l'argent*. Paris.

Hanuschek, Sven. 2017. *Keiner blickt dir hinter das Gesicht. Das Leben Erich Kästners*. Munich: Carl Hanser Verlag.

Hobsbawm, Eric J. 1994. *The Age of Extremes: A History of the World 1914–1991*. London: Michael Joseph and Pelham Books.

Horvath, Michael. 2011. "Vielfalt der Deutungen statt exakter Modelle? Möglichkeiten und Grenzen des interdisziplinären Dialogs zwischen Ökonomik und Kulturwissenschaft." In *Finanzen und Fiktionen. Grenzgänge zwischen Literatur und Wirtschaft*, ed. Christine Künzel and Dirk Hempel, 45–65. Frankfurt a.M.: Campus Verlag.

Jeßing, Benedikt, and Ralph Köhnen. 2003. *Einführung in die Neuere deutsche Literaturwissenschaft*. Stuttgart: J.B. Metzler.

Jürgs, Britta. 1995. "Neusachliche Zeitungsmacher, Frauen und alte Sentimentalitäten: Erich Kästners Roman *Fabian. Die Geschichte eines*

Moralisten." In *Neue Sachlichkeit im Roman: Neue Interpretationen zum Roman der Weimarer Republik*, ed. Sabine Becker and Christoph Weiß, 195–211. Stuttgart: Metzler.

Kästner, Erich. 1932. *Fabian: The Story of a Moralist*. Trans. Cyrus Harry Brooks. London: Cape.

———. 2007. *Fabian. Die Geschichte eines Moralisten*. Munich: Deutscher Taschenbuchverlag.

———. 2013. *Going to the Dogs: The Story of a Moralist*. New, reset edn (without omissions). Trans. Cyrus Brooks. Intro. Rodney Livingstone. New York: New York Review of Books (orig. London: Libris Books, 1990).

———. 2018a. *Emil und die Detektive*. Hamburg: Atrium Verlag.

———. 2018b. *Das doppelte Lottchen*. Hamburg: Atrium Verlag.

———. 2018c. *Pünktchen und Anton*. Hamburg: Atrium Verlag.

———. 2018d. *Das fliegende Klassenzimmer*. Hamburg: Atrium Verlag.

Kracauer, Siegfried. 1980. *Die Angestellten. Aus dem neuesten Deutschland*. With a review by Walter Benjamin. Frankfurt a.M.: Suhrkamp Verlag.

Künzel, Christine. 2014. "Imaginierte Zukunft: Zur Bedeutung von Fiktion(en) in ökonomischen Diskursen." In *Literarische Ökonomik*, ed. Iuditha Balint and Sebastian Zilles, 143–57. Paderborn: Wilhelm Fink.

Martin, Felix. 2013. *Money: The Unauthorized Biography*. London: Bodley Head, 2013.

Marx, Karl. 1998. *Capital: A Critique of Political Economy*. Vol. 1. Trans. Samuel Moore and Edward Aveling. Ed. Frederick Engels. London: ElecBook (orig. 1887).

Mauss, Marcel. 2002. *The Gift: The Form and Reason for Exchange in Archaic Societies*. Foreword by Mary Douglas. London: Routledge Classics (orig. *L'Annee Sociologique, seconde série*, 1923–24).

Plumpe, Werner. 2013. *Wirtschaftskrisen: Geschichte und Gegenwart*. Munich: C.H. Beck.

Radcliffe-Brown, A.R. 1922. *Andaman Islanders: A Study in Social Anthropology*. London: Cambridge University Press.

Reckwitz, Andreas. 2006. *Das hybride Subjekt: Eine Theorie der Subjektkulturen von der bürgerlichen Moderne zur Postmoderne*. Göttingen: Velbrück Wissenschaft.

Ritter, Henning. 1990. "Die ethnologische Wende: Über Marcel Mauss." In *Die Gabe: Form und Funktion des Austauschs in archaischen Gesellschaften*, by Marcel Mauss. Trans. from French to German by Eva Moldenhauer, 188–207. Frankfurt a.M.: Suhrkamp.

Schütz, Erhard. 1986. *Romane der Weimarer Republik*. Munich: W. Fink.

Seitz, Emanuel. 2015. "Lesehinweis zu Simiand." In *Schriften zum Geld* by Marcel Mauss, ed. Hans Peter Hahn, Mario Schmidt, and Emanuel Seitz. Trans. from French by Eva Moldenhauer, 64–67. Berlin: Suhrkamp.

Simiand, François. 2015. "Das Geld, eine soziale Realität (1934)." In *Schriften zum Geld* by Marcel Mauss, ed. Hans Peter Hahn, Mario Schmidt, and Emanuel Seitz. Trans. from French by Eva Moldenhauer, 68–119. Berlin: Suhrkamp.

Spitz, Markus Oliver. 2015. "Die Koordinaten des 'politischen Feldes': Pierre Bourdieus konstante Weigerung, Politik allein den Profis zu überlassen." *literaturkritik.de* 7 (July). *Politik und Geschichte*. Retrieved 17 May 2022 from https://literaturkritik.de/id/20783.

Streeck, Wolfgang. 2012. "Wissen als Macht, Macht als Wissen: Kapitalversteher im Krisenkapitalismus." *Merkur* 66 (760/761): 776–87.

Urbatsch, Katja. 2011. "'Aber ich weiß nicht mehr, was Geld ist' – Mensch, Geld und Markt in Don DeLillos *Cosmopolis* (2003) aus der Sicht des *New Economic Criticism*." In *Finanzen und Fiktionen: Grenzgänge zwischen Literatur und Wirtschaft*, ed. Christine Künzel and Dirk Hempel, 235–50. Frankfurt a.M.: Campus Verlag.

Vogl, Joseph. 2015. *The Specter of Capital*. Trans. Joachim Redner and Robert Savage. Stanford, CA: Stanford University Press.

Willke, Gerhard. 2006. *Kapitalismus*. Frankfurt a.M.: Campus Verlag.

Wrobel, Dieter. 2005. "Mediensatire wider die Entpolitisierung der Zeitung: Journalismuskritik in Romanen von Gabriele Tergit und Erich Kästner." In *Laboratorium Vielseitigkeit. Zur Literatur der Weimarer Republik*, ed. Petra Josting and Walter Fähnders, 267–86. Bielefeld: Aisthesis Verlag.

PART II

German Narratives of Work and Unemployment

CHAPTER 5

Unemployment as Crisis

Past and Present German-Language Sociological Narratives on the Loss of Work

ANNEMARIE MATTHIES

Work has been a central topic of sociology since its establishment as a social science discipline in the late nineteenth century. Sociology's founding fathers—especially Auguste Comte, Herbert Spencer, and Emile Durkheim—attributed to work an essential human function, defining it as the link between society's members that makes society possible. The reverse is also true: generally speaking, sociologists adhere to the underlying premise that an individual contributes to society by means of his or her labor, and therefore exists as a functional member. Unlike sociologists in the twentieth century and today, the founders of sociology were noticeably not preoccupied with the effects of the widespread absence of work, although the Industrial Revolution produced several waves of unemployment in Europe during their lifetimes.[1] In establishing the field of sociology, they did not focus empirically on this phenomenon of mass unemployment. Instead, authors such as Durkheim, who played an important role in Germany, were concerned with theorizing the concept of work as an important component of social integration (Durkheim 1893; Schmid 1989). The results were theories decidedly opposed to Karl Marx's perspective (Berger 1995). Whereas Marx strove to explain the antagonism between workers and capitalists, focusing on the detrimental economic bases of society related to labor, emerging sociologists devoted themselves to proving the opposite: that work promotes social integration, which results in social solidarity (see Brambora in this volume).

This sociological perspective did not change fundamentally for decades, even when the Great Depression struck in 1929. In the wake of this monumental economic crisis, however, when sociology as a discipline was confronted with the massive release of people from paid work, it eventually reacted by adapting its existing theoretical tools. In so doing, sociologists began to conceive of economic crises and their material effects as "social crises" in two senses: at first they believed that the unemployed individual as a "social being" was in crisis, but they soon began contemplating society also as an object of crisis. This chapter reconstructs the principal narratives surrounding unemployment in German-language sociology, first formulated in the early 1930s, up to the early twenty-first century. In doing so, it spotlights sociological research connecting unemployment and social crisis. The stages presented here are, by necessity, laid out briefly. Nevertheless, one essential common feature permeates them: viewed from a broad historical perspective, the field of sociology reveals itself to be concerned specifically with economic effects on the emergence and overarching societal impact of social crises. This perspective distinguishes its findings and narratives from those of the other sciences as well as from those of the literary texts presented in this volume, which tell economic crisis narratives from individualized, fictional viewpoints.

This chapter begins by addressing the 1933 Austrian case study *Marienthal: The Sociography of an Unemployed Community* (Jahoda, Lazarsfeld, and Zeise 1975), which reached beyond the German-speaking discourse and yet was not translated into English until 1971. This case study provided the basis for the socio-psychological concept of work's function for the individual and society underlying all later sociological theories of work. In studies developed after World War II, conducted in the 1950s, 1960s, and 1970s, the central premises of the 1930s can still be found. These decades—during which work appeared more as a marginal than a central topic in public discourse as well as in sociology—are thus given less attention here compared to the decades from the 1980s until the global crisis year 2008 and beyond. This focus on more recent times has a reason: soon after the oil crisis of 1973, a new debate about work and unemployment arose in sociology. Although the grounds of this dispute resembled those of the 1930s, a notable transformation can be observed, from initially viewing loss-of-work crises as individual to later considering society itself to be in a state of crisis. After tracing the history of German-language sociological narratives of unemployment more generally, this chapter concludes with socio-structural perspectives on unemployment in Germany produced since the turn of the twenty-first century. It thereby sheds light on how German-language sociology has altered its views of socio-structural crises within the constraints of its disciplinary lens.

Sociological Narratives from 1930 to 1950: *Marienthal* and Its Consequences

As already mentioned, *Marienthal: The Sociography of an Unemployed Community* is a case study published in 1933 by social psychologist Marie Jahoda, sociologist Paul Lazarsfeld, and sociologist/legal scholar Hans Zeisel. Working with a team of over a hundred assistants, these three researchers studied the effects of short- and long-term unemployment on citizens in the small town of Marienthal, east of Vienna, after its main source of employment, a large textile factory, was closed in 1930. *Marienthal* is a seminal work that significantly shaped the German-speaking sociological discourse surrounding unemployment.[2] Sociologists still cite its conclusions, though nearly a century filled with various economic crises has passed since its publication (Vonderach 2002b).

The interpretations of work and unemployment that form the basis of the *Marienthal* study provide a perspective on unemployment that still feeds into contemporary sociological discourse. The aim of the study was "to depict a socio-psychological fact objectively" (Jahoda, Lazarsfeld, and Zeise 1975: 11) and thus fill a gap that existed in the early 1930s between statistical analysis and individual case studies (15). The *Marienthal* researchers wanted to make the "result of unemployment" visible (24) by "experiencing" (28) it firsthand.

This objective reveals a prototypical dilemma of sociology. The experiences of others, including the reasons behind their thoughts and actions, have to be interpreted. Such interpretations can thus convey a bias, if the researcher's perspective interferes with others' statements and experiences. What applies to everyday "hermeneutic circles," which can never be entirely free of the observer's perspective, also proves problematic for empirical social research. This dilemma is exemplified in the *Marienthal* study. Before this study, unemployment had been framed particularly, though not exclusively, by Durkheim's theories. Work was seen primarily as an important factor in the social integration of an individual. The results of this otherwise unspoken premise became apparent, especially in the chapter when the *Marienthal* researchers presented the results of their observations and surveys. The authors devote nearly twenty pages to the "attitude" of Marienthal's citizens. The majority of their daily activities, influenced predominantly by their economic situation, are interpreted as an expression of morality. This moral attitude can, according to the researchers, represent an individual's "wholeness" or "brokenness" (71ff.). The individual and his or her subjective perspective was thus, for the first time, made the focus of an unemployment study. In contrast to the frowned-upon Marxist perspective, the researchers were not interested in revealing the political or economic structures or other causes underlying their subjects' unemployment. They concentrated instead on the differences in how Marienthal's inhabitants coped with unemployment.

The *Marienthal* study was not unique in its time. Researching unemployment from a socio-psychological perspective also emerged as a new approach in French, British, and American sociology in the 1930s. E. Wight Bakke's *The Unemployed Man: A Social Study* (1933), conducted in Great Britain, displays similar research methods and aims. It was the *Marienthal* study, however, that convinced researchers to devote more time to studying unemployment, thereby moving it from a marginal to a central research topic. Co-author Paul Lazarsfeld, who later became a professor at Columbia University, shaped German-language sociology as well as American sociology significantly. The power of this new perspective lay in interpreting unemployment not only as the result of an overarching economic crisis, but also as a series of individual biographical crises that could eventually erode social connections. Its wide-reaching implications can be seen in the fact that the *Marienthal* researchers' work was read by German politicians. Chancellor Willy Brandt wrote the Foreword to Jahoda's 1983 book, *Wieviel Arbeit braucht der Mensch? Arbeit und Arbeitslosigkeit im 20. Jahrhundert* (How Much Work Does a Person Need? Work and Unemployment in the Twentieth Century).

Unemployment as a (Nearly) Unproblematic Topic in Empirical Social Research, 1950–1980

After World War II, German-speaking sociology needed to reinvent itself. Despite the high postwar unemployment, other topics were more pressing in the early 1950s. At the center of these debates were questions of how to construct a new self-image for the discipline, and where it should fit between the "humanities" and the "sciences" as the empirical analysis of social structures (Lepsius 1979). The two-volume study "Unemployment and the Need for Jobs for Young People" (1952), commissioned by the German Federation of Trade Unions (Deutscher Gewerkschaftsbund), is a notable exception that shows the impact of the socio-psychological research from the 1930s. Under the leadership of Helmut Schelsky, the goal of this study—which surveyed more than two thousand young adults—was to research their "attitudes" toward unemployment and careers. The term "attitudes," as well as the interview method focusing on individual reactions to unemployment, were taken from the *Marienthal* study. In Schelsky's survey, work is granted an existential significance, as it is understood to be important for the moral orientation of young adults, and thus also for maintaining social solidarity. Many of the sociologists who conducted this 1952 study, such as Heinz Kluth and Fritz Rudolph, later went on to become influential industrial sociologists. Thus, it can be assumed that its hypotheses shaped later research—even though there was a significant time gap between it and subsequent major German unemployment studies.

The fact that the topic of unemployment was for the most part ignored in German-speaking sociology from the late 1950s to the early 1970s (Brinkmann and Schober 2002: 32) can be explained by the nearly 100 percent employment rate in Germany and Austria in these postwar years. The postwar economy was quickly ramped up, producing the so-called "economic miracle," which resulted in a manpower shortage that lasted until the oil price crises struck in the early 1970s.

Sociologists reacted to the rapidly rising unemployment figures produced by the first oil price crisis in 1973 not with theory-building—the empirical foundations of which were twenty years old by then—but instead with *empirical* social research, which is nowadays institutionally anchored in institutes such as the Institut für Arbeitsmarkt- und Berufsforschung (IAB; Institute for Employment Research), founded in 1967 as the research unit of the Bundesagentur für Arbeit (Federal Employment Agency). The "development research" carried out by the IAB during the 1970s and 1980s, however, served as a point of reference for many later theoretical works. Its researchers carried forward the 1930s socio-psychological perspective on work, as this perspective served as the basis for many of their empirical studies, in which unemployment was treated from the perspective of its absence resulting in a "psychological burden." This hypothesis was built into the researchers' interview questions. In several such studies, for example, the free time that unemployment generated was defined as a problem for the individual (see Brinkmann and Schober 2002: 37), although it seems obvious that his or her financial situation should be decisive in determining whether or not life without work is perceived as a crisis. After all, free time in the case of a wealthy person leading an idle life is generally perceived to be neither an individual nor a social problem. Follow-up studies, such as Erich Kirchler's *Arbeitslosigkeit und Alltagsbefinden: Eine sozialpsychologische Studie über die subjektiven Folgen von Arbeitslosigkeit* (1984; Unemployment and daily life: A socio-psychological study of the subjective consequences of unemployment), show that the conclusions drawn from observations and surveys of the unemployed citizens of Marienthal continued to serve as the basis for German-language sociological studies into the 1980s. It is a more or less unquestioned presumption in most studies that work is so significant to an individual that its absence is experienced as a crisis.

Unemployment through the Lens of Sociology, 1980–2008 and Beyond

In the 1980s, a paradigm shift took place in sociological studies featuring the topic of unemployment. Along with the socio-psychological research continuing to be conducted on the individual experience of unemployment, the formulation of new theories began on a large scale. At the twenty-first Deutscher Soziologentag (German sociologists' conference), hosted in 1982 in Bamberg by the German Society for Sociology under the theme "Crisis of Working Society?," a discussion of unemployment-related issues appeared for the first time in fifty years. The diverse presentations ranged from examining work as a "key sociological category" (Claus Offe) to "socioeconomic structural problems" (Stefan Hradil, Martin Baethge) to the "crisis of the welfare state" (Warnfried Dettling), as well as a discussion of the "exclusion of workers and psychiatrization" (Wolfgang Bonß and Barbara Riedmüller). It is important to point out here that the topic of this *Soziologentag*—which determined the focus of all presentation topics and discussions—began with the word "crisis" and expanded its scope to encompass all of society. In the fifty years prior, the word "crisis" in combination with the topic of work had mainly only been used by sociologists to refer to the individual experience of unemployment as a personal life crisis. This perspective shifted noticeably in the early 1980s.

Many presentations at the 1982 *Soziologentag* were devoted to what was considered to be a crisis in working society. The term "working society," which can be traced back to Hannah Arendt (1958), was picked up by Ralf Dahrendorf in 1980. In his oft-quoted essay, "Is the work society running out of work?," Dahrendorf presents his trepidation regarding the evolution of job markets toward the use of technology and a reduction of human labor, not only in Germany but also in other Western nations. The organizers of the German *Soziologentag* extracted the topic of their conference from his thesis that work is necessary for the individual. Dahrendorf, who participated in the *Soziologentag*, asserted: "[T]ake away work and most people's lives would fall apart, leaving little more than meaningless bits of social relations" (1980: 282). At the same time, however, if we look back to the beginnings of the sociological narrative of unemployment in the 1930s, a change has occurred. The object of concern among German sociologists in the 1980s is no longer primarily the individual without work but also society as a whole, which is bound together by its citizens' labor.

This dual perspective on labor, established in the early 1980s, remained unchanged in the German-speaking sociological discourse for many years, including the decade following German reunification in 1990. In 1993, Martin Kronauer, Berthold Vogel, and Frank Gerlach argued in their book, *Im Schatten der Arbeitsgesellschaft: Arbeitslose und ihre Dynamik sozialer Ausgrenzung* (In the shadow of the work society: The unemployed and the dynamics of social exclusion), that sociologists researching unemployment should pay attention to exclusion and the threat of societal division resulting from it.[3] In their chapter in the 1998 edited volume *Alte Ungleichheiten – neue Spaltungen*, Kronauer and Vogel ask: "Does unemployment divide society?"—but the answer had already been given. The verdict was that work functions as a means both for the individual to lead a purposeful life and for society to maintain collective unity. Conversely, if work is lacking, not only the socio-psychologically affected individual, but also society's collective sense of unity, will be thrust into a crisis.

The *Hartz-Reformen* and the Division of Society

The discourse surrounding dilemmas such as the end of the working society, the threat of societal division, and the crisis of society caused by mass unemployment, grew in intensity in the early 2000s. This intensification was triggered by the so-called *Hartz-Reformen*, which were enforced as an integral part of the *Job-AQTIV-Gesetz* (Job-AQTIV-Law)[4] of 2002–10, and had far-reaching consequences in several areas. The objectives of these government policies were to modify work relationships, work forms, and the organizational practices of work processes such as hiring and firing;[5] to set new, minimum fixed-wage amounts and income;[6] and to enable the unemployed to find jobs in an evermore competitive job market. These new policies also sparked heated debates in mass media and scientific discourse related to the new world of work. In light of the high numbers of unemployed (especially long-term unemployed) in Germany following reunification and the dot-com stock market crash of 2000–2002, the German government decided to take an active role in influencing the job market (Bescherer, Röbenack, and Schierhorn 2009: 145), the consequences of which became the subject of public contention.

It is important to differentiate between the stipulations of these political measures that required actions to be taken (see Hartz et al. 2002)[7] and the implicit premises behind such measures. Kai Marquardsen (2007: 263) describes the nature of the German *Aktivierungspolitik* as follows: "According to activating job market policy, the individual behavior of the unemployed becomes the reference point of political intervention related to the job market. Activation means to prevent unwanted behavior and ensure wanted behavior by means of appropriate behavioral incentives." Such policies blame unemployment on unwanted behavior, implying that one's employment status can be modified by means of "proper" behavior. Concrete re-education programs and policy measures therefore promote the assumption of "individual responsibility" and the "ability to work," both of which support and oblige "an active role of the individual with the marketing of one's own capacity for work" (ibid.). This positive semantics of implementing support initiatives—including job application training, continuing education and consultation, and the consolidation of equal opportunities for men and women—is coupled with the requirement that individuals accept the employment offers accompanying these initiatives. If they do not, they face financial sanctions.

The media reaction up to the mid-2000s was for the most part uniform in its arguments, taking sides both with and against the unemployed. The Sarrazin debate, which erupted in 2008, can be seen as the climax of this public media discourse on long-term unemployment. Former Deutsche Bank executive board member and Berlin state finance senator Thilo Sarrazin and his followers turned against the unemployed by characterizing them—partly implicitly, partly explicitly—as "parasites" who do not want to work and who actually live off the work of other members of society (see, e.g., Seils 2009; Sarrazin 2010). Opponents pointed out that most unemployed people want to work, but that there was not enough labor market demand. In the wake of this debate, recipients of the unemployment benefits that were referred to colloquially as Hartz-IV came to be described under a new definition. Grouped collectively under this definition, the unemployed were characterized as subjects who had gotten off track and needed activation to get back to work. The descriptors used for the unemployed by their German detractors speak for themselves: "lazy," "poor," "unnecessary" (Baron and Steinwachs 2012).

Sociologists reacted to this discourse by looking critically at government and media judgments. Responding to the debate about "the unnecessary" (Bude and Willisch 2008), "the superfluous" (Sondermann, Ludwig-Mayerhofer, and Behrend 2009), and "the excluded" (Bude 2008), sociologists studied a cross-section of unemployed people and concluded that they are neither passive, lazy, nor unwilling to work. Instead, they are people who suffer not only from having lost their jobs but also from the negative judgments of society. The object of primary concern in the detractors' narrative is not the unemployed person, but rather the collective of the unemployed, who are put in a marginal position by their financial needs and thus bring about a "divided society."[8] What this misleadingly implies, however, is that society before the Hartz reforms and their consequences had supposedly not been divided but intact and united. This false reasoning can also be revealed by recalling the sociological narratives of the 1980s, which referred to the crisis of working society and the end of societal cohesion.

The East German as a Special Case in the German Narrative of Unemployment

A special case in the government and media negotiations related to unemployment is "the East German," referring to former citizens of the socialist German Democratic Republic (GDR). Although the focus in public discourse on differentiating between the cultures of unemployed East and West Germans has subsided in Germany in recent years, it did play a prominent role in the first decade after the GDR was absorbed into the capitalist Federal Republic of Germany (FRG). Roughly speaking, two opposing narratives can be identified. On the one hand was the one primarily established by East German sociologists and intellectuals that characterized the confrontation of former GDR citizens with the free-market working world in the form of unemployment as a crisis of identity (see Engler 2002, 2005). On the other hand, a narrative led by West Germans, which arose immediately after reunification, asked what should constitute appropriate behavior by East Germans working in their new environment. Both narratives treated the major economic changes in the lives and employment situations of former GDR citizens, caused by the reunification, primarily as a socio-psychological challenge for the individual (*Arbeitsmoral*), not as a responsibility of the government or society.

Apart from the high number of political and social science studies that examine the transformations that followed reunification, in the late 1990s and early 2000s numerous works by East Germans appeared,[9] in which the authors discussed the empirical change of systems from their perspective. One main tendency in this literature can be seen in the work of sociologist Wolfgang Engler: the GDR appears in retrospect in the form of a "home" that got lost after reunification.[10] From Engler's point of view, work is less important as an economic relation than as a constitutive element of a social entity that conveys personal meaning and identity. Engler's 1999 book *Die Ostdeutschen: Kunde von einem verlorenen Land* (The East Germans: Tale of a Lost Land) encapsulates what constitutes a "working society" in the late twentieth century in a nutshell: "The working society forms the polemic counterpart to a proletarian [i.e., capitalist] working society and thanks to this polemic a working society *sui generis*; a society in which everyone works . . . and work belongs to everyone individually" (ibid.: 199). As the owner of work—work is defined as a valued possession—the "working human being" in the GDR could perceive him- or herself to be a "child of fortune" (ibid.: 205). Engler continues:

> He did not have to be anything to become something, did not have to become anything to be something. Because everything that he had to be and could be, he already was: an acknowledged member of community. . . . He did not get a certain job or lose it again, change from one work relationship into another, but his long-term relationship with work remained untouched by that. . . . As long as he worked, he did not serve but rule, he submitted neither to the directions of his superior nor to the wishes of the consumers. (Ibid.: 206)

Setting aside the actual, ideologically domineering socialist political interests of the state, the working world of the GDR seems in this stylized description like the expression of a positive social order, the uniting force of which is work. Although Engler references the political demands of the Socialist Unity Party (SED), which were no longer valid in 1999, he goes beyond these demands at the same time, because to him, being an "East German" worker not only means working in and for the state. On the contrary, political and economic demands are articulated as the "abuse" of work (ibid.: 207), whereas a working person's rightful exercising of his power to work fulfills work's actual meaning: work exists to make it possible for the individual to be in harmony with him- or herself and society.

While Engler's *East Germans* can be read as an ethnography of the East German mentality, his book *Bürger, ohne Arbeit* (Citizens, without work), published in 2005, reimagines an ideal working society, and compares it to the capitalist present. Here, too, Engler refers to the particular case of the working world of the GDR and the resulting identity crisis of the East Germans after reunification. However, his findings now claim to be valid across systems:

> Wage work is neither one-dimensional nor empty in itself, nor is it held together simply by a look at the pay. It has depth, content, substance in itself. Just like a spider weaves its web, it also weaves, apart from the scarf that will be created, a closed-meshed, widely branched web of individual and societal relationships and references, the entirety of which indispensably includes financial earnings. (Engler 2005: 55)

This description of work holds a specific criticism of unemployment. Without the established "depth" and "content" of wage work, an individual is at the disposition of every meaningful authority. To "make the pain that comes with the loss of work understandable" (ibid.: 10) is thus not the only goal of this narrative; Engler argues that the practice contains the solution in itself. If unemployment is painful, more work must be provided for people to perform. In this regard, East and West German sociologists' views for the most part converge.

Unemployment after the 2008 Financial Crisis—Not a Topic for Sociology?

The discourses surrounding the *Hartz-Reformen* as well as unemployed East Germans as victims reveal several main sociological premises about the role of work in society. In the aftermath of the 2008 financial crisis, however, German sociologists began focusing less on the topic of unemployment as a contemporary issue. Although they continue to refer to Germany as a divided society, their discussions about unemployment are directed less at the present state of affairs than at a predicted future, which resembles a horror scenario. The reason for this pessimism is not the current unemployment rate, which has not decreased since the beginning of the financial crisis. Today the hot topic is instead the ongoing digitalization of labor, referred to by the term "Industry 4.0," which will not only change the way people currently work, but also lead to the elimination of many existing jobs.

There is a reason why this discourse of a future with different types of jobs and less available work is outlined here only briefly: in fact, there are hardly any narratives left in German sociology about a *concrete* society "without work." Any reference to unemployment seems sufficient to conjure up various horror scenarios. This pessimism suggests that the premise that work is indispensable for a harmonious coexistence of individual and society—that its absence therefore constitutes a *crisis*—is now taken for granted. Recent studies on the "substantial transformation of the work society" that Industry 4.0 is bringing about (Matuschek 2016a), as well as overviews of the publications on this subject (Matuschek 2016b), no longer record any positive function of work. The prospect of its absence, on the other hand, appears all the more negative.

Working with the Topic of Unemployment—and Narrative Solutions

As noted in the introduction to this chapter, the field of sociology has been characterized from the start by its "theoretical lens," through which numerous aspects of life are interpreted as contributing to a collective social unity. From the beginning, one of its main topics has been human labor. German-speaking sociologists have striven since the 1930s to produce a narrative of work that attributes to it an absolutely necessary socio-psychological function for the individual. It is of little consequence, in this context, that sociologists mostly refer to paid work that is offered in exchange for money and dependent on the interests of the employer. Sociological studies generally grant more importance to the fact that social unity is mediated through work, and that it thus possesses a collective significance.

This overarching narrative, interpreting unemployment as a crisis of society and/or of the individual, extends into the present day and is becoming evermore prominent. References to work as necessary for social cohesion are still the subject of government and media debates in Germany, as the working society appears to be under continual attack by the automation and digitalization of production processes. This threat and the narratives describing it are not new, however, as the economist Robert J. Shiller (2019: 174–211) and contributors to the edited volume *The Digital Transformation of Labor* (Larsson and Teigland 2020) testify. A 1982 report by the Club of Rome concerning the automation of work and how it was transforming the working world caused a great public stir in the European Union throughout the 1980s. The authors of the report concluded that new, electronically produced products were not only supplanting mechanically manufactured products, but also making the jobs yielding these products superfluous. Although human labor is required for the development and production of information technology and automated manufacturing machines such as robots, this labor is only needed for a short period and is not equivalent to the vacant jobs that are "eliminated" (Friedrichs and Schaff 1982: 2ff.).

The fact that technological progress goes hand in hand with a rationalization of wage labor was not only articulated by the authors of the Club of Rome report, however. Its conclusions continue to be discussed and researched. In his 2002 book *Erwerbsarbeit in der Krise?* (Employment in the crisis?), Jörg Althammer explicitly asks about the consequences of technological progress for the job market, referring to a paradox: as the jacket blurb states, the labor market policy discourse of the early 2000s has been characterized by a peculiar dichotomy. Long-lasting, structurally entrenched unemployment is interpreted as being caused by a secular trend in developed industrial societies that casts doubt on socioeconomic policies centered on gainful employment, making a return to full employment appear utopian. At the same time, fears are being voiced that a labor shortage could occur. Other sociologists, in particular German sociologists of work such as Klaus Dörre, Stephan Lessenich, Stefan Kühl, and Hartmut Rosa, point out that the discourse on unemployment and technological developments is paradoxical. On the one hand, unemployment is depicted as an inevitable threat to society; on the other, it is subject to political control and the state's desire to balance conflicting interests. Thus, sociologists in the early 2000s agreed that the loss of work is not a "natural development," and nor is it the unintended result of technological progress left to its own devices. Its rationalization, managed intentionally by nation states, is instead, paradoxically, an explicit goal of the so-called "working society." Sociological studies that acknowledge this constantly progressing, destructive situation offer but one solution: that people should find creative ways to work, even if this work is being eliminated constantly in its traditional forms and always becoming something new.

Working with Work and Unemployment

In light of the conclusions drawn in sociological narratives about the various threats to working society, or even its end, it seems paradoxical—though the fact cannot be denied—that since the sociological "discovery" of work's role in maintaining social cohesion, the German federal government's political policies have by no means prevented companies from rationalizing work processes or dismissing workers. On the contrary, rationalization is continually being carried out by those authorities who "give work" (factories, service industries, and public institutions), and it receives hefty government support. One sociological discourse of the past four decades, related to this rationalization, treats critically what is called the "Taylorization" of work (for more recent debates, see Moldaschl 1997; Moldaschl and Voß 2003). This discourse refers to the use of management techniques based on optimization (Bröckling 2017); state-of-the-art machinery and technology; innovative engineering; and the acceleration of work processes—all of which have been known since the dawn of capitalism to speed production—to simplify human labor and above all to make it superfluous. Such rationalization, as it relates to the work process, is being carried out continually, for example, by introducing new quality management systems and cost-saving measures such as outsourcing.

This rationalization, which has been applied to the economy for decades, is not being reined in by politicians. Nowadays, in fact, it is increasingly being supported by governing bodies. One can observe this support in current initiatives being implemented by the so-called "Industry 4.0" (Frey and Osborne 2013). The business networks needed for this digital revolution were created by the German government, and, at the World Economic Forum in Davos in 2016, all major industrial nations came together under the topic "The Fourth Industrial Revolution" to plan not only the consequences, but also the carrying out, of the next big rationalization. It is anticipated that this digitalization of work will produce an enormous number of unemployed people. Because of its desire to compete economically on the international stage, which is considered far more relevant than "saving workplaces," the German government does not view this digitization as an obstacle. Political support for rationalization can also be found in other institutions; for example, nearly every German university now offers a major in "Allgemeine Betriebswirtschaftslehre" (Business Administration Studies). At its core, this major prepares students theoretically and scientifically to carry out such rationalization measures.

What is shown with these brief explanations is the following: in any society defined by sociology as a working society, various institutions are continually striving politically and economically toward the goal of making labor—the unifying factor and creator of identity—as cheap as possible, at the expense of cutting workplaces. From a sociological perspective, therefore, political institutions and private businesses can be considered *generators* of societal states of crisis. The dominant narrative describing political institutions and the economy presents them as part of the solution to the crisis of social cohesion, which was produced by the loss of labor as a vital binding component. However, many critical voices in sociology, engaging in research as "work on work," have formulated objections to the prevailing idea of a working society, and have tried to think beyond it.

Alternatives to the Working Society from a Sociological Perspective

The fact that so-called technological progress threatens any working society was already discussed by sociologists Heinrich Popitz, Hans Bahrdt, Ernst Jüres, and Hanno Kesting in *Technik und Industriearbeit* (1957). In work and industrial sociology, the connection between technology and unemployment has always been present. However, in light of the systematic production of unemployment caused by Industry 4.0, not all sociologists agree that this constant menace should be accepted without seeking alternatives. Since the 1980s, theorists have argued for replacing the working society, which is constantly in crisis mode, with another type of society. One prominent representative of such an alternative narrative is Ralf Dahrendorf. In the context of the 1982 *Deutscher Soziologentag*, he proposed: "Two key questions have to be answered. The first is why the way back to the work society is blocked for us. The answer is that the work society produced the forces to dismantle itself. The second question is which alternatives exist, and where the path leads that starts with the fearful work society" (Dahrendorf 1982: 34). This quest for alternatives in facing the inevitable was present, though not central, in sociological narratives from the 1980s to the early 2000s. It is a question that German sociologists today are not (yet) asking, although it shines through in Germany's public discourse, for example, in the form of demands for an unconditional basic income.

Referring to the value of work, the alternative that Dahrendorf presented in the first question above is especially interesting. Even though Dahrendorf explicitly assumes that society will run out of work, his hope is based in the fact that "work will continually be substituted with activity" (ibid.). From his perspective, in the rationalization of work also lies an opportunity that moves away from work directed by others toward active, self-determined activity, which also seems indispensable because the structure of society appears to him to be endangered without the "discipline through the organization by work" (ibid.). In a way, Dahrendorf wants to keep the work society—even without paid work. A similar alternative to the work society was created by the Austrian-French social philosopher André Gorz, who had a strong influence on German-language sociology. Best known for his treatise *Kritik der ökonomischen Vernunft* (Critique of economic reason, 1989), he later produced *Arbeit zwischen Misere und Utopie* (Labour between misery and utopia, 2000). Sharing Dahrendorf's diagnosis on the end of the work society and the need for a realistic alternative, Gorz presents the idea of a "multi-activity society" (2000: 102). In such a society, human activity (not entirely equivalent to work) constitutes the primary focus. Free time, created by the inevitable mass unemployment, is a boon for society in that individuals have the opportunity to display their full potential: "In other words, individuals can develop abilities (for creating, discovering, planning, and intellectual revelation) that give them nearly endless productivity. . . . Only the free time for their own improvement allows them to set the goal of the free development of individuals" (ibid.: 133). Contrary to Dahrendorf, however, Gorz asserts that the work society, based on wage labor, never did justice to its function of making social cohesion, as well as a meaningful life, possible for the individual (ibid.: 79). The type of work that would be necessary to fulfill these functions differs fundamentally from non-autonomous work for pay.

Gorz's alternative shows that, on the one hand, sociologists have indeed developed perspectives that go beyond the point of view that wage labor is necessary, and that society must do everything to preserve it. On the other hand, this thinking beyond the norm also refers to the necessity of work as professed by sociologists since the 1930s. The premise that the central function of work is to maintain societal connections persists, hence demanding that other forms of work be created as wage labor continues to disappear.

Conclusion

This chapter on the construction of economic crises related to work and unemployment as "social" crises calls attention to two vital features of the sociological narrative on this topic. Diagnosing the lack of work as a state of social crisis results from viewing it through sociology's particular theoretical lens: by defining wage labor solely as a functional element for social cohesion allows its absence to be considered a social crisis. Naively speaking, though, and contrary to this idea, the semblance of "paradise" could be created in a place where no one has to work anymore. Following this logic, in the case of a society whose material wealth increases without more work being required, one could rightly speak of a positive development. To put it somewhat bluntly, however, the specific sociological view of society and its resulting narrative disallow this utopian perspective. Thus, we see the importance of examining crisis phenomena scientifically, based on specific disciplinary premises.

In setting aside this theoretical lens, figuratively speaking, some parts of the sociological narrative of unemployment also prove to be paradoxical. If work is indeed a constitutive element for society, we need to explain why society is constantly and vehemently working on its rationalization. One explanation for this process is that wage labor and other types of work, often not fully distinguished from each other by German-speaking sociologists, have different functions. Thus, one might argue, the central function of work in capitalism does not lie in creating meaning and a cohesive society. Some sociologists—in light of continual rationalizations and in view of a decades-long constructed narrative of crisis, danger, breaks, and social division—simply note this paradox in a "sociological" way. They search for solutions and take into consideration the difference between wage labor and "work for work's sake." Thus, even the alternatives they sketch maintain that work, as an "activity," is a vital element of society to be endorsed. Their discussions show that dealing with the subject of economic crisis requires a differentiated discussion of the topic of work. It is indispensable to distinguish between different forms of work and the diverse reasons for their rationalization.

German-language sociology discussing the topic of work and unemployment has to date not modified its discipline-oriented lens, focusing principally on "the societal" and its functions. Numerous empirical studies exist that convey that (1) the loss of work itself has less of a crisis effect on the individual than the cutting off of their wages; and that (2), in reality, work is not treated by political, economic, or other societal institutions as a force that constitutes society. Nevertheless, the basic judgment of society remains: work creates individual meaning and a collective society. Evidence of these functions of work is not only found in the numerous studies conducted from the 1930s until today that examine working society and the numerous threats it faces. Even scholars who argue in opposition to this viewpoint adhere to the notion that work serves positive individual and societal functions. Their conclusions demonstrate the need to focus on the point of view from which economic crisis narratives are told. Otherwise, it is all too easy to tell a story of how an economically induced crisis transforms into a social crisis.

Of course, it cannot be predicted how the sociological narrative of work and unemployment will develop. Different scenarios are possible; for example, in light of the current debate on digitalization and the anticipated mass unemployment connected with it, the focus of sociology might shift toward the idea that rationalization is desirable and appears non-negotiable. Another important topic of debate could be the purposes capitalist economies pursue, and by which means. It is also possible that sociologists will continue to weave their current narrative of crisis, and focus on anticipating other types of societal erosion and individual loss of meaning. Last but not least, another possibility is that the ideas of Gorz and Dahrendorf could be reactivated. The public discussion about a general basic income provided by the state, which has gained currency in Germany in the past few years, makes this option seem likely.

Annemarie Matthies is Professor of Social Sciences/Social Work at the IU International University in Berlin. Before completing her PhD in Sociology in 2015, she worked as an instructor and researcher in various adult education fields. From 2016 to 2020, she was a research assistant at the Institute for Sociology in Halle, working on "academization" in education. Her book *Spielbälle: Neuverhandlungen der Arbeitswelt im Medium Literatur* was published in 2017, and she recently edited an issue of the journal *Hochschule* on the topic of *Wissenstransfer (in) der Sozialen Arbeit*. Her teaching and research interests include occupational and educational policy, and social work methods.

Notes

1. A male breadwinner was furthermore the default assumption at that time.
2. All citations that follow are from the 1975 Suhrkamp edition.
3. A chapter of this book was published in English by Kronauer and Vogel in 1993 in the *International Journal of Political Economy*.
4. The acronym "AQTIV" stands for "Aktivieren, Qualifizieren, Trainieren, Investieren, Vermitteln" (Activate, qualify, train, invest, facilitate).
5. Regarding new ways of working and practices related to the work process, see the numerous sociological studies pertaining to work and organizations. These studies discuss the imperative of technological innovation as it relates to the accompanying changes in work processes (for example, see the many findings of labor sociologist Sabine Pfeiffer, as well as numerous research studies conducted at the "ISF München"). In regard to the new types of employment produced since the turn of the millennium—atypical employment, subcontracted and temporary work contracts, permanently renewable fixed-term contracts, Ich-AGs (government subsidized self-employment), and mini jobs—see Sommer, Dörre, and Schneidewind 2005. The evolution in the means of production and thus also in employment relations and forms based on new industrial competition goals is also featured in a 2007 volume edited by the Bundeszentrale für politische Bildung.
6. See also the weekly report of the Deutsches Institut für Wirtschaftsforschung, which documents real net income levels since reunification, as well as a trend toward a decrease in wage costs, especially since the turn of the millennium (esp. figures 1–3 in Brenke 2009: 552f.). Apart from the general decrease in inflation-adjusted net wages, Brenke records a shift in the distribution of income in favor of the self-employed and recipients of investment income, but to the detriment of the income of people engaged in several other types of employment (554, 558).
7. For a compact analysis including an extensive bibliography on the topic, see, for instance, Marquardsen 2007.
8. The term "exclusion" acquires a more powerful meaning when binary word pairings such as "rich vs. poor" and "employed vs. unemployed" are used in public and private discourse (Lessenich and Nullmeier 2006).
9. An overview can be found in Fögen 2004. Of course, this does not suggest that this perspective was uniform or that there has been a monolithic "East German point of view." See Gehrke and Rüddenklau 1999 for a collection of diverse critical and affirmative points of view on reunification.
10. Wolfgang Engler's *Die Ostdeutschen: Kunde von einem verlorenen Land* (1999) and *Die Ostdeutschen als Avantgarde* (2002) have attracted widespread attention, along with Daniela Dahn's *Westwärts und nicht vergessen: Vom Unbehagen in der Einheit* (1996) and *Vertreibung ins Paradies: Unzeitgemäße Texte zur Zeit* (1998). Besides works by well-established East German intellectuals, many other now nearly forgotten texts

were published on similar topics in the first years after reunification. Some of these texts refer to the GDR as a lost home and discuss it from a semi-documentary (workers') perspective. See, for example, Panitz and Huhn 1994.

References

Althammer, Jörg. 2002. *Erwerbsarbeit in der Krise? Zur Entwicklung und Struktur der Beschäftigung im Kontext von Arbeitsmarkt, gesellschaftlicher Partizipation und technischem Fortschritt*. Soziale Orientierung 13. Berlin: Duncker & Humblot.

Arendt, Hannah. 1958. *The Human Condition*. Chicago: University of Chicago Press.

Bakke, E. Wight. 1933. *The Unemployed Man: A Social Study*. London: Nisbet.

Baron, Christian, and Britta Steinwachs. 2012. *Faul, frech, dreist: Die Diskriminierung von Erwerbslosigkeit durch BILD-Leser*innen*. Münster: Edition Assemblage.

Berger, Johannes. 1995. "Warum arbeiten die Arbeiter? Neomarxistische und neodurkheimianische Erklärungen." In *Zeitschrift für Soziologie* 24(6): 407–21.

Bescherer, Peter, Silke Röbenack, and Karen Schierhorn. 2009. "Eigensinnige 'Kunden' – Wie Hartz IV wirkt . . . und wie nicht." In *Prekarität, Abstieg, Ausgrenzung*, ed. Robert Castel and Klaus Dörre, 145–56. Frankfurt am Main: Campus.

Brenke, Karl. 2009. "Reallöhne in Deutschland über mehrere Jahre rückläufig." *DIW Wochenbericht* 33: 550–60.

Brinkmann, Christian, and Karen Schober. 2002. "Verlaufsuntersuchungen bei Arbeitslosen 1974/75 und 1981/83." In *Arbeitslose im Blick der Sozialforschung*, ed. Gerd Vonderach, 32–43. Münster: LIT.

Bröckling, Ulrich. 2017. *Gute Hirten führen sanft: Über Menschenregierungskünste*. Suhrkamp-Taschenbuch Wissenschaft 2217. Berlin: Suhrkamp.

Bude, Heinz. 2008. *Die Ausgeschlossenen: Das Ende vom Traum einer gerechten Gesellschaft*. Munich: Hanser.

Bude, Heinz, and Andreas Willisch, eds. 2008. *Exklusion: Die Debatte über die "Überflüssigen."* Suhrkamp-Taschenbuch Wissenschaft 1819. Frankfurt am Main: Suhrkamp.

Bundeszentrale für politische Bildung. 2007. "Unternehmen und Produktion." *Informationen zur politischen Bildung* 293 (1 January): 1–67.

Castel, Robert, and Klaus Dörre, eds. 2009. *Prekarität, Abstieg, Ausgrenzung: Die soziale Frage am Beginn des 21. Jahrhunderts*. Frankfurt am Main: Campus.

Dahn, Daniela. 1996. *Westwärts und nicht vergessen: Vom Unbehagen in der Einheit*. Berlin: Rowohlt–Berlin Verlag.

———. 1998. *Vertreibung ins Paradies: Unzeitgemäße Texte zur Zeit*. Reinbeck bei Hamburg: Rowohlt.

Dahrendorf, Ralf. 1980. "Is the Work Society Running Out of Work?" *Omega* 8(3): 281–85.

———. 1982. "Wenn der Arbeitsgesellschaft die Arbeit ausgeht." In *Krise der Arbeitsgesellschaft? Verhandlungen des 21. Deutschen Soziologentages in Bamberg 1982*, ed. Joachim Matthes, 25–37. Frankfurt am Main: Campus.

Deutscher Gewerkschaftsbund, Bundesvorstand, Düsseldorf, Hauptabteilung Jugend. 1952. Erarbeitet von der Sozialwissenschaftlichen Arbeitsgemeinschaft zur Erforschung von Jugendfragen unter der wissenschaftlichen Leitung von Helmut Schelsky, ed. *Arbeitslosigkeit und Berufsnot der Jugend*. 2 vols. Cologne: Bund.

Durkheim, Emile. 1893. *De la division du travail social*. Paris: Félix Alcan.

Engler, Wolfgang. 1999. *Die Ostdeutschen: Kunde von einem verlorenen Land*. Berlin: Aufbau.

———. 2002. *Die Ostdeutschen als Avantgarde*. Berlin: Aufbau.

———. 2005. *Bürger, ohne Arbeit: Für eine radikale Neugestaltung der Gesellschaft*. Berlin: Aufbau.

Fögen, Thorsten. 2004. "Ostdeutschland nach der Wende: Ankunft der Zonenkinder in der neuen Mitte?" *Orbis Linguarum* 25: 251–59.

Frey, Carl Benedict, and Michael A. Osborne. 2017. "The Future of Employment: How Susceptible are Jobs to Computerisation." *Technological Forecasting and Social Change* 114 (January): 254–80.

Friedrichs, Günter, and Adam Schaff, eds. 1982. *Microelectronics and Society: For Better or for Worse. A Report to the Club of Rome*. Pergamon International Library of Science, Technology, Engineering and Social Studies. Oxford: Pergamon Press.

Gehrke, Bernd, and Wolfgang Rüddenklau, eds. 1999. *. . . das war doch nicht unsere Alternative: DDR-Oppositionelle zehn Jahre nach der Wende*. Münster: Westfälisches Dampfboot.

Gorz, André. 1989. *Kritik der ökonomischen Vernunft: Sinnfragen am Ende der Arbeitsgesellschaft*. Berlin: Rotbuch.

———. 2000. *Arbeit zwischen Misere und Utopie*. Edition Zweite Moderne. Frankfurt am Main: Suhrkamp.

Hartz, Peter, et al. 2002. *Moderne Dienstleistungen am Arbeitsmarkt: Vorschläge der Kommission zum Abbau der Arbeitslosigkeit und zur Umstrukturierung der Bundesanstalt für Arbeit*. Berlin: Kommission "Moderne Dienstleistungen am Arbeitsmarkt" der Bundesanstalt für Arbeit. Retrieved 17 May 2022 from https://www.sozialpolitik-aktuell.de/files/sozialpolitik-aktuell/_Politikfelder/Arbeitsmarkt/Dokumente/hartzteil1.pdf.

Jahoda, Marie. 1983. *Wieviel Arbeit braucht der Mensch? Arbeit und Arbeitslosigkeit im 20. Jahrhundert*. With a Foreword by Willy Brandt. Weinheim: Beltz.

Jahoda, Marie, Paul F. Lazarsfeld, and Hans Zeisel. 1975. *Die Arbeitslosen von Marienthal: Ein soziographischer Versuch über die Wirkungen langandauernder Arbeitslosigkeit. Mit einem Anhang zur Geschichte der Soziographie*. Frankfurt am Main: Suhrkamp.

Kirchler, Erich. 1984. *Arbeitslosigkeit und Alltagsbefinden: Eine sozialpsychologische Studie über die subjektiven Folgen von Arbeitslosigkeit.* Linz: Universitätsverlag Rudolf Trauner.

Kronauer, Martin, and Berthold Vogel. 1993. "Experiences with Unemployment Today: Between Temporary Opportunity and Social Exclusion." *International Journal of Political Economy.* Special Issue: Unemployment in Western Europe: Individual and Social Consequences 23(3): 70–94.

———. 1998. "Spaltet Arbeitslosigkeit die Gesellschaft?" In *Alte Ungleichheiten – neue Spaltungen,* ed. Peter A. Berger and Michael Vester, 333–50. Opladen: Leske + Budrich.

Kronauer, Martin, Berthold Vogel, and Frank Gerlach. 1993. *Im Schatten der Arbeitsgesellschaft: Arbeitslose und ihre Dynamik sozialer Ausgrenzung.* Frankfurt am Main: Campus.

Larsson, Anthony, and Robin Teigland, eds. 2020. *The Digital Transformation of Labor: Automation, the Gig Economy and Welfare.* New York: Routledge.

Lepsius, M.R. 1979. "Die Entwicklung der Soziologie nach dem Zweiten Weltkrieg 1945 bis 1967." In *Deutsche Soziologie seit 1945: Entwicklungsrichtungen und Praxisbezug,* ed. Güntger Lüschen, 25–70. Opladen: Westdeutscher Verlag.

Lessenich, Stephan, and Frank Nullmeier, eds. 2006. *Deutschland – eine gespaltene Gesellschaft.* Frankfurt am Main: Campus.

Marquardsen, Kai. 2007. "Was ist 'Aktivierung' in der Arbeitsmarktpolitik?" *WSI-Mitteilungen* 5: 259–67. Retrieved 19 May 2022 from https://www.wsi.de/data/wsimit_2007_05_marquardsen.pdf.

Matuschek, Ingo. 2016a. "Industrie 4.0, Arbeit 4.0 – Gesellschaft 4.0? Eine Literaturstudie." *Studien im Auftrag der Rosa-Luxemburg-Stiftung* 2 (March): 1–84. Retrieved 14 October 2019 from https://www.rosalux.de/publikation/id/8754/industrie-40-arbeit-40-gesellschaft-40/.

———. 2016b. "Substanzielle Umgestaltung der Arbeitsgesellschaft: Zu den politischen Herausforderungen des Rationalisierungskonzepts 'Industrie 4.0.'" *Standpunkte* 2 (January): 1–4. Retrieved 14 October 2019 from https://www.rosalux.de/publikation/id/8642/substanzielle-umgestaltung-der-arbeitsgesellschaft/.

Moldaschl, Manfred. 1997. "Betriebliche Rationalisierungsstrategien und ihre Auswirkungen auf den Arbeitsprozeß." In *Handbuch Arbeitswissenschaft,* ed. Volpert Luczak, 685–91. Stuttgart: Schäffer-Poeschel.

Moldaschl, Manfred, and Günter Voß. 2003. *Subjektivierung von Arbeit.* Munich: Hampp.

Panitz, Eberhard, and Klaus Huhn. 1994. *Mein Chef ist ein Wessi.* Berlin: Spotless-Verlag.

Popitz, Heinrich, Hans Bahrdt, Ernst Jüres, and Hanno Kesting. 1957. *Technik und Industriearbeit: Soziologische Untersuchungen in der Hüttenindustrie.* Soziale Forschung und Praxis 16. Tübingen: Mohr.

Sarrazin, Thilo. 2010. "Klartext-Politiker Thilo Sarrazin über Hartz IV: Es wächst eine weitgehend funktions- und arbeitslose Unterklasse heran." Bild.de, 27 August. Retrieved 11 August 2021 from https://www.bild.de/politik/2010/es-waechst-eine-arbeitslose-unterklasse-heran-13762150.bild.html.

Schmid, Michael. 1989. "Arbeitsteilung und Solidarität: Eine Untersuchung zu Emile Durkheims Theorie der sozialen Arbeitsteilung." In *Kölner Zeitschrift für Soziologie und Sozialpsychologie* 41(4): 619–43.

Seils, Christoph. 2009. "Abgang des Sparminators." Zeit Online, 29 January. Retrieved 11 August 2021 from https://www.zeit.de/online/2009/05/berlin-thilo-sarrazin.

Shiller, Robert J. 2019. *Narrative Economics: How Stories Go Viral & Drive Major Economic Events*. Princeton, NJ: Princeton University Press.

Sommer, Michael, Klaus Dörre, and Uwe Schneidewind, eds. 2005. *Die Zukunft war vorgestern: Der Wandel der Arbeitsverhältnisse: Unsicherheit statt Normalarbeitsverhältnis?* Oldenburger Universitätsreden 162. Oldenburg: Bibliotheks- und Informationssystem der Universität.

Sondermann, Ariadne, Wolfgang Ludwig-Mayerhofer, and Olaf Behrend. 2009. "Die Überzähligen – Teil der Arbeitsgesellschaft." In *Prekarität, Abstieg, Ausgrenzung*, ed. Robert Castel and Klaus Dörre, 157–70. Frankfurt am Main: Campus.

Vonderach, Gerd, ed. 2002a. *Arbeitslose im Blick der Sozialforschung: Ausgewählte Studien aus der Geschichte der empirischen Arbeitslosenforschung im deutschsprachigen Raum*. Sozialforschung, Arbeit und Sozialpolitik 9. Münster: LIT.

———. 2002b. "Klassiker der Arbeitslosenforschung." In *Arbeitslose im Blick der Sozialforschung*, ed. Gerd Vonderach, 11–22. Münster: LIT.

CHAPTER 6

Cruel Optimism as Plot Driver in German and Austrian Economic Crisis Novels with Adult and Child Protagonists Thrust into Poverty

JILL E. TWARK

Economic crises in Germany and Austria have been propelled by global stock market crashes, wartime overspending and the loss of two world wars, among other causes. Such crises have spawned abundant literary narratives that convey public and private responses as individualized stories. Fiction writers often tune into a climate of privation in their texts as a way to process current events and draw attention to those in need. In the decade following the 2007/8 financial crisis, a group of contemporary German and Austrian authors, all born in the 1970s and thus a generational cohort, published social novels that highlight the plight of disadvantaged adults and children thrust into poverty. André Pilz's *Man Down* (2010), Inger-Maria Mahlke's *Rechnung offen* (Open invoice, 2013), Christoph Dolgan's *Ballastexistenz* (Burdensome existence, 2013), and Thomas Melle's *3000 Euro* (2014) depict ethnic German or Austrian working-class characters living in difficult economic circumstances in contemporary urban settings, whereas Matthias Nawrat's *Unternehmer* (Entrepreneurs, 2014) is set in an isolated region of the Black Forest.[1] These writers recognize "how the literary presentation of poverty is intimately related to the act of presentation that allows for us to see poverty at all" (Greany 2008: 7). Whether their novels are explicitly or implicitly embedded in the shadow of the 2007/8 financial crisis, they narrate poverty as it affects working-class individuals and families, spotlighting complex emotional reactions to personal and social injustices rooted in neoliberal capitalist societies.[2]

In recognizing the need to narrate stories of poverty to make it visible, authors who do so encounter particular conundrums in their choice of literary strategies. It is easy to produce lurid, voyeuristic stories along the lines of tabloid press blurbs, but difficult to write an extended narrative that keeps the reader's attention and invokes compassion along with horror and disgust, as these novels do. One predominant narrative strategy the novelists deploy to tell enlightening contemporary tales of economic privation can be interpreted as built on what Lauren Berlant (2011) calls cruel optimism. "Cruel optimism" is a psychological state of mind, akin to an obsession, that begins with the unfulfilled (and often unfulfillable) craving for a particular object such as a rewarding job or a political goal. Such a desire becomes cruel when it makes you feel hopeful that it can be achieved, but then "actively impedes the aim that brought you to it initially" (1–3). Berlant describes cruel optimism as a historical sensorium that developed in the second half of the twentieth century as the social welfare state and its promise of providing widespread access to the "good life" became eroded. She analyzes texts from various media that depict fraying fantasies, which include "upward mobility, job security, political and social equality, and lively, durable intimacy" (3). These fraying fantasies, and the psychological damage they induce, pervade much contemporary German and Austrian literature,[3] evincing how the current neoliberal system can contribute to perpetuating poverty.

Pilz, Melle, Mahlke, Nawrat, and Dolgan present their adult characters as falling prey to the cruel optimism of wanting what they are unable to acquire in a neoliberal capitalist society in a state of impasse:[4] equitable employment, debt resolution after losing a job, and stable emotional attachments to a partner or parent. As the parents in Mahlke's, Nawrat's, and Dolgan's novels succumb to the quest for these unachievable objects, however, their children take center stage as secondary victims of cruel optimism. It drives the narratives as a snare keeping the poor from rising up out of poverty, as all characters suffer tragic loss, injury, or death in striving to improve their lives. The emotions tied to their conflicted situations, expressing misery but also the hope for a way out, are depicted along a wide spectrum, from understandably strong feelings of anger, fear, frustration, and depression to what Sianne Ngai (2007) refers to as the persistent "ugly feelings" of irritation and paranoia, often hidden from view. Revealed as driving self-destructive behaviors, these emotions are depicted empathetically. Their trajectory intensifies as the narratives play out, however, in ways tied to the financialization[5] and bureaucratization of the current neoliberal capitalist system, but also to economic class division and a social compartmentalization that inhibits the granting of durable assistance to those in need.

As these adult and child characters strive to improve their lives by acquiring money through various means, specific features of the neoliberal system exclude them from engaging in meaningful, reputable, and non-exploitative labor. These features include the low wages paid for unskilled, demeaning jobs in the service industry, which are contrasted with the much higher wages paid in the sex industry or for drug dealing, in which workers are subjected to even greater psychological and physical abuse. The discount supermarket cashier and single mother Denise in *3000 Euro* acts in a pornographic film and envisions using the 3,000 euros she has been owed for months by the porn film director to pay off the homeless protagonist Anton's debts so they can travel to New York City together. Her sorely anticipated earnings do not, however, alleviate her paranoia over having allowed herself to engage in sexual acts streamed on a popular Internet porn site. In fact, her film—indicating the role of the mass media in perpetuating the cruel optimism of capitalism—incites some of her supermarket customers to ogle and harass her sexually, and her earning power and caring nature do not compel the mentally unstable Anton to form a lasting relationship with her. In *Open Invoice* the chain-bakery cashier and single mother Manuela yearns to discard her identity and motherly obligations, and start a new life in another town; but when she carries out this plan, she is arrested by the police and loses custody of her son. The teenage narrator's single mother in *Burdensome Existence,* a discount store cashier, seeks escape from her tyrannical boss and the titular "burden" of her son by turning to alcohol, and she dies prematurely from her addiction.[6] The family in *Entrepreneurs* discusses saving the profits from their scrap-metal scavenging to immigrate to New Zealand, but their perilous metal part extractions set them back rather than moving them forward toward this goal. Cruel optimism is a persistent, emotionally charged mental state that drives the plot in these novels, motivating the characters' decisions and actions, and affecting how they treat their children.

This chapter first explores how cruel optimism propels the action and critiques of neoliberal capitalism in *Man Down* and *3000 Euro,* in which two young male protagonists dig themselves deeper into debt while hoping for a resolution to their debt crises. In the second section, Mahlke's, Nawrat's, and Dolgan's stories of destitution are assessed for the socially critical and literary-aesthetic ways they present economic crises as affecting the children of parents afflicted with cruel optimism. Both types of crisis narrative condemn neoliberal capitalism for exacerbating class divisions and social compartmentalization, but approach the likelihood of a systemic shift to a more equitable socioeconomic order pessimistically. Cruel optimism can deliver forceful characters and plots, providing suspense and continuity to otherwise episodic or fragmentary narratives. Such tales, delving into the wide-reaching effects of economic crises on working-class people, provide a necessary counterbalance to journalistic, scholarly, and other data-driven narratives that tend to focus on the governments, financial institutions, and economic leaders that influence the macroeconomy.

Cruel Optimism in *Man Down* and *3000 Euro*

In the plots spun around the male protagonists in *Man Down* and *3000 Euro*, the deleterious effects of cruel optimism unfold by tying a yearning for the unattainable explicitly to economic crises produced by financialized and bureaucratized capitalism. Both novels begin *in media res*, after Pilz's Austrian protagonist, Kai Samweber, who lives in Munich, and Melle's character Anton from Berlin, both in their twenties, have lost their jobs. The complex reasons the authors give for their unemployment include the cash-strapped situation of their bosses and creditors due to the bank-lending crisis that began in 2008, but also the protagonists' emotional lability and sheer bad luck. Their cruelly optimistic hopes of being compensated financially through the German legal system inhibit their ability to seek or maintain a steady job. Rejected by and consciously rejecting "the system" (Pilz 2010: 113; Melle 2014: 44)—the official capitalist economy—they continue to imagine themselves back in it, subsisting on minimal support from what is depicted as an ineffectual, overly bureaucratic German welfare system, and committing crimes to survive that make them both perpetrators and victims of violence. Along with emphasizing the social injustices they face, the authors explore how their emotional reactions contribute to their downward spiral, conveying a fatalistic view of life in poverty in contemporary urban Germany.

The worldwide financial crisis of 2007/8 sets Pilz's narrative in motion. Although financial crises can appear as abstract phenomena emerging from an unintelligible mass of Internet stock trades, *Man Down* makes the socioeconomic effects of this crisis visible and visceral. These effects play out in a US gangster-style urban setting not usually associated with the wealthy Bavarian city of Munich, among a motley cast of characters that includes a family of brutally stereotyped Turkish drug dealers. The author sets the tone with a verse epigraph from the song "Nie ein Rapper," from the controversial German rappers Bushido and Baba Saad's 2005 album *Carlo, Cokxxx, Nutten II*. Indicating a personal transformation that is both a fall from innocence and a turn to seriousness, anger, and violence, the epigraph reads: "Ich hab mein Lachen verlor'n/Eine ganze Generation besteht aus Waffen und Zorn."[7] Paired with the book's English title, *Man Down*, referring to a wounded or dead soldier, Pilz ties his protagonist's fate metaphorically to that of other young socioeconomic "losers," who fail at fighting life's battles.

The roofer Kai feels a righteous indignation after he falls from a rooftop, becomes physically disabled, and is not paid six-months' back wages after his employer goes bankrupt following the financial crisis. His perpetual indebtedness, first to his bank, then to his Turkish drug-dealer friend Shane, fuels this rage, described powerfully in the novel's introductory paragraph:

> I was head over heels in debt back then. I was constantly receiving letters from my bank, sometimes two or three a week. I crossed out my name and wrote "address unknown" on the envelopes, then I threw them in the next mailbox. The bank people called me, but I told them I was not myself. I wasn't there. . . . A few months earlier the bank had gone bankrupt by speculating on businesses in the US, and the government jumped in with a couple million to help out. The bosses responsible for it were let go with a huge severance package and a stately pension. *60,000 Euros a month for the Chief Indian. . . . Till he drops dead.* (Pilz 2010: 7, italics in original)

Comparing his indebtedness with that of the "responsible" bosses in Germany—who did receive severance pay and large pensions despite engaging in risky financial speculation in the United States and bankrupting their banks (Jungbluth 2008; Herterich 2018)—immediately draws sympathy to Kai as an unwitting financial crisis victim. Kai's refusal to acknowledge receipt of the bank letters shows how becoming economically disadvantaged can induce feelings of being hunted as a criminal. Denying his identity by crossing out his name foreshadows Kai's shift in identity from an ordinary working-class roofer to a criminal drug courier, living in the underground economy and constantly fearing arrest.

Author Pilz tells Kai's story as a tale of cruel optimism by having Kai expect unrealistically to receive the six-months' back pay he is owed by his bankrupt boss and trust the intentions of his ostensible "best friend" Shane, who exploits him as a marijuana courier. Kai struggles to find a legitimate job, subsisting on €278.15 of welfare a month, supplemented with money borrowed from Shane and thus sinking ever deeper into debt. Pilz depicts Kai as an intelligent, sensitive, and tragic victim of circumstances who gradually transforms into a repulsive criminal castaway as he engages in evermore insidious criminal activities. In between crimes, Kai interjects social criticism in letters written but never sent to the brother for whose death he is responsible, as well as in rhetorical questions addressed to the reader. He calls the capitalist system and its credit relations into question, projecting a hypothetical vision of acute economic class warfare:

> *What would happen if we all went down? If we all went broke, all except for those at the top who pocketed everything and are laughing their asses off now, turning up their noses at us idiots, the rabble in the dirt? If they defend their riches with claws and teeth, with their private armies and lobbyists? What happens if my body never heals, if the pain in my back never goes away and I'm dependent on them forever?* (Pilz 2010: 143, italics in original)

Kai's raw criticism of socioeconomic inequality is tied here to the symbolic and real enslavement of his broken mind and body in the exploitative capitalist creditor–debtor relationship. Maurizio Lazzarato's (2012: 59) summary of

Marx's (2005: 215–16) and Nietzsche's (1994: 43–45) analysis of this relationship helps explain the way it dominates Kai, turning him into an archetypal "indebted man":

> Credit entails the creditor's 'moral judgment' of the debtor, that is a 'subjective' measure of value. But not only are the skills and know-how of the worker evaluated, so too are the poor man's actions in society (social 'virtues,' 'conduct,' 'reputation'), that is, his lifestyle, his social behavior, his value, his very existence. It is through debt that capital is able to appropriate not only the physical and intellectual abilities the poor man employs in his labor, but also his social and existential forces.

Pilz critiques this creditor–debtor relationship for sabotaging debtors by demonstrating how his protagonist Kai becomes an ever-greater victim of his indebtedness. Kai not only condemns the poor moral choices he is compelled to make, but also comes to perceive his entire existence as a series of unrepayable debts. In *Man Down*, the cruel optimism attached to the futile anticipation of receiving a legitimately earned salary gradually warps into a cruel pessimism when Kai accepts the fact that the struggle to repay his debts has turned him into a criminal.

Depression and other mental illnesses exacerbate the existential precarity of protagonists such as Kai and Anton in contemporary German-language social novels, as a further reason provided for why people descend into or remain in poverty. In *3000 Euro*, another debt-driven fictional biography, Melle depicts his homeless protagonist Anton as unable to hold a job and suffering from cruel optimism because of his emotional lability. Emotionally labile people experience heightened feelings of happiness or sadness, sometimes inappropriate to a situation, and often exhibit harmful or destructive behavior (Salters-Pedneault 2020). Anton's emotional lability leads him to latch onto a series of cruelly optimistic lures, ranging from his thwarted adolescent desire for a beautiful girlfriend, to his aborted university law degree, and to hoping for a cancellation of the over 5,000 euros he owes to the financially challenged Deutsche Bank.[8] A month-long partying and drinking binge, which he himself cannot justify, leaves him indebted and facing a court trial that will determine whether he is mentally stable enough to be held responsible for these debts. The thread of hope for a favorable ruling inhibits him from seeking serious employment, until a negative verdict shocks him into realizing that he will never be able to dig himself out of his debt, which, with court costs, reaches 10,600 euros:

> Then it's over. There are no more events, Anton thinks, there are only results in my life, the results from events that I can hardly remember, and the results of the results of things that got lost and reappear on some random sheets of paper

> and in letters, and the results of results of results, which add an unbearable sum of interest to life. (Melle 2014: 187)

Like Pilz, Melle expands the meaning of debt collection notices hyperbolically to show how what initially seem only to be "random sheets of paper" and "letters" can come to overwhelm debtors with their "unbearable sum of interest." As this interest accrues, debtors can become paralyzed by the inability to comprehend the cause-and-effect relationship between their own actions and this ever-rising debt. On the one hand, Melle demonstrates how a person's mental state can lead to financial success or failure, exposing society's need to address the underlying psychological roots of poverty. On the other hand, he highlights how poverty can exacerbate or lead to mental health issues, thereby presenting the neoliberal capitalist system as unjust, regardless of one's psychological state.

Melle condemns the modern social-welfare state for placing hurdles in front of destitute individuals like Anton, who need financial assistance and struggle to follow rules they perceive as personally invasive. When Anton's friend Cathrin suggests he declare personal insolvency (*Privatinsolvenz*) as a solution to his debt, he reacts with revulsion: "[J]ust hearing that word makes Anton nauseated, because it means more bureaucracy, more observation, more administration and coercion, more of everything that he wants to get rid of" (Melle 2014: 187). From the perspective of underprivileged, excluded characters who face constant financial and bureaucratic setbacks, contemporary society appears dystopian. The underground economy exists in a constant state of micro-crisis, in tandem with the macro-crises of the neoliberal official economy.

Although the official economy appears impenetrable to Anton and Kai, depicted as powerless to bring about equitable legal or political resolutions to their financial problems, *Man Down* concludes with Kai crossing the socioeconomic class divide by confronting his former employer, Herr Meyer, with his crime of having withheld Kai's back wages. The confrontation occurs at the office of the lawyer who misled Kai into believing he would represent him fairly and yet hid his friendship with Herr Meyer:

> "When you made yourself scarce after the bankruptcy, I took a look at your house in Herlaching [an upper-class Munich neighborhood].[9] Can you imagine how mad I got when I stood in front of that thing?"
>
> [Meyer:] "Yeah, yeah, envy is a dog."
>
> "Envy? I don't hate you because you're rich, Meyer. I hate you because your heart is poor. I'm a cripple because of you! I'm broke because of you! I lost everything, everything! And when I stood in front of that huge house, I finally realized that you cheated me. That you're a swindler, a crook." (Pilz 2010: 269)

When Meyer offers to pay Kai 4,000 euros out of his wallet, however, it is too late: "Fuck your money, Meyer. I want you," Kai says, forcing Meyer and the corporate lawyer Rensing at gunpoint to climb out onto the window ledge of Rensing's high-rise office building. *Man Down* ends with Kai lighting a joint and saying coolly to these two representatives of "the system": "I've got time, a whole lot of time" (ibid.: 275). Kai's anger, directed at his boss, his false friends, and the capitalist system, culminates in an act of revenge. This violent attack is calculated to make wealthy representatives of the official economy, who sometimes cheat the poor and thus are revealed to be the "real criminals" in this story, feel a similar powerlessness and fear. Only through such a violent act of revenge, which Pilz renders with a crime-story suspense, can Kai finally relinquish his cruel optimism. In giving up his quest for justice by legal means, however, he instigates a tragic end.

Man Down and *3000 Euro* both narrate biographical plots motivated by cruel optimism that indicate an affinity between it and the assumption of debt. Borrowing money grants borrowers the optimism of being able to pay their bills and perhaps attain better living conditions. But it is also cruel, because it can make the debtor feel guilty or even morally inferior to his or her creditor (Nietzsche 1994: 43–45). When people incur debt that they cannot repay, this debt thwarts their efforts to improve their lives. Possessing a logic that propels both creditors and debtors to act—creditors strive to recoup debts, and debtors work to repay or to avoid payment—this debt relationship can serve as a narrative device. It provides a way for Pilz and Melle to tell stories of the poor as fantasized visions of their life stories that nevertheless explain their pathways into destitution so that readers can empathize with others who suffer similar fates.

Child Victims of Economic Crisis

The young adult characters Kai, Anton, Manuela, and Denise struggle with adulthood: they lash out in immature temper tantrums or suffer bouts of depression that express the cruelly optimistic futility of fighting for socio-economic independence when a national or personal economic crisis strikes. The child protagonists in the novels by Mahlke, Nawrat, and Dolgan are their younger counterparts. As minors, they represent the one in five children living in poverty today in Germany and Austria (Menne, Funcke, and Lentzler 2020). Their families are depicted as victims of precarious, abusive working conditions; their parents mistreat them; and the German or Austrian child protective services provide only delayed, ineffective assistance, if any at all. None of these child protagonists experience light-hearted joy, and all suffer the loss by death or the removal of parental rights of one or both parents. Eight-year-old Lucas is neglected and then abandoned by his mother, Manuela, as she seeks a life free from her monotonous job and motherly responsibilities; fourteen-year-old Lipa continues to run the family business after her father sinks into depression and dies prematurely; and the unnamed, suicidal teen narrator in *Burdensome Existence* is transported by ambulance to an unknown destination, likely a mental institution, after his mother dies of alcoholism. Although these characters are children, the authors depict their speech and thoughts in an adult language, for, as Lukács (1983: 196) writes: "Artistic truth consists in correctly rendering the feelings, ideas and thoughts of a child in a language in which all this can be readily understood by the adult reader." Speaking through child protagonists as "vehicles of moral and cultural interrogation" (Locke 2011: 4), allows the authors to critique socioeconomic injustices that lead to or compound poverty and child abuse. Whereas Pilz's and Melle's fatalistic stories at times distance their readers from their perpetrator–victim characters, the narratives of Nawrat, Mahlke, and Dolgan elicit profound compassion for exploited or neglected youth.

The economic crisis narrative surrounding the child protagonist Lucas in Mahlke's *Open Invoice* is calculated to evoke the reader's sympathy as it unfolds episodically, switching back and forth between his story and those of the other residents in his run-down apartment building. Lucas faces evermore difficult hurdles when his depressed single mother neglects and then abandons him, and his neighbors do not intervene. Lucas survives for several weeks alone, buying groceries with some cash she left behind. His solitary coping, in a frightening, imaginary world of aliens and Native American Indians bearing scalps (Mahlke 2013: 227), parallels the social compartmentalization of his neighbors from each other and their own families. This alienation is captured in a dialogue between Lucas and his neighbor with Alzheimer's disease, Frau Elsa Streml, who should have been moved to a nursing home several years before, yet persists in inviting her neighbors over for "dust-particle" tea with stale cookies (225). Frau Streml asks Lucas:

> "And is your family doing well?"
> "My mother," Lucas hesitated, "isn't there," he said finally.
> "Well," she said, and said it reproachfully, "that's no reason to cry."
> "I'm not crying at all," he felt his cheeks, they were dry.
> "The pixies haven't come over yet," she said, "maybe next time."
> Lucas nodded, didn't trust himself to ask, finally took a cookie, she seemed satisfied.
> "My mother is gone," he tried again, "for a long time already."
> "Maybe she's out bartering."
> "Bartering?"
> "At the Brandenburg Gate, at the black market, that takes a while, but it's not for children." . . .

"No, that's not it, she's gone for good."
Frau Streml nodded, pointed at his tea.
"It's getting cold. My mother was [in] a bomb strike. The whole street." (Mahlke 2013: 225)

This disjointed conversation resembles a comedy routine in that Frau Streml does not and, indeed, cannot understand Lucas. In her mind she is still living in wartime Germany and associates his mother with her own, who died in a bombing raid; Lucas later observes her being carried out of her apartment on a stretcher. While visiting her, he reacts to a television newscast mentioning the financial crisis: "They spoke of a crisis with the finances; finances means money" (ibid.: 224). He grasps the connection between finances and the money he uses to buy food, but global events mean nothing to him as a child. The humor and compassion in this dialogue is the exception to the otherwise trenchant stance Mahlke takes in depicting alienation, miscommunication, and neglect of the elderly and children among the characters in *Open Invoice*. They are motivated by cruel optimism, valuing personal freedom, material goods, and dietary gluttony over their family or neighbors, and their mentality is presented as unaltered by the global financial crisis.

In *Entrepreneurs*, Nawrat critiques overly pragmatic attitudes toward labor in particular, and neoliberal capitalism more generally, by exploring what might happen if parents who view work as the only meaningful life activity let this attitude dictate how they socialize their children. In his novel, two siblings—the fourteen-year-old girl Lipa and her ten-year-old brother Berti—toil under their father's strict tutelage for their family's survival by scavenging abandoned industrial sites in the Black Forest for scrap metal, which they sell to a nearby junkyard. The father, a landfill maintenance worker who used to live in "the big city" and had wanted to become an engineer (Nawrat 2014: 33), was fired from his job and solves this economic crisis by teaching his children to view the family's scavenging activities as a business and themselves as entrepreneurs. Their thoughts and actions, which comprise the novel's plot, reflect how their identities are dominated by a practical economic worldview: they believe with cruel optimism that earning money must be life's primary focus, ignoring the value of any approach to education that does not contribute to this goal.

Entrepreneurs critiques this worldview with dark irony by transposing economic language, logic, and corporate structures to a family microcosm. The novel's title introduces this theme. As Lipa and Berti ride with their father in their deceased grandfather's old green Mercedes, discussing their roles as scrap-metal scavengers, Berti complains about the division of labor: "Can't I be the assistant once too?" "You're our specialist, father says. Your sister is the best assistant we've ever had" (ibid.: 9). Like the word "entrepreneur," "specialist" is a euphemism for Berti's position in the company, in which he uses his thin arms and small hands to extract valuable copper, tungsten, and tantalum parts from abandoned factory machines and other technical equipment. He had previously lost an arm when it became trapped in a pipe, and later he loses both legs in extracting a uranium fuel rod from a decommissioned nuclear power plant destroyed by dynamite set off by a competing family of scrap-metal scavengers. Nawrat's cynical transposition of economic logic to his fictional family's mindset continues when Berti recovers the fuel rod, despite having lost his legs, and his sister exclaims proudly:

> Berti, in the meantime, our specialist, holds the most valuable thing in the air, a triumph for entrepreneurship. He is truly the next Employee of the Month, maybe of the whole year. . . . Despite all mastery of the art of dynamite blasting, true entrepreneurship begins in the heart. And has to do with courage. . . . Berti is the model for all generations of entrepreneurs to come after us. (Nawrat 2014: 97–98)

Lipa's enthusiastic account of Berti's accident resembles a pep talk given by the manager of a fast-food or supermarket chain that uses Employee of the Month recognition to motivate employees. Nawrat's grotesque satire exposes the absurdity of economic narratives that engage in "sensemaking" after a catastrophe, giving the disaster a positive spin so that a company can avoid or reduce disciplinary actions and continue operating (Weick 1995; Carucci 2019).

This fanatical attitude toward work also influences Berti's and Lipa's perspective on education. When asked by a woman at a gas station why he is missing an arm, Berti responds: "My arm is missing because a business demands sacrifices. . . . And no one learns stuff in school that is worth anything in real life" (Nawrat 2014: 9). Neither Berti nor Lipa attend school for long, because their family believes schools are merely holding pens for unemployed children, occupying them with unproductive activities until they can work and earn money. "[S]chool is a place for the unemployed," Lipa thinks, when her father falls ill and tells her he is sending her back (ibid.: 108). Sitting in her teacher Mr. Gombrowicz's math class, Lipa describes school as an institution whose sole purpose is to train students for the future workplace:

> [B]ecause the unemployed are recording all that stuff in their inventory notebooks, I record it along with them and must admit that the so-called class lesson bears a similar dual nature within itself. On the one hand, it's the site at which the preparation for future work takes place; on the other, it's already work, but without a recognizable business profit, so that I have to think of it as a successful dramatic performance while I'm writing down Mr. Gombrowicz's explanations. For why are the unemployed here writing down anything at all if not to act as if they were working? (Nawrat 2014: 113)

Too sophisticated to represent the thoughts of an average fourteen-year-old, the practical economic logic expressed here indicates that Nawrat speaks through Lipa. He demonstrates what could happen if school curricula are no longer viewed as important media for inculcating humanist educational ideals and producing well-rounded citizens, but instead delivered purely to produce efficient wage-earners.

In both the school and scrap-metal industry microcosms, depicted in a distantiated manner through Lipa's pragmatic lens, the characters act with a paradoxically forced autonomy. Their emotional needs are subsumed to their quest for economic survival, and parents and teachers (as state-employed job trainers), carry out the demands of a dystopian society in which a person's value as a human being is determined by their ability to work and earn a wage. Although the main characters possess the cruel optimism of escaping eventually from their situation by using their earnings to emigrate to New Zealand, the fatalistic, satirical plot does not permit a happy ending.

Alexander Preisinger (2009) writes that in contemporary German literature "the frenzied activity of a social Darwinist cut-throat competition dominates. Competitive situations become the dominant elements motivating the plot." Nawrat transposes economic logic, attitudes, and language to his hyperbolic, fantastical narrative in *Entrepreneurs* to demonstrate how destructive social Darwinist attitudes toward the working poor and the unemployed in Germany and other industrial societies can be if they permeate even the mentality of impoverished children for whom a school education should represent the main path to a better life. Dolgan's novel *Burdensome Existence* reinforces this stance by granting his first-person teen narrator an incisive intelligence similar to Lipa's that permits him to articulate his quite different status as an economic "burden" to his mother and to Austrian society.

Like Nawrat, Dolgan tells a morally ambiguous tale of a child living in a crisis situation to provoke thought on what it means to live with the awareness of one's role in a family and society in which economic value takes precedence over human value. Dolgan's suicidal narrator, diagnosed with borderline personality disorder, is abused by his parents (Dolgan 2013: 9) and engages in destructive behaviors such as smashing all lightbulbs in his apartment (136) and shaving off his hair (143–44). His alcoholic mother's continuous downward trajectory following his father's premature death provides the narrative scaffold on which the narrator hangs his fragmentary first-person observations of his and her life. Her alcoholism and abuse derive at least partly from the tyrannical treatment of his father and in her job as a discount-store cashier. Dolgan invents a grotesque branch-wide regulation for a fictional Austrian discount store chain requiring all women to wear a red cap during their menstrual cycle, and only allowing three caps to be shared in each store on any given day, "or they avoid their menstruation by becoming pregnant. Then they will be fired and the branch manager says: 'Now you can bleed whenever you want, and you can wear whatever you want'" (20). Because she must support her son and fears societal reprobation for becoming unemployed, the narrator's mother is trapped:

> "They make an illness out of unemployment. A moral illness for which there is no cure. You are, they say, an asocial piece of shit who needs to take care of himself. Whoever is unemployed is ill, they say, and whoever is ill is guilty [*schuld*]." (Dolgan 2013: 70)

In German, *schuld* can mean both "guilty" and "indebted." This metaphorical chain tying unemployment to a "moral illness" and illness to guilt/indebtedness does not excuse the mother's alcoholism or mistreatment of her son, but it does indicate how a society's attitudes toward the unemployed can undermine both those who work and those who lose their jobs. When anxiety drives people to accept abusive labor conditions for fear of becoming unemployed and facing social condemnation, their anxiety can erupt in self-destructive behaviors and discourage them from demanding better working conditions. Being unemployed would be one type of "burdensome existence" referred to in the novel's title.

The other "burdensome existence" is the narrator himself, whose mother views him as a liability. He distances himself from her in the way he uses language to approach their relationship:

> She's talking about the clod, the burden that she has to schlep around with her, she's talking about me. "If you weren't here, I wouldn't have to do all this. If you weren't here. But you are anyway. You're still here." I don't know who is behind this "you" of my mother and imagine: "We call each other 'Mr.' and 'Mrs.'" (Dolgan 2013: 79)

Displaying an awareness of himself as an unloved "other," the narrator detaches himself from his mother by claiming he does not know who is behind the "you" his mother blames for having to take care of him. To dissociate himself from her hurtful words, he imagines they are merely acquaintances, addressing each other with the formal "*Sie*" pronoun instead of the familiar German "*du*" commonly used among family members.

Dolgan's narrator describes his life and mental state as depressing and violent with detachment, but also at times with a gut-wrenchingly beautiful language. This poetic language—acquired by having read literary and theoretical texts at a local bookstore—evokes compassion and admiration, adding value to his "valueless" life. In colorful, visceral tropes, he gives body parts a synesthetic ability to manifest his constant fear, and that of his neighbors:

> Fear is audible, fear is the noisy setting as a constant background reality, atonal and uninterrupted. In the vibration of my ear drums, the others' fear becomes a physical certainty, the chronic goosebumps are the notation imprinted on me. (I'm the pin drum of the music box, the world as its chiming comb is rusty. I'm the old song and the droning return of the refrain. And sheet music isn't thrown away.) The so-to-speak raw power of language is the background rhythm here in the projects. Screams and the whimpering that follows, choked back with your own hand. . . . People say it casually and self-evidently that one is not the self in which something shatters. But I heard it break, loud and clear I heard it, how something in and upon me shattered. And I hear it breaking still, because it's still breaking in and upon me, constantly. . . . For this sadness as the remainder of my emotions is the soundproofing that lets the anger in my mouth run dry. Contradicting would only be possible with words, at whose edges another aggregate state begins. (Dolgan 2013: 52–53)

Like the other destitute characters in these novels, the unnamed child narrator in *Burdensome Existence* expresses the repetitive, merciless nature of a life lived in poverty. Here the metaphor is tied to this life as "the old song and the droning return of the refrain" (52). The repetition of the words "Angst," "Lärm," "hören," and "Tod" throughout the novel captures its abrasive, nihilistic monotony. The suicidal boy also describes the experience of his psyche shattering repeatedly into pieces, later on the same page referencing Virginia Woolf as the source for his understanding of how the "I" is just a comfortable expression for someone who does not actually exist (53). He recognizes the possibility of resisting his situation—the cause of his sadness, fear, and anger—by expressing his feelings in words, but he believes these words only form a senseless, loosely compacted aggregate of fragments. The novel itself is composed of a loose aggregate of the narrator's fragmented reflections, cut off soon after his mother dies, leaving him to fend for himself like Lukas in Mahlke's *Open Invoice*. Dependent on his mother, then the Austrian state, for survival, Dolgan's narrator communicates his status as a socioeconomic "burden" paradoxically by producing a text with a high socio-aesthetic value.

Conclusions

These five German and Austrian social novels chronicle the lives of individuals and families facing economic crises in twenty-first-century Europe for various reasons. Some of these crises are blamed on the 2007/8 financial crisis, but others are depicted as the result of more general economic injustices endemic to capitalism, including institutionalized mistreatment by an employer, low wages, employment precarity, and long-term unemployment. They show how attachments motivated and undermined by cruel optimism can lead to the worsening of an already difficult financial situation. What ties these characters' fates together is that the more they or their parents contribute labor, raw materials, time, and their own bodies to the system, the more the system pushes them down. Neoliberal capitalist society appears to be so compartmentalized in these fictional milieus that neither extended family members nor local neighbors serve as a sufficient safety net: only the state can help, and only if need is recognized and the social welfare system is equipped to respond appropriately. The fates of the child characters expose these social gaps most powerfully, giving voice to those in the real world who often cannot speak up for themselves.

These novels indicate a post-millennial trend of German-language authors focusing on serious social problems (see Hahne 2004; Romeiß-Stracke 2010; Eichhorn 2013: 9; Drees 2019), while elevating the aesthetic and psychologically penetrating merits of literary fiction above journalistic or scholarly treatments of unemployment and poverty. Statistics and reports sum up the collective crisis results, but fiction writers bring to life the individual fates behind the data:

> It's not that characters who are 'made up' are by definition frivolous or arbitrary or self-indulgent. . . . It's that non-fiction must do without the novel's great aesthetic advantage—the ability to inhabit the interior lives of other people—and thus cannot move the encounter between rich and poor . . ., child and adult, or white and brown past its uneasy reality. (Dee 2017)

Delving into the psychology and life experiences of their characters, novelists can dig beneath the surface and promote identification with the oppressed and down-and-out.

These narratives, in fact, call on us to assess what it means to live a working-class or unemployed life. Zygmunt Bauman (2004: 5) conceives of modernization's working-class and unemployed lives as "wasted." That physical labor has become devalued in the twentieth and early twenty-first centuries is "an inescapable side-effect of *order-building* . . . and of *economic progress*." All of these protagonists suffer the fate of those whose "wasted lives" are the "new normal," and yet they are depicted as possessing a high value in their ability to articulate the causes and realities of their situation. They speak in an at times blunt and at other times complex, aesthetic, "artistic" language. Their (albeit fictional) lives are "wasted" in that they have sometimes been "unprofitably used, made, or expended" (Merriam-Webster), but they contradict the definition of "wasted" as "used or expended carelessly, extravagantly, or to no purpose." Do people who live in "real-existing poverty" (should they possess such a heightened self-awareness or not) deserve to have their lives labeled "wasted"? In drawing attention to destitute people, these authors expose otherwise hidden, overlooked, or consciously avoided nuances of their existence.

Jill E. Twark is Associate Professor of German at East Carolina University in North Carolina. Her research interests include twentieth- and twenty-first-century German literature and culture, including the representation of history in German film. She has published widely on humor and satire, including the book *Humor, Satire, and Identity: Eastern German Literature in the 1990s* and the edited volume *Strategies of Humor in Post-Unification German Literature, Film, and Other Media*. She focused on social justice dilemmas in the volume *Envisioning Social Justice in Contemporary German Culture*. She serves as a German Studies editor for *The Literary Encyclopedia*.

Notes

1. All five authors have received accolades and awards for their texts. *Man Down* was voted one of ten best novels to read in 2015 by *Focus* magazine, and was adapted into a theatre play (Brand 2015). Mahlke has received various writing stipends and literary prizes, including the 2012 Ernst Willner Prize for *Rechnung offen* at the Tage der deutschsprachigen Literatur, at which Nawrat also won the Kelag Prize for *Unternehmer*. Dolgan earned a manuscript award and writing prize for a successful literary debut from the Austrian Federal Ministry of Education, Arts and Culture in 2013 for *Ballastexistenz*. Melle's *3,000 Euro* was shortlisted for the German Book Prize in 2014.
2. For a detailed account of the extent to which the European Union has adopted neoliberal economic policies, see Hermann 2007.
3. Two other groups of contemporary German and Austrian novels cover related topics. One group depicts formerly successful white-collar professionals who have become unemployed and must cope with their new, disorienting circumstances (see Seddig 2010; Potente 2014). Another group depicts the gentrification of metropolitan areas that is displacing low-income residents and forcing them to the peripheries, thereby excluding them from participating in urban life (see Beck 2013; Mahlke 2013 [discussed below]; Seidl 2014; Wenke 2014). Matthies (2016) discusses how unemployed or working-class characters with precarious jobs are depicted as victims of the neoliberal New Economy in German literary fiction from the 1980s to 2009.
4. Berlant (2011: 4–5) defines an "impasse" as "a time of dithering from which someone or some situation cannot move forward." She refers to it more specifically in her textual analyses as "a stretch of time in which one moves around with a sense that the world is at once intensely present and enigmatic, such that the activity of living demands both a wandering absorptive awareness and a hypervigilance that collects material that might help clarify things, maintain one's sea legs, and coordinate the standard melodramatic crises with those processes that have not yet found their genre of event." It resembles a "holding pattern" that takes the form of "temporary housing."
5. Palley (2007: 2), citing Epstein (2001: 1), defines "financialization" as "the increasing importance of financial markets, financial motives, financial institutions, and financial elites in the operation of the economy and its governing institutions, both at the national and international levels." Its primary effects, according to Palley,

are to: "(1) elevate the significance of the financial sector relative to the real sector; (2) transfer income from the real sector to the financial sector; and (3) contribute to increased income inequality and wage stagnation." Financialization may "render the economy prone to risk of debt-deflation and prolonged recession" (Palley 2007: 3).

6. The young mothers in *Open Invoice, Burdensome Existence,* and *3000 Euro* are depicted as struggling with their caregiving roles, and they often wish they did not have children. They mirror women in real life who live in poverty, because women who live as a socioeconomically subordinate group experience shame more often than men (Harris-Perry 2011; Walker 2014: 83; Kokoli 2018: 488).
7. I've lost my laughter/A whole generation is made of weapons and rage.
8. See Schmidt's chapter on the history of Deutsche Bank in this volume.
9. In the context of this novel, as the place where the "villain" resides, Herlaching may take on an ironic, aptronymic meaning as "Herr Lachen" (Mr. Laughter), who retains the ability to laugh as a financial crisis winner.

References

Bauman, Zygmunt. 2004. *Wasted Lives: Modernity and its Outcasts.* Cambridge, UK: Polity Press.

Beck, Zoë. 2013. *Brixton Hill.* Munich: Heyne Verlag.

Berlant, Lauren. 2011. *Cruel Optimism.* Durham, NC: Duke University Press.

Brand, Jobst-Ulrich. 2015. "Geschenktipps: Die Bücher des Jahres." *Focus.de.* 11 May. Retrieved 17 May 2022 from http://www.focus.de/kultur/buecher/tid-20660/geschenktipps-fuer-harte-jungs_aid_579234.html.

Carucci, Ron. 2019. "4 Ways Lying Becomes the Norm at a Company." *Harvard Business Review,* 15 February. Retrieved 17 May 2022 from https://hbr.org/2019/02/4-ways-lying-becomes-the-norm-at-a-company.

Dee, Jonathan. 2017. "The Lives of Others: Does the Social Novel Have a Future?" *Harper's Magazine.* September. Retrieved 17 May 2022 from https://harpers.org/archive/2017/09/the-lives-of-others/.

Dolgan, Christoph. 2013. *Ballastexistenz* [Ballast existence]. Graz and Vienna: Literaturverlag Droschl.

Drees, Jan. 2019. "Neue Ernsthaftigkeit in der Literatur." Deutschlandfunk.de. 19 October. Retrieved 17 May 2022 from https://www.deutschlandfunk.de/frankfurter-buchmesse-neue-ernsthaftigkeit-in-der-literatur-100.html.

Eichhorn, Kristin, ed. 2013. *Neuer Ernst in der Literatur?: Schreibpraktiken in Deutschsprachigen Romanen Der Gegenwart.* Bern, Switzerland: Peter Lang.

Epstein, Gerald. December 2001. "Financialization, Rentier Interests, and Central Bank Policy." Manuscript, Department of Economics, University of Massachusetts, Amherst, MA. Retrieved 17 May 2022 from https://peri.umass.edu/fileadmin/pdf/financial/fin_Epstein.pdf.

Greany, Patrick. 2008. *Untimely Beggar: Poverty and Power from Baudelaire to Benjamin*. Minneapolis: University of Minnesota Press.

Hahne, Peter. 2004. *Schluss mit lustig! Das Ende der Spaßgesellschaft*. Lahr/Schwarzwald: St. Johannis.

Harris-Perry, Melissa V. 2011. *Sister Citizen*. New Haven, CT: Yale University Press.

Hermann, Christoph. 2007. "Neoliberalism in the European Union." *Studies in Political Economy* 79(1): 61–90. DOI: 10.1080/19187033.2007.11675092.

Herterich, Wolfgang. 2018. "Finanz- und Wirtschaftskrise vor 10 Jahren." Landeszentrale für politische Bildung Baden-Württemberg. Retrieved 17 May 2022 from https://www.lpb-bw.de/finanz-und-wirtschaftskrise.

Jungbluth, Rüdiger. 2008. "Rundum sorglose Bank-Manager." *Die Zeit*, 3 April. Retrieved 17 May 2022 from http://www.zeit.de/2008/15/IKB.

Kokoli, Alexandra. 2018. "*Free Lunch with the Stench Wench*: Toward a Synaesthetics of Poverty and Shame in Catherine Hoffmann's Performance." *Hypatia* 33(3) (Summer): 485–99.

Lazzarato, Maurizio. 2012. *The Making of the Indebted Man*. Translated by Joshua David Jordan. South Pasadena, CA: Semiotext(e).

Locke, Richard. 2011. *Critical Children: The Use of Childhood in Ten Great Novels*. New York: Columbia University Press.

Lukács, Georg. 1983. *The Historical Novel*. Translated by Hannah and Stanley Mitchell. Lincoln: University of Nebraska Press (orig. Boston: Beacon Press, 1963).

Mahlke, Inger-Maria. 2013. *Rechnung offen* [Open invoice]. Berlin: Berlin Verlag.

Marx, Karl. 2005. "Comments on James Mill—*Élémens d'économie politique*, Translated by J.T. Parisot—Paris, 1823." In *Karl Marx, Friedrich Engels: Collected Works*. Vol. 3. *Marx and Engels: 1843–1844*. Translated by Jack Cohen. New York: International Publishers. 211–28.

Matthies, Annemarie. 2016. *Spielbälle: Neuverhandlungen der Arbeitswelt im Medium Literatur*. Konstanz: UVK Verlagsgesellschaft.

Melle, Thomas. 2014. *3000 Euro*. Berlin: Rowohlt Berlin Verlag.

Menne, Sarah, Antje Funcke, and Tobias Lentzler. 2020. "Kinderarmut – was heißt es in Deutschland arm aufzuwachsen?" Vielfalt leben – Gesellschaft gestalten blog, Bertelsmann Stiftung, 19 October. Retrieved 17 May 2022 from https://blog.vielfaltleben.de/2020/10/19/kinderarmut-was-heisst-es-in-deutschland-arm-aufzuwachsen/.

Ngai, Sianne. 2007. *Ugly Feelings*. 1st paperback edn. Cambridge, MA and London, UK: Harvard University Press.

Nietzsche, Friedrich. 1994. *On the Genealogy of Morality*, ed. Keith Ansell-Pearson, trans. Carol Diethe. Cambridge: Cambridge University Press.

Palley, Thomas I. 2007. "Financialization: What It Is and Why It Matters." Political Economy Research Institute Working Paper Series, no. 153. Amherst, MA: University of Massachusetts Amherst. 1–38. Retrieved 17 May 2022 from https://scholarworks.umass.edu/peri_workingpapers/135/.

Pilz, André. 2010. *Man Down*. Innsbruck: Haymon Verlag.
Potente, Franka. 2014. *Allmählich wird es Tag* [The day is breaking gradually]. Munich: Piper.
Preisinger, Alexander. 2009. "Ökonomie als Poetologie. Der literarische Realismus des Neuen Kapitalismus." *Literaturkritik.de*, 5 May. Retrieved 17 May 2022 from https://literaturkritik.de/id/13089.
Romeiß-Stracke, Felizitas. 2010. "What Comes After the Fun Principle?" In *Trends and Issues in Global Tourism 2010*, ed. Roland Conrady and Martin Buck, 153–58. New York: Springer.
Salters-Pedneault, Kristalyn. 2020. "Mood Lability and Borderline Personality Disorder." Verywell Mind, 12 April. Retrieved 17 May 2022 from https://www.verywellmind.com/what-is-mood-lability-425304.
Seddig, Katrin. 2010. *Runterkommen* [Coming down]. Reinbek bei Hamburg: Rowohlt.
Seidl, Leonhard M. 2014. *Letzte Ausfahrt Giesing* [Last exit Giesing]. Munich: ars vivendi.
Walker, Robert. 2014. *The Shame of Poverty*. Oxford: Oxford University Press.
Weick, K. E. 1995. *Sensemaking in Organizations*. Thousand Oaks, CA: Sage.
Wenke, Astrid. 2014. *Windmühlen auf dem Wedding* [Windmills on the Wedding]. Berlin: Verlag Krug & Schadenberg.

CHAPTER 7

John von Düffel's *Ego* (2001) as a Seismographic Recorder of the Neoliberal Crisis of the Self

JOHANNA TÖNSING

The monumental financial crisis of 2008 has often been described and perceived as an earthquake (Kahler and Lake 2013: 7). This metaphor does not just contribute innocently to the analysis of an economy otherwise understood abstractly, however; it also serves as an instrument for stakeholders who have a vested interest in maintaining the neoliberal system in its current form. Conceptualizing the financial crisis as a natural disaster such as an earthquake or tsunami brings with it the advantage of allowing probing questions to be avoided about its underlying societal, economic, political, and cultural causes (ibid.: 14). Regarding the financial crisis as an isolated, unpredictable, singular event does not shake our belief in what Joseph Vogl (2010: 25–27) calls "oikodicy": the ideology of the market as beneficial. Since the rise of economic liberalism in the eighteenth century, this ideology has been deeply entrenched in Western societies.

This chapter thus considers the 2008 financial crisis as more of a "turning point," as Kahler and Lake (2013: 11) describe it, rather than as a singular catastrophe. It is seen as the result of fundamental changes and adaptations in an entire economic system, which can only be viewed retrospectively in their full breadth and with a good amount of objectivity. The crisis must also be viewed as an event symptomatic to neoliberalism for it to be discussed from a properly critical perspective. As a new form of capitalism,[1] neoliberalism led to major societal and workplace changes in Germany, which came to fruition in the 1990s.

Boltanski and Chiapello (2003: 80–144) examine the turn from Fordist and Taylorist methods of production toward evermore common flat and flexible hierarchies in current work environments. Their empirical analysis of around sixty influential management texts published in the 1960s, comparing the contents with around the same number of texts from the 1990s, demonstrates that these hierarchies have been flattened; that there has been an increase in individual freedom at the workplace; and that these developments have led to changes in the mechanisms of control. Control is now directed toward the entire subject (worker/employee). This transformation can be traced back to the pressures of globalization, which require factories to produce a wide variety of products in small batches in ever shorter time frames. Boltanski and Chiapello see proof of their central thesis in that capitalism tends to implement critiques and make them useful for its market-driven purposes. Thus, for example, what used to be a subversive criticism, such as that capitalism does not permit the free expression of creativity, self-actualization, or autonomy, has now been turned on its head: these attributes have become a part of the new work environment.

The initially promising revolution in the workplace accompanying the spread of neoliberalism—one need only recall the buzzwords related to self-actualization achieved at work, flexible work schedules, and flat hierarchies—has led to a rise in evermore precarious employment relations, even in Germany with its relatively strict employment laws (Menz 2005: 33–48). These new employment conditions have been accompanied by an increase in pressure on the individual. The dream of a wonderful new working world ended, however, along with the dot-com bubble, at the turn of the twenty-first century at the latest (Biendarra 2011: 73).

These socioeconomic developments, which can only be conceptualized abstractly, nevertheless affect actual, subjective human behavior. Judith Butler examined the interconnectivity between society and the individual, and how their interplay affects the creation of the self, in *The Psychic Life of Power* (1997). Butler describes how an individual's relationship to the self cannot be conceived independently from the predominant discourse in which he or she lives. Identifying with a social norm is the necessary precondition for entering into any relationship with oneself. Only if a person can place an imagined solidity in opposition to his or her mortal, decaying body, can that person gain the self-consciousness of a subject. The "unchangeable consciousness" (ibid.: 48) governs over the changeable part (i.e., the physical body) and, in denying this mutability, gains its status as a thinking self. The formation of the self is thus based on an act of denial, because it ignores the transitory nature of the physical body. The subordination of the subject to the dominant discourse can also be equated with the creation of the self: "Power not only *acts on* a subject but, in a transitive sense, *enacts* the subject into being" (ibid.: 13; italics in original). Along with the conscious part of identity building, there is also a part that eludes our awareness. The dominant norm, in this case, does not precede the creation of the subject, but is instead adopted by the self; only after the self is created can this norm be materialized. The self, then, embodies this norm to a certain degree. Because the creation of the self is not fully predetermined, however, there is always a possibility of creating a self that differs in some ways from the dominant discourse.

Based on Butler's theory of the subject, one can conclude that there must be a connection between any economic developments in Germany and the individual constitution of German citizens as subjects. In fact, since neoliberal economic policies were implemented in Germany in the 1990s, multiple sociological studies have detected the logic of neoliberalism evermore prominently in the ways Germans relate to their self.[2] Although the new neoliberal working conditions were initially depicted positively in literary texts, this perspective shifted toward a more critical assessment as job security and income levels began to decline. Thus, not only German reunification in 1990, but also the advent of the New Economy in a reunified Germany, are considered to mark the start of a new epoch in German literary history. Literary historians categorize texts produced since this time either as welcoming the New Economy and portraying it affirmatively, or as interpreting it from a critical perspective. Some of these literary historians claim that, as employment precarity in the New Economy grew, the critical engagement with it also became more pronounced in literary texts (Probst 2013). This chapter, with a literary text as its focus, thus analyzes one author's strategies of narrating a personal crisis rather than any specific economic crisis, although the personal crisis narrative is assessed as being caused by neoliberal economic developments in German society. The perpetual growth imperative of neoliberalism—considering the fact that natural resources and human capital are finite—inevitably leads to financial crises. Such crises are encoded in the neoliberal system and, on an individual level, the constant working on and improving of the self can, sooner or later, lead to a personal crisis. Individuals furthermore possess limited resources to draw on, and the optimization of one's mental and physical strength and performance cannot be pursued indefinitely.

John von Düffel's 2001 novel *Ego*[3] depicts the protagonist's personal crisis as dependent on neoliberal employment relations. Before the global financial crisis of 2008 occurred, von Düffel revealed the predisposition of the neoliberal system to produce such crises on a microcosmic, individual level. The novel's significance thus lies in its questioning of a financial-political system that, on a personal human level, led to a crisis long before 2008. It is from this personal perspective that *Ego* can be viewed as a seismographic recording instrument of the impending global financial crisis. As a work of literature, the novel displays sensitivity in regard to the subtle effects of these economic developments in Germany. By critiquing neoliberal developments, it moreover functions as an agent in the web of discourse. The text foreshadows the macrocosmic financial crisis that arrived several years later, and at the same time it demonstrates the inescapability of the all-encompassing neoliberal system.

Literary narratives such as von Düffel's novel expose the origins of crisis tendencies in the neoliberal system without getting lost in abstract theories about economic developments. Here, the abstract system of neoliberalism is experienced vicariously by means of a character with whom readers can identify. Inducing empathy for a protagonist as he or she faces a personal crisis may increase the power of literary critiques of neoliberalism, because such texts delve into both rational and irrational levels of perception.

Düffel's protagonist, Philipp, lives in a world in which there is no boundary between work and free time. Philipp works as a business consultant in the New Economy, where the maxims for optimization are not limited to the professional arena, but also define his relationships with women, his friends, and himself. "He knows," in playing the role of a business consultant also in his private life, "what matters: increasing profits and maximizing gains" (Leipprand 2001). His body and the constant improvement of it provide the anchor for his definition of self. This constant work on his body is structured according to capitalist optimization logic (see Balint 2013: 93–107). In the three days of his life narrated in the novel, he anticipates being promoted to a junior partner in his company. After a brief pang of doubt, he eventually accepts the position and acquiesces to the apparent inevitability of the neoliberal system. The novel thus not only depicts a "neoliberal subject," but, with this expression of doubt, also assumes the task of showing a part of Philipp's concept of self that eludes his otherwise conscious identificatory experience. It thus makes the reader aware of the more subtle effects of the neoliberal crisis on its pawns. In this chapter, I assess how and why Düffel depicts Philipp as the prototypical neoliberal subject. I also analyze how the author manages to give voice to that part of Philipp that escapes neoliberal priming, thus undermining the system's apparent hegemony.

Optimizing the Neoliberal Subject

Optimization is an approach to solving economic problems using mathematical methods and models. When speaking of optimization, one refers to an economic problem that is solved sensibly and efficiently by drawing on a linear function equation, and determining the extreme values associated with it.[4] Although originally applied only to the processes of increasing economic efficiency in companies providing goods or services, optimization processes have now diffused into all areas of daily life. As stated above, neoliberalism has dissolved the boundary between work and free time, so the idea that people can optimize all aspects of their lives is now producing a new type of self-conceptualization (Bröckling 2015). In his influential book, *The Entrepreneurial Self: Fabricating a New Type of Subject*, first published on the cusp of the financial crisis in 2007, sociologist Ulrich Bröckling refers to this new concept of the individual as the "entrepreneurial self."

John von Düffel's novel *Ego* supplies a satirical yet not entirely unrealistic paradigm for the transformative inertia of this neoliberal, entrepreneurial self as it narrates its existence. The personal story of the protagonist, Philipp, testifies to the ways the neoliberal economy might become incorporated into a self-image similar to his. Analogous to optimization processes, the quantification of his life forms the basis of the events Philipp narrates, and his actions are motivated by his constant efforts to improve this life. His tangible, physical presence is the main reference point for his self-perception and, at the same time, a command to test the limits of the possible for the future. The novel begins by demonstrating how the depth of Philipp's navel plays a significant role in determining his perception of self-worth:

> Five millimeters more. I can't think about the fact that at first it was seven—or more at the time, when I hadn't started measuring yet! I should actually be really satisfied. But I'm not. I want to get my navel down to zero. I hate staring into a hole when I look at my stomach. A damn pit. Or a dimple, in the meantime. It distracts from my stomach muscles. I absolutely have to work on the depth of my navel. (von Düffel 2001: 9)

Reducing the indentation of his navel means improving himself. In a structural analogy to the optimization process, the goal is constant improvement that can only ever be complete temporarily. The current measurement represents the culmination of a certain amount of labor and, for a short while, conveys a feeling of satisfaction. At the same time, however, an imperative is built into this measured value: more work is needed to improve one's measurements in the future. The current quantification always opens up the possibility of greater progress.

Because *Ego* is narrated autodiegetically (i.e., the story's narrator is also its protagonist), its organizational structure reflects this protagonist's concept of himself. Each chapter relates one day in his life, and each day begins with Philipp measuring the depth of his navel. His state of mind and physical condition can be determined by reading the line chart that shows how they implicitly parallel the narrative (see Figure 7.1). This diagram, illustrating the reduction in Philipp's navel depth, reveals much more than a simple physical quantification. Such a graphic illustration makes it easier to show how his state of mind parallels his physical condition: Philipp's self-esteem rises when the line curves downward, and it goes down when the line moves up. Philipp's actions and feelings are motivated solely by his goal to reduce the depth of his navel as a concrete sign of his level of physical fitness. His ego is constituted by a linear curve produced by the adjustable variables of his physical measurements and their optimization.

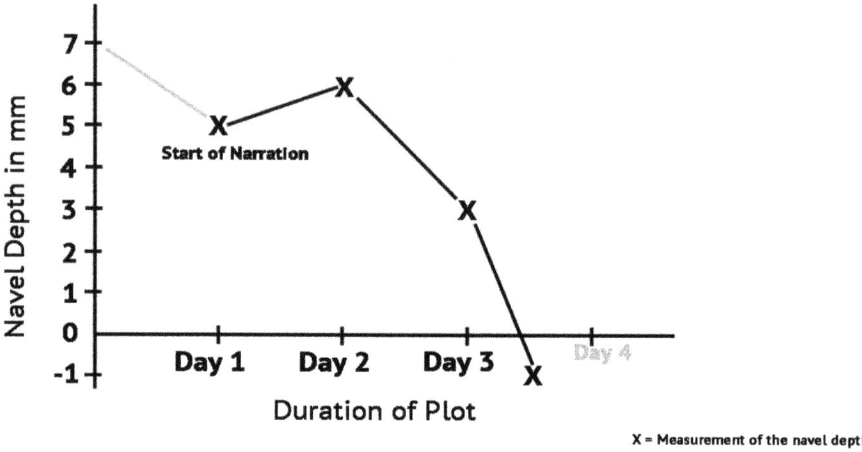

Figure 7.1. Philipp's physical fitness as represented by his navel depth in millimeters. Created by Johanna Tönsing.

The Satirical Enactment of Philipp's Body as the Agonal Setting of Neoliberal Subjectivity

The novel *Ego* takes on the task of making that part of Philipp's self-concept visible that eludes him in his everyday identificatory experiences. In doing so, von Düffel critiques the archetype of the neoliberal subject. Although Philipp's story is told from a first-person perspective, which often encourages the reader's identification and sympathy with him, von Düffel uses various satirical devices to distance his reader from his protagonist. One such device consists of having the protagonist narrate his corporeal reactions to his situation to undermine the man's self-image and the decisions he makes in order to optimize his life. This type of narrative, allowing the narrator's body to "speak" for him and thereby contradict his conscious thoughts, allows for critical reflection on the extreme, occasionally self-destructive actions that neoliberal optimization can prompt a person to take.

Philipp's body in particular becomes a concrete site where neoliberal subjectivity is negotiated. Whatever the first-person narrator consciously states about himself is told in the present tense during the three days he describes. On the second day, however, a past event is described in such a way that its narration suddenly rattles his self-image. When the Weinheimer couple invite him to dinner to thank him for having saved Mr. Weinheimer's life while he was on vacation the year before, Philipp is inadvertently reminded of this earlier incident. Its memory, forced upon him, plays an essential role in the novel, as the later presentation of Philipp's body at dinner would otherwise not appear plausible. My summary of the event below is thus a prerequisite for understanding the analysis that follows. The switch in verb tense here from the present to the simple past tense marks grammatically the deviation from Philipp's usual self-image, which is focused on the presence of his body. The plot interruption takes the form of a flashback that reveals some information about Philipp's self-image, but also allows the reader to draw conclusions about a part of this image that is not represented explicitly. Remarkably, Philipp views the fact that he saved Mr. Weinheimer's life as a failure to live up to the expectations he has of himself:

> Yet whatever I wanted to prove in the water, I was disappointed by my body. I was powerless. It's hard to be smarter than one's own mirror image and not believe what one sees. Just like Mrs. Weinheimer, I had fallen in love with an image of myself, perhaps not as uncritically as she had, but deeply enough that I was blinded. In the ocean, all of a sudden, I was forced to realize that this image did not actually exist. My victory was an illusion, in reality I couldn't do anything. And although this was a comparatively small part of the problem, considering what was at stake, it was not unimportant. It was that part of the problem that prompted the Weinheimer crisis. (von Düffel 2001: 48)

Philipp later learns that this incident had actually been a suicide attempt by Mr. Weinheimer resulting from his awareness that his wife, Isabell, was having an affair with Philipp. After the trip, Mr. Weinheimer comes to symbolize all the thoughts and emotions that Philipp had repressed by means of focusing on his self-image.

Every encounter with Mr. Weinheimer thus becomes a painful reminder of Philipp's awareness of a part of his self that exists outside the hegemony of neoliberal logic. When Philipp tries to explain to his girlfriend (Isabell) why he is disgusted in Weinheimer's presence and thus having difficulty accepting the man's dinner invitation, he is momentarily rendered speechless with emotion:

> "I can't, I can't . . ." It irritates me a little that I'm unable to speak in complete sentences, but at least it sounds sincere. "I – Isabell, I'm disgusted by him. . . . It's just his gratefulness, that . . ." For a moment I hope Isabell understands me without my having to put it in words. I take a deep breath. "It's too – clingy." (Ibid.: 76)

Julia Kristeva's psychoanalytical theory helps explain the disgust that Philipp feels for Mr. Weinheimer (see Kristeva 1982; Suchsland 1992: 121–33; Menninghaus 1999: 516–67). According to Kristeva, the feeling of disgust sets up a barrier between the "I" and the other, where at first this barrier was permeable, and allows the "I" to perceive itself as distinct and coherent. Kristeva's theory also accounts for the fact that Philipp is so overcome by his feeling of disgust that he grasps for words. This emotional state transports the subject back to an earlier developmental level in which his or her language acquisition is not complete. The "clingy" feeling brings back the early childhood experience with bodily secretions, which Kristeva refers to as the "abject" (Kristeva 1982: 1–11). A child begins to be disgusted by sticky or gooey things when it starts to perceive itself as a unified whole. Disgust and the sticky feeling that Mr. Weinheimer evokes in Philipp testify to the self-fracturing power that Weinheimer exerts over Philipp's psyche.

The second day of Philipp's tale marks the first anniversary of the vacation during which he saved Mr. Weinheimer's life. The dinner to which the Weinheimers invite him in order to thank him for his good deed is staged, however, as a satirical attack on Philipp's self-image. His body appears as an entity that, unbeknownst to him, exposes his narrative about himself as an internalization of societal power structures. Philipp's conclusion at the end of the evening—"I vomit surprisingly substantially" (von Düffel 2001: 192)—can thus be understood as a kind of metapoetical clue for readers. The contents of his stomach and its regurgitation, interpreted symbolically, indicate that Philipp's body can be viewed as an entity that speaks. In the following section, I refer consciously to this act as "puking" (*Kotzen*), as opposed to "vomiting" (*sich übergeben*), because the former, cruder term emphasizes more forcefully that this corporeal reaction defies societal conventions. The term "to puke" furthermore conveys the connotation of "to puke one's guts out" (*sich auskotzen*), which, in German, refers to the act of expressing criticism in a way that lies outside normative social constraints. In research studies on literary texts, it is, moreover, common practice today to use the less cultivated term so as to emphasize the drastic nature of the act, and the significance it carries in its interpretation.[5]

The contents of his stomach consist in part of Philipp's breakfast. In the morning on that same day, Philipp had an appointment with his new boss and hoped to be promoted to a junior partner at his firm. Mr. Weinheimer asks Philipp at dinner about the results of this meeting:

> "He's making it suspenseful." Weinheimer glances meaningfully at Isabell, but she shrugs it off. "If a junior partnership had come out of your breakfast, we would have heard about it before lunch."
>
> I look up from my plate, Isabell and Weinheimer watch me expectantly. I feel a lot like puking. "It was . . .," I have to swallow twice, "it was really heavy [*mächtig*]." (Ibid.: 185)

The wordplay here with the double meaning of "heavy" (*mächtig*)—as "fatty" and also as "powerful" (*mit Macht ausgestattet*)—is a premonition of the ambivalent meaning that Philipp's later vomiting takes on.

Because of its high fat content, Philipp's breakfast breaks with his usual eating habits. This infraction of his strict diet can be interpreted as his otherwise adhering to the logic of optimization, and thus his puking can be seen as his body's rebellion against the fatty breakfast food. But Philipp ate the fatty breakfast for opportunistic, careerist reasons. From this perspective, the purging of his breakfast might be viewed as an unconscious "disembodiment" of the neoliberal ideology. The otherwise rigorously disciplined body, acting independent of conscious self-control, is made to speak in protest of this treatment by means of involuntary regurgitation.

The double coding of Philipp's vomiting is reinforced by the evening meal served by the Weinheimers, which also takes on symbolic meaning:

> Weinheimer leans over the table and fills us up. A slap of ash-gray broth lands in my soup plate, sprinkled with chunks of crumbled meat, thumbnail-sized mussels and a crab claw. "I kept the soup as fat-free as possible and refrained from adding any cream at all. Of course, a few extra fat percentages would complement the flavor of the fish better. But like this, I think, just with the spices, it tastes like the ocean. I mean, really: the ocean. Not like anything else. Bon appetit!" . . . Weinheimer shovels entire fish cadavers into himself. (Ibid.: 185)

Weinheimer made the fish soup to commemorate Philipp's lifesaving act, keeping it low-fat to help Philipp stick to his diet. From this perspective, yet another ambivalence can be found in Philipp's symbolic regurgitation of it. On the surface, this purge eliminates the burdensome memory of this past event. On a deeper level, however, the fish confronts Philipp with a physicality he cannot control: it affects a part of his body that is unable to be disciplined according to neoliberal logic, and thus eludes conscious self-control. This subtextual reading of regurgitation as rebellion is plausible, considering the fact that Philipp's nausea becomes more intense when Isabell and Weinheimer discuss his anticipated promotion to junior partner:

> I slowly let the spoon sink back down. I can't eat any more.
>
> "It's a difficult decision, of course," says Weinheimer, as if he were in my position. "I mean, junior partner, that would be a career leap! But what about your private life? Not to mention physical activity! The question is really—"
>
> "You can't talk about having a private life," interrupts Isabell. . . . "I think the concept of having a 'private life' is dubious. As if one had several lives to choose from!" (Ibid.: 186)

Philipp becomes nauseated, quite literally, from this analysis of his future job and the accompanying neoliberal elimination of the boundary between work and free time that it would entail. The text enacts an intensification of this nausea, connecting it directly to Philipp's thoughts about becoming a junior partner in his firm: the initial feeling of nausea is first experienced as a "shudder of disgust" (ibid.: 188), then it becomes a "column of vomit up to his tonsils," and, later, a stomach pumping up bile (ibid.: 189). Philipp pukes at the height of the conversation, when Weinheimer—who represents Philipp's repressed memories—adds an existential meaning to the neoliberal optimization imperative:

> "You think you're not like that, don't you? You think you don't just live for power and an annual salary. You like losers, you can also just laugh and look past people who show their weakness; that's what you think, don't you, Isabell?"
>
> I'm thinking only about her stomach. "But you would never want to have children with a man whom you consider a loser, a genetic dud. Would you? People can delude themselves however they want, but the fun stops when they get down to the chromosomes!"
>
> I really wanted Weinheimer to change the topic fast. I'm already in the REM-phase, when Isabell's stomach suddenly starts bloating up. At first, I think I still have it under control. But it keeps swelling, and her navel turns itself inside out like a bony little finger pressing from the inside against her abdominal wall.
>
> "When the body makes the decision, Isabell," Weinheimer lowers his voice, and it sounds as if he is going to threaten her, but he looks at me as he says, "when biology, the instinct, strikes, it always decides in favor of whoever is strongest. That's the way we're wired, let's be honest, that's who knows how many thousands of years of evolution." (Ibid.: 192)

Weinheimer turns the pursuit of professional success into a natural human predisposition by depicting it as a physical instinct. He draws on the theory of evolution to argue that the way self-optimizers constitute themselves as subjects must be a natural process.

Michel Foucault describes how arguments based on the theory of evolution are often used to make optimization discourses appear to be based on nature, and that this line of argumentation contributes to how the process of subject-formation is governed:

> And as soon as a society poses itself the problem of the improvement of its human capital in general, it is inevitable that the problem of the control, screening, and improvement of the human capital of individuals, as a function of unions and consequent reproduction, will become actual, or at any rate, called for. So, the political problem of the use of genetics arises in terms of the formation, growth, accumulation, and improvement of human capital. (Foucault 2008: 228)

Weinheimer's argument fits Foucault's conclusion; if Philipp were to stop optimizing himself, he would not only lose his job, but also his girlfriend and, with her, his place in human evolution:

> "Listen, Isabell,"—it's Weinheimer speaking for me, I close my eyes and concentrate on the image I have of her stomach—"let's be honest, you couldn't

> stand to be with a man who failed at the decisive point in his life." (von Düffel 2001: 191)

Weinheimer's remarks cause Philipp to sink into a daydream in which he imagines Isabell to be pregnant. Because he only possesses the ability to control his own body, he is afraid of Isabell having a child inside her womb that "presses against her abdominal wall" (ibid.: 192) and thereby assumes control over her body. Weinheimer's comments thus signify to Philipp in many ways a loss of control. His words also grant a Darwinian evolutionary meaning to Isabell's desire to have a child—though Philipp does not find out until later in the novel that she is actually pregnant—and thereby intensify the pressure Philipp feels to optimize his body. It is not surprising that Philipp, after hearing these words, must literally turn his insides out and "throw up," for the discrepancy is too great between the demands made on him and his ability to work even more on improving himself. His character flaw of misrecognizing himself becomes a metaphor that he only begins to recognize "dimly . . . in the wastewater" (ibid.: 192), before he pukes and his body forces him to acknowledge that part of himself that did not fit into his prior identificatory experience.

The act of vomiting anticipates on a physical level what Philipp recognizes consciously on the day after the dinner party: a significant part of his self does not fit the logic of optimization of which he has become an object. At this point, he considers not accepting the position of junior partner at his firm, because it would destroy what remains of the "human" in him. The sudden awareness that he had misrecognized his former self-image does not lead to positive consequences, however. When he attempts to tell his girlfriend Isabell about his career doubts, she responds as if she were a mouthpiece of neoliberalism:

> "But you know as well as I do that there are no more jobs where you can just let the door fall shut and lock automatically behind you. Every position that requires at least some responsibility demands a certain amount of involvement and commitment." (Ibid.: 236)

Isabell demonstrates to Philipp that it is pointless to resist neoliberal imperatives. She is the one who drives him to the interview with his future boss, despite the doubts he has regarding his identity, and, in the end, forces him to continue working on himself and his career. It is no coincidence that Philipp abruptly realizes during the ride to his office building that Weinheimer had been trying to commit suicide when Philipp saved his life:

> Suddenly I get it. "Isabell"— I didn't notice this before—"he didn't go swimming yesterday, the party was a year ago yesterday. The actual anniversary is today. Today is the date he died!" Do I really have to tell you what that means? "He'll try it again." (Ibid.: 209)

Seen in the context of the association of Weinheimer with Philipp's prior repression of a part of his unconscious self, it is credible that Philipp finally realizes during the ride to his promotion interview that Weinheimer had wanted to commit suicide. That Isabell throws her photographs of Weinheimer out the car window can also be understood symbolically. At this point in the narrative, Philipp not only had the opportunity to get out of the car and once again prevent Weinheimer from attempting suicide; in a metaphorical sense, he could also have exited from the neoliberal system and thereby avoided further repressing those parts of his personality that do not accord with the perpetual process of self-optimization. But this window of opportunity to prevent two types of self-destruction is thwarted. During the ride to his promotion to junior partner at his firm, Philipp's thoughts jell ultimately into the recognition that the neoliberal system in which he finds himself is inescapable, because it has already permeated all areas of his life.

After Philipp assumes the position as junior partner, von Düffel shifts the narrative style from a first-person to a third-person perspective. Philipp now observes himself from an external viewpoint, thus making his resulting feeling of self-alienation apparent. This switch illustrates how much like a marionette a person can become when captured in such a hermetically sealed system. It is not just a coincidence that Philipp comments on his promotion with the following words: "He is ready to accept his death sentence, the sooner, the better" (ibid.: 228). The association he makes between his promotion and a death sentence reveals once again the important place in his psyche that Weinheimer's suicide occupies—successful on his second attempt a year later, the day after the dinner party. In sum, one can say that the novel *Ego* narrates a professional promotion within the neoliberal system in such a way that its violent dimensions are revealed. This violence consists of the compulsion to throttle those parts of one's self that cannot be integrated into the framework of optimization.

Although the novel depicts a protagonist who can and does recognize his self-alienation, this crisis of the self does not lead to a reorientation of his self-perception and behavior, but instead produces the opposite result: Philipp quickly shifts back to his former state of mind, accepting optimization's maxims unconditionally. After a brief period of feeling alienated from his self, he stifles his short-lived rebellion and begins to overidentify with the system whose apparent insubvertibility he had come to recognize:

> One millimeter! I put the measuring tape on several times and adjust myself to the correct position in the mirror—exactly one millimeter, I'll stick with that. And strictly speaking, it's not exactly the depth of my navel, but instead the height of my navel lip that curls in a slight curve over the muscles covering my stomach. And with that, I've not only reached my goal, but I'm beyond zero. My navel is sublime! It's especially easy to see when it's freshly shaved. (Ibid.: 238)

Philipp has not only reached a navel depth of zero, but he has also exceeded his own expectations of his performance. The elimination of all that was human about himself has turned him into an optimization machine.

The novel *Ego* illustrates the neoliberal strategy that Bröckling describes as taking that which starts as a critique of the system, incorporating it, and thereby using it to perpetuate its existence. This strategy immunizes the system against attack. Von Düffel additionally draws attention to the failure of the universal remedy of emancipating workers from the alienation from their labor, as Karl Marx (1959) described it, in the twentieth century by promising them new freedoms such as the aforementioned flexible schedules, flat heirarchies, and the ability to achieve self-actualization at work. Contrary to such promises, work has not become an extension of free time, but instead turned into the reverse: free time has become work. *Ego* attempts to come to terms with the neoliberal crisis of the subject and his/her relationship to labor on a personal level by telling the story of its systemic violence, which compels individuals to forcefully stifle certain aspects of their psyches.

Ego can thus be considered a parody of a *Bildungsroman*. Although it is a "narrative depiction of the path of a central figure through mistakes and crises to self-discovery and active integration into society" (Jacobs 1997: 230), it inverts the main premise of this genre. Whereas the *Bildungsroman* is based firmly on the idea that the individual acts independently and freely, *Ego* posits that the self can no longer be constituted outside the confines of the optimizing logic of neoliberalism. From the "complete development of the individual out of all available possibilities" and the "emancipation from immaturity" (Delhey 2016: 296), von Düffel's novel offers the bitter realization that contemporary concepts of education and self-actualization are predicated on the integration of the individual into the neoliberal system. Instead of presenting the intellectual and spiritual growth of an individual, von Düffel shows a self that is forced to fit into this system.

The great number of intertextual references to the 1991 novel *American Psycho* by Bret Easton Ellis, in particular, allow von Düffel's text to bear witness to a discursive history that, in its global dispersal of neoliberal logic, has come to permeate the private sphere. In Europe, apparently, the spread of neoliberalism has initiated an ever-increasing alienation of the subject from his/her self. The parallels between the protagonists in both of these novels, Philipp and Ellis's investment banker/serial killer Patrick Bateman, indicate that, despite their strong social-welfare systems, European countries have allowed neoliberal logic increasingly to spread to the private sphere, where it can produce disastrous consequences for those who fall victim to it. Friedhelm Marx thus calls Philipp the "German Psycho" (Marx 2010: 108).

Bateman and Philipp resemble each other in their search for an identity outside neoliberal maxims and suppression of something inside themselves. Philipp does not prevent Weinheimer, and all he represents, from carrying out his second suicide attempt. Bateman becomes a serial killer, taking out his anger on others at being unable to develop a self, outside the confines of Wall Street and its optimization logic. Both are cogs in the wheels of a real-existing neoliberal system. Bateman is a member of the 1980s Wall Street scene while Ronald Reagan is implementing economic reforms in the United States, cutting taxes and eroding the power of workers' unions (see Voßmann 2002: 116–29; Vöing 2013: 365–82; Mitterer 2016: 28–29). Philipp participates in the developing New Economy of the late 1990s and early 2000s in united Germany. Both incorporate the optimization logic of their times, and suffer from an internal emptiness. They are united in that both enter into a "symbiosis" of "body and career," in which "the production of beauty" is considered "economic capital" (Balint 2017: 187). Neither can escape from the neoliberal society in which he lives. As a member of the 1980s Wall Street, New York milieu, Patrick Bateman is depicted as a subject of the newly emerging turbo-capitalism who appears not to exist as an individual outside the optimization logic that dominates his life. Bateman exists, like Philipp, only as a performing body:

> I worked out heavily at the gym after leaving the office today but the tension has returned, so I do ninety abdominal crunches, a hundred and fifty push-ups, and then I run in place for twenty minutes while listening to the new Huey Lewis CD. I take a hot shower and afterwards use a new facial scrub by Caswell-Massey and a body wash by Greune, then a body moisturizer by Lubriderm and a Neutrogena facial cream. (Ellis 1991: 76)

Like Philipp, Bateman carefully quantifies his performance at the fitness studio as it progresses ("I spent two hours at the gym today and can now complete two hundred abdominal crunches in less than three minutes" [ibid.: 180]) and identifies with this progress. The optimization of his body duplicates the Wall Street logic of the emerging modern financial capitalism of the 1980s, and marks the diffusion of the economy into private life in the United States. The disappearance of individuality behind commodities (Scheck 2019) characterizes the internalization of consumer society in American neoliberalism. This comparison with Ellis's novel shows how the neoliberal crisis has spread, from its source in the United States, worldwide.

Johanna Tönsing is a Postdoctoral Fellow at the University of Paderborn. She holds a PhD in German Literature, and wrote her dissertation on "Self-Optimization as a Figure of Subjectivity in Contemporary German Literature." Her postdoctoral project, "Gender-Related Experiences in

Human Zoos around 1900 – Reconstructing Unheard Voices of Colonial and Migration History," is situated within the fields of postcolonial studies, gender studies, and the poetics of knowledge.

Notes

1. Deleuze (1992) speaks of a substantial mutation in the capitalist system that has taken place since the end of World War II. A major characteristic of this mutation is the transition from the factory to the corporation. Workers are now no longer controlled by administrators, but oversee themselves instead. This type of control is thus "continuous" and "without limit" (ibid.: 6).
2. See Tönsing (2021: 25–61) for an overview of this research.
3. The novel *Ego* has to date not been translated into English; all direct quotes below were translated by Twark.
4. It is interesting that the term "optimization" is only used by mathematicians when calculating the profitability of business decisions. They do not generally use it to solve minimization or maximization problems in linear function equations (Merz and Wüthrich 2013: 512).
5. See, for example, the chapter "Zum Kotzen" in the volume on emotions in literary texts edited by Alexandra Pontzen (2005: 74–97), as well as the special issue of the *Zagreber Germanistischen Beiträge* titled "Schöne Scheiße. Konfigurationen des Skatologischen in Literatur und Sprache" (Breuer 2018).

References

Balint, Iuditha. 2013. "Innenraum und Oberfläche: Inkorporierte Ökonomie in Werken von John von Düffel, Ernst-Wilhelm Händler, Ewald Palmetshofer und Elfriede Jelinek." In *KörperÄsthetiken: Allegorische Verkörperungen als ästhetisches Prinzip*, ed. Cornelia Logemann, Miriam Oesterreich, and Julia Rüthemann, 93–107. Bielefeld: transcript Verlag.

———. 2017. "Die Frage literaturhistorischer Genrezuordnungen. Erika Runges *Bottroper Protokolle* (1968) und Kathrin Rögglas *Wir schlafen nicht* (2004)." In *Kathrin Röggla*, ed. Iuditha Balint, Tanja Nusser, and Rolf Parr, 15–32. Munich: edition text + review in the Richard Boorberg Verlag.

Biendarra, Anke. 2011. "Prekäre neue Arbeitswelt: Narrative der New Economy." In *Das erste Jahrzehnt: Narrative und Poetiken des 21. Jahrhunderts*, ed. Julia Schöll and Johanna Bohley, 69–82. Würzburg: Königshausen & Neumann GmbH.

Boltanski, Luc, and Eve Chiapello. 2003. *Der neue Geist des Kapitalismus*. Konstanz: UVK.

Breuer, Ingo. 2018. "Schöne Scheiße. Konfigurationen des Skatologischen in Literatur und Sprache." Special Issue. *Zagreber Germanistische Beiträge* 27.

Bröckling, Ulrich. 2015. *The Entrepreneurial Self: Fabricating a New Type of Subject*, trans. Steven Black. Los Angeles: Sage Publications (orig. *Das unternehmerische*

Selbst: Soziologie einer Subjektivierungsform. Frankfurt am Main: Suhrkamp, 2007).
Butler, Judith. 1997. *The Psychic Life of Power: Theories in Subjection*. Stanford, CA: Stanford University Press.
Deleuze, Gilles. 1992. "Postscript on the Societies of Control." *October* 59 (Winter): 3–7.
Delhey, Yvonne. 2016. "Was heißt Bildung des Individuums? Judith Schalanskys *Der Hals der Giraffe*." In *Der Bildungsroman im literarischen Feld. Neue Perspektiven auf eine Gattung*, ed. Katrin Dennerlein and Elisabeth Böhm, 283–302. Berlin: De Gruyter.
Düffel, John von. 2001. *Ego: Roman*. Munich: dtv.
Ellis, Bret Easton. 1991. *American Psycho*. New York: Vintage Open Market.
Foucault, Michel. 2008. *The Birth of Biopolitics: Lectures at the Collège de France 1978–1979*, trans. Graham Burchell. London: Palgrave Macmillan.
Jacobs, Jürgen. 1997. "Bildungsroman." In *Reallexikon der deutschen Literaturwissenschaft*. Vol. 1. Ed. Klaus Weimar, 230–33. Berlin: De Gruyter.
Kahler, Miles, and David A. Lake. 2013. "Introduction: Anatomy of Crisis: The Great Recession and Political Change." In *Politics in the New Hard Times: The Great Recession in Comparative Perspective*, ed. Miles Kahler and David A. Lake, 1–24. Ithaca, NY: Cornell University Press.
Kristeva, Julia. 1980. *Pouvoirs de l'horreur. Essai sur l'abjection*. Paris: Seuil (English: *Powers of Horror: An Essay on Abjection*, trans. Leon S. Roudiez. New York: Columbia University Press, 1982).
Leipprand, Eva. 2001. "Fitnessprosa. John von Düffel über den modernen Helden." *Literaturkritik.de. Rezensionsforum* 10(3). Retrieved 13 June 2019 from https://literaturkritik.de/id/4167.
Marx, Friedhelm. 2010. "Körper, Kunst, Bildung. John von Düffels Roman EGO." In *Familien erzählen. Das literarische Werk John von Düffels*, ed. Stephanie Catani and Friedhelm Marx, 99–112. Göttingen: Wallstein Verlag.
Marx, Karl. 1959. *Economic and Philosophic Manuscripts of 1844*, trans. Martin Milligan, rev. Dirk J. Struik. Moscow: Progress Publishers.
Menninghaus, Winfried. 1999. *Ekel. Theorie und Geschichte einer starken Empfindung*. Frankfurt am Main: Suhrkamp.
Menz, Georg. 2005. "Auf Wiedersehen, Rhineland Model: Embedding Neoliberalism in Germany." In *Internalizing Globalization: The Rise of Neoliberalism and the Decline of National Varieties of Capitalism*, ed. Susanne Soederberg, Georg Menz, and Philip G. Cerny, 33–48. London: Palgrave Macmillan.
Merz, Michael, and Mario V. Wüthrich. 2013. *Mathematik für Wirtschaftswissenschaftler. Die Einführung mit vielen ökonomischen Beispielen*. Munich: Vahlen.
Mitterer, Nicola. 2016. *Das Fremde in der Literatur. Zur Grundlegung einer responsiven Literaturdidaktik*. Bielefeld: transcript.
Pontzen, Alexandra. 2005. "Zum Kotzen." In *EGB. Emotionales Gesetzbuch. Dekalog*

der Gefühle, ed. Rainer Maria Kiesow and Martin Korte, 74–97. Cologne: Böhlau.

Probst, Inga. 2013. "Überwindet Arbeit alles oder wird sie überwunden? *Narrative der Arbeit* – aktuelle Forschungsperspektiven eines virulenten Themas." In *Omnia vincit labor?: Narrative der Arbeit—Arbeitskulturen in medialer Reflexion*," ed. Torsten Erdbrügger, Ilse Nagelschmidt, and Inga Probst, 17–48. Berlin: Frank & Timme.

Scheck, Dennis. 2017. "Diesem Yuppie sind die Menschen wurst." *Die Welt online*, 10 May 2017. Retrieved 22 January 2019 from https://www.welt.de/kultur/literarischewelt/article164347047/Diesem-Yuppie-sind-die-Menschen-wurst.html.

Suchsland, Inge. 1992. *Julia Kristeva zur Einführung*. Hamburg: Junius.

Tönsing, Johanna. 2021. *"Hallo, wer spricht? Hallo, wer spricht!" Über die Poetik der Selbstoptimierung in deutschsprachiger Gegenwartsliteratur*. Bielefeld: Aisthesis.

Vogl, Joseph. 2010. *Das Gespenst des Kapitals*. 2nd edn, Zurich: diaphanes Verlag.

Vöing, Nerea. 2013. "Zwischen Affirmation und Leerstelle. Richard Sennetts Theorem des 'Drift' in der Gegenwartsliteratur." In *Repräsentationen von Arbeit. Transdisziplinäre Analysen und künstlerische Produktionen*, ed. Susanna Brogi, Carolin Freier, Ulf Freier-Otten, and Katja Hartosch, 365–82. Bielefeld: transcript.

Voßmann, Ursula. 2002. *Paradise Dreamed: Die Hölle der 80er Jahre in Bret Easton Ellis Roman American Psycho*. Essen: Die blaue Eule.

PART III

German “Exceptionalism” in Contemporary European Crisis Situations

CHAPTER 8

Germany's Compromises

The Impact of Crisis Narratives on the European Central Bank and Euro Governance

SARA KONOE

The European Central Bank (ECB) was established to unite currencies and monetary policies for EU member states that adopted the euro. When the Economic Monetary Union and the ECB were formed in the 1990s, price stability became an absolute priority for the ECB's monetary policy principles, upon Germany's insistence. This stability could not be compromised for other economic policy purposes, as stipulated in the Treaty on the Functioning of the European Union (Article 127).[1] In the pre-euro crisis years, indeed since its establishment, the ECB had adhered to these conservative monetary policies, which were considered of paramount necessity for stable management of the eurozone. The euro crisis, however, starting in 2010, induced changes in the ECB's roles that expanded its ability to stabilize the economy. Which conflicts did this crisis give rise to among eurozone countries? How did the crisis influence the policy community in Germany—a nation that had initially expressed the strongest reservations about expanding the ECB's role—to tolerate a wider discretion for the ECB to implement financial stabilization policies in the crisis's wake?

When the 2007/8 global financial crisis and the 2010 euro crisis hit Europe and the eurozone, it became clear that constraining average rates of inflation would hardly be sufficient to maintain the region's financial stability. The 2007/8 global financial crisis was perceived to be, and also described as, more or less externally driven, although risky European bank investments in the United States were, in fact, one of its core causes. The EU and its member states had failed to monitor their large banks' activities abroad, and, in response to the crisis, the ECB made expanded liquidity available to these banks in order to keep European financial markets afloat. The euro crisis erupted soon after, and this crisis was also narrated by creditors, including the German government, as an event that had been externally driven, resulting from problems with the debtors' fiscal management outside the creditors' territorial borders. Thus, the eruption of the crisis per se did not provide enough reason for creditors to accept policy changes that could lead to a relaxation of lending conditions. Yet, according to critics, in the lead-up to the crisis, French and German banks had also financed unsustainable consumption and investment booms in eurozone periphery states such as Greece and Spain. From this perspective, the crisis must also be viewed as a failure of creditor governments for having allowed their banks to permeate periphery countries' booming markets beyond a sustainable level. Regardless of divided opinions on who was to blame for the crisis, it became clear that timely action was necessary to regain stability and foster economic growth in the eurozone. When the ECB injected further liquidity into European banks, it assumed the role of a de facto *lender of last resort* by expanding its long-term lending operations and securities purchases. It even went so far as to announce its unlimited commitment to purchasing government bonds issued by periphery states under prescribed conditions.

According to Europeanization literature, in the *uploading* process—that is, the phase of integrating economic policy preferences from member states to the European level—policy outcomes do not solely reflect or sum up national preferences and interests at the European level. These national preferences and interests are subject to changes resulting from economic or political shocks and the acquisition of knowledge, and it is essential to identify European factors that induce policy learning and affect domestic preferences (Bulmer and Radaelli 2013: 373). Thus, analyzing how the euro crisis unfolded, along with how European institutions functioned in attempting to manage it, is essential for understanding the changes in member state practices and narratives, including those of Germany concerning the management of the crisis.

In examining changes in ECB practices and narratives during and after the euro crisis, the first section of this chapter assesses the divergent reactions of the German government and German ECB representatives to these changes. The context in which the ECB accelerated its active policies of striving for financial stability beyond price stability is also taken into consideration here.

The second section analyzes underlying economic narratives and policy preferences in Germany's crisis responses during and immediately following the euro crisis. It first discusses various explanations for the euro crisis, and illustrates how a particular narrative, called the "moral hazard frame," initially became dominant in forming crisis responses in Germany. Problems in focusing on the crisis from such a frame are also discussed here. These two sections expand the arguments made in the Introduction of this book that a particular perspective on crisis causes and responses, along with the subsequent narrative developed to explain the events as they unfolded, affected Germany's and Europe's reactions to the crisis.

The third section looks at how the positions of the German Bundesbank and government evolved with respect to the role of the ECB, as well as how the euro crisis influenced Germany's general policy direction and stance on this role. The ECB's efforts to defend the euro's credibility, along with other eurozone members' demands for the ECB to expand its scope, eventually convinced Germany to accept the ECB's widened discretion during this period of crisis management, despite its original preference for giving the ECB a narrowly focused mandate pertaining to price stability. Such a compromise became possible as part of broader agreements on post-crisis euro governance reforms that incorporated Germany's demands in the handling of the euro crisis. As this section shows, German chancellor Angela Merkel directed such compromises, with extreme hesitancy at the beginning of the crisis, by associating the government's new stance with ordoliberal rhetoric to appease the German public. Overall, this chapter focuses on how an expanded ECB liquidity provision was tolerated politically, while policy stringency was implemented in exchange, as concomitant ways to reform euro governance. In spite of the alleged limitations of such crisis responses, new narratives concerning euro governance served to broaden the economic policy options for eurozone countries by enabling concessions from Germany.

The Euro Crisis and the ECB's Changing Practices

The policymaking environment for financial supervision and crisis management in the European Union was transformed during the 2007/8 financial crisis and the 2010 euro crisis. This transformation was partially driven by the ECB's efforts to fill a power vacuum, as the euro governance body lacked crisis management schemes, and serious disagreements in the Council of the European Union inhibited timely and decisive actions. As Verdun (2017: 214–17) argues, the ECB presidents Jean-Claude Trichet (2003–11) and Mario Draghi (2011–19) played a vital role in recovering trust and liquidity in the financial markets. Trichet and Draghi lengthened the maturity period for longer-term refinancing operations, the ECB's three-month lending to banks in normal times.[2] They also implemented the Securities Market Programme from 2010 to 2012, which enabled the ECB to purchase bonds, especially sovereign bonds, to ensure depth and liquidity in debt securities markets. Draghi went even further in 2012 by permitting the ECB to engage in outright monetary transactions—that is, unlimited purchases of government bonds from the secondary market. Such purchases were solely contingent on the issuing countries' compliance with the rules of the European Stability Mechanism (ESM)—a newly built post-crisis institution for emergency lending to euro member states. After these two ECB presidents made these bold moves, the

Governing Council of the European System of Central Banks and its member states followed suit. In addition, the ECB decided to publish abridged accounts of the Governing Council's meetings to enable greater public transparency. This change occurred in 2014–15, right before a quantitative easing program began in March 2015 with the ECB's commitment to purchase large assets from commercial banks to provide sufficient financial liquidity and enhance economic growth (European Central Bank 2014a, 2014b).

During the euro crisis, as analyzed by Schmidt (2016: 1039–42), the ECB changed its discourse and policy emphasis from one of credibility, in which it had adhered strictly to measures that contained inflation, to one of stability, to legitimize a bond-buying program and bring financial turmoil under control. Although Draghi (2012a) never claimed overtly that the ECB would function as a lender of last resort, his pledge in London on 26 July 2012 that "[w]ithin our mandate, the ECB is ready to do whatever it takes to preserve the euro" was perceived as a commitment to functioning as a lender of last resort, thus calming the panicked market. The ECB's stance thus shifted under Draghi's leadership, although its Governing Council members held intensely divided opinions about this shift. It is noteworthy that the president of the Bundesbank (Germany's national central bank), Jens Weidman, was the only ECB Governing Council member to vote against the ECB engaging in outright monetary transactions (McBride and Alessi 2015). The Bundesbank's opposition was based on its concerns about monetary finance (the central bank's financing of government debt), which contradicted the Treaty and could lead to inflation.[3] In response, the ECB and proponents of the ECB's expanded role in maintaining financial stability argued that bonds purchased from a secondary market (a trading market) instead of an issuance market could not be considered a form of monetary finance (Grauwe 2018: 184–85).

In 2012, ECB leaders claimed that its new administrative policy and expanded range of operations could ensure the proper conditions and environment for its core mandate—maintaining price stability. For example, in a September 2012 speech, Draghi emphasized that the ECB had been addressing "financial fragmentation," which created different costs of credit (i.e., borrowing costs) among eurozone member states, as such divergences were often "larger than justified by individual credit risk." These measures aimed to preserve the "singleness of monetary policy," and thereby improve investor confidence, which would ultimately lead to "greater overall stability" for the euro area as a whole. Draghi asserted:

> In exceptional times, regaining stability sometimes requires exceptional measures. We cannot always look to the past for answers. We may need to take new steps to achieve longstanding goals . . . For the ECB, new steps have been needed to maintain price stability in the face of fragmented financial markets. These new steps are not a departure from our mandate . . . In the current

circumstances, the greatest risk to stability is not action, but *inaction*. This is why the ECB has acted. (Draghi 2012b; emphasis in original)

As for the ECB's undertaking of quantitative easing in 2015, Draghi stressed its effectiveness in supporting demand for credit and investment, and increasing potential output, as seen in his speech at the hearing at the European Parliament's Economic and Monetary Affairs Committee. After explaining that this operation could serve price stability by elevating low inflation rates close to 2 percent, Draghi stated:

> [T]he expansive potential of the monetary policy measures that had been decided between June and October was seen as uncertain. This was because they were largely dependent on banks' own decision to borrow Eurosystem funds and lend them on to their customers . . . Therefore, the monetary impulse had to be reinforced . . . Our interventions have accelerated a trend that had been evident [for] some time. A steady process of re-integration across financial markets and jurisdictions had been under way . . . What is new today, however, is that lower interest rates in capital markets are increasingly being transmitted through the entire financial intermediation chain . . . In the short-run, this should sustain the demand for credit and investment . . . In the longer-term perspective, this will increase potential output. (Draghi 2015)

Similarly, the ECB's new policy direction—associated with its traditional mandate, price stability—was confirmed by several studies that compared or analyzed new narratives created by the ECB or other central banks in response to recent financial crises. According to Nerghes et al. (2015: 7–8, 13–18), who conducted a semantic network analysis based on ECB press releases from 2006 to 2013, structural differences can be found in the use of language before and after the euro crisis began.[4] Two dimensions were calculated based on keywords mapped to show their roles in the semantic network. The total degree centrality of each keyword ("the number of other nodes incident to the focal node") was an indicator of popularity, and the betweenness centrality of each keyword ("the frequency with which a particular node is on the geodesic path between any other two nodes in the network") was an indicator of connectivity. After the euro crisis started and deepened in spring 2010, the word *growth* increased somewhat in popularity and increased significantly in connectivity, which could mean that a desire for greater economic growth prompted connections to be forged between otherwise disparate issues and measures during the euro crisis. By contrast, the word *inflation* had low connectivity during the euro crisis, after a short-term increase in the word's connectivity during the global financial crisis that preceded the euro crisis. In the face of the global financial crisis, the word *inflation* was possibly invoked to defend the ECB's various responses and attitudes. After the eruption of the euro crisis, this word no longer played a significant role in connecting various issues. This shift in language use accords with the way the ECB refocused its objectives beyond its conventional priority to price stability.[5]

Regarding central bankers' use of languages and narratives, Braun points out post-crisis shifts across the major affected countries, including those in the eurozone. Before the crisis (and for some years after it had erupted), the perception of money as a quantity—the quantity theory of money, the gist of monetarism—had been strategically reinforced by the ECB. This strategic emphasis was meant to enhance the credibility of the central bank by assuming that it could effectively protect the value of money against inflation. The quantity theory of money does not distinguish, however, between outside money (cash and commercial bank reserves in central bank accounts) and inside money (money created in a general market by private bank lending), and it wrongly assumes that money is created and controlled exclusively by a central bank (Braun 2016: 1073–80). This discourse began to shift with the massive crisis-driven increase in liquidity provision, facilitated by open market operations and quantitative easing programs. As monetarist assumptions made people believe (with a critical eye) that such liquidity provision gave banks "free money" and could spark the fear of inflation, central banks, including the ECB, the Federal Reserve, and the Bank of England, began to change their discourse or open up new communication channels to the public (ibid.: 1080–83) in order to correct such misperceptions or misunderstandings.

The Bank of England, for example, "let the cat out of the bag" by admitting the central bank's limited ability to control the amount of money in circulation and acknowledging the importance of people's willingness to borrow in determining this amount (Graeber 2014).[6] While disregarding monetarist thinking based on a quantity theory of money, this revelation assured citizens that an increase in the central bank's lending would not be translated directly into money expansion or inflation.

With the Maastricht Treaty, price stability and central bank independence became enshrined in an institutional structure of the ECB that followed the German Bundesbank model (Padoa-Schioppa 2004: 67). These principles assumed a paramount importance in central banking with the aid of monetarism as the dominant school of thought. This monetarist stance had been reflected in the Bundesbank's monetary policies before monetary authorities were transferred to the ECB, as well as in the Bundesbank's continuous resistance to the ECB's responses to the recent crises (see Young 2017).[7] The Bundesbank resisted the ECB's active involvement in enacting its massive liquidity provision because the Bundesbank was concerned about the fiscal implications and inflationary impacts of such responses. The German government did not stick to monetarist positions, however, as can be seen from the fact that Chancellor Merkel did not object to the ECB's announcement of its engagement in outright monetary transactions. At a press conference in

Ottawa, Canada, on 17 August 2012, she stated that "the ECB followed the same line [with the European heads of government] in spite of its institutional independence" (Bundesregierung 2012b; Young 2017: 230–31). Her accounts were supportive of, or at least did not contradict, the ECB's increasingly active role in enhancing financial stability, while such a compromise was arguably used as a tool by the German government to impose conditions in exchange for its acquiescence (Meiers 2015: 37).

The pledge to execute outright monetary transactions if necessary was an ECB guarantee that it would purchase an unlimited amount of sovereign debt bonds issued by distressed countries in secondary markets, but this purchase was contingent on the countries' compliance with conditions specified under the ESM. Around that time, eurozone governments agreed to create and support the ESM to lend money to indebted countries on condition that they agreed to meet specific fiscal and economic conditions. Unlike the ESM, which has been utilized to support debtors, the outright monetary transactions announced by the ECB were not actually put into operation. This announcement alone, however, had a strong reassuring impact on the European financial market.

The next two sections shed light on how a specific crisis interpretation in Germany, in combination with the European-wide learning process that took place as the crisis developed, formed Germany's policy stances toward euro governance, including the role of the ECB. I argue here that a crisis narrative (rather than a dominant school of thought, including ordoliberalism, per se), along with the redefined role of the ECB in euro governance, influenced Germany's attitude toward the proposed crisis responses. The first of these sections discusses various explanations for the euro crisis, and points out problems with Germany's dominant narrative of it, which can be described as a *moral hazard frame*. The next section then discusses how this moral hazard frame influenced Germany's general stance on crisis responses, taking into consideration its long-standing position on the monetary union and its learning processes. This section also examines the ways Germany's narratives shifted in accordance with how the crisis was unfolding.

Interpreting the Euro Crisis and Its Impact on Germany's Positions

Various crisis interpretations have been put forth in the wake of the eurozone crisis, one of which is particularly dominant in Germany and affected its positions on the post-crisis responses. The three main explanations for the cause of this crisis can be summarized as follows: (1) fiscal profligacy, especially in the case of Greece; (2) the competitiveness gap and large payment imbalances within the eurozone (Johnston 2016); and (3) financial market vulnerability and fear contagion (Jones and Underhill 2014). These three explanations can be referred to as the *moral hazard frame*, *export frame*, and *contagion frame*, respectively.[8]

Germany's policy positions on the handling of the euro crisis and post-crisis reforms were to a large extent influenced by one main crisis interpretation. Among the three explanations summarized above, the dominant narrative in Germany was the moral hazard frame, which presumes that a lack of control over government budgets, together with private citizens' overreliance on debt (i.e., risky fiscal decisions) led to the crisis (Newman 2015: 121–23). This position emphasized moral hazard issues related to the euro and eurozone crisis responses, as well as their implications for current and future fiscal problems. After the introduction of the euro, periphery countries were able to borrow more than they could afford, as their bonds received higher credibility in bond markets due to investors' increased confidence in the unified currency zone. If creditor nations lend more money to debtors suffering from a debt crisis, debtors' overspending tendencies can intensify, based on their expectations of an eventual bailout when fiscal conditions again deteriorate. This is a moral hazard problem stemming from a lack of incentives to restrain overspending behavior. In crisis responses by the ECB and other European-level institutions, creditors—Germany in particular—requested that debt restructuring and structural reforms (i.e., an austerity policy) be implemented stringently in eurozone periphery nations such as Greece, Ireland, Portugal, and Spain.

The moral hazard frame explanation for the euro crisis does not pertain to cases other than that of Greece, however. Whereas the Greek crisis developed after data documenting its public finances was revealed to have been falsified (Barber 2010), Spain fell into a financial crisis despite its low deficit and debt levels in the pre-crisis period (see figures 8.1 and 8.2). In Spain and Ireland, government finance problems rapidly mounted because their banks began failing after the bursting of real estate bubbles. Thus, the causes of the crisis in these latter two countries should be attributed to the private-sector financial system rather than to governmental fiscal policies. The moral hazard frame does not explain well the case of Italy either, where the government budget deficit increase (as annual flow) remained modest despite its high government debt (as stock from accumulated debt).

Regardless of its limited applicability to other countries, the moral hazard frame remained a relevant narrative for Germany in explaining how the eurozone crisis came about. Its persistence is partly due to the German Basic Law, based on which the German Constitutional Court demands the Bundestag's (the German federal parliament) direct control over Germany's budget. The Treaty on the Functioning of the European Union also prohibits a member state from assuming the debt of other member states' public entities (Article

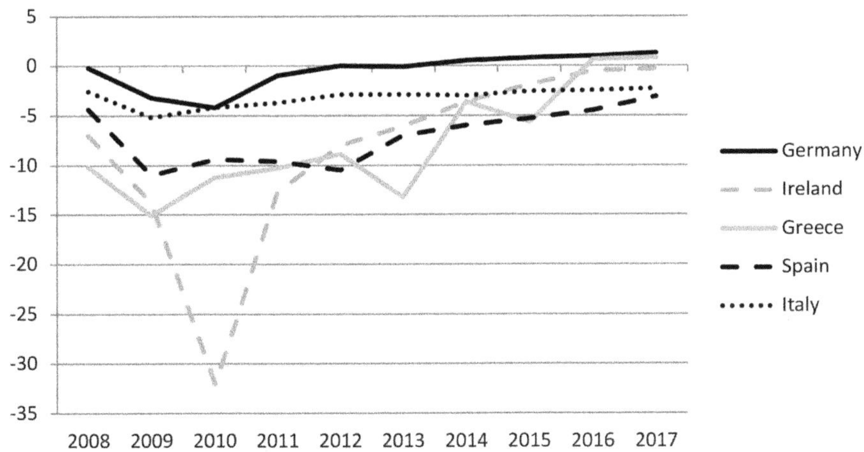

Figure 8.1. Government deficit (percentage of GDP). Source: Eurostat. Created by Sara Konoe.

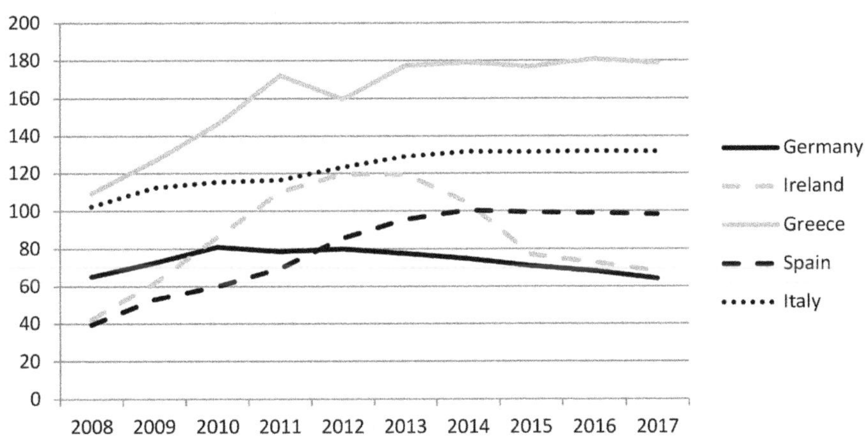

Figure 8.2. Government gross debt (percentage of GDP). Source: Eurostat. Created by Sara Konoe.

125). This treaty needed to be interpreted in a way that did not contradict the principles enshrined in the German Basic Law.[9] Thus, according to this viewpoint, debt service cost needed to be borne in principle by each member state, without financial assistance from the other members. This principle of self-responsibility for fiscal policy matched the moral hazard frame, as this frame suggests debtors assume responsibility for their own debt, regardless of the reasons for any debt overhang.

The second explanation for the euro crisis, the export frame, only partially influenced the German stance. As a crisis interpretation, the export frame focuses on payment imbalances in the eurozone that may have driven massive, risky cross-border financial inflow to debtors in the pre-crisis period. Divergent inflation rates, especially after the introduction of the euro, led to diverging levels of competitiveness, as seen in harmonized competitiveness indicators—a European version of real effective exchange rates, which resulted in widening payment imbalances. In addition to the moral hazard frame, Germany accommodated a part of the export frame interpretation to justify the need for structural reforms on the part of debtors to make labor markets and production processes more efficient (Jacoby 2015: 191–93). Although this frame could also have been invoked to request that creditors stimulate domestic consumption or investment as a way of supporting debtors' economies that suffered under severe, Europe-wide downturns, creditors' potential roles in correcting imbalances were often pushed aside or denied during the negotiation process, as Jacoby (ibid.: 192) points out. A relative lack of attention paid to creditor responsibilities often limited the crisis response options; it was thought that crises needed to be resolved not through mutual adjustments but instead by imposing austerity policies and structural reforms on debtors. This asymmetrical stance resulted in irate responses and resistance to such policies in debtor countries.

The third frame, the contagion frame, emphasizes the role of precarious cross-border financial flows and their contagious effects between member states' sovereign bond markets in the eurozone. This is the flip side of the export frame argument, although the causal link is upside down. According to the contagion frame, depletion of financial inflow into periphery countries, rather than these countries' loss of market competitiveness, is considered to be the root cause of the crisis. Euro member states may face a sovereign risk crisis, not because of their lack of competitiveness in trade, but because of a ripple effect generated by the deteriorating credibility of other member states. As insufficient attention was given to the role of financial flows, negotiations were prolonged and liquidity provisions delayed, in turn making crisis responses more costly. Improvements in public finance and the economic performance of debtors helped stabilize the bond markets in the eurozone but did not necessarily address the fundamental vulnerability at the core of the currency union's financial market in the long run: financial flight could still recur as a result of unexpected contagion in a time of crisis. Emergency lending programs were enacted after the euro crisis erupted, but the strict conditionality and lengthy political negotiation process for these programs inhibited timely responses with a sufficient level of funds to calm a crisis-prone market.

As Jones and Underhill (2014: 7) point out, in the cases of Ireland and Italy, their then current account deficits were not excessive, and were even improving, when the euro crisis hit them (see Figure 8.3). Although they did not have significant problems with payment imbalances, their financial systems experienced a sudden surge in borrowing, as shown in the Trans-European Automated Real-time Gross Settlement Express Transfer System (the so-called TARGET 2) balance, which reflects the claims and liabilities of euro area national central banks vis-à-vis the ECB. Following Greece and Ireland, whose TARGET 2 balances were negative, Italy then recorded a sudden deterioration in August 2011, and its balances largely remained negative in the following years (see Figure 8.4). This downturn cannot be explained by deficit, debt, or current account figures, as no major changes in those figures occurred at around that time.

Still, the German government's crisis response arguments generally followed their traditional pattern, especially in the initial phase of the euro crisis: the eurozone should stay away from fiscal transfers to debtors and debt forgiveness because such arrangements could worsen debtors' moral hazard problems, which are the root cause of the euro crisis. This account, however, does not reflect the fact that the causes and progression of the euro crisis differed widely across countries. Many national problems, a significant portion of which were not directly related to debtors' public debt or export competitiveness issues, were rooted in the nature of the overarching financial market, which extended beyond the scope of each individual nation. Greece's problems emerged in fall 2009 from its fiscal situation and the worsening credibility

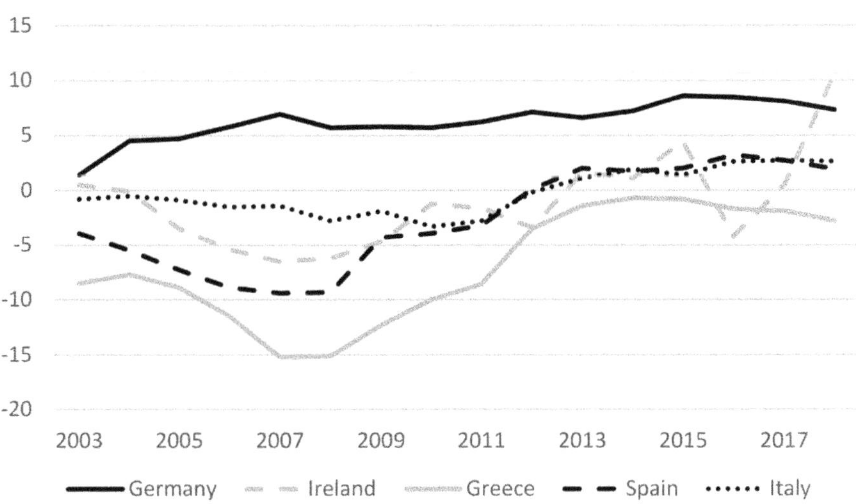

Figure 8.3. Current account balances in the Eurozone (percentage of GDP). Source: Eurostat. Created by Sara Konoe.

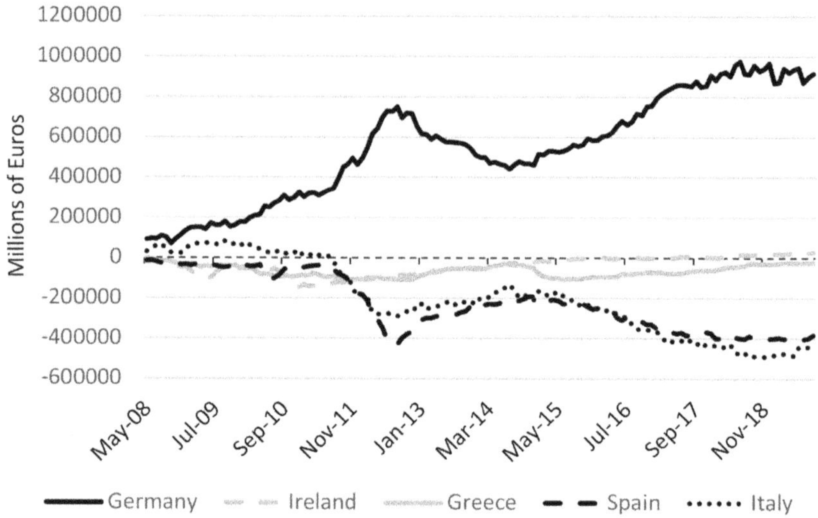

Figure 8.4. TARGET 2 balances 2008–2018 (millions of euros). Source: European Central Bank Statistical Data Warehouse. Created by Sara Konoe.

among investors, especially after Chancellor Merkel denied that Germany bore a responsibility to save Greece (see Traynor 2010; Bertram 2010). Greece's externally financed consumption and credit growth could not be sustained after the Lehman shock of 2008, as many financial institutions faced financing difficulties and began withdrawing their money from periphery countries. Spain's and Ireland's problems originated in their banking systems, which had made too many investments in real estate and risky financial products during the boom. These countries' bubbles were sustained and fueled by the cross-national financial flow in Europe, which was cheap and accessible, but eventually burst as credit conditions shrank in 2007/8. Although the Italian economy experienced a credibility loss due to underlying debt problems, a rigid economic structure, and political scandals, its sudden depletion of money was closely intertwined with contagious cross-national capital flow reduction as a result of an augmented investors' fear in the midst of the euro crisis.

Although each euro member state can recount a different story of what sparked its financial crisis, all periphery countries have a common denominator in their exposure to the crisis: their participation in a boom–bust cycle aided by a rapid, heavy cross-border financial flow entering and leaving. This heavy financial traffic is susceptible to fluctuating credibility and investor concern. Thus, the contagion frame is perhaps the most comprehensive account of the cause of the crisis, as such financial flows were accelerated by fiscal profligacy, overconsumption, lack of price competitiveness, and asset bubbles in periphery states. Pre-crisis financial inflow into periphery states was due either to a slightly higher premium set on these states' government bonds (despite the relative convergence of yields before the euro crisis) or to attractive private investment opportunities. Evidence of such investor inflow can be found in records showing the significant investment of creditor countries' banks (e.g., German and French banks) in periphery countries' bonds (Kirkegaard 2010; Blyth 2013: 86).

As the crisis developed, spread throughout the periphery, and began to threaten even core member states, the German government slowly departed from a simple version of the moral hazard frame and incorporated some discussions from the other frames to address post-crisis reform demands. Regardless of this apparent allowance for a diversity of explanations, claims relating to a moral hazard frame often re-emerged during the negotiation process to limit the extent to which costs and responsibilities were transferred and managed at the European level. At the same time, legal cases were brought to the German Constitutional Court and European Court of Justice, questioning the constitutionality or legality of crisis responses.

Germany's Monetarist Tradition and Its Adjustments

To understand narrative shifts on policies toward the euro in Germany, one should look at past narratives that framed the formation of euro governance. How can Germany's positions on handling the crisis be traced back to its past positions on this governance? Looking at the negotiation process surrounding the introduction of the euro in the late 1980s, one can see that the German public authorities did not always speak univocally. Note that the German federal government position often collided with that of the Deutsche Bundesbank, as it did in the context of the more recent euro crisis responses. Careful attention needs to be paid to their respective positions on the euro and euro crisis responses to explain the euro governance's institutional development.

In the late 1980s, Chancellor Helmut Kohl (1982–98), with strong support from Foreign Minister Hans-Dietrich Genscher, took a rather active stance in introducing a regional common currency to replace the regional currency stabilization mechanism, the European Monetary System. Compared to the chancellor's office, the Bundesbank was much more skeptical about whether the timing was right to introduce a common currency in Europe. Bundesbank leaders insisted that countries comply with strict conditions before being allowed to adopt a common currency.

In the Bundesbank's 1988 annual report, published at the time the Delors Report was announced (as a blueprint for the introduction of the euro), the

Bundesbank reiterated its long-standing position since the 1970s that an economic and political foundation would have to be built before introducing a single European currency.[10] The Bundesbank's annual report states:

> [T]here seems to be no reason for subjecting oneself or being subjected to time pressure when taking the remaining . . . irrevocable steps towards an economic and monetary union, since integration is proceeding more or less continuously in the markets and is creating the appropriate foundation for the lasting attainment of these long-range goals. (Deutsche Bundesbank 1989: 8)

The Bundesbank's stance was cautious and reserved compared to the German government's position, although the Bundesbank did not ultimately oppose the formation of an economic and monetary union.

The German federal government, however, was the agent responsible for managing foreign exchange rates and their realignment in the European Monetary System (1979–98). Kohl prioritized Germany's foreign policy goals of enhancing multinational ties with its EU partners at the time of the end of the Cold War and German reunification. Beyond this political context, the European Monetary System became increasingly dysfunctional in resolving adjustment problems in foreign exchange markets as massive cross-national capital flows associated with the depreciating dollar in the late 1980s created pressure on European currency rates to diverge. A move toward the full liberalization of capital controls, which was agreed upon in 1988, was expected to drive more speculative money flow and worsen tensions and conflicts over adjustments.[11] Eventually, Kohl succeeded in integrating the Bundesbank into the euro project by locking "Bundesbank representatives into the framing process for both the Delors Report and the Maastricht Treaty" (Leaman 2001: 230). Whereas the German government's initiative, in close cooperation with other member states (France, in particular), made the introduction of the euro possible, the Bundesbank's cautious approach was enshrined in the ECB's institutional structure. Bundesbank's influence can be seen in the ECB's limited mandates, mainly focused on price stability.

Regarding the issue of financial supervision and crisis management, the Bundesbank had been reluctant to give the ECB a wide scope of mandates to enforce financial stability. During the negotiation process of drafting the Maastricht Treaty and setting up the ECB, a Bundesbank representative wanted to make the ECB highly independent in its mandate to maintain price stability, while also desiring to "avoid references to an explicit role for the ECB in supervising banks" out of fear that the bank could be viewed falsely as a lender of last resort (James 2012: 292).[12] As a result, more specific references to the ECB's role in financial supervision than the ones agreed upon in the final version of the Maastricht Treaty, adopted in 1992, were removed from its draft at the Committee of Governors of the Central Banks of the Member

States of the European Economic Community. The Bundesbank put forth these policies because it had concerns related to conflicts of interest and moral hazard, as discussed below.

Those Bundesbank representatives critical of giving the ECB a wider range of roles maintained that a conflict of interest could arise if a central bank held a guardian role over both price stability and financial stability. If the ECB were to be endowed with financial supervisory authority or a lender-of-last-resort role from the start, it might place a high priority on liquidity and financial stability, and implement low interest rate policies for a longer period than necessary. If this were to happen, these policies would lead to inflation and compromise the ECB's role as a guardian of price stability.[13] Critics also argued that the existence of a lender of last resort at the European level could worsen the moral hazard problem. If private banks expected to be bailed out if anything went wrong, they would be deprived of the proper incentives to restrain their risky investment activities. Thus, the Bundesbank wanted the ECB to be created without mandates related to financial stability that might possibly facilitate irresponsible credit expansion or conflict with the ECB's mandate to maintain price stability.

The Bundesbank's position in the Maastricht Treaty negotiation process cannot be explained, however, solely by a general argument pertaining to a conflict of interest or moral hazard. In its domestic context, the Bundesbank itself engaged in financial supervision in cooperation with federal supervisory agencies, such as the *Bundesaufsichtsamt für das Kreditwesen* (BAKred) and the *Bundesanstalt für Finanzdienstleistungsaufsicht* (BaFin). The BAKred conducted financial supervision of banks from 1962 until 2002—the year in which its role was replaced by and consolidated into the BaFin. The BaFin was created to supervise three financial sectors—banks, securities, and insurance. During the decision-making process of consolidating financial supervisory powers over these sectors in the early 2000s, the Bundesbank even proposed a plan to absorb financial supervisory authorities under its umbrella (Frach 2008: 66). Thus, the Bundesbank's adherence to a limited mandate for the ECB can be considered to have originated in its concern over inflationary pressures from the Mediterranean countries, including France and Italy, as these countries were historically exposed to higher inflation than the Federal Republic of Germany (especially before 1983).

Well into the euro crisis, in mid-2012, the eurozone countries negotiated the Banking Union, in which they aimed at integrating financial supervisory powers into the ECB, providing a new mechanism for restructuring troubled banks, and harmonizing deposit insurance funds at the European level. At that time, the Bundesbank wanted to create a separate, independent supervisor outside the ECB. This could not be done, however, not only because of treaty restrictions (the so-called Meroni principle),[14] but also because Chancellor Merkel had already hinted at the possibility of the ECB undertaking this supervisory task. In her speech on 14 June 2012 at the Bundestag before her trip to the G20 Summit, Merkel pointed out a problem with the new European banking supervisor, the European Banking Authority (EBA), a then-candidate for the position of European financial supervisor, in conducting a stress test—that is, an assessment of banks' solvency in a scenario of economic and financial stress.[15] In particular, Merkel condemned the EBA for being heavily influenced by its national supervisors and national interests, and for having overlooked Spanish bank problems. Merkel further stated: "I don't have anything against the ECB's stronger role in financial supervision so that we can avoid national influence continuing to be a problem" (Bundesregierung 2012a). Moreover, as shown above, in her speech on 17 August 2012, Merkel did not argue against the ECB conducting outright monetary transactions—that is, the ECB's de facto role as a lender of last resort. In other words, the German federal government began allowing or even supporting the ECB's wider functions as the crisis developed, against the Bundesbank's cautious positions on the ECB gaining new mandates.

When the German government tolerated the ECB's active engagement in promoting financial stability, it also called for the formation of a political union among EU nations to enable closer cooperation in dealing with the crisis. In her speech on 14 June 2012, Merkel admitted that forming such a political union would be a "Herculean" task, but argued that it was unavoidable. This political union should include a fiscal union with tighter monitoring powers over the budget. The Six Pack (2011), Two Pack (2013), and Fiscal Compact (2013), intended to strengthen the Stability and Growth Pact, had already fostered a closer fiscal union. For the union to function properly, a consolidation of financial supervision at the European level was also required, and this consolidation was later agreed upon as a part of the Banking Union. The ECB's expanded functions in promoting financial stability became politically admissible, at least in creditors' eyes, as part of the broader euro governance reform.

The fiscal union and banking union are institutional structures based on core lessons learned from the euro crisis related to a lack of control over sound fiscal policy and the vicious circle that arose between nation states and banks. Germany's emphasis on tighter fiscal control initially emerged from its adherence to a simple version of the moral hazard frame that condemned debtors' overspending and debt accumulation, but this frame soon expanded to incorporate additional arguments related to financial market risk as the euro crisis worsened. The experience of the looming fiscal crisis in Spain in 2012 that originated from its banking sector prompted the eurozone to agree on tightening and consolidating control over the banking sector, because this sector's problems alone could undermine the member states' public finances.

In her June 2012 speech, Merkel delivered the strong message that "*Haftungen und Kontrollen gehören zusammen*" (liabilities and controls belong together). This statement carries forth the ordoliberal ideology that has buttressed government economic policies in the Federal Republic of Germany since it was founded after World War II.[16] Merkel repeated the importance of enhancing European financial and fiscal control in exchange for providing a series of emergency loans to debtor countries. Although the ECB's crisis responses were implemented on its own initiative, based on its independent status, its active involvement and reinterpretation of its original operational rules were enabled only along with increasing political support for its enhanced role in promoting financial stability, at least among policymakers, as part of the euro governance reform.[17]

In contributing to the management of the euro crisis, this position of the German federal government led to Germany's demand for debtors to implement tight fiscal policies and structural reforms in their countries. As Jacoby (2015: 195) summarizes it, "whenever Germany has innovated on the monetary policy side, it flanks this with stubbornly conservative policies on fiscal and structural issues," even in the middle of a crisis. Germany led creditor demands for strict conditions to be imposed on recipients of emergency loans provided by the European Financial Stability Facility and ESM. In general, Merkel's response to the euro crisis received strong support in Germany. According to the Pew Research Center (2013), 74 percent of respondents in Germany supported her handling of the crisis in 2013—the year when the euro crisis began to abate after financial turmoil, and after the implementation of various crisis response initiatives in 2012. In that year, Merkel was re-elected as chancellor with strong voter support.[18]

Creditor countries absorbed a significant portion of the crisis management costs for the eurozone, including the ECB's liquidity provision, while requesting that tighter rules be imposed on the European level. The redefined links between the ECB's role and euro governance can typically be seen in the announcement of outright monetary transactions, according to which the ECB can purchase government bonds without limit if the countries that issue these bonds submit to the control of the ESM. The ECB's new initiative, as well as emergency liquidity support such as the ESM, increasingly gained political support among the eurozone countries, including Germany, as the crisis worsened to a disastrous level, and euro governance reform needed to progress to prevent future crises. The new arrangements provoked serious political dissatisfaction at times, however, among both creditors and debtors, and continue to do so. In Germany, a simple version of the moral hazard frame periodically sneaked into and took over the public discourse, igniting emotional resistance against any increase in liquidity support, and ignoring the actual, complex mechanisms of crisis development in the monetary union.

While the moral hazard frame, with its persistent influence, took root in constitutional and legal constraints in Germany, this narrative was also invoked as an emotional expression of citizen dissatisfaction with economic circumstances, in which German taxpayers were forced to pay for the mistakes or misfortunes of other nations. Because arguments associated with the export frame or contagion frame were often too technical to be understood widely by the general public, the responsibilities of creditors or currency union members remained unclear to citizens, and were only occasionally called into question.

Conclusion: Germany and Euro Governance Reforms

Against the backdrop of the worsening 2008 financial crisis and the 2010 euro crisis, the ECB initiated a widening of its role to engage in expanded longer-term refinancing operations, the Securities Market Programme, outright monetary transactions, and quantitative easing programs, in order to restore financial stability and promote economic growth in the eurozone. In facing the crisis, the German government accommodated the ECB's new initiatives despite opposition from its national central bank, the Bundesbank. It compromised on its long monetarist tradition, which considers rule-based central banking with a focus on price stability to be of paramount importance. Germany gave its support to the ECB's new roles in exchange for tighter political control over the budget and banks at the European level.

Germany's positions during the two major crisis periods were based on its interpretations of the euro crisis and crisis developments. In particular, Germany's emphasis on the moral hazard frame gave primary importance to the creation of a fiscal union and attaching conditions to emergency loans. Post-crisis austerity policies often drew criticism from other eurozone member countries and those outside the eurozone for worsening the economic situation. The austerity measures originated from Germany's perception that debtors' fiscal profligacy problems (the moral hazard frame) and their lack of competitiveness (a variant of the export frame), shown in payment imbalances, were core causes of the euro crisis. The export frame argument, however, which could have led to the implementation of a more symmetrical set of policies, did not produce this result. Such a mutual adjustment plan would have required both deficit and surplus countries to take on adjustment costs. Deficit countries' efforts to restrain excess demand and enhance their competitiveness (to support their exports), as well as surplus countries' efforts to stimulate domestic demand and consumption while encouraging more inbound investment, might have helped mitigate this payment imbalance. Instead, a one-sided recognition of the export frame led to the limited enactment of policy tools for financial stabilization.[19]

Germany's demands in the negotiations related to the Banking Union also reflected its reading of the crisis. Schimmelfennig (2015: 189–90) points out Germany's asymmetrical interest: it preferred the consolidation of the Single Supervisory Mechanism at the European level (the "control" element, which could be more burdensome for debtors) along with an intergovernmental solution for the Single Resolution Mechanism (the "liability" element, which could be more burdensome for creditors). In the end, regarding the Single Resolution Mechanism, the Council of the European Union as an intergovernmental body has the final say when the European Commission objects to a decision of the Single Resolution Board—the agency that decides on a resolution plan for failing banks in the Banking Union.

The limitations facing the Banking Union originate from the limited role that the contagion frame played in informing German government decisions, despite its representatives' enhanced recognition of this issue after the euro crisis worsened in 2012. What have been insufficiently undertaken to date are reforms necessary to address the fundamental risks in a monetary union composed of different fiscal and economic authorities, along with enormous cross-national financial flow. This deficit can be seen in the lack of a clearly defined role for the lender of last resort/investor of last resort (i.e., emergency liquidity provision and fiscal backup for financial crises), as well as the lack of other effective tools to mitigate the contagious effects of investors' concerns and unsynchronized boom-and-bust cycles in the eurozone.

In part, these problems were addressed in the Single Supervisory Mechanism, which provides for European-level monitoring of systemic risk stemming from cross-border financial transactions. Whether the Single Supervisory Mechanism functions better for the member states of the Banking Union than the pre-crisis system of supervisory colleges (cooperation between home and host supervisors) or the post-Lehman shock financial governance architecture, which is composed of European Supervisory Authorities (e.g., the EBA) and the European Systemic Risk Board, remains to be seen.[20] The issues related to cross-national financial flows and businesses were also addressed with the creation of the Single Resolution Mechanism and the ESM, in which major bank resolution cases can be processed at the European level, and emergency liquidity can be provided for crisis-ridden countries under prescribed conditions to avoid or mitigate financial panic. These new safety-net institutions and policies, however, are far from sufficient (see Varela 2015; Lybeck 2016). Complicated procedures may still impede timely responses, and a Europe-wide deposit insurance has not yet been created. Furthermore, solid progress has yet to be made in addressing the imperfect mobility of production factors, and in enabling some forms of fiscal transfer to mitigate asymmetric economic shocks for the common currency area.[21]

Incomplete features of the Banking Union are due to insufficient political will and support among eurozone countries for strengthening financial stability in the region, and a limited role of narratives associated with the contagion frame that could justify or even demand such changes. The contagion frame originates from the recognition of financial risk common to all member countries within a financial and monetary union. Creditor countries were hesitant to assume such risk after the crisis erupted and the cost became a reality. There were not enough renewed reflection and narratives assessing which risks and responsibilities eurozone countries should have shared in the first place, at the point of creating a common currency for the sake of long-term monetary and financial stability. The deepening euro crisis indeed brought eurozone countries together to agree on the Banking Union and the ESM, but specific arrangements within these institutions often suggest creditor countries' reluctance to share risks relating to regional financial stability policies beyond national borders.

Although ordoliberal or monetarist thinking must have influenced the German government's narratives and policies toward the euro crisis, these ideologies do not necessarily explain the government's specific policy positions and compromises at each phase of the euro crisis. One should instead consider Germany's specific interpretation of how this event occurred in explaining the position it took on how to manage it. From an ideational perspective, Germany entered into a compromise to permit the ECB's discretionary functions and expanding role in promoting financial stability in the eurozone. Germany reluctantly compromised and adjusted its monetarist stance, because the crisis necessitated intervention for the survival of the euro. The German government agreed to elevate a degree of risk sharing, as shown in the creation of the Single Resolution Fund, based on the lessons learned from the disastrous spread of financial risk in 2012, as seen in the vicious circle argument recognized between the sovereign debt and banking crises (contagion frame). In exchange for such compromises, the German government asked for closer monitoring and structural reforms, based on moral-hazard and one-sided export frame crisis explanations. Although the German government's positions incorporated views from all of the aforementioned three frames in one way or another, particular emphasis was often placed on the moral hazard frame, as can be seen in its consistent call for debtor countries to take responsibility in implementing austerity policies. Based on the crisis narratives describing how the crisis occurred, developed, and spread, various forms of liquidity provisions were accommodated as part of a broader euro governance reform.

So, what is the current situation? Despite the fact that some progress was made in recent years, with a new agreement on revising the ESM treaty to backstop the Single Resolution Fund, the Banking Union project remains incomplete. Whether the agreement on an over €800 billion coronavirus recovery fund for the EU (the so-called Next Generation EU, ratified in June 2021) can facilitate future fiscal cooperation in the eurozone is uncertain. Recent turmoil, including the 2015 European refugee crisis, COVID-19, and the Russian military attack on Ukraine, depleted and may continue to limit member countries' scarce political resources for negotiating further euro governance reform.

Acknowledgments

I thank the Japan Society for the Promotion of Science for providing me with Grants-in-Aid for Young Scientists (B) 17K13695 (from April 2017 to March 2019) to support this research. This publication has benefited from my research stays at the Max Planck Institute for the Study of Societies in Cologne, Germany from February to March 2018, and at GESIS, Leibniz Institute for the Social Sciences, also in Cologne, from October 2019 to March 2020. I appreciate the helpful comments of Jill Twark, Reinhard Schmidt, Gregory W. Noble, Kenneth McElwain, and anonymous reviewers.

Sara Konoe is Professor in the Faculty of Economics of Kansai University in Japan. She received her PhD at the Paul H. Nitze School of Advanced International Studies (SAIS) of Johns Hopkins University in May 2009. She published her first monograph, *The Politics of Financial Markets and Regulation: The United States, Japan, and Germany,* in 2014 with Palgrave Macmillan. Her second book, *Politics of Financial Integration: Unbalanced Development of the European Financial and Monetary System,* was published by Iwanami Shoten in 2020 (in Japanese). Her research focuses on international political economy, the politics of financial regulation, and European integration.

Notes

This contribution is partly based on my book (Konoe 2020, in Japanese).

1. See the text, retrieved 19 October 2021 from https://eur-lex.europa.eu/legal-content/EN/TXT/PDF/?uri=CELEX:12012E/TXT&from=EN.
2. The maturity period for ECB lending to banks was extended for longer-term refinancing operations from 3 months in normal times to 6 months (March 2008), 1 year (June 2009), and then 3 years (December 2011, February 2012).
3. After a serious confrontation concerning the Securities Market Programme, the president of the Bundesbank, Axel Weber, and an ECB Executive Board member, Jürgen Stark, resigned.

4. As Nerghes et al. 2015 focus on the role of the global financial crisis (a crisis period considered to be from 2008 to 2009) in central bank communication, the euro crisis periods (2010–11 and 2012–13) are categorized as *post-crisis* and *recovery* phases. As this chapter's interest is on the role of the euro crisis, the *pre-crisis* (2006–7) and *crisis* (2008–9) phases are recategorized as before the euro crisis, and the *post-crisis* (2010–11) and *recovery* (2012–13) phases as after it. Interpretation here reflects such recategorization.
5. The ECB did not explicitly foster financial stability up to the 2007/8 global financial crisis, as monetary policies supporting financial stability are considered different from those used to maintain price stability. For the purpose of financial stability, a central bank may need to increase liquidity (money supply and credit) in an interbank market, which may undermine price stability and lead to inflation. Moreover, the ECB's reinterpretation of price stability in 2003, based on a Governing Council decision, indicates its initial realization that economic problems can originate not only from inflation but also from other issues, such as deflation. Price stability was previously defined as "growth in consumer price inflation of below 2 percent for the year," whereas the new rule is to "keep inflation rates below, but close to, 2 percent over the medium term" (Kaltenthaler 2006: 73–74).
6. See also this article on the Bank of England website: https://www.bankofengland.co.uk/quarterly-bulletin/2014/q1/money-creation-in-the-modern-economy.
7. Young (2017: 226–27, 230–31) attributes Germany's post-crisis attitudes not to ordoliberalism (see Note 16), but instead to the dominance of New Institutional Economics, which informed the German Bundesbank's monetarist stance.
8. This naming of crisis interpretations follows Newman 2015, who uses them as a way to describe the various crisis responses.
9. For the German Constitutional Court's rulings on these matters, see Poptcheva 2014.
10. This policy is called the "crown theory," as a common currency can only be introduced as a "crown" after all other economic convergences are attained. The Bundesbank's position can, in general, be called *economist*, in contrast to the French *monetarist* position, which emphasizes the essential role of a common currency in promoting economic convergence (Marsh 2011: 45–46). The monetarist position justified the introduction of the euro at an early stage, in parallel with the formation of a single market policy.
11. The full liberalization of capital movement—a prominent goal long advocated by some member states, particularly Germany, as a way of reinforcing the disciplinary effects on member states' economic policies (e.g., containing inflation)—became one of the four main pillars of the EU's single market policy. This created an important context for reaching an agreement on the introduction of the euro (see Bakker 1996: 159, 167, 211).
12. When a central bank acts as a lender of last resort, it is expected to provide emergency loans to illiquid private banks when these banks cannot borrow money from other private banks because of their declining credibility or shrinking liquidity (money) in an interbank market.
13. An equivalent logic can be applied when a monetary authority pursues economic growth, because a zero-interest-rate policy and quantitative easing to restore investment and economic health may also lead to inflation. The Maastricht Treaty stipu-

lates that economic policies, including growth-related ones, shall be supported by the ECB, but that price stability cannot be compromised for these policies.

14. A 1958 ruling of the European Court of Justice limited the extent to which the European Commission could delegate administrative tasks to independent administrative agencies (Moloney 2014: 909).
15. The EBA was an institution created in 2011 in response to the 2007/8 global financial crisis in order to enhance coordination among national financial supervisors in their monitoring of multinational financial firms, and to strengthen financial supervision at the European level. The EBA was given the power to mediate differences between national supervisory practices.
16. Ordoliberalism as an economic ideology, developed in the Weimar Republic by the so-called Freiburg School scholars, was widely discussed and more or less implemented in rebuilding the postwar West German economy. This ideology is opposed to that of a controlled economy, such as under socialism or National Socialism, though it also questions laissez-faire policies. It emphasizes the role of the state in forming market rules, including competition rules, while distancing itself from Keynesian demand management. While some scholars point out the role of ordoliberalism in explaining Germany's handling of the euro crisis (Blyth 2013; Schäfer 2016), others are more skeptical of the direct linkage (Young 2017). Yet, it can be said that any reference to ordoliberal principles has the rhetorical power to reach its core audience in Germany's policy-making circle.
17. It was also essential that the ECB's outright monetary transactions were admitted only for the cases under the control of ESM, in which creditor countries held strong voting power. Such conditionality was reiterated at the European Court of Justice's ruling on this new ECB initiative.
18. At the same time, a new right-wing party, the *Alternative für Deutschland* (AfD), was founded in Germany in 2013, based on the statement "*Deutschland braucht den Euro nicht*" (Germany does not need the euro) (Spiegel Online 2013). This party enhanced its power especially after the 2015 refugee crisis. In the 2017 federal elections, the AfD put forth anti-immigrant and anti-Islam positions (BBC 2020) and surpassed the 5 percent threshold of votes necessary to have representation in the Bundestag, winning 94 out of 709 seats (Deutscher Bundestag 2022: 27).
19. Whether or not Germany's recognition of this frame was one-sided, note that limitations remain for accepting the export frame as a core explanation for the euro crisis, as discussed earlier.
20. For further analysis of the implementation of the Banking Union, see Konoe 2020.
21. Free mobility of production factors (e.g., labor and capital) is a condition for an optimum currency area (i.e., an optimal area for using a common currency), according to Mundell 1961. When an asymmetric shock occurs in several countries in a monetary union or fixed exchange rate regime (e.g., a positive demand shock in country A and a negative demand shock in country B), the free mobility of production factors promotes labor movement from one country to another (from country B to country A, in this example). This move will mitigate inflationary pressures in country A while mitigating unemployment problems in country B. Free mobility of production factors can be a substitute for adjustment through exchange rates, which countries in a common currency area cannot enjoy (by contrast, under a flexible exchange rate system, the aforementioned asymmetric demand shocks in two countries can lead to

currency appreciation in country A and depreciation in country B, so that economic imbalances can be adjusted through the fluctuation of exchange rates). The European single market did not bring about a sufficient level of production factor mobility, as can be seen in the imperfect labor mobility inside the eurozone, thus making the necessary adjustment associated with asymmetric demand shocks difficult. Adjustment is still possible if there is some degree of fiscal transfer from country A to country B to stimulate the country under negative demand shock. Without sufficient funding at the European level (at present, the EU budget is quite limited), however, the EU/eurozone is incapable of implementing such a fiscal transfer for the purpose of economic adjustment.

References

Bakker, Age F. P. 1996. *The Liberalization of Capital Movements in Europe: The Monetary Committee and Financial Integration, 1958–1994*. Dordrecht: Springer.

Barber, Tony. 2010. "Greece Condemned for Falsifying Data." *Financial Times*, 12 January. Retrieved 21 December 2021 from https://www.ft.com/content/33b0a48c-ff7e-11de-8f53-00144feabdc0.

BBC. 2020. "Germany's AfD: How Right-Wing is Nationalist Alternative for Germany?" BBC News, 11 February. Retrieved 21 December 2021 from http://www.bbc.com/news/world-europe-37274201.

Bertram, Christoph. 2010. "Griechenland-Hilfe: Das doppelte Versagen der Angela Merkel." *Zeit Online*, 7 May. Retrieved 19 October 2021 from https://www.zeit.de/politik/deutschland/2010-05/merkel-griechenland.

Blyth, Mark. 2013. *Austerity: The History of a Dangerous Idea*. Oxford: Oxford University Press.

Braun, Benjamin. 2016. "Speaking to the People? Money, Trust, and Central Banking Legitimacy in the Age of Quantitative Easing." *Review of International Political Economy* 23(6): 1064–92.

Bulmer, Simon, and Claudio M. Radaelli. 2013. "The Europeanization of Member States Policy." In *The Member States of the European Union*, 2nd edn. Ed. Simon Bulmer and Christian Lequesne, 57–83. Oxford: Oxford University Press.

Bundesregierung. 2012a. "Regierungserklärung von Bundeskanzlerin Merkel zum G20-Gipfel am 18./19. Juni 2012 in Los Cabos (Mexico)." 14 June. Retrieved 9 May 2022 from https://www.bundeskanzler.de/bk-de/aktuelles/regierungserklaerung-von-bundeskanzlerin-merkel-zum-g20-gipfel-am-18-19-juni-2012-in-los-cabos-mexiko--1007564.

———. 2012b. "Pressekonferenz von Bundeskanzlerin Angela Merkel und dem kanadischen Premierminister Stephen Harper." 17 August. Retrieved 19 October 2021 from https://www.bundeskanzler.de/bk-de/aktuelles/pressekonferenz-von-bundeskanzlerin-angela-merkel-und-dem-kanadischen-premierminister-stephen-harper-846492.

Deutsche Bundesbank. 1989. "Report of the Deutsche Bundesbank for the Year 1988." Retrieved 19 October 2021 from https://www.bundesbank.de/resource/blob/702918/c06222ad906f3677b6503b734c8f939c/mL/1988-annual-report-data.pdf.

Deutscher Bundestag. 2022. "Kapitel 1.8 Wahlergebnisse nach Ländern (Sitzverteilung)." 9 June. In Datenhandbuch 1. Wahlen zum Deutschen Bundestag. Retrieved 23 June 2022 from https://www.bundestag.de/resource/blob/196098/213b0510d3385a30a5400369ff4ce35a/Kapitel_01_08_Wahlergebnis_nach_L__ndern__Sitzverteilung_-data.pdf.

Draghi, Mario. 2012a. "Speech by Mario Draghi at the Global Investment Conference in London." 26 July. Retrieved 19 October 2021 from https://www.ecb.europa.eu/press/key/date/2012/html/sp120726.en.html.

———. 2012b. "Speech by Mario Draghi at the annual event 'Day of the German Industries' organized by the Federation of German Industries in Berlin." 25 September. Retrieved 19 October 2021 from https://www.ecb.europa.eu/press/key/date/2012/html/sp120925.en.html.

———. 2015. "Speech by Mario Draghi at the Hearing at the European Parliament's Economic and Monetary Affairs Committee in Brussels." 23 March. Retrieved 19 October 2021 from https://www.ecb.europa.eu/press/key/date/2015/html/sp150323_1.en.html.

European Central Bank. 2014a. "ECB to Adjust Schedule of Meetings and to Publish Regular Accounts of Monetary Policy Discussions in 2015." Press release, 3 July. Retrieved 19 October 2021 from https://www.ecb.europa.eu/press/pr/date/2014/html/pr140703_1.en.html.

———. 2014b. "ECB to Publish Accounts of Monetary Policy Discussions from January," Press release, 18 December. Retrieved 19 October 2021 from https://www.ecb.europa.eu/press/pr/date/2014/html/pr141218.en.html.

Frach, Lotte. 2008. *Finanzaufsicht in Deutschland und Großbritannien: Die BaFin und die FSA im Spannungsfeld der Politik* [Financial supervision in Germany and the UK: BaFin and FSA in the tense area of politics]. Wiesbaden: VS Verlag für Sozialwissenschaften.

Graeber, David. 2014. "The truth is out: money is just an IOU, and the banks are rolling in it." *The Guardian*, 18 March. Retrieved 19 October 2021 from https://www.theguardian.com/commentisfree/2014/mar/18/truth-money-iou-bank-of-england-austerity.

Grauwe, Paul de. 2018. *Economics of Monetary Union*. 12th edn. Oxford: Oxford University Press.

Jacoby, Wade. 2015. "Europe's New German Problem: The Timing of Politics and the Politics of Timing." In *The Future of the Euro*, ed. Matthias Matthijs and Mark Blyth, 187–209. Oxford: Oxford University Press.

James, Harold. 2012. *Making the European Monetary Union: The Role of the Committee of Central Bank Governors and the Origins of the European Central Bank*. Cambridge, MA: The Belknap Press of Harvard University Press.

Johnston, Alison. 2016. *From Convergence to Crisis: Labor Markets and the Instability of the Euro*. Ithaca, NY: Cornell University Press.

Jones, Erik, and Geoffrey Underhill. 2014. "Theory of Optimum Financial Areas: Retooling the Debate on the Governance of Global Finance." *SWIFT Institute Working Paper* no. 2013-001. Retrieved 19 October 2021 from http://www.swiftinstitute.org/wp-content/uploads/2014/11/SWIFT-Institute-Working-Paper-No-2013-001-Theory-of-Optimum-Financial-Areas-Jones_v4-FINAL.pdf.

Kaltenthaler, Karl. 2006. *Policymaking in the European Central Bank: The Masters of Europe's Money*. Lanham, MD: Rowman & Littlefield.

Kirkegaard, Jacob Funk. 2010. "The 'Shamed Seven' EU Banks Open Their Books." Peterson Institute for International Economics. Retrieved 19 October 2021 from https://www.piie.com/blogs/realtime-economic-issues-watch/shamed-seven-eu-banks-open-their-books.

Konoe, Sara. 2020. *Kinyu Togo no Seiji gaku: Oshu Kinyu/Tsuka Sisutemu no Hukinnko na Hatten* [Politics of Financial Integration: Unbalanced Development of the European Financial and Monetary Systems]. Tokyo: Iwanami Shoten.

Leaman, Jeremy. 2001. *The Bundesbank Myth: Towards a Critique of Central Bank Independence*. Basingstoke: Palgrave Macmillan.

Lybeck, Johan A. 2016. "Resolution of Failing Banks in the European Banking Union: Finishing the Job or Going Back to the Drawing Board?" In *European Banking Union: Prospects and Challenges*, ed. Juan E. Castañeda, David G. Mayes, and Geoffrey Wood, 184–207. London: Routledge.

Marsh, David. 2011. *The Euro: The Battle for the New Global Currency*. New Haven, CT: Yale University Press.

McBride, James, and Christopher Alessi. 2015. "The Role of the European Central Bank." Council on Foreign Relations, 9 July. Retrieved 19 October 2021 from https://www.cfr.org/backgrounder/role-european-central-bank.

Meiers, Franz-Josef. 2015. *Germany's Role in the Euro Crisis: Berlin's Quest for a More Perfect Monetary Union*. Cham, CH: Springer.

Moloney, Niamh. 2014. *EU Securities and Financial Markets Regulation*. 3rd edn. Oxford: Oxford University Press.

Mundell, Robert A. 1961. "A Theory of Optimum Currency Areas." *The American Economic Review* 51(4): 657–65.

Nerghes, Adina, Ju-Sung Lee, Peter Groenewegen, and Iina Hellsten. 2015. "Mapping Discursive Dynamics of the Financial Crisis: A Structural Perspective of Concept Roles in Semantic Networks." *Computational Social Networks* 2(16). Retrieved 19 October 2021 from https://computationalsocialnetworks.springeropen.com/articles/10.1186/s40649-015-0021-8.

Newman, Abraham. 2015. "The Reluctant Leader: Germany's Euro Experience and the Long Shadow of Reunification." In *The Future of the Euro*, ed. Matthias Matthijs and Mark Blyth, 117–35. Oxford: Oxford University Press.

Padoa-Schioppa, Tommaso. 2004. *The Euro and Its Central Bank: Getting United after the Union*. Cambridge, MA: The MIT Press.

Pew Research Center. 2013. "The New Sick Man of Europe: The European Union." 13 May. Retrieved 19 October 2021 from http://www.pewglobal.org/2013/05/13/the-new-sick-man-of-europe-the-european-union/.

Poptcheva, Eva-Maria. 2014. "German Constitutional Court Decisions on EU Anti-crisis Measures." *European Parliament Research Service*, briefing in July. Retrieved 19 October 2021 from https://www.europarl.europa.eu/RegData/bibliotheque/briefing/2014/140568/LDM_BRI(2014)140568_REV1_EN.pdf.

Schäfer, David. 2016. "A Banking Union of Ideas? The Impact of Ordoliberalism and the Vicious Circle on the EU Banking Union." *Journal of Common Market Studies* 54(4): 961–80.

Schimmelfennig, Frank. 2015. "Liberal Intergovernmentalism and the Euro Area Crisis." *Journal of European Public Policy* 22(2): 177–95.

Schmidt, Vivien A. 2016. "Reinterpreting the Rules 'by Stealth' in Times of Crisis: A Discursive Institutionalist Analysis of the European Central Bank and the European Commission." *West European Politics* 39(5): 1032–52.

Spiegel Online. 2013. "Alternative für Deutschland: Protestpartei startet Anti-Euro-Wahlkampf." 14 April. Retrieved 19 October 2021 from https://www.spiegel.de/politik/deutschland/alternative-fuer-deutschland-gruendet-sich-und-beschliesst-programm-a-894277.html.

Traynor, Ian. 2010. "Angela Merkel Dashes Greek Hopes of Rescue Bid." *The Guardian*, 11 February. Retrieved 19 October 2021 from https://www.theguardian.com/theguardian/2010/feb/11/germany-greece-merkel-bailout-euro.

Varela, Justo Corti. 2015. "Direct Recapitalization of Banks and Sovereign Debt: The ESM Direct Recapitalization Instrument and its Impact on Sovereign Debt." In *European Banking Union: The New Regime*, ed. Luis M. Hinojosa-Martínez and José María Beneyto, 121–35. Alphen aan den Rijn, NL: Kluwer Law International.

Verdun, Amy. 2017. "Political Leadership of the European Central Bank." *Journal of European Integration* 39(2): 207–21.

Young, Brigitte. 2017. "Is Germany's and Europe's Crisis Politics Ordoliberal and/or Neoliberal?" In *The Birth of Austerity: German Ordoliberalism and Contemporary Neoliberalism*, ed. Thomas Biebricher and Frieder Vogelmann, 221–37. London: Rowman & Littlefield.

CHAPTER 9

Housing Crises and the Crisis of Housing

German Experiences with Neoliberal Reforms

PAULETTE KURZER AND ALICE H. COOPER

During the seismic economic shift referred to as the Great Recession, a housing bubble fueled by a decades-long credit boom burst, resulting in a widespread loss of housing value—from 2007 in the United States, and from 2009 in many European housing markets. The bursting housing bubble and the associated crisis of the financial system were instrumental in bringing about the broader recession that followed. Although the Great Recession also affected Germany—because of its banks' involvement with the international financial market and the severe drop in German exports—a housing market crisis was *not* a component of Germany's economic difficulties. Consequently, the subsequent German narrative of the causes of the economic crisis stressed heedless speculation and excessive spending in other countries.

Although Germany steered clear of the debt-fueled consumption that was rampant in other countries' housing markets, and therefore avoided a housing bubble—which in turn spared it the full impact of the global financial crisis and helped its economy recover relatively quickly—Germany has *not* managed to avoid a different sort of crisis with housing. Like a number of other countries, Germany too suffers from a notable lack of affordable housing, particularly in large cities, partly driven by sluggish home construction, a scarcity of rent-stabilized units, and, in its particular case, hindrances to purchasing a home with mortgage credit. The coronavirus pandemic has worsened this affordability crisis as more households are looking to buy, while institutional investors are buying up large blocks of dwellings to take advantage of higher rents. In Berlin alone, the local government estimates that it will need two hundred thousand additional apartments, and it hopes that half of these units will be built by the public sector and governed by social housing rules (Nienaber and Johnson 2021).

Historically, homeownership has been a rare form of housing tenure in northwestern Europe, with only farmers and the wealthy owning their own

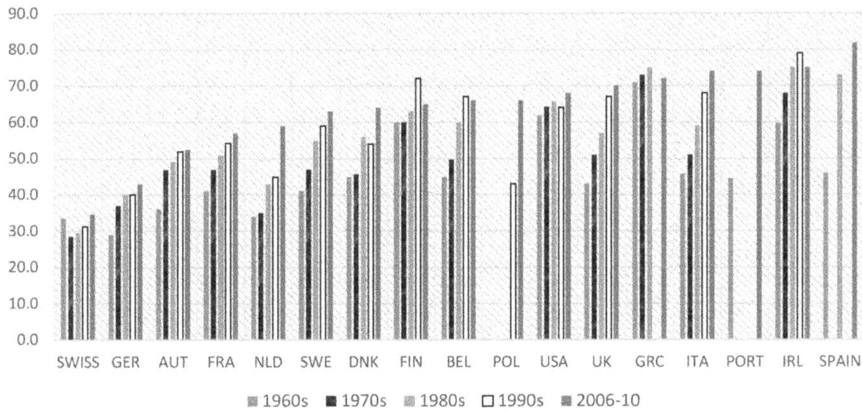

Figure 9.1. Homeownership, percentages of housing stock, various years, from low to high. Source: Sebastian Kohl, Homeownership, Renting and Society: Historical and Comparative Perspective (https://www.sebastiankohl.com/data). Created by Paulette Kurzer and Alice H. Cooper.

homes. Until the 1980s, many European countries had relatively low homeownership rates (i.e., owner-occupied housing; see Figure 9.1). Homeownership rates ranged from less than 50 percent in various northern countries (including Germany) to around 60 percent in Ireland and southern Europe. This pattern shifted fundamentally, however, starting in the 1980s. Homeownership rates now range from over 60 percent to around 80 percent, and homeownership has become the dominant type of housing tenure. Germany, however, is a notable exception to this general trend, with homeownership rising only into the 40 percent range, and almost half of all households renting their residence in 2018. In terms of housing stock, only about 45 percent of all housing there is owner-occupied.

This rise in European homeownership rates paralleled shifts in government policy and narrative. As we will elaborate more fully below, after World War II the turn to a social-welfare ideology in Europe led to strong government support for *rental* housing above all, with the promotion of homeownership considered to be of secondary importance. In the 1980s, however, many governments made expanding *homeownership* an explicit priority, and scaled back support for rental housing dramatically. This policy shift in housing was part of a general shift toward neoliberal economic reforms, which strove to reduce state intervention in favor of extending market relationships, based on the view that markets stimulate competition, economic efficiency, and choice. The neoliberal policy paradigm, broadly, includes three objectives. First, it promotes economic deregulation in the name of market efficiency. Second, it involves cutting back social policy programs and welfare spending. Finally, it relies on a discourse of individual responsibility and entrepreneurialism to justify these new policy measures. In housing, these neoliberal transformations were paired with a new neoliberal narrative tied to homeownership and to reducing direct support for home construction, rent regulation, and subsidized housing.

Germany also enacted neoliberal reforms, adopting a concomitant neoliberal narrative in several policy areas, starting in the 1980s and becoming more pronounced in the 1990s, following the reunification of East and West Germany. Unlike many West European countries, however, Germany largely did *not* dramatically extend neoliberal policies to the housing market or expand government support for homeownership. The focus of this chapter is thus to describe an odd phenomenon: the fact that German officials did not promote homeownership with either policy or narrative after the 1980s, given that it was pursuing at the same time many other neoliberal objectives. Countries generally similar to Germany, including the Netherlands, Denmark, and Sweden, launched market-based reforms intended to restructure social security programs, labor market institutions, product markets, *and* housing. Governments in these countries encouraged the sale of nonprofit housing, deregulated mortgage lending, approved new mortgage products, and incentivized middle-class households to enter the homeownership market. Market-based reforms thus characterized the labor market, the pension system, *and* the housing market. In Germany, the labor market was likewise deregulated and social programs became less generous. German officials also restructured the pension system in order to deter older workers from seeking early retirement. Along with other countries, Germany gradually raised the retirement age while encouraging an expansion of individual retirement provisions in order to reduce the burden on occupational retirement funds and the public pillar.

The neoliberal stress on financial self-sufficiency by becoming an "asset holder" was thus *not* brought to bear on housing in Germany nearly to the extent it was in the Netherlands, Sweden, and Denmark. Although the German government did reduce direct support for housing, German leaders were *not* trying to create a nation of homeowners and did not adopt policies that induced households to borrow (excessively) in order to enter the homeowner market. Moreover, the German narrative regarding housing did not center on pushing households to take on credit in order to become homeowners (Reisenbichler 2022).

In this chapter we first discuss the "homeowner ideology," and explain how it and related public policies were embraced by other European corporatist welfare states like Denmark, Sweden, and the Netherlands. We then describe major differences in the main political parties' dominant housing narratives in the Netherlands, Sweden, and Denmark, comparing them with the policies and narratives in Germany to illustrate how these policies affected these nations' economies during and after the financial crisis of 2008–10. All four countries are generally considered to share common characteristics as corporatist welfare states, but we show that Germany differed from the other three in its government policy and narrative regarding housing markets. In the second part of the chapter, we assess the emergence of a crisis in housing and housing affordability in Germany, despite the fact that it, unlike the other three countries under discussion, did not fully liberalize the housing market and/or mortgage lending—indeed, its narrative continues to downplay the benefits of homeownership.

The Rise of "Homeownership Ideology" in the Netherlands, Sweden, and Denmark

After 1945, governments in all West European countries adopted a social-welfare ideology and significantly increased their social-welfare state provisions, including the supply of affordable housing. In the postwar period, this ideology often led to government support for rental housing in order to provide quality dwellings for working-class families. Both European center-left and center-right governments provided vast subsidies for the construction of public or social housing;[1] maintained strict rent regulation and tenant protection laws; and treated housing as a social right (together with education, health care, and employment) (Kohl 2018).

Yet by 2000, most European governments had ceased subsidizing social housing, relying instead on market forces to steer housing infrastructure. Taking the lead, center-right governments actively promoted homeownership. They developed a narrative arguing that homeownership would result in a broader distribution of wealth and a better housing supply, foster social stability, and promote individual self-sufficiency. Their narrative also proclaimed the advantages of homeownership for individual families, asserting that it afforded greater control over living arrangements, enhanced savings for retirement and emergencies through equity accumulation, and served as a status symbol (Ronald 2008). By the early 2000s, center-left governments had also embraced homeownership, owing to widespread homeownership among their voters and to pressures to control public spending.

The promotion of homeownership and the decline of government support for rental and non-profit housing were part of the wave of neoliberal reforms of the social-welfare state, beginning in Europe in the 1980s. Whereas, in the first decades of the post-1945 era, European governments had provided public goods and services to guarantee the well-being of the population, neoliberal reforms reversed that trend. Welfare state reforms usually involved privatizing caring functions such as eldercare, hospitals, and child care, formerly performed by the state. For their part, labor-market activation policies aimed to increase incentives for working-age adults to enter the workforce (Lodemel and Moreira 2014).

One important emphasis of neoliberal housing market policy involved a new approach to public or social housing. Center-right governments pioneered the sale of public rental housing to sitting tenants, the elimination of direct housing construction subsidies, and the deregulation of capital markets. The most famous example was Britain under prime minister Thatcher, where the 1980 "Right to Buy" law raised homeownership as a share of housing tenure by around 15 percent (Forrest and Murie 1988). The success and popularity of the British privatization of public housing inspired liberal and conservative parties in other European countries to sell public housing, aiming to foster a property-owning democracy.

The Netherlands, Sweden, and Denmark all embraced this homeownership model. In the Netherlands, the Christian democratic-liberal coalition elected in 1989 broke with the past and proposed the sale of social housing (representing nearly 40 percent of housing stock) to sitting tenants, the elimination of all direct subsidies to the social-housing sector, and the transfer of financial responsibilities for construction and maintenance to non-profit governmental housing corporations. In 1995, a new Dutch law officially divorced the social-housing sector from the state; housing associations, which owned and managed the social housing sector, were then also told to be more profit-oriented and commercial (Priemus 1995).

In the 1990s, Dutch politicians also reformulated the narrative on housing by treating owner-occupied housing, instead of housing in general, as a public good (Ronald and Dol 2011). The commodification of housing shaped the political discourse. Conservative politicians argued that middle-class households should embrace the values of personal responsibility, freedom of choice, and improved neighborhoods, as well as the prospect of asset gains (van Gent 2013), and Social Democratic Party leaders agreed with this assessment. In an interview in 1996, Rik van der Ploeg, a member of the Dutch parliament and a prominent Social Democratic spokesperson on housing, explained that "home ownership is like car ownership or a steak on Saturday. It is a fundamental right for people to own a home." He continued by pointing out that it is not fair that high-income households can become homeowners, when this opportunity is unavailable to low-income households (Bijlo and Welgraven 1996).

In Sweden, social housing owned by municipalities was at the core of the "Swedish People's Home" and the postwar welfare state. From the 1930s to the 1970s, social democratic governments provided housing subsidies and regulated mortgage interest rates. The Swedish Social Democratic Party, which was the architect of Sweden's postwar housing policy, formulated a welfare state housing model popularly known as *Folkhemmet* (the people's home). It upheld an image of a home built on solidarity and efficiency (Grundström and Molina 2016). As a social democratic commentator pointed out in 1945, "to this generation of Swedes, housing is becoming the panacea for all social evils" (qtd. in Dickens et al. 1985: 55). The Social Democratic Party also regulated municipal housing companies, which were told what and where to build, and at what cost for the end user. Spending on housing reached new heights after the Social Democrats launched the Million Homes program and literally built a million homes—mostly apartments—between 1965 and 1974 (Hall and Vidén 2005).

The 1990s were an era of transition in Swedish housing. In 1991, Prime Minister Carl Bildt led the first center-right (conservative-liberal) government since the 1930s, which set out ambitious reforms for the Swedish housing market. The new government argued that state steering was inefficient and that individuals should make their own choices without government intervention. New rules cut back direct subsidies to builders, and urged municipal housing companies to sell part of their inventory (Holmqvist and Turner 2014). With the withdrawal of the state, a housing market based on competition was supposed to bring lower prices, lower building costs, and easier entry to homeownership. The new Bildt government narrative contended that politics should support favorable market conditions, which in turn would improve the functioning of the housing market and increase private sector profits (Grundström and Molina 2016). Whereas in the past, Swedish housing policy had espoused an ideology of universal fairness, the post-1990 narrative focused on providing the educated professional class with an array of housing choices. In 1997, the minister of finance, Erik Åsbrink (Social Democratic Party) stated that there was no difference between housing and cars or other commodities: "We don't have a ministry in charge of trucks and lorries, nor a minister of trucks and lorries. So why should we have one for housing?" The role of the government, he claimed, was to provide suitable market conditions so that the housing market would operate efficiently. Like cars or trucks, housing took on new functions as a status symbol and a means of expressing values and taste (qtd. in ibid.: 327).

A decade later in Denmark, a Liberal-Conservative coalition won the 2001 election—the first center-right majority since 1924. The new government, led by Anders Fogh Rasmussen, immediately set about transforming the housing market, accompanied by a new narrative and new priorities (Bruun 2018). The minister of economic and business affairs, Bendt Bendtsen, a member of the conservative People's Party, published a government report in 2002, with the title: More Housing: Growth and Innovation in the Housing Market. The minister claimed in the report to introduce reforms that aimed at "a long-term effort . . . to make the housing market work better under market conditions and, to a greater extent than today, to support the economic growth of the society" (qtd. in Larsen and Lund Hansen 2015: 266). With the election of a liberal-conservative government, the minister of economics and business affairs finally had the support of government and parliament to introduce more market forces and less state intervention in the Danish housing market. One early measure passed by this neoliberal coalition was legislation that turned not-for-profit private cooperatives, constituting 7 percent of the housing stock, into private homeownership.

Until 2001, the Danish narrative had stressed housing as a social right and sought to protect tenants. But the center-right coalition elected in 2001 pushed a new approach that celebrated the benefits of property ownership. A senior member of the Danish Conservative People's Party spoke in favor of the "strengthening of property rights in the public housing sector" (Larsen and Lund Hansen 2015). Thus, in both Denmark and Sweden, center-right governments moved away from the social-democratic, solidaristic vision of housing and from support for rental and cooperative housing. Instead, they linked an expansion of homeownership with the idea that people should become more self-sufficient (Ronald 2008). When the left returned to power, it crucially did not reverse these housing policies. The buzzwords became consumer choice, efficient market forces, and lower prices.

A second major area of neoliberal housing policy reform involved the liberalization of mortgage lending, which the expansion of homeownership required. In the Netherlands, after 1993, buyers could obtain a mortgage without any down payment, and loan-to-value ratios were routinely over 100 percent. Dutch bank regulators approved such new rules in order to lower entry costs into the housing market, especially as prices rose. With average Dutch house prices doubling between 1998 and 2008, the total outstanding mortgage credit/debt for the Netherlands rose from 40 percent of GDP in 1995 to over 100 percent after 2005 (Elsinga, Priemus, and Boelhouwer 2016). The Dutch tax code also allowed a generous deduction of mortgage interest payments. Until reforms took place in 2013, homebuyers could obtain a mortgage that had a loan-to-value (LTV) of more than 100 percent, which meant that a new homeowner could borrow more than the value of the house. This stimulated the "overconsumption" of mortgage debt, because it made fiscal sense to take on a huge loan as homeowners could deduct the interest payments from their taxable income (Andrews, Caldera Sánchez, and Johansson 2011). In addition, until 2013, it was possible to take out a non-amortizing mortgage in which the homeowner only paid the interest payments and did not touch the principal until the end of the loan term. Klaas Knot, president of the Dutch Central Bank, warned in 2011 that "the enormous mortgage debt owed by Dutch households constitutes a major risk to the financial system" and that people "take out large mortgages" but do not "hurry to pay back the actual loan capital" ("Dutch central bank's mortgage warning"). In 2013, the Dutch government heeded such warnings, passing new legislation that banned interest-only mortgages, and began to introduce limits on mortgage interest deductions.

In Sweden, mortgage market liberalization also gave buyers many new financing options in the 1990s, with the launching of the single currency (euro) and increased integration of European capital markets. Buyers were permitted to take out larger loans with long maturity terms (informally, up to eighty years). Moreover, after the financial liberalization, 70 percent of all mortgages had an adjustable interest rate, which added instability to the Swedish housing market. Homeowners furthermore began to enjoy tax relief for interest payments (Andrews et al. 2011) and the ability to withdraw equity and use it for other consumption goals. With these incentives, it is no surprise that over 90 percent of Swedish homeowners held a mortgage loan in the early 2010s (Stenfors 2014). Similarly, in the Netherlands, 75 percent of homeowners had a mortgage in 2013. By contrast, homeowners in Germany faced very different incentives, and so only 40 percent of homeowners held a mortgage in 2013 (Kelly, Le Blanc, and Lydon 2019).

In Denmark, to ease the opening of the market for cooperative apartments, the Liberal-Conservative coalition government under the leadership of prime minister Anders Fogh Rasmussen (2002–5; 2005–7; 2007–11) approved new mortgage products such as interest-only loans. The government also allowed tax appraisers to assess the value of the cooperatives based on the open market, which by 2006 had contributed to a rise in housing prices of 155 percent in metropolitan areas (Bruun 2018). As prices continued to rise, commercial banks topped up mortgage loans issued by specialized mortgage banks, adding an additional loan to the initial amount borrowed. Thus, as in the Netherlands (until the law changed again in 2005), some Danish homebuyers put no money down at all. Denmark also began to offer interest deductibility on taxes (Andrews et al. 2011). All these factors led to real home prices in Denmark rising by 140 percent between 1994 and 2007.

In all three of these countries, the restructuring of the housing market was couched in terms that were antithetical to the social-democratic ideology. Center-right and conservative coalitions highlighted gains in efficiency, a wider variety of choices, the virtues of self-sufficiency, and the benefits of owning a "concrete asset." Rising prices, moreover, cultivated an investment attitude among many homeowners, who viewed their home as a long-term asset to fall back on in old age or during an emergency (Poppe, Collard, and Jakobsen 2016). Even the center-left parties in these countries, when they were back in power, did not reverse the commodification and privatization of housing. While social-democratic parties had not initiated the first wave of reforms, commodification led to appreciating house prices, which in turn stirred excitement and convinced more people to join the housing ladder, including typical social-democratic voters. As more center-left voters became homeowners, center-left parties started contributing to the political narrative defending homeownership and financialization (Anderson and Kurzer 2020). Homeowners, moreover, tend to have higher voter turnout rates, which the center-left could not ignore (André, Dewilde, and Luijkx 2017). The Danish social democratic prime minister Helle Thorning-Schmidt, in power from 2011 to 2015, expounded in a *Financial Times* interview: "It's still true that the market is a lousy master but a good servant, and that means that we still have to have a market economy, but we have to control it and regulate it to the benefit of everyone" (qtd. in Milne 2014). Social-democratic parties thus tried to extend homeownership advantages to low-income and working-class voters by initiating special subsidies for first-time homebuyers and those with low incomes, but they no longer propped up social housing or promoted the new construction of affordable homes.

The neoliberal push for increased homeownership was quite successful in the Netherlands, Sweden, and Denmark, especially when compared to Germany, but this growth in homeownership had both positive and negative consequences. As Figure 9.1 showed, homeownership rates increased significantly in all three countries between 1980 and 2010, compared to very modest growth in Germany.[2] Figure 9.2 shows, however, that by 2008 mortgage debt

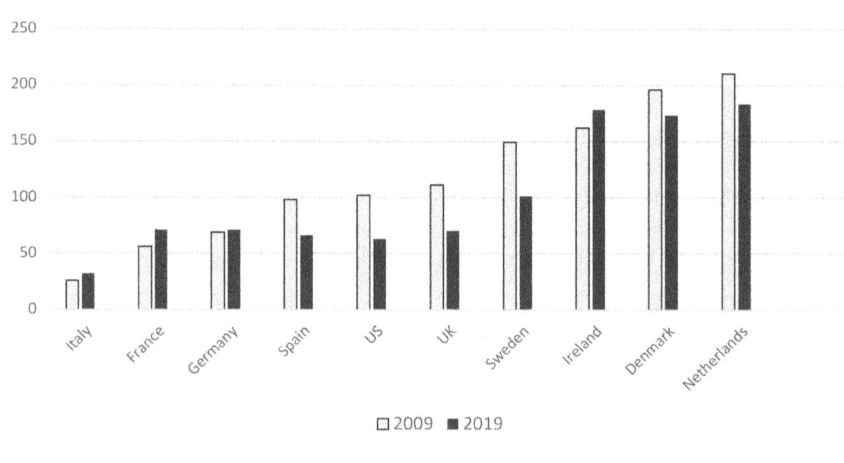

Figure 9.2. Total outstanding residential loans as percentage of disposable income of households. Source: European Mortgage Federation, Hypostat 2020 (November 2020). Created by Paulette Kurzer and Alice H. Cooper.

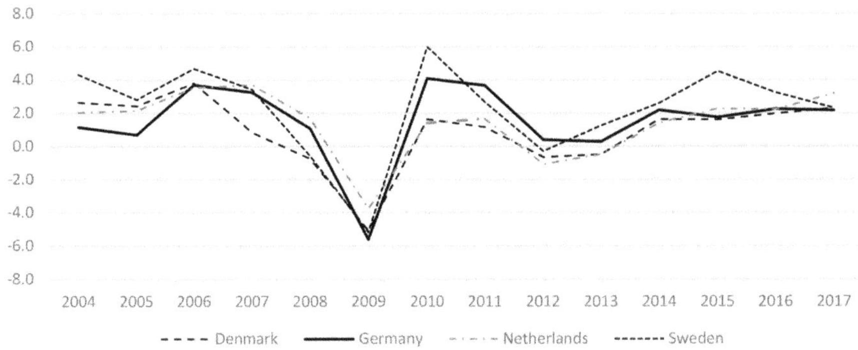

Figure 9.3. Annual growth rates of GDP, in percentages. Source: OECD, https://stats.oecd.org/ (2018). Created by Paulette Kurzer and Alice H. Cooper.

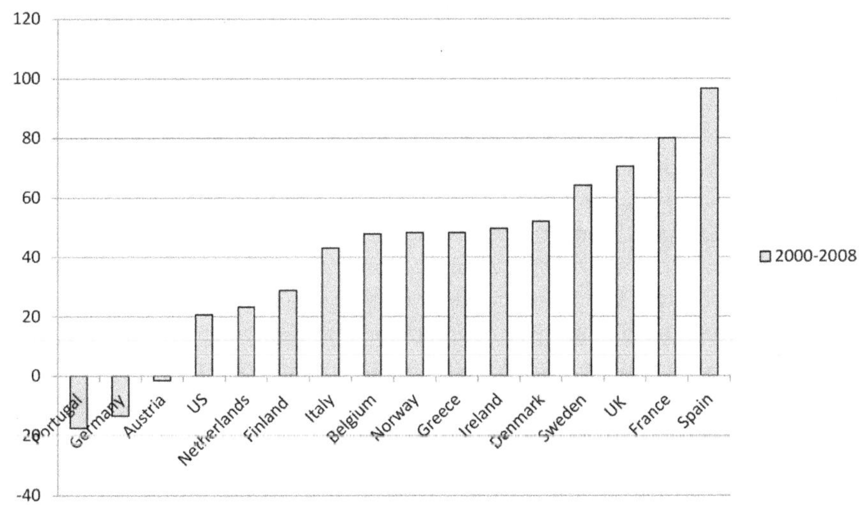

Figure 9.4. Real housing price growth: 2000–2008. Source: OECD, https://stats.oecd.org/ (2018). Created by Paulette Kurzer and Alice H. Cooper.

had also grown quite high in those three countries, exceeding 100 percent of household disposable income in Sweden, and approaching 200 percent in Denmark and the Netherlands, which was much higher than in Germany. Annual GDP growth rates were, moreover, mostly on the rise as of 2006, as Figure 9.3 shows. In much of Western Europe, the liberalization of mortgage-lending regulations stimulated consumer spending and economic growth, as homeowners could withdraw equity thanks to house price appreciation.

Until the recession hit Europe in 2009/10, GDP growth rates were concomitantly higher in the Netherlands, Sweden, and Denmark than in Germany. Finally, an unintended consequence of neoliberal housing policies was that the housing supply did not keep up with the rising demand for owner-occupied housing, and thus house prices rose steadily in all three countries. As Figure 9.4 shows, from 2000 until the global financial crisis, Denmark and Sweden recorded notable increases in house prices. This was also true, but to a lesser extent, in the Netherlands, where house prices had already risen substantially in the 1990s.

German Housing Policy from the 1950s to the 1990s

From roughly 1980 on, Germany's housing policies began to diverge from those implemented in the other three countries discussed here (Cooper and Kurzer 2020). As we will see, Germany did not develop a neoliberal financialized approach to housing reforms, despite introducing dramatic changes in other areas of the economy.

Economists from the Freiburg School, who had developed their ideas in the 1930s, influenced the West German government's approach toward postwar reconstruction. They emphasized an economic order founded on competition, price stability, private property, and economic predictability. At the same time, the Freiburg School prescriptions were tempered by an ethical ideology called the "social-market" economy. The main goal of this ideology was for the new, postwar German economy to be both efficient and fair, with a strong state that could guarantee competition and monetary stability but also ensure that people could expect a decent quality of life (Berghahn and Young 2013). The main objective of Germany's postwar government was, therefore, to achieve a social balance by coordinating different spheres of society—the private market, state governments, and social groups—and to establish a middle way between market freedom and social protection. In addition, the "subsidiarity" principle mandated that social policies be carried out at the lowest possible level of government (Rieter and Schmolz 1993; Sally 1996). In the 1950s, the social-market economy and the subsidiarity principle also guided housing policy. While the federal government provided much of the financing for new housing construction starting in 1950, state and municipal governments were able to steer federal housing subsidies according to their particular housing priorities and local needs.

During World War II, nearly half of Germany's housing stock was destroyed or damaged (Kofner 2014). After the war, one of the Adenauer government's top priorities was to overcome the desperate housing shortage. In line with social-market thinking, subsequent German governments continued to employ an array of policy instruments to address housing shortages and affordability. These instruments included federal financial support for social housing and the overall rental market, but they also offered opportunities to private investors to help provide this support, and they gave state governments some leeway to pursue their own priorities. The First and Second Housing Laws of 1950 and 1956 provided massive subsidies for the construction of new rental and owner-occupied housing. Subsidies were made available to public-sector actors, non-profit housing companies, factory-related housing provided by industrial firms, private investors, and prospective individual homeowners (Voigtländer 2009; Droste and Knorr-Siedow 2014).

As in the other three European countries discussed here, the German narrative after World War II portrayed housing predominantly as a social right. The CDU's *Düsseldorfer Leitsätze* (Düsseldorf guiding principles) of 1949 noted with great concern the desperate postwar housing shortage. They called it a threat to the spiritual, moral, and physical foundations of Germany's collective life as a people and a state. Although the party preferred single-family housing and small-scale developments, large numbers of small apartments with affordable rents were also deemed essential to address general housing needs (CDU 1949). As for the SPD, its *Godesberger Programm* (Godesberg program) of 1959 tellingly discusses housing policy in the section titled "Social Responsibility." It notes that the citizens' right to adequate housing must not be subject to the profit motive. Moreover, social housing should be supported and a social perspective should influence rent levels (SPD 1959). Thus, despite the center-right parties' ideological preference for homeownership, government support for housing in general as a public good enjoyed a consensus among all mainstream German parties in the initial postwar decades (Bartholomaei 2004).

Starting with the various Adenauer governments of the 1950s, the construction of rental units was subsidized in Germany, and considerable support was given to homeowners in the form of various tax subsidies for owner-occupied housing. Homeowners were able to deduct mortgage interest from their taxes up to 1986. They were also allowed to claim depreciation until 1996, at which point Germany switched to a tax allowance called the *Eigenheimzulage* (homeownership subsidy). These subsidies, however, were less generous and more restrictive than in the Netherlands, Sweden, and Denmark. The *Eigenheimzulage* allowance could only be used once or twice by any given household, which discouraged frequent buying/selling or "trading up" to more expensive housing. Moreover, tax subsidies for homeownership were lower than in many other countries, and did not influence the rate of homeownership as much (Voigtländer 2009). Finally, in contrast to many other countries' ongoing fiscal subsidies for homeownership, Germany eliminated the *Eigenheimzulage* altogether in 2006 (Reisenbichler 2022). The

Social Democrats had long opposed it as primarily benefiting upper-income groups. Moreover, certain CDU-governed states also lent critical support in the Bundesrat for its eradication, because the states had historically co-funded the *Eigenheimzulage*, and many states were looking for ways to reduce budget deficits. Finally, there was an overall concern about the growing disparity in wealth levels between the new and old states, and tax subsidies for homeowners contributed to that disparity, given low homeownership rates in the eastern states (Reisenbichler 2016). The last remaining tax subsidy for homeownership is embedded in a post-1990s change to Germany's pension policy. In 2002, the SPD-Green government adopted a program that encourages private, tax-advantaged, individual pension savings contracts, which became known colloquially as the "Riester-Rente" (Riester pension, named after labor minister Walter Riester), to complement government and workplace-based pensions. In 2008, the CDU-SPD government passed the Eigenheim-Rente law, which allowed Riester-Rente savings to be applied toward the purchase of an owner-occupied home (*Manager Magazin* 2008).

The private rental sector has also enjoyed generous government support in Germany since World War II. Tax breaks include both a capital-gains exemption for new construction of private rentals, and tax relief for repairs and upgrades to existing stock. Until 2005, depreciation rules were also relatively generous, allowing landlords to write off 40 percent of the purchase price or construction cost in the first ten years of rental property ownership (Kofner 2014, 2016). These rules encouraged investment in private rental property, and contributed significantly to its supply. They fit the idea that, while competition has a vital role to play in the housing market, vulnerable populations should be protected from market forces.

Limited Neoliberal Reforms in the German Housing Market after 1990

Along with many other countries, Germany also enacted neoliberal reforms from the 1980s to the early 2000s, based on the neoliberal narrative advanced by Great Britain and the United States that such reforms would stimulate economic activity and reduce unemployment. Under Chancellor Gerhard Schröder, the SPD-Green government adopted far-reaching legislation to liberalize and deregulate the labor market and to reform social security benefits in 2002–5 (Hartz/Agenda 2010 reforms). These reforms were intended to increase employment by making it easier for firms to hire workers and workers to find jobs, retrain, or start their own businesses. In addition, the Agenda 2010 legislation reduced unemployment benefits and social-welfare assistance, as well as adding the Riester-Rente plan discussed above to the defined-benefits system to encourage private savings for retirement (Boersch-Supan and Juerges 2011). Some of these reforms fit with the discourse on increasing households' financial self-sufficiency and reducing their reliance on the state. This narrative partly drove the liberalization of housing policy in other countries, in addition to neoliberal reforms of pension systems and labor markets. But in Germany, despite neoliberal reforms in other areas, there was no real debate on restructuring the housing market, and households were not encouraged to achieve greater financial autonomy and independence through homeownership.

To be sure, Germany reformed social housing dramatically, and ultimately eliminated the federal government's role in regulating and subsidizing it. Although the state governments furthermore withdrew from ownership of social housing, private landlords who purchased such units received subsidies so they could continue to operate the newly privatized dwellings as a functional equivalent to social housing for a defined period of time (Kofner 2017). At the same time, tax deductions for homeownership and depreciation allowances for rental property were reduced or eliminated, disincentivizing homeownership. Neither the Kohl, nor Schröder, nor Merkel governments adopted housing policies that clearly privileged homeownership over renting.

The German government's foray into reforming social housing began with the abolition of the public interest housing law (*Wohngemeinnützigkeit*) in 1989. This meant that factory-related and public housing organizations, the most important providers of social housing, lost their tax advantages, on the one hand, but gained entrepreneurial freedom on the other. Subsidies for social housing were also largely ended by the SPD-Green government in 2001 (Droste and Knorr-Siedow 2014), which shifted the government's focus from supporting affordable housing for large segments of the population to supporting only people in need. The 2006 federalism reform, furthermore, shifted full authority for allocating social-housing funds to the states and to local governments, removing the federal government from this policy area altogether (Kofner 2017; Reisenbichler 2021).

In the 1990s, moreover, the federal government and many state and local governments began to privatize publicly owned housing. Such privatization was particularly common in the new East German states (Elsinga, Stephens, and Knorr-Siedow 2014). Unlike in countries such as the United Kingdom, the Netherlands, Sweden, and Denmark, selling social housing to sitting tenants was never a major goal of the German government, however, and few tenants there showed much interest in purchasing their apartments. Instead, much rental property was purchased by private investors (often individual families residing in the formerly West German states) and then rented out. By contrast, although declining support for large-scale social housing had a neoliberal ideological grounding, German governments still generally accepted the need for a stable, affordable rental sector. The federal government still finances the *Wohngeld* program, whereby low-income families can qualify for government housing allowances intended to enable them to afford housing in the private rental market and to enjoy strong tenancy protection (Droste and Knorr-Siedow 2014).

As with its public housing policies, many enduring features of the German credit (i.e., mortgage) market also have a decidedly ordoliberal character. The proponents of ordoliberalism advocated economic predictability and a rule-based legal approach to household credit, along with fiscal policy and price stability more broadly. Whereas other countries liberalized and deregulated mortgage lending in the 1990s to enable households to acquire housing assets by accumulating debt, German authorities took a different approach and discouraged "asset speculation" (Berghahn and Young 2013).

Along with possible tax considerations, the nature of the mortgage market plays an important role in household homeownership decisions. Traditional norms and values have thus far preserved conservative mortgage lending practices in Germany, and thereby also restricted the expansion of homeownership relative to other countries. Germany's mortgage-lending institutions discouraged debt-financed entry into homeownership. Down-payment requirements were high, and most homeowners spent many years building up adequate savings. High standards for the creditworthiness of borrowers made obtaining mortgages difficult for middle-class households. In Germany, banks finance only 60–80 percent of the purchase price of a home, and buyers must supply the rest from personal savings, loans from a building society, or contractual savings plans with specialist banks known as *Bausparkassen* (Voigtländer 2009; Kofner 2014; Wijburg and Aalbers 2017).

German banks got into trouble during the global financial crisis because of their involvement in international financial markets such as the American mortgage market. However, their conservative mortgage lending practices had remained largely unchanged at home prior to the crisis, and, after it ended, they did not expand access to mortgage capital for the ordinary aspiring homeowner. High loan-to-value loans, interest-only mortgages, and adjustable-rate mortgages have never been widely available. Most mortgage credit continues to come from traditional sources such as deposits and mortgage bonds, rather than from securitization. Various changes such as abolishing public guarantees for public sector banks, along with eliminating the specialist bank principle for mortgage banks, seem to have reinforced traditional German lending practices, reducing the appetite for increasing lending risk or extending the product range. Thus, in contrast to other countries, Kofner (2016: 197) maintains that "the German system of housing finance has undergone no fundamental change in the last 25 years." This consistency contributed to the stability of German housing prices throughout the global financial crisis (Kofner 2014; Kofner 2016). Stable housing prices in turn encourage Germans to continue to view owner-occupied housing as a consumption good, rather than as an opportunity to amass wealth by treating it as an asset class (Voigtländer 2014).

The Weakness of German Homeownership Ideology from the 1990s to the 2010s

The early twenty-first-century German narrative surrounding housing has remained remarkably consistent with its past discourse. Reflecting the dominant thinking about preserving stability in the housing market and discouraging private credit accumulation, the election platforms of many political parties in Germany have neither prioritized homeownership expansion nor the liberalization of mortgage lending. What is striking is what is *not* said (or what gets only occasional mention) about the lack of a growing emphasis on neoliberal housing priorities. German political actors have not lent support to private credit accumulation, homeownership, or financial liberalization of the housing industry (Mertens 2017). In short, politicians there have expressed no appetite for households accumulating debt and tying their wealth to housing. Such activities would jeopardize the predictability of economic policy, and add an element of uncertainty in dealing with unexpected downturns. Above all, they would make curbing inflation more complicated, which German voters and officials continue to prioritize even when that threat is remote (Jacoby 2014). Through their policies, German authorities continue to incentivize renting over buying, and to "punish" homeownership by, for example, imposing high transfer taxes on buying real estate.

Although various German governments since the early 1990s have changed a number of policies related to housing, the dominant narrative has not changed. The discourse on housing lacked excitement about potential wealth accumulation, risk-taking, or financial self-sufficiency that characterized the housing reforms in the Netherlands, Sweden, and Denmark. Instead, we observe a continuation of the traditional narrative: although the CDU/CSU, SPD, and FDP all support homeownership and sometimes propose measures to stimulate it, none of their suggestions amounts to a strong neoliberal attempt to transform German society by dramatically increasing homeownership. Moreover, although homeownership is occasionally seen as a way for people to provide for themselves in retirement, it is rarely mentioned with regard to old-age provision. We will illustrate this perspective here by drawing on electoral platforms and coalition agreements that featured the most significant discussions of housing policy from the 1990s to the 2010s.

From the center-right perspective, the 1994 CDU/CSU-FDP coalition agreement presented a "new initiative for asset accumulation," which aimed to stimulate homeownership by increasing income limits for subsidized homeownership savings contracts (*Bausparförderung*). Housing policy also received considerable attention at this time in the discussion of "family policy." The focus here was on affordable housing for families with children, including homeownership. Interestingly, while the "new initiative for asset accumulation" got one short paragraph, five separate mentions of homeownership as part of "family policy" got more than twice as much space, suggesting that this rather traditional conservative concern underlay much of the desire to promote homeownership (CDU/CSU-FDP 1994).

In the CDU/CSU's platform for the 2009 election, the CDU/CSU note their desire for more people to be able to fulfill their aspiration for homeownership. Later, in a section on provisions for old-age financial security, private savings are mentioned as one of its three pillars, along with government and workplace-based pensions. However, there is no mention of homeownership as a component of such private savings, let alone measures to encourage it. This policy contrasts strongly with the idea in many other countries that homeownership should be a major component of retirement savings (CDU/CSU 2009).

Like the CDU/CSU, the SPD maintained much of its traditional narrative after 1990, based on the social-market ideology, whereas in countries like the Netherlands the Social Democratic Party got on board with the massive promotion of homeownership, rooted in neoliberalism. In its *Grundsatzprogramm*, approved in 1989 and amended in 1998, the SPD discusses housing in a section on social justice and social solidarity, and calls housing a fundamental social right on par with work and education. It also calls for restrictions on treating land as an object of speculation (SPD 1998a). The SPD platform for the 1998 election discusses three pillars of old-age provision, including private savings, "for example," in the form of homeownership and life insurance policies. Thus, the SPD considers homeownership to be a possible component of old-age provision, but neither necessary nor central to it. The party reiterates its traditional support for social housing, rent control, and housing allowances (SPD 1998b).

The coalition agreement for the first SPD-Green government in 1998 continues along these traditional party lines. There is some support for homeownership, along with the occasional mention of homeownership as a means to providing for old age, but many other housing policy goals are equally prominent. The 1998 agreement advocates selling federally owned housing to local governments and "tenant privatization" as a path to accumulating assets for old-age provision (SPD-Greens 1998). But in the 2002 coalition agreement, the SPD and Greens agree that renting and homeownership have equal rights as types of housing. They support homeownership, especially for families with children, and they express the desire to better integrate homeownership and provision for old age. However, housing allowances and environmental protection/energy efficiency get equal billing with these other housing policy goals (SPD-Greens 2002).

A Housing Affordability Crisis and the Election Narrative of the Political Parties

Up to the global financial crisis, the German property market did not experience the boom-and-bust characteristics of many other Western countries in the 1990s and 2000s (see Figure 9.1). The rate of homeownership remained concomitantly stagnant, both in comparison to other European countries and to past German homeownership rates. In addition, in the absence of measures to promote homeownership, the mortgage indebtedness of German households remained manageable relative to other countries (see Figure 9.2). While this policy may have contributed to Germany's slower economic growth in the early 2000s than countries such as the Netherlands, Sweden, and Denmark (see Figure 9.3), it also allowed Germany to avoid the rise in housing prices which culminated in the housing bubble and its subsequent collapse elsewhere in the mid-2000s (see Figure 9.4). This, in turn, allowed Germany to recover more quickly from the global financial crisis than the Netherlands and Denmark. Sweden also made a remarkable recovery because it likewise did not have a housing bubble before 2007, although mortgage lending was deregulated and house prices there have increased dramatically since 2010.

It should be noted that, although German housing prices have risen considerably since 2010, this increase was not in response to government policies intended to stimulate homeownership. Instead, rising prices resulted from low interest rates, which spurred private equity groups and hedge fund managers in search of better investment opportunities to settle on German real estate, which was relatively cheap compared to that of neighboring countries. For this reason, Germany faces another sort of housing crisis today, which has different features from traditional crises such as the bursting of a housing bubble. It is instead a slow-moving, "creeping" crisis, driven by social and economic changes in the past thirty years. Germany's current housing crisis derives from a lack of housing availability and affordability for people in the middle- and lower-income brackets, especially in the large urban areas that attract young professionals and migrants (Kaschel 2021). This housing dearth is acknowledged as an urgent problem, and the various German political parties have proposed a number of countermeasures.

In brief, the German housing crisis has resulted from an expanding demand for housing but with a limited supply, and has culminated in sharply rising housing prices for (aspiring) homeowners and renters alike. When indexed to 100 for 2010, as of 2020–21 rents of existing rental contracts had risen relatively modestly to 115. This increase was dwarfed, however, by rents for new leases, which stood at around 147 for Germany as a whole, and at around 156 for seven major cities. Moreover, rent-to-income ratios as of 2021 reached 27 percent (on average), the upper end of what is considered affordable. Regarding supply in recent decades, new construction fell dramatically around 2008–9. Since then, supply has suffered from slow "completions" of new housing stock, because of skilled labor shortages, the complexity of the building code, and high land prices (Schmidt 2021). Compared to demand, particularly for the lower price segments, supply has been tightest in major urban areas.

Part of this housing supply problem can be traced back to the 1990s, when state governments retreated from the housing market and privatized public housing stock. This led, over time, to a drop in privately owned social-housing dwellings, because private landlords only had to abide by social-housing rental terms for a defined period of time. As more dwellings landed outside the parameters of the functional equivalent of social housing, rents rose and affordability fell. Given Germany's overall housing shortage, increasing rents are also due to demographic changes: large urban areas have become a magnet for young professionals and migrants. The rising demand for affordable housing has furthermore met with a shrinking or at least stagnating supply in large cities. Moreover, like many other advanced industrialized countries, Germany is aging rapidly and counts a growing number of single-person households, which has also increased the demand for affordable housing.

Since the 1990s, moreover, incomes have failed to keep up with the rising housing costs for major segments of the population. Until the 1990s, most workers could expect full-time employment during their working life and pension benefits that represented true wage replacement. Since then, pension reforms and other catalysts have reduced statutory, occupational, and private pension benefits. In addition, labor market changes have created many irregular, non-standard employment patterns that can depress people's incomes during their active working years, and their retirement benefits later (Hinrichs 2021). These developments have generated greater housing cost burdens.

All major German political parties have noted this affordability crisis in their election platforms, starting in the 2010s. The affordability crisis became such a salient political issue that Chancellor Angela Merkel held a *Wohngipfel* (housing summit) in 2018, and declared that "for many, one of the most pressing themes of our time is finding affordable housing" ("Chancellor Angela Merkel," 26 May 2018, authors' translation). Correspondingly, the narratives of the main political parties involved in governing (CDU/CSU, SPD, Greens, and FDP) reflect the growing urgency to reduce housing costs, thereby acknowledging rising voter frustration. Since the 2010s, housing affordability has become the dominant theme by far, yet the solution is not sought in expanding owner-occupied housing by liberalizing mortgage financing or increasing tax incentives for homebuyers. Neither do the political parties view homeownership as an important contribution to old-age provision or wealth building, in spite of shrinking pension entitlements in the wake of labor market reforms and pension restructuring (e.g., CDU/CSU 2013; SPD 2021).

Starting with the 2009 election, the CDU/CSU platforms have put a great deal of emphasis on addressing housing shortages. On the one hand, the sister parties affirm their commitment to homeownership for those who want it, and stress in particular that measures are needed to facilitate homeownership for families with children. For example, the party's 2017 platform discusses three such measures, including a new provision of 1,200 euros per child, annually for ten years, for families that purchase or build a house after July 2017. Similarly, the 2021 platform proposes adjusting loans and subsidizing interest rates based on the number of children in any given family (CDU/CSU 2021). On the other hand, the rental market receives much greater attention, primarily pertaining to its affordability. The 2021 platform proclaims that the best tenant protection lies in sufficient availability. It sets the goal of having 1.5 million new housing units built by 2025, mostly via market-oriented measures such as investment incentives (expanded tax deductions for new rental units), speeding up planning and approval processes, and reducing building code regulations. The CDU/CSU also proposes to expand social housing and housing allowances, to remodel housing to suit the elderly, and to increase the energy efficiency of older structures (ibid.), all while increasing the housing supply.

For FDP politicians, too, the main problem is the affordability of both rental and owner-occupied housing. The party's twin goals are to help aspiring homeowners purchase homes and to increase affordability for renters. Like the CDU/CSU, the FDP focuses on expanding the housing supply as the best means to these ends, mostly through private-sector avenues. In terms of homeownership, the FDP proposes reducing a specific property tax (the *Grunderwerbsteuer,* a real estate transfer tax) for owner-occupied housing. The party also advocates reducing regulations and speeding up the approval process, in order to cut the costs and time associated with new construction. Rather than subjecting the owners of rental units to traditional forms of rent control (e.g., the *Mietendeckel* [rent freeze] and *Mietpreisbremse* [rental price control]), the FDP proposes favorable tax treatment such as allowing a faster depreciation for rental property. The party also proposes measures to facilitate new construction on empty lots or land that could be repurposed. Finally, the FDP advocates increasing rent allowances for low-income renters so that they may more easily rent apartments in the private rental sector (FDP 2021).

For its part, the SPD platform for the 2013 election, along with its 2018 party resolution, both reaffirm the party's support for affordable housing, rent control, and control of land use and prices—without explicitly mentioning support for homeownership. The 2018 resolution declares that "the lack of affordable housing is the social question of our time" (SPD 2013, 2018, authors' translation). The housing section of the 2021 election platform is titled "affordable housing," and the rental market is by far the dominant focus. The SPD's prescriptions have a fairly non-market cast. They advocate the annual construction of one hundred thousand social-housing units and the creation of an additional non-profit segment of the housing market. The party advocates various rent control measures such as restricting rent increases to the rate of inflation, along with measures to eliminate land speculation and strengthen local government control over buildable land. Homeownership is briefly mentioned and, for the first time, acknowledged as a component of old-age provision, but the SPD's support for homeownership takes the form of strengthening housing cooperatives and "rent-to-own" programs (SPD 2021).

The Greens have the most "moralizing" stance of the mainstream German political parties. In its 2021 election platform, the party advocates anchoring a right to housing in the Basic Law. It proposes a national "housing first" summit on housing and rent rates, with the participation of all stakeholders such as renters, builders, and various levels of government. When it comes to rental housing, the Greens take a relatively non-market approach. They call for increased investment in social housing, and eliminating its sale to private investors; fair rent rates maintained by various forms of rent control and by strengthening tenants' rights; curbing real-estate and land speculation; and redirecting buildable land toward affordable housing by ending profit-oriented forms of landownership. When it comes to homeownership, the Greens advocate facilitating it for owner-occupiers (as opposed to large housing firms) through rent-to-own programs, reducing real-estate transaction costs and property taxes for owner-occupiers, and strengthening housing cooperatives. Finally, like the CDU/CSU and SPD, the Greens advocate more environmentally friendly and climate-friendly building practices and techniques (Die Grünen 2021).

Conclusion

This chapter has discussed housing crises and policy narratives in four advanced welfare states. Our analysis shows that a combination of neoliberal housing policies and narratives have characterized the housing markets of the

Netherlands and Denmark, with Sweden also showing these tendencies. In contrast, the absence of policies and incentives that treat housing as a vehicle for wealth accumulation have helped Germany avert a housing market bubble and thus a subsequent collapse. In the past four decades, most West European countries have given primacy to homeownership and disinvested in the rental market, and their narratives overwhelmingly celebrated the idea of becoming and enjoying the status of being a nation of homeowners. Yet this "ideology of homeownership" has not characterized housing reforms in Germany, despite the fact that German center-left and center-right coalition governments introduced extensive reforms in its labor markets, social security, and pension systems. In the absence of financial liberalization and favorable tax deductions, homeownership has not dominated the national housing narrative.

Yet the German policies and narratives reviewed here have not rendered Germany immune to all types of housing crises. Low interest rates and the relative inexpensiveness of German property, at least up until 2010, attracted substantial inflows of capital from investment companies and private equity firms, driving prices up. At the same time, the influx of young professionals and migrants into large urban areas has put pressure on local housing markets. The lack of construction and investment in rental housing has resulted in rising rental costs that are hurting young professionals, retirees, and low-income households. Voter outrage is directed at the lack of affordable rental options, not at missed opportunities for homeownership. The coronavirus pandemic has, in fact, worsened the situation, because investors have continued to buy up residential properties in large cities, while many households working from home are looking to upgrade their home office by renting a larger space. Nevertheless, "some things never change," and, compared to many other countries, German political policy and narratives continue to place less emphasis on homeownership and more on the need to maintain a healthy rental market.

Paulette Kurzer is Professor of Political Science at the School of Government and Public Policy at the University of Arizona, where she also directs the MA in International Security Studies. She has written widely on consumer protection policies, public health, and housing markets in West European countries and the European Union. Her latest publication is *Bricks in the Wall: The Politics of Housing in Europe*, co-edited with Alison Johnston (Routledge, 2021), and a study on EU health reforms after the pandemic is forthcoming.

Alice H. Cooper is Professor of Political Science at the University of Mississippi. She has studied social movements, various aspects of social policy in the EU and Germany, and more recently housing market policy. She has published in *German Politics, German Politics and Society, Comparative Political Studies, European Journal of Political Research,* and various other journals.

Notes

1. The difference between US 'public housing' and European 'social housing' is that, although the latter is subsidized, it serves middle-class as well as low-income households, thereby avoiding the stigmatization of America's public housing (Lewis 2013).
2. Unification resulted in severe imbalances in the German housing market in the 1990s because of the large movement of East Germans into West Germany, and the resulting high number of vacancies in the East. But the demise of socialism did not result in a new commitment to homeownership; in fact, the federal government abolished the tax break for homeowners in order to address growing wealth and income differences between the old and new federal states (Reisenbichler 2016).

References

Anderson, Karen M., and Paulette Kurzer. 2020. "The Politics of Mortgage Credit Expansion in the Small Coordinated Market Economies." *West European Politics* 43(2): 366–89.

André, Stéfanie, Caroline Dewilde, and Ruud Luijkx. 2017. "The Tenure Gap in Electoral Participation: Instrumental Motivation or Selection Bias? Comparing Homeowners and Tenants across Four Housing Regimes." *International Journal of Comparative Sociology* 58(3): 241–65.

Andrews, Dan, Aida Caldera Sánchez, and Åda Johansson. 2011. *Housing Markets and Structural Policies in OECD Countries.* OECD Economics Department Working Papers, No. 836 (25 January): OECD Publishing, https://doi.org/10.1787/5kgk8t2k9vf3-en.

Bartholomaei, Reinhart. 2004. "Die Entwicklung des Politikfelds Wohnen." In *Wohnungspolitik in Deutschland,* ed. Bjorn Egner et al., 15–34. Darmstadt: Schader-Stiftung.

Berghahn, Volker, and Brigitte Young. 2013. "Reflections on Werner Bonefeld's 'Freedom and the Strong State: On German Ordoliberalism' and the Continuing Importance of the Ideas of Ordoliberalism to Understand Germany's (Contested) Role in Resolving the Eurozone Crisis." *New Political Economy* 18(5): 768–78.

Bijlo, Esther, and Co Welgraven. 1996. "Het Biefstuksocialisme op Herhaling: Iedereen zijn eigen Huis." *Trouw* (29 June). Retrieved 30 September 2021 from https://www.trouw.nl/home/het-biefstuksocialisme-op-herhaling-iedereen-zijn-eigen-huis~a1cd572e/.

Boersch-Supan, Axel H., and Hendrik Juerges. 2011. "Disability, Pension Reform and Early Retirement in Germany." *NBER Working Paper No. 17079* (May).

Bruun, Maja Hojer. 2018. "Social Imaginaries and Egalitarian Practices in the Era of Neoliberalization." In *Egalitarianism in Scandinavia: Approaches to Social Inequality and Difference*, ed. Synnøve Bendixsen et al., 135–55. New York: Palgrave Macmillan.

CDU. 1949. "Düsseldorfer Leitsätze." Retrieved 2 May 2022 from http://www.kas.de/wf/de/71.8940/.

CDU/CSU. 2009. "Wir haben die Kraft gemeinsam für unser Land. Regierungsprogramm 2009–2013." 2009–2013_Regierungsprogramm_Wir-haben-die-Kraft_Gemeinsam-fuer-unser-Land.pdf. Retrieved 2 May 2022 from http://www.kas.de/wf/de/71.8940/.

———. 2013. "Gemeinsam erfolgreich für Deutschland. 2013–17." 2013-2017_regierungsprogramm.pdf. Retrieved 2 May 2022 from http://www.kas.de/wf/de/71.8940/.

———. 2021. "Das Program für Stabilität und Erneuerung: Gemeinsam für ein modernes Deutschland." Retrieved 22 July 2021 from https://www.bundestagswahl-2021.de/wahlprogramme/.

CDU/CSU-FDP. 1994. "Das vereinte Deutschland zukunftsfähig machen." Koalitionsvertrag1994.pdf. Retrieved 2 May 2022 from http://www.kas.de/wf/de/71.9390/.

"Chancellor Angela Merkel Tackles Housing Shortfall, Tenancy Hikes." 2018. Dw.com. 26 May. Retrieved 18 September 2021 from https://www.dw.com/en/chancellor-angela-merkel-tackles-housing-shortfall-tenancy-hikes/a-43940831.

Cooper, Alice, and Paulette Kurzer. 2020. "Similar Origins–Divergent Paths: The Politics of German and Dutch Housing Markets." *German Politics*, https://doi.org/10.1080/09644008.2020.1764541.

Dickens, Peter, Simon Duncan, Mark Goodwin, and Fred Gray. 1985. *Housing, States and Localities*. London: Methuen.

Die Grünen. 2021. "Deutschland. Alles ist drin. Bundestagswahlprogramm 2021." Retrieved 21 July 2021 from https://www.bundestagswahl-2021.de/wahlprogramme/.

Droste, Christiane, and Thomas Knorr-Siedow. 2014. "Social Housing in Germany." In *Social Housing in Europe*, edited by Kathleen Scanlon, Christine Whitehead, and Melissa Fernandez Arrigoitia, 183–203. Hoboken, NJ: Wiley-Blackwell.

"Dutch Central Bank's Mortgage Warning." 2011. Expatica. 2 November. Retrieved on 30 September 2021 from https://www.expatica.com/nl/uncategorized/dutch-central-banks-mortgage-warning-15499/.

Elsinga, Marja, Hugo Priemus, and Peter Boelhouwer. 2016. "Milestones in Housing Finance in the Netherlands, 1988–2013." In *Milestones in European Housing Finance*, ed. Jens Lunde and Christine Whitehead, 255–72. Oxford: John Wiley & Sons.

Elsinga, Marja, Mark Stephens, and Thomas Knorr-Siedow. 2014. "The Privatisation of Social Housing: Three Different Pathways." In *Social Housing in Europe*, ed. Kathleen Scanlon, Christine Whitehead, and Melissa Fernández Arrigoitia, 388–413. Hoboken, NJ: Wiley-Blackwell.

European Mortgage Federation (EMF). 2020. *Hypostat 2020*. Brussels: EMF.

FDP. 2021. "Nie gab es mehr zu tun: Wahlprogramm der freien Demokraten." Retrieved 1 August 2021 from https://www.fdp.de/nie-gab-es-mehr-zu-tun.

Forrest, Ray, and Alan Murie. 1988. *Selling the Welfare State: The Privatisation of Public Housing*. London: Routledge.

Grundström, Karin, and Irene Molina. 2016. "From Folkhem to Lifestyle Housing in Sweden: Segregation and Urban Form, 1930s–2010s." *International Journal of Housing Policy* 16(3): 316–36.

Hall, Thomas, and Sonja Vidén. 2005. "The Million Homes Programme: A Review of the Great Swedish Planning Project." *Planning Perspectives* 20(3): 301–28.

Hinrichs, Karl. 2021. "Recent Pension Reforms in Europe: More Challenges, New Directions. An Overview." *Social Policy & Administration* 55(3): 409–22.

Holmqvist, Emma, and Lena Magnusson Turner. 2014. "Swedish Welfare State and Housing Markets: Under Economic and Political Pressure." *Journal of Housing and the Built Environment* 29(2): 237–54.

Jacoby, Wade. 2014. "The Politics of the Eurozone Crisis: Two Puzzles behind the German Consensus." *German Politics & Society* 32(2): 70–85.

Kaschel, Helena. 2021. "COVID Worsens Germany's Housing Shortage." *Deutsche Welle*. 21 February. Retrieved 28 July 2021 from https://www.dw.com/en/covid-worsens-germanys-housing-shortage/a-56618601.

Kelly, Jane, Julia Le Blanc, and Reamonn Lydon. 2019. *Pockets of Risk in European Housing Markets: Then and Now*. ECB Working Paper Series No. 2277 (May). Retrieved 10 May 2019 from https://www.ecb.europa.eu/pub/pdf/scpwps/ecb.wp2277~4093901f33.en.pdf?ef051cf99a2b003c0e73f88bcd669bdc.

Kofner, Stefan. 2014. "The German Housing System: Fundamentally Resilient?" *Journal of Housing and the Built Environment* 29(2): 255–75.

———. 2016. "Milestones in the Development of the German Housing Finance System in the Last 25 Years." In *Milestones in European Housing Finance*, ed. Jens Lunde and Christine Whitehead, 183–99. Oxford: John Wiley & Sons.

———. 2017. "Social Housing in Germany: An Inevitably Shrinking Sector?" *Critical Housing Analysis* 4(1): 61–71.

Kohl, Sebastian. 2018. *A Small History of the Homeownership Ideal* (No. 18/6). MPIfG Discussion Paper. Retrieved 30 September 2021 from https://www.econstor.eu/handle/10419/180216.

Larsen, Henrik Gutzon, and Anders Lund Hansen. 2015. "Commodifying Danish Housing Commons." *Geografiska Annaler: Series B, Human Geography* 97(3): 263–74.

Lewis, Roger K. 2013. "Let's Go from 'Public Housing' to 'Social Housing.'" *The Washington Post*, 3 May. Retrieved 30 April 2022 from https://www.washingtonpost.com/realestate/lets-go-from-public-housing-to-social-housing/2013/05/02/2f96427e-b1a7-11e2-baf7-5bc2a9dc6f44_story.html.

Lodemel, Ivar, and Amilcar Moreira, eds. 2014. *Activation or Workfare? Governance and the Neo-Liberal Convergence*. Oxford: Oxford University Press.

Manager Magazin. 2008. "Altersvorsorge Wohn-Riester beschlossen." 20 June. Retrieved 2 August 2018 from https://www.manager-magazin.de/finanzen/artikel/a-561005.html.

Mertens, Daniel. 2017. "Borrowing for Social Security? Credit, Asset-based Welfare and the Decline of the German Savings Regime." *Journal of European Social Policy* 27: 474–90.

Milne, Richard. 2014. "Lunch with the FT: Helle Thorning-Schmidt." *Financial Times*, 7 February. Retrieved 30 September 2021 from https://www.ft.com/content/6a2010fa-8e51-11e3-98c6-00144feab7de.

Nienaber, Michael, and Simon Johnson. 2021. "Pandemic Surge in European House Prices Raises Fears of New Bubble." *Reuters*. 10 May. Retrieved 30 September 2021 from https://www.reuters.com/world/europe/pandemic-surge-european-house-prices-raises-fears-new-bubble-2021-05-10/.

Poppe, Christian, Sharon Collard, and Turf Böcker Jakobsen. 2016. "What Has Debt Got to Do with It? The Valuation of Homeownership in the Era of Financialization." *Housing, Theory and Society* 33(1): 59–76.

Priemus, Hugo. 1995. "How to Abolish Social Housing? The Dutch Case." *International Journal of Urban and Regional Research* 19(1): 145–55.

Reisenbichler, Alexander. 2016. "A Rocky Path to Home Ownership: Why Germany Eliminated Large-Scale Subsidies for Homeowners." *Cityscape: A Journal of Policy Development and Research* 18(3): 283–90.

———. 2021. "Housing Finance between Social Welfare and Growth Strategies." In *Growth and Welfare in Advanced Capitalist Economies*, ed. Anke Hassel and Bruno Palier, 320–47. London: Oxford University Press.

———. 2022. "Entrenchment or Retrenchment: The Political Economy of Mortgage Debt Subsidies in the United States and Germany." *Comparative Politics* 54(4): https://doi.org/10.5129/001041522X16314500561319.

Rieter, Heinz, and Matthias Schmolz. 1993. "The Ideas of German Ordoliberalism 1938–45: Pointing the Way to a New Economic Order." *The European Journal of the History of Economic Thought* 1(1): 87–114.

Ronald, Richard R. 2008. *The Ideology of Home Ownership: Homeowner Societies and the Role of Housing*. London: Palgrave Macmillan.

Ronald, Richard R., and Kees Dol. 2011. "Housing in the Netherlands before and after the Global Financial Crisis." In *Housing Markets and the Global Financial Crisis: The Uneven Impact on Households*, edited by Ray Forrest and Ngai Ming Yip, 93–112. Cheltenham, UK: Edward Elgar Publishing.

Sally, Razeen. 1996. "Ordoliberalism and the Social Market: Classical Political Economy from Germany." *New Political Economy* 1(2): 233–57.

Schmidt, Carolin. 2021. "Strong Tenant Protections and Subsidies Support Germany's Majority- Renter Housing Market." Brookings Institution. Retrieved 21 July 2021 from https://www.brookings.edu/essay/germany-rental-housing-markets/.

SPD. 1959. "Grundsatzprogramm der Sozialdemokratischen Partei Deutschlands."

Godesberger_programm.pdf. Retrieved 2 May 2022 from https://www.spd.de/partei/organisation/das-grundsatzprogramm/.
———. 1998a. "Grundsatzprogramm der Sozialdemokratischen Partei Deutschlands." Berliner_ Program.pdf. Retrieved 2 May 2022 from https://www.spd.de/partei/organisation/das-grundsatzprogramm/.
———. 1998b. "Arbeit, Innovation und Gerechtigkeit." wahlprogramm_bundesparteitag_leipzig_1998.pdf. Retrieved 2 May 2022 from https://www.spd.de/partei/beschluesse/.
———. 2013. "Das WIR Entscheidet: das Regierungsprogram 2013–2017." 20130415_ regierungsprogramm_2013_2017.pdf. Retrieved 2 May 2022 from https://www.spd.de/partei/beschluesse/.
———. 2018. "Für eine gerechte und moderne Wohnungsbaupolitik in Bund und Ländern – die Wohnungsbauoffensive des Bundes konsequent fortsetzen." B2_Fu__r_eine_gerechte_und_moderne_Wohnungsbaupolitik_in_Bund_und_La__ndern_-_die_Wohungsbauoffensive_des_Bundes_konsequent-fortsetzen-2.pdf. Retrieved 2 May 2022 from https://www.spd.de/partei/beschluesse/.
———. 2021. "Aus Respect vor deiner Zukunft." Retrieved 21 July 2021 from https://www.bundestagswahl-2021.de/wahlprogramme/.
SPD-Greens. 1998. "Aufbruch und Erneuerung – Deutschlands Weg ins 21. Jahrhundert." koalitionsvertrag_bundesparteitag_bonn_1998.pdf. Retrieved 2 May 2022 from https://www.spd.de/partei/beschluesse/.
———. 2002. "Erneuerung – Gerechtigkeit – Nachhaltigkeit. Für ein wirtschaftlich starkes, soziales und ökologisches Deutschland. Für eine lebendige Demokratie." koalitionsvertrag_bundesparteitag-berlin-2002.pdf. Retrieved 2 May 2022 from https://www.spd.de/partei/beschluesse/.
Stenfors, Alexis. 2014. *Financialisation and the Financial and Economic Crises: The Case of Sweden*. FESSUD Studies in Financial Systems, No. 27.
Van Gent, Wouter. 2013. "Neoliberalization, Housing Institutions and Variegated Gentrification: How the 'Third Wave' Broke in Amsterdam." *International Journal of Urban and Regional Research* 37(2): 503–22.
Voigtländer, Michael. 2009. "Why Is the German Home Ownership Rate So Low?" *Housing Studies* 24(3): 355–72.
———. 2014. "The Stability of the German Housing Market." *Journal of Housing and the Built Environment* 29(4): 583–94.
Wijburg, Gertjan, and Manuel B. Aalbers. 2017. "The Alternative Financialization of the German Housing Market." *Housing Studies* 32(7): 968–89.

PART IV

The Tricky Question of Cause and Effect

CHAPTER 10

Literature against the "Profit-Friendly Ideological Defense System"

Entertainment and Sociopolitical Enlightenment in Uwe Timm's Headhunter

MONIKA ALBRECHT

From Miles Kahler and David A. Lake's (2013: 1) proposal to describe the 2007/8 global financial crisis with the metaphor of an "economic earthquake," to Joseph Vogl's (2015: ix) critical glance at the "spectrology" of political economy and his endeavor to deconstruct the phrases used to describe it, scholars from a range of fields such as the Social and Political Sciences, and Culture and Literary Studies, aspire to grasp and explain financial activities. They focus on how these activities are manifested in our imagination and mediated through language. How does literature respond to economic issues? What kinds of stories are told and for what purposes? Do the authors have alternative scenarios in mind, or do they warn against risks to help prevent future calamities? Perhaps most importantly, how do they convey the contingency, seeming irrationality, and impenetrability of economic processes, and how do they call our attention to systemic problems? The German writer Uwe Timm contributes substantially to tackling these issues with the various stories he tells in his 1994 novel *Headhunter* (translated from the German original, *Kopfjäger—Bericht aus dem Inneren des Landes*, 1991), which revolve around these questions and negotiate possible answers. What is more, there is good reason to read *Headhunter* as a novel that describes attitudes that led to the 2007/8 financial crisis.

Headhunter was written in the late 1980s, at a time when the effects of deregulated financial capitalism were only beginning to emerge. Yet Timm apparently foresaw what would happen as a result of unrestrained financial activities. Twenty years before Joseph Vogl's *The Specter of Capital*, the novel *Headhunter* criticized the very narrative strategies of justification and obfuscation that produce the economic reality of capitalism. In this reality, the status quo of financial affairs appears natural and without any alternative. As Timm put it aptly in a speech presented upon accepting the Carl Zuckmayer literature prize in 2012, these narratives are all part of a "profit-friendly ideological defense system" (Timm 2012). In *Headhunter,* he exposes the well-functioning mechanisms of these narratives, not by pointing a moral finger, but by depicting how the mist clouding his narrator's view gradually lifts, allowing him to acknowledge his active participation in the flawed system of financial capitalism. In the end, the narrator realizes that this system not only creates grotesque social injustice but also obscures its destructive forces with great effort, rewriting them so that they appear to be natural processes or unfathomable mysteries that can only be explained using "chaos theory." Against the backdrop of the work done by the aforementioned and other scholars, this chapter will analyze how *Headhunter* depicts the narrator's learning process, thereby revealing the all-too-willingly repressed knowledge that the simple law of cause and effect still serves well to explain international financial activities and how they impact society.

The narrator's learning process is closely linked to a strand of motifs revolving around a curious, historical wooden figurine. The destruction of this precious figurine early in the novel and its broken pieces, which serve as a constant reminder of this destruction, are successively revealed as signifiers for this process of learning. *Headhunter* opens with the narrator, Peter Walter, an investment adviser from Hamburg, on the run because he is "charged with fraud and misappropriation" (H 117; K 136),[1] specifically the "embezzlement" (H 309; K 347) of "23 million marks in commodity futures trading" (H 26; K 37). Hiding out at his isolated vacation home in Spain, Walter reports the contents of a phone call from his mother the evening before that left him edgy and irritated. The result of this call is that he is no longer able to continue working on his "book about Easter Island" (H 2; K 9) and instead starts writing the *Report from the Interior of the Country,* referred to in the subtitle of the German version of the novel:

> I went back to my desk. Once again, my mother had succeeded in disturbing me, in effectively stopping me working. I sat down again at my desk, in front of me La Pérouse's account of his travels in 1797. In irritation, or rather in rage, I pushed it aside against another book, the movement continued in accordance with the law of kinetics to a writing pad which in turn passed it on to the wooden figure—and pushed it off the table.
>
> It broke, no, shattered on the tiled floor into a thousand pieces. (H 6f.; K 15)

What follows is a kind of slow-motion effect, a seemingly quiet contemplation: "I hadn't realized wood could shatter like porcelain, even when it was as old and dried out as this piece;" and then a violent outburst: "I crawled on the floor and I shrieked in dismay [outrage[2]], shrieked in rage and disappointment"

(H 7; K 15). This unintentional destruction of a wooden figurine and the narrator's seemingly strange overreaction make up a key scene in the novel, and this scene has accordingly attracted numerous interpretations. First, the sense of a great loss is understandable, even on the surface of the text, because this ancient figurine from Easter Island is not only of historical value but also considerable material value. "[N]ot quite three years ago" (H 7; K 16), Walter paid 230,000 German marks for it, a "criminally high price" (H 309; K 347), at a time when he actually could not afford it and had to take out a loan to pay for it. The fact that he bought this wooden figurine—brought to England by "Cook's ship doctor" (H 8; K 17) at the end of the eighteenth century—"without even hesitating" (H 309; K 347) imbues it with additional symbolic and sentimental value. The extent of this value is revealed little by little throughout the course of the novel (Schöll 2007: 44).

It is also obvious that the figurine—"transformed by an artist with an obsidian knife into this bird man" (H 8; K 16)—bears an intrinsic philosophical meaning, because the narrator describes him as "a human being halfway between heaven and earth" (H 8; K 16): "Now he lies on the ground, his hands held as if bound behind his back, and with all his strength seems to be lifting the upper part of his body and the lower part that ends in a bird's tail. But you can see he'll never quite be able to lift himself off the ground" (H 8; K 16f.). Beyond that, this bird man, as the wooden figurine is called throughout, has also been interpreted as related to the narrator's concept of his identity. On the occasion of the phone call that preceded the bird man's destruction, Walter learned that his "writing uncle" (H 59; K 72) is looking for him and, as he repeatedly exclaims, intends to write about him (H 9; K 18). It is indeed striking, as Julia Schöll (2007: 144) observes, that the wooden figure "splinters at the very moment when Peter Walter sees himself in danger of becoming a narrated object." Although these interpretations are plausible, they leave questions unanswered, especially that of the underlying meaning of the specific way the mysterious bird man is destroyed.

In her study on the "de-mythologizing of German history" in Uwe Timm's works, Kerstin Germer speaks of a "double- or multi-layered encoding of the narrated or written words, which equally refers to the individual biography and to the collective pattern of past and present" (Germer 2012: 174). This observation also applies to the destruction of the bird man. In what follows I provide a new reading of this key scene of the novel against the backdrop of the motif of "outrage" (*Empörung*). In particular, I ask the question why this key motif from Timm's literary works, which usually appears in 1968 contexts,[3] is, as it seems, employed differently in the novel *Headhunter*. In fact, this motif is assigned to a literary character who can hardly be associated with the "red of outrage" (*Rot der Empörung*) (Timm 2001: 311) of the left-wing, anticapitalist 1968 student protest movement, as Timm referred to it a decade later.

On the contrary, what Peter Walter "got from the student movement" was, according to him, only what he saw through the shop window of the department store at which he was working as a window dresser. He observed from behind this shop window—a visible representation of the capitalist system as well as Walter's position in it—as in a protected bubble, that "outside on the Jungfernstieg the demonstrators passed by"[4] (H 84; K 100). It is important that the motif of "outrage" (*Empörung*) is introduced early in the novel and tied to the wooden figurine, and the specific way it is destroyed. As the narrative progresses, the bird man evolves into a string of motifs. The narrator reflects on the previously undamaged wooden figurine, tells its story, always keeps a small bag with its remains within view of his desk, and carries it with him on the various stages of his flight from the police.[5]

The present-day plot strand of *Headhunter* is set in 1989, the year of the fall of the Berlin Wall,[6] and the novel appeared on the book market in 1991. Referring to the German subtitle, an early critic pointed out that the writer Timm in those early days identified the true *Interior of the Country* as the economic and financial world, which is deprived of its material correlate (tangible commodities) and only concerns money as an abstract basis for exchange (Petersenn 2005: 12f.). Likewise, Monika Shafi (2012: 150) remarks that "rereading *Kopfjäger* twenty years after its publication one is certainly struck by its prescience and insight into global networks of commerce and trading. After all, in 1991, . . . the contours of deregulation and the unprecedented scope of investments, . . . were only beginning to emerge, but they are given center stage in *Kopfjäger*." I would go a step further than Shafi and argue that the novel actually prophesies what came to pass after around fifteen years of minimally restrained financial capitalism: the 2007/8 financial crisis. As the authors of *The Financial Crisis Inquiry Report* (2011: xviii) concluded, "widespread failures in financial regulation and supervision proved devastating to the stability of the nation's financial markets. . . . More than 30 years of deregulation and reliance on self-regulation by financial institutions . . . had stripped away key safeguards, which could have helped avoid catastrophe." Timm made his prophesy public by putting it into the mouth of another of *Headhunter*'s fictional characters, Manfred Kubin, the "economic editor of a well-known magazine," who "lived opposite [Peter Walter] on the same floor" (H 291; K327) of a luxury apartment building. When Kubin and his wife invite Walter and his wife Britt to dinner one evening, the slightly drunk Kubin gives them all a crash course in economics:

> you see, there is overcapitalization, there's too much capital and it's all rushing to all kinds of weird places, . . . to van Goghs, to loans, to future trading; never mind, it's beautiful chaos, it's creative, you see, until at some stage it all collapses. Third World countries living on credit, on their last legs, banks in

> America collapse, Wall Street wobbles, London, Frankfurt . . ., then capital is going to get sucked into these voids as if they were black holes. . . . Capital constantly needs black holes. (H 299; K 335f.)

While using the phrases that serve Peter Walter and his fellow brokers to justify and obfuscate what is going on in their world of finance—"it's beautiful chaos, it's creative" (H 299; K 335)—Kubin simultaneously predicts the inevitable outcome of what may look to some as merely a "creative" and "beautiful" game.

This clairvoyant prognosis of a crisis that results from unrestrained financial capitalism is not coincidentally part of one of Kubin's numerous statements on the topic of "chaos." In Kubin, the various narrative threads of the chaos motif come together—a further motif that plays an important role in the novel, along with scattered references to so-called chaos theory. Directly after the just-quoted monologue, Kubin's wife brings up the relevant keyword in the group's discussion by accusing him over dinner: "You and your chaos ideology" (H 299; K 336). However, Kubin could not be further from adhering to this ideology, and so he rightly rejects her accusation. This economic editor and, as the novel elsewhere states, subscriber of the newspapers "*taz* and *konkret*" (H 292; K 328), is above all an "uninhibited critic of our own economic system" (H 292; K 328). When Kubin sings the praises of "beautiful chaos" on the just-quoted private occasion (H 299; K 335), it is primarily a cynical outburst and does not mean he is its advocate. Contrary to Kubin, Walter already dreamed of being a "concept artist on the stock exchange," someone "who accelerates capital," "a master of chaos" (H 144; K 167), when he was still living in a depressingly small, bare, newly built apartment and selling life insurance for a living. Accordingly, throughout most of the novel he appears sympathetic to the idea of chaos. He recognizes it in the context of his profession as a financial adviser, in his research into the culture of Easter Island (H 155, 209; K 178, 239), and not least when he misunderstands the chaos theory expert, Kubin, time and again—or rather, would prefer to misunderstand him (see below).

Chaos as a metaphor for economic processes, like the bird man motif, is introduced early in the novel (H 10; K 19), and it usually appears along with other metaphors. At one point Walter, prompted by his lawyer to reveal the location of the embezzled money, suggests that it "disappeared . . . in the crazy, unpredictable, incomparable maelstrom of the flow of capital," or, alternatively, "it's become a part of the chaos, so to speak, disappeared into the black holes of the capital market" (H 66f.; K 81). It is no coincidence that this sounds like another version of Joseph Vogl's characterization of the political economy as "spectrology" (Vogl 2015: ix), because it is exactly with this aim in mind that the relevant metaphors, terminology, and concepts are also employed in *Headhunter*. Much of Vogl's study *The Specter of Capital* is about pointing to a narrative method that interprets economic occurrences as natural processes, related to occurrences in the natural world such as earthquakes or floods. Vogl writes that "price fluctuations in financial markets," for instance, are described as "turbulent currencies" (ibid.: 12). These allegedly natural processes are in turn associated with basic patterns of human experience: "Financial markets in a state of turmoil mirror zones of elemental danger. Together, they shape a narratological program that converts the dynamics of exchange rates into a pattern of epic fatefulness, making the advent of the unlikeliest outcome appear utterly inevitable" (ibid.: 8). A critique of such interpretive methods runs through many of Timm's other literary works. The rogue businessman Morris in the novel *Morenga* whitewashes his business practices by philosophizing about "an invisible hand" that "will create humanistic acts out of even the most selfish motives" (Timm 2003: 150; Timm 1978: 174).[7] The '68-generation character Aschenberger in the novel *Rot* moreover characterizes media coverage as "meteorology," because economic and social evils are depicted as being as natural as the weather (Timm 2001: 350). In his Zuckmayer prize acceptance speech, Timm (2012) phrases his criticism yet more clearly: "The paradigms of the economy are not natural laws, as they have solidified in our consciousness, but [are] instead identifiable and modifiable."

In *Headhunter*, the idle talk of a "crazy, unpredictable incomparable maelstrom of the flow of capital," "chaos," and "black holes," is just a smokescreen for the embezzlement of money. Other characters in the novel recognize this smokescreen as well. Walter's clever defense lawyer, for instance, strongly advises his client not to use these metaphors when he appears in court. The lawyer says this would be "too picturesque, too alchemical, it's for poetically inclined observers" (H 66; K 81). One of the guards who escorts Walter from his prison cell to the courtroom is likewise not impressed by the claim that the 26 million just disappeared in a black hole, but instead counters: "Ha ha, I don't believe it" (H 277; K 311). But strangely enough, the metaphorical talk about chaos and black holes seemingly enabled Walter to obfuscate his business practices even to himself over a long period of time. Although he is perfectly aware of the destructive energies of the economic system—like most people in the novel and in real life—*Headhunter* shows why he nevertheless takes part in this system—just as in reality most people do, to a greater or lesser degree. In this spirit, the novel traces the development of cognitive processes—from the shriek of outrage at its beginning to the mysterious claim at its end: "I'd arrived. At last" (H 402; K 448). Its focus is not on the moral purification of the protagonist or his self-criticism in line with the charge of fraud and evasion of the law, but instead about his participation in a system that takes great pains to make these destructive energies look like forces of nature, or, as Vogl (2015: 8) puts it, "converts" them so that they "appear utterly inevitable."

The motif of chaos as a metaphor for economic processes is just one of a range of recurring strategies by which the protagonist justifies his unethical business practices. These strategies are part of the "profit-friendly ideological defense system," the well-oiled economic mechanism of masking and repressing that *Headhunter* scrutinizes. Some of these strategies aim to affirm and justify the economic system, whereas others refer to the particular business operations that the protagonist developed together with his business partner Dembrowski. There is also frequent cross-fading of both realms, the legal and the illegal, for instance, when Walter first starts embezzling funds at his brokerage firm, and comments: "We'd in any case have kept the money we'd failed to invest. Why should we pay out what had disappeared in the whirlpool of the great flow of capital?" (H 310; K 348). The protagonist's preference for using chaos as a metaphor for economic affairs, here in the form of a "whirlpool," has its counterpart in his statements on Easter Island (H 155, 209; K 178, 239). Time and again, Walter furthermore feels vindicated by his neighbor, the economic editor Kubin, in the latter's fascination with chaos. Even when Kubin calls the transfer of chaos theory to the economy "our metaphysics" (H 321; K 360), Walter does not wish to understand Kubin's praise of "beautiful chaos" (H 299; K 335) as ironic. It is, however, particularly revealing when he writes about the last weeks before his arrest that he missed Kubin for having assuaged his conscience (H 350; K 392): "when he . . . sat in our kitchen at night he was the one who took away my doubts, not by encouraging me to continue taking the money off people—we never spoke that directly about it—but because he sang the praises of entropy, of chaos" (H 351; K 393). At this point in his development process, the narrator appears to admit that he was still very much capable of deceiving himself, even by listening to someone who pokes fun at his wishful thinking.

In the spirit of the "profit-friendly ideological defense system," it is a rather effective strategy to continually conjure up "beautiful chaos" and thereby silence questions about cause and effect. If the economy and financial markets appear to be merely creative chaos, and allegedly the origins of processes and developments cannot be detected, then it is likewise easy to believe in "the miracle of self-multiplying money" (H 283; K 318). Not only the investors in Timm's novel want to believe in this delusion, however. One reviewer of *Headhunter* from the newspaper *Die Zeit* stated quite clearly what "every intelligent human being is able to recognize," namely, that

> money cannot multiply by itself. . . . Profit is only possible if you cheat others. The stock exchange is based on this principle. . . . The innate goal of the speculation on the stock exchange is to wrangle money out of each other, to cheat

> on one another. For this reason, at the stock exchange there cannot only be winners. Losers are needed off whom the winners can feed. (Perina 1991)

In *Headhunter*, praise of creative chaos is part of a strategy of justification that serves to confirm the economic system as such in its supposed naturalness; at the level of individual actions, such as diverting a client's money, other forces of whitewashing are at work. In her essay on the novel, Sabine Wilke (2004: 118) points out that Peter Walter's "work on the book about the mysterious culture of Easter Island seems to be a mere pretense to think through problems of his own existence." Admittedly, "one aspect of the discovery of Easter Island . . . especially troubled me: what does theft mean" (H 22; K 32). Walter's thoughts on exchange transactions in Easter Island society ultimately aim at an "alternative logic of interchange" (Wilke 2004: 120), and in his role as a broker, Walter certainly put this "alternative logic" into practice. Just as "the Easter Islanders stole with a clear conscience" from the Europeans, "they took what they coveted, and in exchange offered their women" (H 22; K 32)—so Walter takes money from his clients because they have gotten something in return. He offers them unique, imaginative stories, with which he persuades them indirectly to engage in the investment transactions he recommends. But just as the Europeans did not understand the exchange logic of the people of Easter Island, and wanted the women "from the savages for free" (H 22; K 32), Walter's clients also assumed that his stories were gratuitous. He sees things differently, however. A financial investment of "75,000 marks" (H 183; K 210), which entered and then disappeared from Walter's bank account, receives the following comment: "He paid dearly for the story, but I think it's worth the price" (H 184; K 210). Walter likewise talks often about "our hard-earned money" (H 288, 352; K 324, 395) and asserts: "I worked hard at it. And I let myself be well paid for it" (H 357; K 400). Applying his own "alternative logic of interchange" to his conduct at his brokerage firm served as a justification for his business methods.

While most of the stories Peter Walter tells about his business do not arouse the reader's pity for these wealthy clients' losses, some of them are revealing in terms of his self-concept in the overall picture he constructs of his life. The fact that he and his partner "plucked . . . people fattened for the occasion . . . like Christmas turkeys" (H 288; K 324) earns them some sympathy. The keywords "Robin Hood" and "redistribution" (H 289; K 324) crop up a few times (H 23; K 34, see also H 66; K 80), and Walter states repeatedly: "It didn't exactly hit the poorest" (H 66; K81 [see also H 208; K 238]). In an interview, Timm himself called his protagonist's attitude "resistance in everyday life": "I am interested for example in desperadoes, white-collar criminals: someone who from within reduces to absurdity the system, which is based on commerce, arm twisting, and selling— . . . and showing to the system what's really behind it" (Timm, qtd. in Stoehr 1995). Timm is, in my view, more critical of his protagonist's conduct in *Headhunter* than his public comments suggest. There seems indeed to be a subversive aspect to the narrative,[8] when a person born into an underprivileged family such as Walter takes matters of distributive justice into his own hands.[9] At least in court, Walter explains that "we'd seen to a certain redistribution, the money would have disappeared one way or another" (H 289; K 324). This testimony contrasts tellingly with a quite different story of redistribution that Walter tells the court he had conveyed to a client. This other story reveals much about his ambivalent attitude toward his business practices. In this version of the redistribution story, he imagines the person who made the client's money disappear (himself, that is) as a *real* Robin Hood—one who steals from the rich and uses the money to benefit society. A hacker crept into their system, Walter maintains, and "transferred the money, what's more to an account of Robin [Wood]"[10] (H 208; K 237), a non-violent action group for nature and the environment founded in 1982.[11] Although this story serves as a source of amusement in court, with it, the protagonist admits implicitly that he does *not* actually deserve the title of Robin Hood.[12] He simultaneously draws attention to the fact that the relevant headlines—"Robin Hood in the dirty money investment business" (H 66; K 80) and "*Robin Hood and his band invest shady money*" (H 289; K 324, italics in original)—may very well have emerged from the wishful thinking of the editors of a "small left-wing paper" (H 289; see also H 66[13]; K 324, see also K 80). In any event, the fact that Walter grapples with the Robin Hood image reveals his wishful thinking and ambivalent attitude toward his business practices.

This ambivalence comes to light throughout the novel whenever he discloses facts about his business that show he was actually not a "Robin Hood in the dirty money investment business" (H 172; K 197). He did not "redistribute" embezzled money with the intention of apportioning wealth more fairly. He not only deceived "people who already had too much money" (H 172; K 197), "spare money" (H 54; K 68), and "[a]ll the people that don't know what to do with their money" (H 298; K 334). In fact, he admits that while the majority of the aggrieved party, "189 altogether," had actually "speculated off the book, with money they weren't actually supposed to have", "69" were able to start "legal proceedings" against his brokerage firm after the fraud came to light (H 327; K 367)—which means that they had earned the embezzled money by legal means. Literature critic Stefan Neuhaus likewise stresses that the protagonist "who is called 'Robin Hood' by a newspaper, has to realize that he also ruined people who do not embody the type of the superficial capitalist" (Neuhaus 2004: 85). Toward the end of the novel, Walter finally tells one remarkable case story from this group of "69" that simultaneously reveals the less funny and playful part of his broker business.

The story of the boat builder demonstrates what reality may look like for the losers of finance capitalism. This noteworthy story appears late in the novel, but its context is important, because as a *Report from the Interior of the Country* it seems both to trace Walter's cognitive process and to expose what has been suppressed. What motivates Walter's storytelling is a reflection immediately preceding it, and this in turn comes at the end of a chain of motifs revolving around the bird man. This chain is initiated at the novel's beginning, shortly before he reports the bird man's destruction, when he calls him "the unique irreplaceable figure" (H 3; K 11). Later in the novel it is carried forward and even more charged with emotion: "The figure that had meant so much to me would never again exist" (H 311; K 349), and finally he mentions once again that "the figure of the bird man" was "unique and irreplaceable" (H 338; K 379). What seem to be Walter's sentimental memories of his forever-lost wooden companion lead directly to one of the most important phases of the cognitive learning process he undergoes throughout the course of the novel. Immediately after—and explicitly with a "fragment" of the unique and irreplaceable bird man "lying here next to the laptop" (H 338; K 379)—he starts to write the boat-builder story, beginning with the sentence: "To be honest, I wasn't indifferent to all the people who testified in court and spoke of their distress. Above all not to the old man" (H 338; K 379). This story thus directly connects the figurine of the bird man and its destruction to Walter's process of learning—a process that here provides insight into the consequences of his business conduct and the human tragedies it can generate.

Before losing all his money by trusting Walter's fraudulent investment advice, this old man had a workshop in which he built, along with one assistant and two apprentices, "surf boat[s] for the Ivory Coast" (H 341; K 382). Walter, who on his last visit meant to encourage this client to keep speculating, is fascinated by his workshop: "[H]ere are people still working by hand" (H 340; K 381).[14] He asks the workers to explain the construction material to him and how the boats are used, and then, to the dismay of Saldin, his employee at the investment firm, Walter lets slip out: ". . . and you want to give all this up" (H 341; K 383). Walter neglects to take into consideration that the man had already been forced to sell his business because of his speculation losses. In the midst of negotiations with this client, something unusual occurs:

> This was the moment, as I fell silent and couldn't think of anything to say, . . . I thought about myself and I found myself repulsive, I thought of myself with revulsion. And if I'm to describe this revulsion, then what comes to mind are the plates that go under the flower pots on window sills, yes, I didn't think, you're a swine, I see the plates under the flowerpots, white plates with little gilt lion's claws at the sides, the gold worn away in the course of time. Britt wanted underplates like these, we were always looking in the antique shops, but never found any. I thought they're sure to sell these plates, I thought for me

> they'd sell them, they'd do it for me. And suddenly this "for-me" struck me as repellent: I'm the one, I thought, who makes money out of the misfortune of these people. (H 342; K 383f.)

By shining the spotlight on decades-old traces of everyday objects, this scene illustrates vividly that financial transactions do not just mean that abstract numbers move simply from one account to another, from that of the loser to that of the winner. Instead, on the loser's side, an entire life may be destroyed, "unique and irreplaceable."

After this point, the novel no longer mentions chaos theory, but instead the straightforward principle of cause and effect. Walter speaks of those who are responsible and of that for which he must take responsibility. This sudden realization of his own and others' culpability may be exactly what flashed into Walter's mind at the moment the bird man was destroyed. The realm in which he acts cannot be explained by chaos theory, and causes and their effects are much easier to identify than he (and many others) might wish to acknowledge. On a whim, you start to push something (a book on your desk or a commodity futures transaction); the impact forces are passed on (to another object or a fellow investor at the stock exchange); and in the end something breaks into pieces beyond repair: a wooden figure of immense historical value, "unique and irreplaceable," or an entire life such as that of the boat builder—or national economies in what was once called the "Third World" helplessly exposed to the game of commodity futures and other speculations. The nonprofit organization *Foodwatch* (Foodwatch Report 2011) documented the link between food speculation at the commodity exchange and increasing food prices, which in turn are the cause of a worldwide increase in hunger and poverty. And even though there is no consensus among critics on this issue, as Lütge (2014) reported in the weekly newspaper *Die Zeit*, "even hedge funds managers confirmed, on the occasion of a hearing in the US Senate, that share prices in the virtual futures market of course play a role when it comes to real business."

It is thus no coincidence that in the key scene at the beginning of the novel the same Peter Walter, who is usually fascinated by chaos theory, all of a sudden speaks of the "law of kinetics." When he pushes the book aside, "the movement continued in accordance with the law of kinetics to a writing pad," and so forth (H 6; K 15). The resulting shock runs so deep that it is not the "beautiful chaos" that he recognizes as undergirding his activities, but instead "the law of kinetics." According to *Dictionary.com*, kinetics is "the branch of mechanics that deals with the actions of forces in producing or changing the motion of masses." Although he never appears in the novel except when Walter speaks of him, Walter's "writing uncle" (H 59; K 72), a well-known German author, is involved significantly in this sudden insight. After all, the message about him at the beginning of the novel caused the very irritation that led Walter to push the book aside in rage and trigger the domino effect. The influence of this "writing uncle" seems to link the motif of cause and effect, of action and taking responsibility for it, in a more general sense to this character. This link becomes more explicit at the end of the novel. When the protagonist leaves the shade of the Easter Island statue, where he had spent several hours, and slowly walks toward a Chilean police officer sent to apprehend him, this further key scene ends with the statement: "I'd arrived, at last" (H 402; K 448). Like the scene with the bird man at the novel's beginning, this scene invites several interpretations. For instance, it has been understood as Walter's acceptance of his fate, or similarly vaguely as his arrival at his beginning (Hielscher 2002: 247), or that Walter arrived at the place that attracted him all his life (Germer 2012: 178). All these options may be valid, but the *specific* events of *this* scene are hardly understandable according to these interpretations.

As Walter walks from the Easter Island colossuses back to his travel guide, a group of children throw small rocks at him—"an old game as I knew from travelers' accounts" (H 401; K 447)—and this reminds him of a similar game from his childhood after World War II "in the ruins of Hamburg when we threw chunks of stone at each other that kept getting bigger." On one occasion there was an accident, *almost incidentally* mentioned in parentheses, when Walter hit his "uncle on the forehead" so that "he still has the scar" (H 402; K 448). Back then blood was also spilled, and on this occasion in his childhood he had to learn that his actions may have consequences, sometimes detrimental to other people. In retrospect, it is the character of the "writing uncle" who symbolizes Walter's early insights into the law of cause and effect, a rule that he forgot as an adult in his investment firm—or at least wanted to forget. When the children on Easter Island throw a stone and hit him on his cheekbone so that "suddenly blood was running down [his] face" (H 402; K 448), he finally arrives at this early insight, "at last."

It seems plausible against this backdrop that, in the scene where the bird man is destroyed, this insight into the cause-and-effect relationship is linked to Timm's central motif of "outrage" (*Empörung*):[15] "I crawled on the floor and I shrieked in dismay [outrage]" (H 7; K 15). Timm never abandoned his claim from the 1970s that literature has its place "Between Entertainment and Enlightenment" (Timm 1970) and certainly the novel *Headhunter*—usually seen in the tradition of the picaresque novel (Petersenn 2005)—can likewise be located in this space. It expresses as much fury about the world of business and finance as the author's novel *Rot* did ten years later, even if the protagonist Walter, unlike the narrator Thomas Linde in *Rot*, does not introduce "outrage" in *Headhunter* but instead has to learn it as the result of a concurrence of events. Nevertheless, as always in Timm's texts, the '68 context is installed like a false bottom, also in *Headhunter*.[16] This false bottom is made apparent by the "writing uncle" who, as Walter's mother tells her son "with some embarrassment," was of course among "the demonstrators" who back then "outside on the Jungfernstieg . . . passed by" (H 84; K 100).

As the German weekly newspaper *Die Zeit* put it in December 2012, "the dogma of our time of permanent crisis reads: 'There is *no alternative*!'" (Rauterberg 2012). In this view, financial crises, such as the 2007/8 global one, are seemingly as natural as the weather. Literature, as a medium in which ethical issues are inevitably negotiated, cannot help but position itself in one way or another in this context. Uwe Timm was always outspoken in advocating for social-political enlightenment, arguing that the "paradigms of the economy are not natural laws" but instead "identifiable and modifiable" (Timm 2012). It is against this background that literature must be understood as an intervention in meaning-making and opinion-forming practices. It can contribute to understanding what is considered real, normal, and "the way things are" in a relevant historical situation and, as such, has the potential to question prevailing social and political conditions and the seemingly unchangeable status quo. In the early 1970s, the Swiss writer Max Frisch discussed yet another aspect of literature's "surplus value" in this respect when he insisted that it can capture "what sociology, what biology cannot"; the "domain of literature" is, in his view, "everything that people experience, sex, technology, politics, but in contrast to science, related to the human being that experiences" these things (Frisch 1976: 89). Timm picked up this line of thinking decades later. Unlike the sciences, he argued, literature makes "the particular, the individual its subject—with all his feelings or even his callousness, his individual language and behavior." And he explained that while the sciences speak abstractly about phenomena, literary texts help the reader to understand and comprehend them emotionally (Timm 2003: 455).

Monika Albrecht is apl. Professor of Cultural Studies at the University of Vechta's Faculty of the Humanities, recently the Faculty of Social Sciences. She has previously held faculty positions in the US, the UK, and Ireland. Her main research areas include twentieth- and twenty-first-century German culture, history, politics, and literature, with particular focus on critical postcolonial studies; memory studies and the politics of memory; multiculturalism and migration; multiculturalism and postcolonialism in comparative perspective; and history, memory, and minorities in literature. Her most recent, relevant publication is "Critical Post-Colonial Studies: Opening Up the Post-Colonial to a Broader Geopolitical View" in the *Oxford Research Encyclopedia of Literature*.

Notes

1. Uwe Timm, *Headhunter,* translated by Peter Tegel (1994), and Uwe Timm, *Kopfjäger—Bericht aus dem inneren des Landes* (1991). In this chapter I quote from the English translation with the letter "H," and the German original with the letter "K."
2. The English translator was seemingly not aware of the key motif of "outrage" (*Empörung*) in Timm's work, and rendered it as "dismay." Later in the novel, however, when the motif of *Empörung* reappears ("Wie hat der Angeklagte Walter reagiert? / Empört. Ja, er hat den Hörer auf den Apparat geknallt," K 231), the translation reads: "How did the accused Walter react? / Outraged. Yes, he slammed down the phone" (H 202).
3. On the topic of "1968" in Uwe Timm's novels *Rot* and *Morenga,* see my "Maybe the Genuine Utopia" (2015); "The Absoluteness of the Knowledge Once Possessed" (2015); "Uwe Timm: *Rot*" (2015); "Das Beispiel Kropotkin" (2012); and "Che Guevara in 'Deutsch-Südwest'" (2006).
4. The English translation reads "demonstrators doubled past," but "the demonstrators passed by" is a more accurate translation of Timm's sentence: "Es war nämlich die Zeit, als draußen auf dem Jungfernstieg die Demonstranten vorbeizogen" (K 100).
5. See H 3 [K 11], 7–9 [15–17], 20 [30], 32 [43–44], 61 [75], 87 [103–4], 138 [160], 139 [162], 166f. [191], 193 [221], 202 [231], 209 [238], 308–11 [345–49], 391 [437].
6. Near the novel's end, Timm refers to "[p]eople dancing on the Berlin Wall" (H 374; K 419).
7. An overt reference to Adam Smith occurs a few pages earlier in the novel (Timm 2003: 147; Timm 1978: 171); see Albrecht 2012.
8. See also Petersenn 2005: 129.
9. According to a reviewer in *Neue Deutsche Literatur,* he achieves this by intervening in the flow of capital and redistributing the money into his own bank account (Langner 1992: 158).
10. The translator was seemingly unaware of the NGO "Robin Wood."
11. See https://www.robinwood.de/, last accessed 18 May 2022.
12. In order to qualify for the Robin Hood title, Peter Walter and his partner should indeed, as one of their employees suggests, "lay down ground rules, whom can we approach and whom not, a charitable investment business, as it were" (H 343) ["Richtlinien herausgeben, wen man ansprechen darf und wen nicht, sozusagen ein karitatives Anlagegeschäft," K 385]. Another one of the employees actually has scruples: he has "no pensioners among his clients because he was of the opinion that only [those] who had spare money should speculate" (H 203) ["unter seinen Klienten keine Pensionäre, weil er der Meinung war, spekulieren dürfe nur, wer überflüssiges Geld habe," K 232], and "he'd always taken care that no client speculated with money he'd put aside for an emergency" (H 204f.) ["daß kein Klient mit seinem Notgroschen spekuliert," K 233].
13. Mistakenly translated as "leaflet."
14. On the importance of physical labor and the handicrafts in *Headhunter,* see Shafi 2012.
15. This motif of *Empörung* already appears in Timm's first novel *Heißer Sommer* (Timm 1974: 56 and passim), is crucial for the development of the character Gottschalk in the novel *Morenga;* and in particular in the novel *Rot* it is turned into a key strand of

motifs (see Timm 2001: 53, 69, 94, 138, 152, 153, 155, 163, 311, 346, 347, 348, 378, 381).

16. For a similar phenomenon, see my essay "Che Guevara in 'Deutsch-Südwest.'"

References

Albrecht, Monika. 2006. "Che Guevara in 'Deutsch-Südwest': Uwe Timms Anti-Kriegsroman *Morenga* aus interdisziplinärer Sicht." In *Schreiben gegen Krieg und Gewalt. Ingeborg Bachmann und die deutschsprachige Literatur 1945–1980*, ed. Dirk Göttsche and Franziska Meyer, 187–202. Göttingen: V & R Unipress.

———. 2012. "Das Beispiel Kropotkin: Umsetzung von '68er Inhalten' bei Uwe Timm." In *Gegenwartsliteratur. Ein germanistisches Jahrbuch / A German Studies Yearbook* 11: 77–102.

———. 2015. "'The Absoluteness of the Knowledge Once Possessed': 1968 Ethics and Consensual Ethics in Uwe Timm's Novel *Rot*." In *Edinburgh German Yearbook 2013* (Vol. VII: *Ethical Approaches in Contemporary German-Language Literature and Culture*), ed. Emily Jeremiah and Frauke Matthes, 13–28. Rochester, NY: Camden House.

———. 2015. "'Maybe the Genuine Utopia': Uwe Timm's Envisioning of Social Justice in His Novel *Rot*." In *Envisioning Social Justice in Twenty-First-Century German Culture*, ed. Axel Hildebrandt and Jill Twark, 47–64. Rochester, NY: Camden House.

———. 2015. "Uwe Timm: *Rot*." In *The Literary Encyclopedia* (August). Retrieved 27 December 2019 from http://www.litencyc.com/php/sworks.php?rec=true&UID=35498.

Foodwatch Report. 2011. *Die Hungermacher: Wie Deutsche Bank, Goldmann & Co. auf Kosten der Ärmsten mit Lebensmitteln spekulieren*, ed. Thilo Bode. Berlin: Foodwatch. Retrieved 27 December 2019 from https://www.foodwatch.org/uploads/media/foodwatch-Report_Die_Hungermacher_Okt-2011_ger_02.pdf.

Frisch, Max. 1976. *Tagebuch 1966–1972*. In *Gesammelte Werke in zeitlicher Folge*. Edited by Hans Mayer, assisted by Walter Schmitz. Vol. VI.1: Frankfurt am Main: Suhrkamp.

Germer, Kerstin. 2012. *(Ent-)Mythologisierung deutscher Geschichte: Uwe Timms narrative Ästhetik*. Göttingen: V & R Unipress.

Hielscher, Martin. 2002. "Der Kannibalismus des Erzählens: Zu Uwe Timms Roman *Kopfjäger*." In *Gegenwartsliteratur. Ein germanistisches Jahrbuch / A German Studies Yearbook* 1: 247–67.

Kahler, Miles, and David A. Lake. 2013. "Introduction: Anatomy of Crisis: The Great Recession and Political Change." In *Politics in the New Hard Times: The Great Recession in Comparative Perspective*, ed. Miles Kahler and David A. Lake, 1–24. Ithaca, NY: Cornell University Press.

Langner, Rainer-K. 1992. "Der Roman aus dem Laptop." *Neue Deutsche Literatur* 40(1): 157–60.
Lütge, Gunhild. 2014. "Zocken hat Zukunft: Die neuen EU-Regeln gegen Spekulanten taugen nichts." In *Die Zeit*, 23 January. Retrieved 27 December 2019 from http://www.zeit.de/2014/05/spekulation-nahrungsmittel.
Neuhaus, Stefan. 2004. "'Plötzlich findest du dich in einem Buch wieder, und du bist ein anderer.' Grenzauflösungen als konstitutives Merkmal von Uwe Timms Werk." In *Grenzen, Grenzüberschreitungen, Grenzauflösungen: Zur Darstellung von Zeitgeschichte in deutschsprachiger Gegenwartsliteratur*, ed. Edgar Platen and Martin Todtenhaupt, 79–92. Munich: Iudicium.
Perina, Udo. 1991. "Die Lust an Lug und Trug" [review of *Kopfjäger*]. In *Die Zeit*, 11 October.
Petersenn, Olaf. 2005. "Ein Schelm in der modernen Wirtschaftswelt. Uwe Timms *Kopfjäger*." In *Der schöne Überfluss, Texte zu Leben und Werk von Uwe Timm*, ed. Helge Malchow, 121–30. Cologne: Kiepenheuer & Witsch.
Rauterberg, Hanno, et al. 2012. "Weltverbesserung: Gesellschaft, was fehlt dir?" In *Die Zeit*, 27 December. Retrieved 27 December 2019 from http://www.zeit.de/2013/01/Weltverbesserung-Gesellschaft/komplettansicht.
Schöll, Julia. 2007. "Zur Anwesenheit des Abwesenden: Erzählen als Erinnerungsbewegung in Uwe Timm's *Kopfjäger*." In *Erinnern, Vergessen, Erzählen. Beiträge zum Werk Uwe Timms*, ed. Friedhelm Marx, 133–49. Göttingen: Wallstein.
Shafi, Monika. 2012. "Discourses of Work: Uwe Timm's *Kopfjäger: Bericht aus dem Inneren des Landes*." In *Gegenwartsliteratur: Ein germanistisches Jahrbuch / A German Studies Yearbook* 11: 149–69.
Stoehr, Ingo R. 1995. "A Trip of Discovery into My Own Consciousness: A Conversation with Uwe Timm." *Dimension²* 2(3): 334–57. Translated from the German by Ingo and Louise Stoehr. Retrieved 18 May 2022 from http://www.dimension2.org/Texts/v2n3-interview.html.
"The Financial Crisis Inquiry Report: Final Report of the National Commission on the Causes of the Financial and Economic Crisis in the United States." 2011. Submitted by the Financial Crisis Inquiry Commission Pursuant to Public Law. Retrieved 27 December 2019 from http://fcic-static.law.stanford.edu/cdn_media/fcic-reports/fcic_final_report_full.pdf.
Timm, Uwe. 1970. "Zwischen Unterhaltung und Aufklärung." *Kürbiskern* 1: 79–90.
———. 1974. *Heißer Sommer*. Vienna: AutorenEdition.
———. 1978. *Morenga. Roman*. Vienna: AutorenEdition.
———. 1991. *Kopfjäger—Bericht aus dem Inneren des Landes*. Cologne: Kiepenheuer & Witsch.
———. 1994. *Headhunter*. Translated from the German by Peter Tegel. New York: New Directions.
———. 2001. *Rot. Roman*. Cologne: Kiepenheuer & Witsch.

———. 2003. "Einfühlungsästhetik wäre ein kolonialer Akt." Ein Gespräch [with Christoph Haman]. *Sprache im technischen Zeitalter* 168: 450–62.

———. 2003. *Morenga*. Translated from the German by Breon Mitchell. New York: New Directions.

———. 2012. "Gesellschaft und Gerechtigkeit: Strammgestanden für den freien Markt." *Der Tagesspiegel*, 30 January. Retrieved 27 December 2019 from http://www.tagesspiegel.de/kultur/gesellschaft-und-gerechtigkeit-strammgestanden-fuer-den-freien-markt/6121446.html.

Vogl, Joseph. 2015. *The Specter of Capital*. Palo Alto, CA: Stanford University Press.

Wilke, Sabine. 2004. "Uwe Timms *Kopfjäger* oder von der erotischen Bedeutung des Geldes." *Literatur für Leser* 27(2): 112–24.

CHAPTER 11

An Imaginary of Blame
The Representation of Crisis, the Crisis of Representation, and Jonas Lüscher's Barbarian Spring

JOEL KAIPAINEN

In November 2008, Minister of Finance Peer Steinbrück addressed the German parliament, visibly flustered: "How do I explain something to the larger population that eludes simple explanations and colloquial meanings of words?" (qtd. in Peter 2011). Steinbrück's reaction to the unfolding financial crisis, just as Alan Greenspan's testimony to the US Congress, expressing a "state of shocked disbelief" (qtd. in Felsenthal 2008), are symptomatic of the disorienting effects the crisis had on policymakers, economists, and the larger public alike. Yet this initial shock, seemingly threatening the neoliberal system as a whole, soon made way for an emerging narrative that pinned the financial crisis on the mismanagement and greed of individual banks and bankers. Culture and fiction came to play a curious role in this reimagination of the crisis that replaced threatening complexity with all-too-human perpetrators: it was chaos with a promised return to stability. The "Masters of the Universe," a term borrowed from Tom Wolfe's 1987 satirical novel *Bonfire of the Vanities*, and Gordon Gekko (as portrayed by Michael Douglas), the icon of greed of two *Wall Street* movies, soon became the most referenced fictional characters in connection with the crisis by journalists, politicians, and even the clergy (see, for example, Rudd 2008; Doyle 2010). In fact, the actor Michael Douglas himself was enlisted by the FBI to make a public-service announcement in a campaign against securities fraud, insisting that "the movie was fiction, but the problem is real" (Federal Bureau of Investigation 2012).

The multiple ways the financial crisis has been construed make up what I call an "imaginary of blame," which influences how people perceive the causes of this event, as well as how artists portray it in their artworks. In this chapter I first discuss how this "imaginary of blame" came about by outlining the way the financial crisis came to be described, soon after it occurred, in economics, politics, and general societal discourse, which includes the mass media and household conversations. The excessive focus on the responsibility and deviance of bankers and other financial professionals was instrumental in capturing public imagination and support, and in (re)creating a sense of continuity and *Ordnung* after this seemingly temporary breakdown of an otherwise stable financial system. To elucidate the role of culture and representation in coming to terms with the financial crisis, the novella *Barbarian Spring* (2015; orig. title: *Frühling der Barbaren*, 2013), by Swiss Author Martin Lüscher, will then be examined in the context of this imaginary. A discussion of the communicative function of cultural production reveals how artworks, in this case fiction-writing, take part in the process of understanding and working through crises. If this mediated form of communication has created a complicity in the dominant imaginary, analyzing cultural production can help scrutinize the prevailing narrative. Studying the cultural production of this particular crisis narrative also sheds light on issues resulting from various forms of representation and complexity reduction, bringing into focus the larger conundrum of how we should understand the financial crisis in hindsight.

Tracking the Narrative Shift from Complexity to Blame

From the beginning, narratives about the economic crisis produced since 2007/8 have been haunted by accounts of ominous complexity. It became a trope that financial markets and their products had gotten so technically and mathematically complex that they could be neither fully understood nor fully explained in plain language. Similarly, it was even more difficult to assess the aggregated risk embedded in finance for the economic system as a whole. In other words, when even the economic experts failed to predict and explain, the crisis seemed to emerge without warning, and it was an event that could not be understood or communicated in straightforward ways.[1] The fallout of these difficulties of understanding and explaining—the disorienting effects of the crisis—came into plain sight when the financial products in question, most importantly mortgage-backed hedge funds, turned out to be as toxic as they were sophisticated, when economic models "collapsed" together with the markets ("Why They Crashed Too" 2014).

With a simultaneous "systemic failure of academic economics" (Colander et al. 2009: 2) and an unanticipated and comprehensive economic meltdown on the horizon, central banks and governments had to act under conditions of uncertainty. The greater public—with jobs, savings, and pension funds in peril—was left with a blurred and unsettling image of distant and unpredictable forces that had suddenly and dramatically determined their fate. It was not a business cycle that had transpired, but instead a shock to both the material and symbolic order of the economic system. In the initial moments of distress, the epistemological dimension of the crisis became clear, and it even inspired some historical comparisons beyond the catastrophe of the world economic crisis of the 1930s, now routinely conjured by politicians and the media. Some commentators suggested a comparison with the great Lisbon earthquake of 1755, predicting a fundamental reassessment of our faith in economic models and finance itself (e.g., Lipshaw 2009). Of course this state of disorientation could not last; as the markets kept falling and long-standing financial institutions started failing, something had to be done, and done quickly. Actions had to be taken, and someone had to be blamed.

A prominent target for assigning responsibility quickly emerged: banks. Not coincidentally, the spectacular insolvency of the global financial services firm Lehman Brothers on 15 September 2008 marked the definite arrival of the economic crisis in public perception. As the heavily mediatized sequence of events quickly made obvious, even before Lehman Brothers went bankrupt, all kinds of financial institutions had played important roles along the way, as the US mortgage crisis turned first into a financial crisis, then a banking crisis, various national fiscal crises, and before long a global economic recession. From uncertain mortgages to dubious derivative financial products, from overleveraged trading to the misuse of bailout money, banks promptly came under scrutiny. But whereas banks recovered fairly quickly, nation states faced historic deficits, and the recession affected the general public for several years after the crash. Whereas the political system returned more or less to a normal state of affairs (e.g., banks were denationalized at a rapid rate, and efforts were ostensibly underway to reregulate the financial sector), the image of banks seems to remain lastingly damaged. The negative image of "Wall Street," as the symbolic nucleus of the crisis, comprises an integral part of the dominant crisis narrative, which cuts from politics to economics, society and culture.

As a consequence of this negative view of the banking industry, the enormously costly regulatory and compensatory fixes administered by swift and heavy-handed government interventions produced their own crisis imaginary. This imaginary, to be unfolded here, consists of a collective reimagination of the events of the crisis that works to (re)organize an otherwise overly complex and threatening economic reality.[2] It becomes clear, as Bob Jessop (2013: 17) argued early on, that even if the crisis was construed in the Global North as "a crisis *of* finance-led accumulation" or more generally as "a crisis *of* neoliberalism," "the neo-liberal economic imaginary remains dominant and continues to shape imagined recoveries." Although competing narratives and imaginaries (e.g., nationalistic, Keynesian, and even Marxist economic) still play an important role in academic discussions and in the way crisis management is appraised by opposing political groups, the dominant response has managed to establish itself as lacking an alternative. But how did we get from this epistemological shock—from a systemic crisis that challenged the dominant economic models, policies, and beliefs—to a situation where "the practical response" has been a "further strengthening of the neo-liberal project"? (Jessop 2012: 39). Indeed, the way this imaginary of blame operates, how it avoids larger systemic questions, and what makes it successful in the competition between crisis explanations and narratives demands further scrutiny.

Representation as Complexity Reduction

The imaginary of blame was spawned when specific sectors of the economy were identified as responsible for the financial crisis. This identification took place in two parallel steps: (1) the disaster was represented as a crisis *of* financial accumulation (one part of the system got out of control, but not the whole system); and (2) the crisis *of* financial accumulation was depicted as a crisis *in* financial accumulation (individual practices in the subsystem were considered to be faulty, but not finance overall as a system of managing economies). These two descriptive modes operate with a series of exclusions that limit alternative readings of the causes of the crisis. Since its creation, this imaginary of blame has often functioned as a primary decisive moment of complexity reduction in financial crisis narratives.

First, as the economist Richard Wolff (2008) has pointed out, the problem with representation starts with the term "financial crisis": "[T]o put an adjective in front of it is an attempt to make it small, to make its impact seem restricted." According to Wolff, this was not simply a crisis produced, shaped, and controlled by Wall Street, but also a larger and older crisis of neoliberal capitalism. Financial crisis suggests a crisis that originated in and spilled over from an isolated financial sector: various investment firms' speculation with mortgage-based products impacted the rest of the system detrimentally. The narrow focus of this imaginary, however, leaves out other potentially critical factors and systemic complexities that led up to the stage of the crisis that indeed concerned the financial industry. More than restricting the causes and impact of the crisis to the financial regime of accumulation, the term "financial crisis" also contains the crisis narrative in a short history that does not warrant an analysis that reaches further back than the generally accepted trigger event of the US subprime crisis.

Second, the fact that financial institutions are at the heart and on the frontline of a large economic crisis is certainly no coincidence. After all, the unprecedented, vital importance of banks and finance for the current economic system should be seen as a logical if not willed consequence of a pre-crisis imaginary that underwrote the financialization and neoliberal deregulation of the past four decades.[3] Although the crisis exposed the risks of these transactions and prompted government interventions that at first may seem contradictory to the neoliberal imaginary, the predominant narrative cover-up consists in portraying the situation as unusual rather than symptomatic, as an excess rather than a norm. Hence, the interventions are not seen as a return to Keynesian policy: they are not addressing a systemic need, but instead represent extraordinary measures in the face of extraordinary circumstances. In the words of cultural scholars Brassett, Rethel, and Watson (2009: 2), "the proffered solution to the crisis pre-empts genuine analysis of its causes by enforcing the characterization of their manifestations as abnormalities." In other words, finding a particular culprit, in lieu of a systemic cause, allows for a discursive appeasement of the potential crisis of the system with the promise that once a small internal problem is eliminated, an otherwise healthy system will remain.

Third, the dominant narrative has to a large extent framed the culpability of banks as a crisis of governance in leadership and corporate culture (see, e.g., OECD 2009: 29–34; SIGTARP 2013). As Brassett et al. observe: "Perhaps predictably in such circumstances, the mantra of good governance . . . has been dusted down and given new life as a catch-all antidote" (2009: 378). As evidence, we see "the rhetoric of 'seriously delinquent' finance" emerging from within the IMF, and the political denouncement of bank behavior—for example, UK chancellor Alistair Darling's reflections on the social irresponsibility of some bankers' "kamikaze manner" (ibid.). This emphasis on corporate governance encourages a shift in focus away from a potentially faulty, unstable financial system toward the irresponsibility and deviance of a limited number of financial actors. In doing so, the leading political efforts to contain the crisis can water down calls for more stringent regulation, or at least dismiss fundamental reforms of the financial sector. Indeed, among the measures immediately taken was the criminal persecution of a surprisingly small number of investment bankers,[4] and the promotion of better federal government oversight to improve corporate governance. These measures suggest, however, that more regulation would not really help against a "toxic culture" already shaped around finding "loopholes" in government regulations (see, e.g., SIGTARP 2013: 5).

In sum, the representation of the 2008–10 crisis in the dominant imaginary as a limited financial crisis, a historic abnormality, and a crisis in financial governance enables the preservation of the pre-crisis imaginary, and thus maintains the status quo. This manageable narrative does not challenge fundamental macroeconomic beliefs, such as an assumed natural equilibrium in accumulation or the self-governing rationality of markets; it dismisses instead a systemic analysis of the crisis altogether.

Retaining the Imaginary of Blame

Although it is difficult to measure the pervasiveness of this imaginary of blame, the 2013 "Global Trust Report" of the Gesellschaft für Konsumforschung (GFK; German society for consumer research), conducted in twenty-five different countries, confirms a fundamental loss of trust in banks and an increase of trust in the government (Lades 2015). This increase in trust, in the case of Germany, for example, allowed the government to "capitalize on crisis management" (qtd. in "Studie: Immer weniger Deutsche vertrauen Banken" 2013). Even amidst the euro crisis, this trend continued in the 2015 report (Lades 2015). Thus, although the crisis and its management created fertile soil for more radical political dissidence, and this event allowed nationalist parties all over the western hemisphere to rise to power, overall the immediate, dominant political response secured popular support. The success of such an interpretive regime hinges on creating a sense of continuation and stability, as it upholds the values and beliefs of the neoliberal project and submits to pre-established patterns of interpretation. Legal prosecutions and the communication of political efforts to regulate banks, however ineffectual in reality, further helped propagate a sense of law and order. In its most narrow manifestation, the rhetorical (rather than analytical) focus on financial leadership is instrumental in capturing the public imagination and retaining the predominant narrative. It is, moreover, what one might call a "moral legibility" of the crisis that wins out over more unsettling imaginaries, and allows for a reintegration of the cataclysmic events into the threatened realm of everyday life.

Tales of greed and excess are seductive and easily brought to bear in pre-established worldviews. Portraying the crisis as being a result of moral and ethical shortcomings of institutions and individuals substitutes anonymous market forces with a seemingly finite number of individualized human perpetrators. This portrayal diverges, for example, from explanations of market behavior and incentives deriving from the perspective of systemic failure. Popular suspicion regarding the ominous world of finance and investment bankers that political denouncement plays into is certainly not new, but is itself an imaginary that is continually revisited and expanded. In the more immediate past, the rise to power of modern-day investment banks can be traced back to the 1980s. The following three decades produced a "golden age of investment banking," during which Wall Street excesses were at the forefront of the popular imagination (Augar 2006: 25). From this time also stems the notoriety of Wall Street investment bankers as "masters of the universe," who tellingly received this name from a work of fiction.

Another factor that helped retain this imaginary is the symbolic place that banks hold on the grid axis of the seemingly "immaterial" derivative financial market, as opposed to the axis of the "material" real economy (i.e., the manufacturing and exchange of goods). Although crisis narratives often resort to describing market forces as far removed and too complex to be understood, banks serve as the visible and material interface for that which supposedly went wrong. Far from being considered neutral intermediaries, banks and their names became symbols of the crisis in the public imagination, as in the now-famous words by journalist Matt Taibbi (2009: 52), who described Goldman Sachs as a "giant vampire squid wrapped around the face of humanity." This symbolic focus on blaming financial institutions for the crisis provides a kind of moral and psychological relief. In its simplest form, it provides an opportunity to point a finger at a specific culprit, despite being confronted with an otherwise faceless threat.

The moral legibility of the crisis, derived from assigning blame to financial actors and institutions, and presented in the predominant discourse surrounding it, also coincides with the fundamental axioms of the dominant pre-crisis imaginary. These axioms presume that markets possess a beneficial self-governing rationality and can thus reach a natural equilibrium. According to such a reading, human flaws such as excessive greed and criminal behavior disturb the otherwise rational machine of the liberal economy. The numerous moralistic (but also occasionally psychological and psychopathological) explanations for the crisis play into a narrative of isolated excess that represents the crisis as a historical abnormality in a single, rational, objective, and atemporal economic system.

Understanding the crisis thus, as a tale of corruption and mismanagement, mobilizes a predisposed process of complexity reduction in representing the events since 2007/8. This complexity reduction is informed by ideologically determined interpretive patterns based on moral rather than analytic approaches. One should not ignore moral concerns regarding the responsibility of individuals or institutions in the financial industry, and it is important to investigate all instances of mismanagement and illegal practices in economic systems. Nevertheless, the excessive focus on the masters of the universe, corporate governance, and greed is too convenient if it externalizes these factors from an economic analysis, avoids reintegrating their underlying motivations into the system as a whole, and invites us to forgo a systemic analysis altogether. While producing a moral legibility of the crisis is essential for upholding an interpretive regime that retains the dominant imagined recovery, it is important to keep in mind that focusing solely on passing moral judgment can distract from the work needed to come to a more comprehensive understanding of its causes and to evaluate its systemic nature.

The Communicative Function of Cultural Production

Finance, a financial crisis, and economic phenomena in general are not isolated from other human domains. Instead, they intersect with, depend on, and are (re)produced by culture, society, and politics. In order to appreciate the more specific intersections between Culture with a capital "C" and the financial crisis, it is helpful to understand works of art as sites of social reflection and imagination. This aesthetic-cultural production contributes to, works to reaffirm or subvert, to stabilize or destabilize, a given or nascent imaginary that underlies any economic order. In this sense, the omnipresent reference to the "masters of the universe" in politics and the mass media not only testifies to an alleged "post-crisis witch hunt against bankers" (Kaletsky 2010), but it also illustrates the ways in which artworks partake in how an economic imaginary comes about. One side of the "communicative function" of aesthetic-cultural production concerns the way it helps a broader audience to reflect on and imagine economic phenomena.[5] In the face of what appears to be an impenetrable complexity and disenfranchisement, cultural production provides images and narratives that address this critically heightened uneasiness toward the often-abstract realm of finance.

Art has the potential to filter into political discussions and to influence collective modes of perception. As Irene Finel-Honigman (2009: 4) suggests in *A Cultural History of Finance*, "semantically and ideologically, banking and financial operations have an intrinsic lack of transparency and accessibility which feed into stereotypes, biases and mythologies." The lack of understanding of the financial system—a deep-seated disconnect between the general population and the world of high finance, experienced widely as a fundamental disorientation and threat in times of economic crisis—makes fictional cultural imaginaries and stereotypes of finance especially attractive and potent. The semiotic complicity of aesthetic-cultural production in the dominant imaginary thus superimposes a moral order over an unraveled financial reality.

The communicative function of aesthetic-cultural production also carries a critical potential in its representative form. If aesthetic-cultural production is taken seriously on its own terms (i.e., not as the site of a moral battle over finance or as a warehouse of rhetorical stock figures and metaphors), its specific form and relationship to reality both elucidate and complicate issues of representation. Fictional and aesthetic works communicate crisis in ways that insist on rather than conceal decisions of selection and complexity reduction. Cultural-aesthetic production is expressive and often self-conscious of the necessary choices that a writer, filmmaker or artist makes in creating fictional places as a way of giving shape to the extra-literary and extra-filmic world. On a conceptual level, paying close attention to "fictional" representations of crisis allows us to rethink the mechanisms of representation, and their implications at work in the imaginary at large.

In the myopic space of public media and cultural memory, the culprits flippantly referred to as "banksters" might have appeared to be a new perpetrator group after 2007/8. Indeed, they resurfaced as a cast of characters seemingly no older than the financial excesses of the 1980s. In fictional literature, however, this depiction of finance certainly does not start with Tom Wolfe's *Bonfire of the Vanities*. Bankers, as perpetrators of social misfortune and personal suffering, have not only long captured the imagination of authors and their readers, but have also staged and shaped the Western cultural perception of finance for the past two centuries. Irene Finel-Honigman goes as far as to suggest a cyclical cultural and psycho-social reaction to financial crises since the mid-nineteenth century of finding various scapegoats and vilifying financiers and bankers (Finel-Honigman 2009: 7). Although perceptions of its complexities and cultural reactions have evolved together with the financial system over time, what is certain is that from authors such as Goethe, Balzac, Dreiser, Dos Passos, Faulkner, and Wolfe there is a rich tradition of what Finel-Honigman calls the "anti-heroes of finance" (ibid.: 6). This cultural and literary tradition with its tropes and cast of characters resurfaced unsurprisingly after 2008.

In the narrative fiction-writing that has emerged in response to the most current financial crisis, a strong continuity can be seen among the representations that historicize the financial system. If, initially, critics bemoaned a lack of literature on the financial crisis (see Müller 2011), it is striking that, in the plethora of fiction generated in recent years, many authors seem either consciously or unconsciously to inscribe their narratives into older financial imaginaries. These authors grapple with ways to adapt pre-existing vocabulary, metaphors, and characterization to a context teeming with derivative financial products and asset-backed securities. Although they frequently shun the magical, demonic attributes historically attached to literary descriptions of finance,[6] they do rely on older motifs, stereotypes, and the moral condemnation of bankers in their crisis narratives. In doing so, their subjects correspond closely to the imaginary of blame invoked in the wider political and media landscape, throughout which an otherwise efficient financial system has been depicted as having been derailed by overconfident and amoral bankers. Jonas Lüscher's *Barbarian Spring* represents just one such text that at the same time thematically relies on, and formally works to subvert, this imaginary of blame.

Jonas Lüscher's *Barbarian Spring*

Swiss writer Jonas Lüscher's literary debut *Barbarian Spring* was published in 2013. At first glance, the story about a wedding party of debased financial professionals appears to be a one-sided take on the titular "barbaric" bankers lending support to the imaginary of blame. A closer look at the novella, however, reveals a more subtle critique of culpability in a world permeated by finance. Rather than a one-sided critique of bankers, Lüscher draws attention to issues of agency in modern financial markets. He moreover uses the literary form of the novella to reflect on the limits of narrative accounts of crisis.

In *Barbarian Spring*, a middle-aged, slightly peculiar Swiss industrialist named Preising, who has become a patient in a mental institution, tells the story of an eventful North African business venture. In Tunisia, while Preising is attending a wedding with a group of financial professionals from London, the British economy suddenly suffers a catastrophic decline on the night of the ceremony. As the wedding guests nurse their hangovers, they learn that Great Britain has had to declare bankruptcy—just one example of Lüscher's fictional reworking of the crisis aftereffects. With their credit cards frozen and their jobs made obsolete, the former bankers are unable to pay for the wedding. Stranded in the middle of the desert, with their world crumbling around them, they take matters into their own hands. When the beer starts running out and they are unable to break open the kitchen storage pantry, the increasingly disinhibited crowd arms itself with kitchen knives to hunt for food. Soon, they find and kill the camel that the bride rode on the night of the wedding. In a grotesque variation of a fabled Bedouin wedding dish, the bankers attempt to stuff the camel with the hotel dog, and the dog with her own puppies. When the pool boy tries to stop this travesty, he is murdered by the frenzied crowd. Using furniture as tinder for their abhorrent meal, they finally set the entire resort aflame. Preising, who witnesses these events, escapes, makes his way through a resumption of the Arab Spring protests, and seeks refuge in the Swiss embassy. He eventually enters the mental institution in Switzerland, from where he tells his story.

Lüscher's rather short text follows the structure of a novella. There is a frame narrative (set during the narrator's walk in the yard of the Swiss mental institution), a novelty (the crisis and turning point), and even a recurring *Novellensymbol* (the camel). Finally, and somewhat unconventionally, along with the narrative voices of Preising and the unnamed first-person narrator (another patient to whom he tells his story), there is the occasional intervention of an omniscient narrator.

Whereas the novella offers a rich set of characters with multiple side stories and conflicts, the unrestrained behavior of the investment bankers (the "barbarians" of the title), both before and after the economic meltdown, takes center stage. The analysts, traders, account managers, and other financial sector professionals are described at length and characterized as a somewhat homogeneous group in both appearance and behavior. They were all "young people in their late twenties and early thirties. Brash and self-confident. Trim and gym-toned" (Lüscher 2015: 30). All follow the same dress code to the point that even when they are clothed scantily at the pool, they seem "like they were in uniform." When among themselves, they are playful and promiscuous, displaying arrogant attitudes toward anyone they perceive to be of lower status. They talk in jargon, brag, show off, drink excessively, and have a taste for fast, expensive cars. In short, Lüscher's "bankers" from London fulfill every cliché. Even a character in the novella, Sanford, a sociologist by profession, is "struck" by "the sheer gusto with which they fulfilled every stereotype in the book" (ibid.: 38–39). The novella's characterization of financial professionals leans heavily on the available clichés, making them highly visible in order to mobilize them on multiple levels.

Once the crisis strikes, the effects of this stereotypical representation seem straightforwardly satirical. As one reviewer writes, "the masks come off" (Hartwig 2013), exposing the bankers' thinly veiled immorality and unrestrained brutality. One of the bankers, "Quicky," who is "a few years older," louder, and more self-confident than the rest, emerges as a natural leader of the excesses (Lüscher 2015: 76). Quicky's career exemplifies the seamless transition from banker to barbarian in the novella. Before Quicky joined the financial industry, he had served in the military in Iraq, first as an SAS soldier of the US-led coalition, then as a mercenary for a private security firm (89–90). If we are to believe his account, it was only a "short step" from soldier to mercenary to financial professional (ibid.: 90). Quicky's adaptable talent led to his nickname, "quick trigger finger. That's why they were all so hot for me: the army, the firm and the bank" (ibid.: 90). Consequently, as the events in the resort suggest, just as effortlessly as a former soldier of fortune can become a banker, a banker can become a killer. Or to put it differently, the analysts, traders, and bankers in Lüscher's novella are implied to have always been barbarians. They performed well in their professions because of their unscrupulous voracity, which in normal times was but thinly disguised by their lingo, tailor-made suits, dresses, and smartphones.

Lüscher's barbarians seem to enter the broader crisis discourse side by side with Gorden Gecko's and the masters of the universe. In fact, with his titular barbarians, Lüscher conjures yet another popular anti-heroic cast by referencing the journalistic book about the leveraged buy-out of Nabisco, *Barbarians at the Gate* by Bryan Burrough and John Helyar (1989). This account of "barbaric" corporate raiders, greed, and excess in the 1980s was further popularized by HBO's TV adaption under the same title (1993). Predictably, the trope of barbarians resurfaced in media discourse at the onset of the financial crisis with the *Guardian* newspaper warning of "Barbarians back at the gate" (2007), and the *Economist* telling us about the arrival of "Barbarians at the vault" (2008), this time destabilizing the entire global financial system.

Given this symbolic activation of anti-heroic stereotypes, it is tempting to read *Barbarian Spring*, as demonstrated above, as a literary endorsement of the dominant crisis imaginary and confirmation of the readers' worst suspicions about bankers. Indeed, the novella has received much media attention and was nominated for both the Deutscher Buchpreis and the Schweizer Buchpreis in 2013. Criticized for its blatant stereotyping (Bucheli 2013), it has also been celebrated as a "most humorous and convincing satire of the ridiculous excesses of those responsible for the financial crisis that began in 2008" (Cohan 2015). The camel, the novella's recurring symbol, might further strengthen such a didactic reading, because "it is easier for a camel to go through the eye of a needle than for a rich person to enter the kingdom of God" (Mark 10:25). This biblical quote, as just one example of the long-standing tradition of associating money with vice, ties the novella's symbolic center to earlier stereotypes of finance.

Like the Bedouin wedding dish, however, Lüscher's carefully crafted text has multiple layers that need to be uncovered. To begin with, the question of responsibility of the bankers for the financial crisis in Britain is never raised explicitly. Rather than looking for those responsible for the novella's fictional economic crisis (a fictitious British default shortly after the "real" financial crisis of 2007/8), the novella merely studies the effects of the crisis on the closed society in the resort. The signs and rumors of the coming financial disaster are, moreover, present throughout the first two-thirds of the book, but the description of the crisis itself is abrupt and brief: "While Preising was sleeping, Britannia sank" (Lüscher 2015: 91). Thus begins the novella's crisis narrative that spans little more than one page. The reader learns that, by nightfall in England, the "London interbank market had already ground to a standstill" (ibid.). As soon as the markets opened in different time zones, other countries had quickly liquidated their British pound reserves. Meanwhile, "the prime minister's cabinet" had met until the early morning hours, but "no consensus had emerged on who was to blame for this appalling mess." In consequence, the government failed to suspend trading for the coming day. By the time the British market opened, the historic descent of the currency had become "a nosedive." Before anyone could react, "computer programs" had annihilated billions in minutes, in a way that "no-one up to now had even thought possible" (ibid.). When the London Stock Exchange closed five minutes after it opened, it became clear that the UK would not be able "to service its horrendous sovereign debt" (ibid.: 92). The declaration of government bankruptcy that follows later that day is a mere formality. This crisis description certainly does not suggest an immediate culpability of the novel's "barbarians."

Although the reader is presented here with a more or less plausible crisis scenario,[7] it is not a critical representation of a financial crisis—let alone "the" financial crisis—that reflects on it in categories of either innocence or guilt. Lüscher's omniscient narrator simply lists the events that make up the crisis, without addressing or evaluating its underlying causes. If the ironic undertones of this account seem to expose the inability of the British government to act, they do so precisely by addressing the British politicians' obsession over the question of responsibility. Notably, "markets" take center stage in the events as faceless, anonymous entities with a swift, far-reaching, and perhaps non-accountable—or no longer accountable—agency. High finance and its protagonists (other than automatic trading as an accelerator) are not mentioned in this crisis description.

Lüscher has thus curiously separated the financial crisis narrative from the representation of bankers. As a result, the events outside the oasis do not suggest that the bankers were once in command but have lost control of the markets. Rather, their fate is simply more immediately tied to their dramatic up and downs. As part of the satire, this narrative strategy of dislocation helps to unmask the hubris and self-assured importance of the characters. However, as a representation of finance, this dislocation significantly departs from, even subverts, the dominant imaginary that has framed the crisis as one of financial governance. Lüscher's fictional description of markets seems to echo a more fundamental, systemic question of governability that asks if financial markets have left their masters behind. The bankers and their professional milieu are at the center of a literary social experiment in a world dominated by finance: what happens if a group of bankers is in an isolated setting and we add a large-scale financial crisis? They are not, however, at the core of the financial crisis narrative as perpetrators. Certainly, the outcome of such an experiment, and the excesses that follow, are not surprising, given the ironic, stereotypical portrayal of the characters in the first place. However, rather than "unmasking" the true nature of bankers (Hartwig 2013), much less holding them "responsible for the crisis" (Cohan 2015), the novella seems to point blame at yet something or someone else.

A closer look at the perspective from which the story is told, and the literary and formal means that establish it, challenges a reading of the novella that would simply place Lüscher's barbarians side by side with the masters of the universe. The barbarians might be here once more, but the gates are elusive. The unfolding financial crisis does not unmask their unchecked power and culpability, but rather their powerlessness. In mobilizing the barbarians, the text simultaneously portrays a more literal violent horde (when faced with their own impotency) and unfolds a more nuanced critique of finance, in the face of crisis, to the attentive reader. The novella's beginning and end should be enough to make us suspicious that there is a simple, clear-cut moral to the story. After all, the frame narrative is set in a mental institution, which calls into question whether Preising's report is based on actual memories or delusions, as well as why he tells it to the narrator at all. *Barbarian Spring* begins with the sentence: "No," said Preising, "you are asking the wrong questions" (Lüscher 2015: 1). It ends 131 pages later with an exchange between Preising and the first-person narrator: "'So what was the point of your story, then' I pressed him, mercilessly. Preising's response seemed pregnant with some secret knowledge on his part, yet also a deep anxiety about what he knew. 'Once again, you are asking the wrong question,' he said" (ibid.: 132). The key to Preising's story lies in what Preising senses but is unable to articulate: the critical thrust of Lüscher's novella is not contained in a synthesis of what is told about the crisis, nor is it likely found in the satire about bankers as such. Rather, the more fundamental critique that *Barbarian Spring* communicates lies in the way the story is told, and by whom. It requires taking the novella's characteristics as a work of literature seriously in order to reconstruct Preising's narrative position and consider the formal strategies that fashion it.

What the first-person narrator and Preising have in common is their inability to act. Yet, while the narrator is being treated for a "common depression," Preising's diagnosis appears more complicated to determine (Lüscher 2015: 10–11). With Preising, Lüscher has created an unusual main character for a literary text insofar as Preising never acts, is utterly incapable of making decisions, and never intervenes in the events he professes to have witnessed. Preising's strangely consistent indecisiveness regarding these events leads to humorously absurd situations and informs the detached, distant way he tells the story of a resort going up in flames. All of this seems to contradict what the narrator observes at the novella's start: "You could never be sure whether Preising's stories were true or not, but that wasn't the point. What mattered to him was the moral of the story. He firmly believed that every tale worth telling had one. For the most part, his stories bore witness to his own prudence, of which he was inordinately proud" (ibid.). Yet, the story that Preising tells destabilizes both the idea that there is an easy lesson to be learned and that his so-called "prudence" is indeed an unambiguously positive quality. Preising is constantly faced with crises that reach from the banal to matters of life and death. Often well aware of the need to make a decision, he is paralyzed by his own permanent state of crisis. If Preising has no answer for the narrator's final question ("So what was the point of your story, then?"), it is certainly no coincidence that Lüscher chose to tell the events in the resort through him. The author does not put stereotypes in motion in order to reassure his readers that the world is just like they all thought—finance is too powerful, bankers are barbarians, etc. Instead, he demonstrates that we are all too familiar with the state of the world, but we will not or are unable to do anything to alter and thereby improve it. Lüscher suggests that, similar to his fictional character Preising, we are not in charge of our economic affairs. A seemingly independent, anonymous system of finance and markets has taken over. In fact, in the face of crisis we all behave like Preising: well-educated and well-meaning, but merely witnessing from a distance and ultimately complicit in our passivity.

The narrative form of *Barbarian Spring* carries forward this self-reflexive, critical inquiry. Apart from its status as a work of fiction, as testified in its genre designation on the book's cover as a "novella," it is the narrative situation of this genre that calls attention to the act of narration itself. The novella form, rather than suggesting an "objective" report of events, stresses that the story inside the frame narrative is told in a particular setting and from a particular position. Preising's unreliability—the instability of his story, combined with the setting of the frame narrative in a mental institution—add a pathology to the crisis narrative that plays out in its plot, tropes, and narrative form.

On the level of plot, this pathology immediately refers to the behavior of the main character as someone who never acts, even when he thinks he should. A critical reading of the text moreover reveals that it depicts the pathological condition of a world in which agency dissolves when confronted with an omnipresent, threatening system of finance, faceless markets, and anonymous forces. Together, these pathologies call into question the possibilities of narration itself. In other words, *Barbarian Spring* recalls the literary trope of the "world as a madhouse" that inverts and dissolves the clearly marked borders between the inside and outside of a mental institution, declaring the world a madhouse and the institution a refuge (see, e.g., Daemmrich and Daemmrich 1995: 368ff.). Preising's curious condition is not an individual mental disorder; it stands for the condition of the entire world. Whereas such an idea might further Lüscher's panoptic vision of finance to the point where there is indeed no longer an outside, it also fundamentally questions the possibility of a critical representation from the inside. The addition of an omniscient narrator, which is an unconventional technique for a novella, exposes the limitations of the subjective perspective of Preising as a narrator. This unknown, third narrator's omniscience—often deployed as a corrective to Preising's account—underscores the unreliability of his narration of the critical events, as well as the impossibility of narration generally to express the world objectively.

This deliberate, necessary "inconsistency" in Lüscher's novella—the impossibility of an omniscient, objective narrator—points to the fundamental representational issues that the financial crisis exposed. Because achieving an omniscient perspective has proven impossible, the diagnoses of the reasons for the crisis have been many, and a consensus has remained elusive since 2007/8 (see, e.g., Lo 2011; Culp 2018). Rather, just like in the novel, the crisis was experienced as a shock, drawing attention to what can and cannot be known about such a complex event. It neither afforded an outside perspective, nor could it be dealt with using a new set of readily available, fundamental truths. Older forms of representation became unreliable and no longer served to capture the events of the crisis adequately, but instead destabilized widespread beliefs and offered little help in deciding which direction to take for solutions. Falling back on earlier political policies and knowledge, as well as experimenting with the radically new, are both predicated on this epistemological shock. If the dominant imagined recovery has focused on the former, and relied on an imaginary of blame as its predominant explanation, this imaginary compensates for the representational difficulties and ignorance the crisis exposed. Lüscher undermines this compensatory effect in his novella. Deploying the imaginary of blame, he ultimately insists that we focus on the problem of knowledge about the financial crisis and its representation, rather than presenting the critique of bankers as a solution or as a return to a stable economic order.

The popular reception of cultural production in the mass media often ignores its communicative function and critical potential, using fictional narratives and imagery uncritically to buttress dominant narratives. Invoking Gordon Gekko from the movie *Wall Street*, the master-of-the-universe metaphor, or Lüscher's barbarians to assign blame to bankers for the financial crisis are three prominent examples of such misappropriation. A careful analysis of such artworks shows not only how the two purportedly separate spheres of culture and the economy profoundly condition each other, but also how they can function together as mutually enlightening. The works must be understood, however, as a communicative intervention of aesthetic-cultural production in a dominant economic imaginary.

Lüscher's rigged literary experiment helps bring into focus what real-life economic events exposed: the instability and power of finance and financial markets. Like the barbarian roast staged by the bankers in Lüscher's novella, an engastration of puppies in a dog in a camel, the author nested multiple crises to construct this effect. The novella's immediate crisis in the resort (bankers becoming barbarians) is the result of a crisis in the UK (financial markets crashing) that is part of a larger systemic crisis of agency and governance (finance and markets controlling every aspect of life). If the dominant imaginary relies on established, negative views of bankers, so does Lüscher's satire at the heart of his novella. The dominant imaginary, with its cast of masters of the universe and barbaric bankers, creates a moral legibility of the crisis that judges individuals, and absolves everyone else from both a critical analysis and a need to act. After all, we believe it is the responsibility of our legal and regulatory systems to manage this kind of crisis. Lüscher's textual strategies—the ways the story is set up as a work of fiction—undermine this moral legibility and criticize our own fatalistic passivity toward economic affairs. The "camel" in the room here, or the problem with asking "the right question," as Lüscher suggests, is not only that this question cannot be raised by Preising, nor in the closed world of Preising's tale. Rather, this difficulty references inadequacies in our interrogations of the crisis that are based on the fundamental representational conundrums and systemic instabilities exposed by the crisis of financialized liberal capitalism.

Joel Kaipainen is an independent researcher and scholar who received his PhD from the Department of German at the University of Wisconsin, Madison, with a dissertation on "Creative Destruction: The Financial Crisis and Cultural Production." He studied at the University of Augsburg, Germany; at Paris IV, France; and at the University of Pittsburgh. His research focuses on how the discourses on finance, globalization, economic change, and crisis are negotiated in contemporary literature, film, and video games.

Notes

1. See, e.g., Richard Dale's essay from November 2008, which draws the following conclusion: "What we have witnessed in recent months is not only the fracturing of the world's financial system but the discrediting of an academic discipline. There are some 4,000 university finance professors worldwide, thousands of finance research papers are published each year, and yet there have been few if any warnings from the academic community of the incendiary potential of global financial markets. Is it too harsh to conclude that, despite the considerable academic resources that go into finance research, our understanding of the behavior of financial markets is no greater than it was in 1929/33 or indeed 1720?" (Dale 2008: 117).
2. I follow the Cultural Political Economy concept of an "Imaginary." For a more detailed discussion of "economic imaginaries" and their role in crisis conceptions, see, for example, Jessop 2012 and 2013.
3. For the deregulation of banks from the 1970s onward, see, for example, Dewatripont, Rochet, and Tirole 2015, especially Chapter 1, "Regulation in a Historical Perspective," 1–3.
4. The *Financial Times* reported in 2018 that forty-seven bankers had been charged with financial crimes—twenty-five from Iceland, eleven from Spain, seven from Ireland, and one each from Germany, the United States, Italy, and Cyprus (Noonan et al. 2018).
5. This communicative function can further be divided into a parallel critical function and a utopian potential of cultural production in confronting the crisis.
6. See, e.g., Finel-Honigman's discussion (2009: 4ff.); other examples include Goethe's *Faust II*, and Norbert Jacques's *Dr. Mabuse der Spieler.*
7. With London as a key node of the financial industry, the outlook for Great Britain was glum in the early crisis years. At the end of 2009, the European Commission predicted a negative GDP growth rate for the UK, together with Spain and Ireland.

Starting in July 2008, the pound sterling had fallen by almost 25 percent against the US dollar and the euro. British currency depreciated at one of the fastest rates in history, hitting a historic low at the end of December and almost reaching parity with the euro ("Pound Hits New Low against Euro" 2008).

References

Augar, Philip. 2006. *The Greed Merchants: How the Investment Banks Played the Free Market Game*. London: Penguin.

"Barbarians at the Vault." 2008. *The Economist*, 17 May. Retrieved 31 August 2021 from https://www.economist.com/leaders/2008/05/15/barbarians-at-the-vault.

Brassett, James, Lena Rethel, and Matthew Watson. 2009. "Introduction to the Political Economy of the Sub-prime Crisis in Britain: Constructing and Contesting Competence." *The British Journal of Politics and International Relations* 11(3) (August): 377–81. Available at: https://doi.org/10.1111/j.1467-856X.2009.00376.x.

Bucheli, Roman. 2013. "Jonas Lüschers Novelle 'Frühling Der Barbaren': Zwei Spaziergänger im Park." *Neue Zürcher Zeitung*, 12 February. Retrieved 4 May 2022 from http://www.nzz.ch/zwei-spaziergaenger-im-park-1.17996726.

Burrough, Bryan, and John Helyar. 1989. *Barbarians at the Gate: The Fall of RJR Nabisco*. New York: Harper & Row.

Cohan, William D. 2015. "Filthy Lucre." Review of *Sweetland* by Michael Crummey, *Barbarian Spring* by Jonas Lüscher, and *The Room* by Jonas Karlssohn. *The New York Times*, 20 March. Retrieved 4 May 2022 from http://www.nytimes.com/2015/03/22/books/review/michael-crummeys-sweetland-and-more.html.

Colander, David, et al. 2009. "The Financial Crisis and the Systemic Failure of Academic Economics." University of Copenhagen, Department of Economics, Discussion Paper No. 09-03. Retrieved 4 May 2022 from http://papers.ssrn.com/abstract=1355882.

Culp, Christopher L. 2018. "A Review of the Academic Literature on the Causes and Evolution of the Credit Crisis." *Studies in Applied Finance* 24 (April): 1–77.

Daemmrich, Horst S., and Ingrid Daemmrich. 1995. *Themen und Motive in der Literatur: ein Handbuch*. Marburg: Francke.

Dale, Richard. 2008. "The Financial Meltdown Is an Academic Crisis Too." VoxEU.org (blog), 27 November. Retrieved 6 September 2022 from https://cepr.org/voxeu/columns/financial-meltdown-academic-crisis-too.

Dewatripont, Mathias, Jean-Charles Rochet, and Jean Tirole. 2015. *Balancing the Banks: Global Lessons from the Financial Crisis*. Trans. Keith Tribe. Reprint edition. Princeton, NJ: Princeton University Press.

Doyle, Jack. 2010. "Wall Street's Gekko 1980s–2010." The Pop History Dig (blog), 4 February. Retrieved 4 May 2022 from http://www.pophistorydig.com/topics/wall-streets-gekko-1980s-2010/.

Federal Bureau of Investigation. 2012. "FBI Announces Public Service Announcement by Michael Douglas on Securities Fraud and Insider Trading." FBI, https://archives.fbi.gov/archives/newyork/press-releases/2012/fbi-announces-public-service-announcement-by-michael-douglas-on-securities-fraud-and-insider-trading.

Felsenthal, Mark. 2008. "Greenspan Shocked at Credit System Breakdown." Reuters, 23 October. Retrieved 4 May 2022 from https://www.reuters.com/article/idINIndia-36122420081023.

Finel-Honigman, Irene. 2009. *A Cultural History of Finance*. New York: Routledge.

Hartwig, Ina. 2013. "Wenn die Masken fallen. Jonas Lüschers beeindruckendes Debüt 'Frühling der Barbaren.'" *Süddeutsche Zeitung*, 22 June. Retrieved 4 May 2022 from https://www.buecher.de/shop/england/fruehling-der-barbaren/luescher-jonas/products_products/detail/prod_id/36495225/.

Jessop, Bob. 2012. "Narratives of Crisis and Crisis Response: Perspectives from North and South." In *The Global Crisis and Transformative Social Change*, ed. Peter Utting, Shahra Razavi, and Rebecca Varghese Buchholz, 23–42. New York: Palgrave Macmillan.

———. 2013. "Recovered Imaginaries, Imagined Recoveries: A Cultural Political Economy of Crisis Construals and Crisis-Management in the North Atlantic Financial Crisis." In *Before and Beyond the Global Economic Crisis: Economics, Politics and Settlement*, ed. Mats Benner, 234–54. Cheltenham, UK: Edward Elgar Publishing.

Kaletsky, Anatole. 2010. "Bankers Are Masters of the Universe Again." *The Times*, 7 September. Retrieved 4 May 2022 from http://www.thetimes.co.uk/tto/opinion/columnists/anatolekaletsky/article2717868.ece.

Lades, Sandra. 2015. "Euro and Grand Coalition in Germans' Good Graces." GfK-Verein.com, 23 March. Retrieved 4 May 2022 from http://www.gfk-verein.org/en/press/euro-and-grand-coalition-germans-good-graces.

Lipshaw, Jeffrey M. 2009. "The Epistemology of the Financial Crisis: Complexity, Causation, Law, and Judgment." *Southern California Interdisciplinary Law Journal* 19(2) (August): 299–351. Retrieved 4 May 2022 from https://dx.doi.org/10.2139/ssrn.1421837.

Lo, Andrew. 2011. "Reading about the Financial Crisis: A 21-Book Review." SSRN Electronic Journal, 27 October. Retrieved 4 May 2022 from https://dx.doi.org/10.2139/ssrn.1949908.

Lüscher, Jonas. 2015. *Barbarian Spring*. Trans. Peter Lewis. London: Haus Publishing (orig. *Frühling der Barbaren*, Munich: C.H. Beck, 2013).

Müller, Uli. 2011. "Krise? Gibt's Hier Nicht." Zeit Online, 24 February. Retrieved 4 May 2022 from http://www.zeit.de/kultur/literatur/2011-02/krise-literatur-essay.

Noonan, Laura, et al. 2018. "Who Went to Jail for Their Role in the Financial Crisis?" *The Financial Times*, 20 September. Retrieved 19 May 2022 from https://ig.ft.com/jailed-bankers/.

Organization for Economic Co-operation and Development (OECD). 2009. *The*

Financial Crisis: Reform and Exit Strategies. Paris. Retrieved 5 May 2022 from https://www.oecd.org/daf/fin/financial-education/43091457.pdf.

Peter, Nina. 2011. "Kollabierende Sprachsysteme: Zwei Strategien sprachlicher Verarbeitung der Geldwirtschaft." In *Finanzen und Fiktionen: Grenzgänge zwischen Literatur und Wirtschaft*, ed. Christine Künzel and Dirk Hempel, 137–54. Frankfurt am Main: Campus.

"Pound Hits New Low against Euro." 2008. BBC, 29 December. Retrieved 5 May 2022 from http://news.bbc.co.uk/2/hi/business/7802981.stm.

Rudd, Kevin. 2008. "The Children of Gordon Gekko." *The Australian*, 6 October. Retrieved 19 September 2019 from http://www.theaustralian.com.au/archive/news/the-children-of-gordon-gekko/story-e6frg7b6-1111117670209.

SIGTARP. 2013. "Quarterly Report to Congress. Office of the Special Inspector General for the Troubled Asset Relief Program." Office of the Special Inspector General, 29 October. Retrieved 4 May 2022 from https://www.sigtarp.gov/sites/sigtarp/files/Quarterly_Reports/October_29_2013_Report_to_Congress.pdf.

"Studie: Immer weniger Deutsche vertrauen Banken—immer mehr der Bundesregierung." 2013. *Frankfurter Allgemeine Zeitung*, 7 February. Retrieved 4 May 2022 from http://www.faz.net/aktuell/gesellschaft/studie-immer-weniger-deutsche-vertrauen-banken-immer-mehr-der-bundesregierung-12054499.html.

Taibbi, Matt. 2009. "The Great American Bubble Machine." *Rolling Stone*, 9 July.

Wachman, Richard. 2007. "Barbarians Back at the Gate – and Thinking Big." *The Guardian*, 18 March. Retrieved 31 August 2021 from https://www.theguardian.com/business/2007/mar/18/privateequity.observerbusiness1.

"Why They Crashed Too." 2014. *The Economist*, 19 June. Retrieved 4 May 2022 from http://www.economist.com/blogs/freeexchange/2014/06/economic-models-and-financial-crisis.

Wolfe, Tom. 1989. *The Bonfire of the Vanities*. Reprint edn. New York: Picador (orig. New York: Farrar Straus Giroux, 1987).

Wolff, Richard. 2008. "Capitalism Hits the Fan." Lecture, Brown University, Providence, RI, 2 December. Retrieved 6 September 2022 from https://www.youtube.com/watch?v=TZU3wfjtIJY.

~: INDEX :~

www.ingramcontent.com/pod-product-compliance
Ingram Content Group UK Ltd.
Pitfield, Milton Keynes, MK11 3LW, UK
UKHW021837100926
8556IPUK00004B/386